Zambia

WORLD BIBLIOGRAPHICAL SERIES

General Editors:
Robert G. Neville (Executive Editor)
John J. Horton

Robert A. Myers   Hans H. Wellisch
Ian Wallace   Ralph Lee Woodward, Jr.

John J. Horton is Deputy Librarian of the University of Bradford and was formerly Chairman of its Academic Board of Studies in Social Sciences. He has maintained a longstanding interest in the discipline of area studies and its associated bibliographical problems, with special reference to European Studies. In particular he has published in the field of Icelandic and of Yugoslav studies, including the two relevant volumes in the World Bibliographical Series.

Robert A. Myers is Associate Professor of Anthropology in the Division of Social Sciences and Director of Study Abroad Programs at Alfred University, Alfred, New York. He has studied post-colonial island nations of the Caribbean and has spent two years in Nigeria on a Fulbright Lectureship. His interests include international public health, historical anthropology and developing societies. In addition to *Amerindians of the Lesser Antilles: a bibliography* (1981), *A Resource Guide to Dominica, 1493-1986* (1987) and numerous articles, he has compiled the World Bibliographical Series volumes on *Dominica* (1987), *Nigeria* (1989) and *Ghana* (1991).

Ian Wallace is Professor of German at the University of Bath. A graduate of Oxford in French and German, he also studied in Tübingen, Heidelberg and Lausanne before taking teaching posts at universities in the USA, Scotland and England. He specializes in contemporary German affairs, especially literature and culture, on which he has published numerous articles and books. In 1979 he founded the journal *GDR Monitor*, which he continues to edit under its new title *German Monitor*.

Hans H. Wellisch is Professor emeritus at the College of Library and Information Services, University of Maryland. He was President of the American Society of Indexers and was a member of the International Federation for Documentation. He is the author of numerous articles and several books on indexing and abstracting, and has published *The Conversion of Scripts and Indexing and Abstracting: an International Bibliography*, and *Indexing from A to Z*. He also contributes frequently to *Journal of the American Society for Information Science*, *The Indexer* and other professional journals.

Ralph Lee Woodward, Jr. is Director of Graduate Studies at Tulane University, New Orleans. He is the author of *Central America, a Nation Divided*, 2nd ed. (1985), as well as several monographs and more than seventy scholarly articles on modern Latin America. He has also compiled volumes in the World Bibliographical Series on *Belize* (1980), *El Salvador* (1988), *Guatemala* (Rev. Ed.) (1992) and *Nicaragua* (Rev. Ed.) (1994). Dr. Woodward edited the Central American section of the *Research Guide to Central America and the Caribbean* (1985) and is currently associate editor of Scribner's *Encyclopedia of Latin American History*.

VOLUME 51

Zambia

Revised Edition

Jan Kees van Donge

Compiler

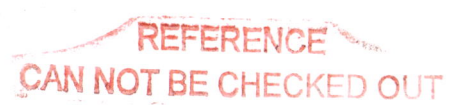

CLIO PRESS

OXFORD, ENGLAND · SANTA BARBARA, CALIFORNIA
DENVER, COLORADO

British Library Cataloguing in Publication Data

Donge, Jan Kees van
Zambia. – Rev. Ed. – (World bibliographical series; v. 51)
1. Zambia – Bibliography
I. Title
016.9´6894

ISBN 1–85109–319–2

ABC-CLIO,
Old Clarendon Ironworks,
35A Great Clarendon Street,
Oxford OX2 6AT, England.

_____

ABC-CLIO Inc.,
130 Cremona Drive,
Santa Barbara,
CA 93117, USA

Designed by Bernard Crossland.
Typeset by ABC-CLIO, Oxford, England.
Printed and bound in Great Britain by print in black, Midsomer Norton.

THE WORLD BIBLIOGRAPHICAL SERIES

This series, which is principally designed for the English speaker, will eventually cover every country (and some of the world's principal regions and cities), each in a separate volume comprising annotated entries on works dealing with its history, geography, economy and politics; and with its people, their culture, customs, religion and social organization. Attention will also be paid to current living conditions – housing, education, newspapers, clothing, etc. – that are all too often ignored in standard bibliographies; and to those particular aspects relevant to individual countries. Each volume seeks to achieve, by use of careful selectivity and critical assessment of the literature, an expression of the country and an appreciation of its nature and national aspirations, to guide the reader towards an understanding of its importance. The keynote of the series is to provide, in a uniform format, an interpretation of each country that will express its culture, its place in the world, and the qualities and background that make it unique. The views expressed in individual volumes, however, are not necessarily those of the publisher.

VOLUMES IN THE SERIES

For Ilse Mwanza
in recognition of stimulating
scholarship on Zambia

Contents

Contents

Contents

Preface

It has been a pleasure for me to work on this bibliography. Not only that, I also found it useful. This seemed odd to a fair number of my acquaintances, who doubted the need for more bibliographies in the age of CD-ROM databases and on-line access to library catalogues. I am of the view, however, that this enormously enlarged access to information makes it all the more necessary to be selective, and for this, one often depends on people who are well read in particular fields. A selected and annotated bibliography fulfils exactly that function.

I admit without hesitation that personal preference played a role in this selection. I was aware, however, that a wider focus than my own preferences would make this bibliography more useful. Therefore, I have included much that is of limited value in my opinion. I have used the annotations not only to give a clear idea of what is to be found in a particular item, but also to pass judgement extensively. My evaluation will be clear from the annotations; if people disagree with me they can take a negative judgement as a recommendation and *vice versa*.

There were however other, more objective criteria for selecting items for this bibliography. It may be helpful if these are spelt out:

As I am a social scientist, it was easier for me to deal with subjects within that field. This may have led to some regrettable gaps in coverage. Geology is of major importance in Zambia because of the large mining sector, but it is beyond me to find and judge the literature. I have, however, included a reference to the Geological Survey in Lusaka, where more literature may be obtained. There is a sizeable literature on the archaeology of Zambia, which is also outside my expertise. In this case, I have referred to a publication by Derricourt containing the most up to date bibliography. Linguistics and medicine are also fields that are beyond my competence. In this bibliography they are represented only by items which are accessible to the general reader.

If a publication was recent, I have included it even if I considered it quite shallow. I looked at older publications much more critically. Even then, I tried to make sure that a user of this bibliography could find their way to these older publications through other items. I have not included, for example, the works by Phyllis Dean, Merle Davis and Hortense Powdermaker on the Copperbelt, but the polemic exchange between James Ferguson and Hugh Macmillan in the *Journal of Southern African Studies* gives an exhaustive review of literature on that region. Similarly, I have not included the reports of the early Portuguese travellers, but these can be accessed through Ian Cunnison's article in the *Journal of African History*.

Expatriates produce most of the writing – and usually the best quality writing – on Zambia. This is regrettable and so I have exercised some positive discrimination. I have treated writings by Zambians more uncritically than those by expatriates.

Academics tend to recycle the same material in many publications. In such cases, I have as a rule tried to concentrate on one book and one journal article, the latter preferably in a widely accessible journal. I have tried to ensure, however, that the bibliographies of the selected items gave access to the literature I ignored.

Only rarely have I mentioned doctoral and masters theses in this bibliography. Their usefulness is limited because they are difficult to access and, in any event, the best parts of theses are usually published. Furthermore, there is an excellent bibliography of theses on Zambia by Ilse Mwanza.

Among the more recent items there is more grey literature, produced within and for organizations, than in the earlier ones. Accessibility was an important criterion in selection and grey literature is not easily accessible. However, consultancy reports have become more and more important media in the past decades. Here also, I have included items not only because of their intrinsic value, but because they can lead to others – for example to the World Bank financed social fund studies.

The World Bibliographical Series of ABC-CLIO addresses itself to a wide public. Tourists and business travellers use the series as well as academics and professionals, and I hope that they will find here what they are looking for. That is my base line, but I shall feel I have really succeeded if their attention is caught by the more academic entries. My hope is to convey that academics can be fun as well!

This bibliography is organized in broad categories, which aim to give an overview of Zambia. Entries are ordered, in so far as it has been possible, alphabetically by author, starting with the author's earliest included publication. Where an author has multiple entries with different authors, the second author's surname, rather than publication date, determines the order within the sub-group. Where it has not been possible to order by author, entries are ordered alphabetically by title, ignoring the definite and indefinite article.

Three indexes are provided – author (personal and corporate), title and subject. The numbers in these indexes refer to bibliographical entry numbers, not page numbers.

Acknowledgements

Bibliographical work depends upon libraries and I am indebted to those I have used. They are, in chronological sequence of use: the library of Chancellor College, Zomba, Malawi; the library of the Institute of Social Studies, The Hague; the library of the Africa Studies Centre, Leiden, The Netherlands; the library of the Royal Institute for the Tropics, Amsterdam; and the special collections of the University of Zambia library.

I thank Dr Robert Neville and Julia Goddard at ABC-CLIO for their patience in waiting for this manuscript. I could not have compiled this bibliography without the support of Catherine O'Dea. She is not only the editor who turns my writing into readable English, but also a critical audience who tirelessly corrects my sloppiness and, above all, a good friend. I owe her special thanks for the work on the subject index. If I had not benefited from the hospitality of Jacob and Ilse Mwanza this bibliography would have lost some colourful and rich items. House-sitting in Lusaka made it possible to access grey literature – including some in their house – which would otherwise have remained outside consideration. Finally, I am grateful to Aafke Justesen who kept me going on the bibliography during a few difficult years.

Jan Kees van Donge
August 2000

Introduction

Zambia is a subject that provokes contradictions and conflicting emotions. Zambia's landscape, for example, is considered by some to be monotonous and boring, while for others the relatively intact savannah landscape – the bush is an appropriate expression – is a treasure to be cherished. Lusaka, the capital, is for some their favourite city because of the great diversity of people to be found there. For those it is thus a cosmopolitan city, while others consider it provincial: a few skyscrapers with surrounding houses and hovels in the bush. The more political the issue is, the sharper the divergence in views. Zambia is castigated as a wastrel among developing countries where development aid is squandered. For others, Zambia's plight – especially its debt burden – qualifies the country as a priority for aid allocation. Zambia was a forerunner in the wave of democratization in Africa during the 1990s, and democracy is seen as entrenched in its political culture. Zambia is at the same time severely criticized because of its human rights record in recent years, and the lack of a democratic culture is seen as the explanation. It is useful to keep these emotional overtones in mind when becoming acquainted with the country. This introduction is meant to serve the latter purpose. It is written as an introduction to the bibliography and aims to bring out the major themes in the literature on Zambia rather than bombarding the readers with facts. The hope is to entice them to read about Zambia rather than to do the reading for them.

Geography

Even the map of Zambia arouses contradictory opinions. The shape of Zambia is arbitrary for many: an amorphous landlocked mass created in the scramble for Africa. For others, its shape is reminiscent of a butterfly, with the railway line from Livingstone to the Copperbelt serving as the country's spine. The latter, more organic view of the country directs attention to Zambia as a major copper producer. The railway line was for a long time the major link connecting this modern industrial complex to the rest of the world. It linked Zambia with the Southern African economic constellation where the big mining complexes are central. But the copper mines are not merely an enclave in the country, as was previously thought. Most of the country was for a long time seen as a traditional and untouched society, but the influence of the modern world throughout Zambia is now widely acknowledged, if only because labour migration to the mines has influenced the whole of the country.

The erroneous impression that large chunks of Zambian society are untouched by the modern world arises also because the Zambian landscape conveys such an impression of emptiness. The long drives from Lusaka to a provincial capital, for instance to Chipata in the East (569 km) or to Kasama in the North (850 km), seem to pass through wide and sparsely populated expanses of mostly umbrella shaped trees, the so-called brachystegia woodlands. Population density in Zambia is still relatively low, although it is increasing fast. More and more land is therefore used for settled agriculture, and shifting agriculture – which uses land extensively – is decreasing rapidly.

Another reason why rural Zambia appears to be less populated than is actually the case lies in the location of the roads. These tend to follow the watershed, while most population concentrations are found in valleys, near rivers. This is also changing as artificial water supplies make it possible for people to settle nearer the roads.

There is a further reason why Zambia seems more empty than it is: the largest rural population concentrations are found near Zambia's borders, for example on the Barotse floodplain near the Angolan border, in the Luapula river valley on the border with Congo, and in the east of the country on the border with Malawi. Zambia is for the most part a plateau lying at about 1,000 m above sea level, and the rural population is often concentrated in the big river systems which are mostly found towards the edges of the plateau.

At the borders, or close to them, one also finds the spectacular scenic beauties of Zambia: the Victoria Falls in the south, the Zambezi floodplain in the west, the source of the Zambezi in the north west, the Bangweulu and Mweru lakes and their swamps in the north west, the Kalambo falls in the north east. Zambia has some of the most spectacular game parks in Africa and these are usually found near rivers. Luangwa and Kafue are names of game parks as well as of rivers. Kasaba Bay in the North is on Lake Tanganyika and Lochinvar is on the Kafue.

These places are ostentatiously spectacular. The brachystegia woodlands also offer rich viewing, but a trained eye is required to see the variations. Zambia has been the scene of pioneering ecological studies that deduce the nature of the soil from vegetation and that is then related to farming systems.

Reading about Zambia's landscapes is highly rewarding for newcomers to Zambia.

Historical overview up to independence

The riverine areas in Zambia were the usual places of early human settlement, although human presence was not exclusively limited to such areas. The earliest human remains found in the country were not discovered near a river: the skull of Broken Hill Man was named after the mine in which it was found in 1921. Most archaeological discoveries have, however, been made in locations such as the Victoria Falls area on the Zambezi or the Itezhi-tezhi area on the Kafue. There is a considerable archaeological literature on Zambia, but this is mostly written for and by professionals. Andrew Roberts's history of Zambia is the most accessible source.

The spread of a settled population over the whole plateau dates from later and was linked to the development of trade, the concentration of people in areas such as the Zambezi floodplain and the military development of some tribes. These led to centralizing processes and state formation. Early European travellers have described some early state formations – the court of Mwate Kazembe was described by the Portuguese Gamitto, and the Zambezi floodplain was an important place in Livingstone's travels. Such state formation is also the subject of important scholarly work in which oral sources are significant. The work by Andrew Roberts on the Bemba is an outstanding example.

The imperial expansion of Western Europe started to affect Zambia from the second half of the 19th century. The Europeans figured among a number of players at that time. It was an unstable era: the slave trade had made big inroads; the fortunes of ruling groups were fluctuating sharply; and loyalties shifted easily. Two Western influences manifested themselves strongly towards the end of the 19th century: missionaries and traders. It was not yet an era of European dominance: missionaries had to treat local authority with respect, and traders had to form alliances with the local forces they met. This changed with the increasing dominance of Cecil Rhodes's British South Africa Company. The origin of western-style government in Zambia is to be found in this private company. In 1900 it appointed its first administrator of the territory, and company rule lasted until 1924. Then the British government formally took over the administration. These first decades did not lead to much imperial activity in the territory, but the area formed part of the whole Southern African complex driven by mining, and wage labour as well as labour migration started to affect the life of Zambians. There was some land alienation and European settlement, but the Zambian economy was never as dominated by settlers as Kenya or Zimbabwe. Lewis Gann's magnificent history of the colonial period is still the best source on this period, and on European politics during the colonial era.

The idea of finding an El Dorado was of course common in colonialism, but at that time less so in Zambia than elsewhere. It is striking that – as Ackson Kanduza has shown – the future of the territory was to be in tobacco grown by European settlers, and mineral wealth was not given consideration. There seemed to be no loss involved when the British South Africa Company handed over the territory to the British government. Despite the handover, however, the shareholders of the British South Africa Company benefited enormously after the copper mines were developed, because the company had retained its mineral rights at the time of the handover in 1924. These were secured in a treaty concluded with the Litunga (chief) of Barotseland, one of the centralized states at the eve of colonization. Copper was found outside Barotseland and the British South Africa Company had nothing to do with it, yet the latter profited from Zambia's copper until 1964. The independent Zambian government simply did not recognize these rights at independence. The question of who is to benefit from mining Zambia's richness remains a crucial issue in the country up to the present day.

The economic importance of the country thus only became obvious in the late 1920s, when the copper mines were developed. This led to great economic optimism, which was almost immediately dampened by the Great Depression of the 1930s. Thereafter there was a continuing boom for the Zambian copper mines until the 1970s. Copper is essential in the manufacture of bullets. It is therefore not surprising that this period covers the Second World War and the Cold War period until the end of the Vietnam War.

The development of the mining complex led to massive labour migration from rural areas and made Zambia the most urbanized country in Africa. Urbanization, labour migration and education provided the background to early assertions of African identity, which led increasingly to opposition to colonial authority. Such assertions appeared early in the churches. Africans split off from mission churches and branched out in many independent ones. These churches incorporated many elements from indigenous religion but the New Testament was a pervading force. The *Book of Revelation* has a particular attraction. Millenarian beliefs – especially as propagated through the Watchtower and Tract Society – struck a deep chord. Zambia is still the country with the highest proportion in the world of Jehovah's Witnesses as a percentage of the population. The most dramatic manifestation of millenarianism was the revolt of Alice Lenshina's Lumpa church on the eve of independence. That dramatic event made an indelible impression on all those involved, and several publications emanating from that experience have appeared in recent years.

Africans also developed an identity as workers, which was not immediately obvious to Europeans. They saw their workforce as villagers, rooted in tribal ways, who worked only on a temporary basis in the modern sector. The mineworkers' revolt of 1935 shook that image. After the war particularly, African trade unionism developed and became accepted, if not stimulated, by the authorities. The trade unions were supported by advice from the British Trade Union Congress after the Second World War. Thirdly, Africans manifested their identity through welfare societies. These were more elitist, and educated Africans found a platform there. They are usually seen as proto-nationalist movements. The more Africans were educated and moved in positions close to Europeans, the more keenly racial discrimination was felt. Nationalist feeling developed most strongly among clerks and teachers.

Many different cultures encountered each other in Zambian society. This was not merely a colonial encounter, as in the cities different African cultures mixed as well. This cultural mix has been memorably described by Clyde Mitchell in his study of the *kalela* dance. Mitchell was one of the directors of the Rhodes-Livingstone Institute, a centre of brilliant anthropological research from the 1940s until just after independence. Research in Zambia may have shown more clearly than elsewhere African societies in a state of flux. Migration and change are more typical of African society than tradition and unchanging tribal identities. When pervasive labour migration exists, it is difficult to maintain a vision of static rural societies. Whereas kinship in African societies tended to be seen as a structuring static element of social life, the research of the Rhodes-Livingstone Institute showed kinship in social action: it is an idiom in which people talk about their society and formulate their social situations. From this perspective, Africans are seen as creatively responding to new influences, rather than obstructing those influences on traditional grounds.

After independence, this anthropological work was – wrongly – associated with colonialism. Many of the themes from this work were studied by historians, however: African history became the subject instead of archaeology and colonial history. This African history was pioneered by anthropologists – for example Barnes in his study of the Ngoni – who stressed African initiative. This was, however, soon considered too benign a view. Zambian society was more and more depicted as being at the mercy of outside forces, despite African initiative. Chipungu's study of agriculture in Southern Province, where farming for the market arose among smallholders despite a policy to contain it, is a clear example of that.

Zambia's more recent history has been rather neglected, despite the great interest in African history in general. This neglect is regrettable as the emergence of Zambia as a nation is relatively recent and inextricably tied up with European politics in the territory, because the more Zambia grew in

Introduction

economic importance based on its mineral wealth, the more its future became a contentious issue. On the one hand, there was a colonial view, which maintained that the country was held in trust in the interest of the native population. On the other hand, there was a growing clamour by the European settler population to amalgamate Zambia (Northern Rhodesia) with Southern Rhodesia and Nyasaland in a federation. Although the arguments were usually made on economic grounds, the actual project behind it was to augment the political power of settler populations. This population was relatively small in Northern Rhodesia as alienation of land had virtually stopped after 1914, while the mining complexes and related industries employed many Europeans but preferred to do so on a contract basis rather than encourage settlement. Amalgamation would boost settler power as the Northern Rhodesian settlers could then join forces with the much more numerous settlers in Southern Rhodesia.

It was thus not surprising that Africans in Northern Rhodesia and Nyasaland opposed federation – all the more so as racial discrimination in Southern Rhodesia was harsher than in the North. The issue of federation galvanized African political opinion as no other issue had, and led to the emergence of genuine nationalist movements. When a Central African Federation was created in 1953, despite strong African opposition, this was a grievous blow to the young nationalist movement. This federation proved to be a highly iniquitous affair. Northern Rhodesia (Zambia) brought in most of the revenue – because of its copper reserves – while Southern Rhodesia profited most from it. This had a racial slant as well because most settlers lived in Southern Rhodesia. African nationalism revived after 1958 under the leadership of a new generation of politicians. Kenneth Kaunda and Simon Kapwepwe were the most prominent among those who broke away from the African National Congress (ANC). They came together in a new, rival political party, called the United National Independence Party (UNIP) which was to lead the country to independence.

The period of federation and the independence struggle is an open field for further scholarship. The literature on the Central African Federation is quite voluminous, but it is written mostly by Europeans involved in the politics of the region at that time. The lack of an African perspective on history in that period is thus particularly conspicuous. A critical study benefiting from the distance created by the passage of time would be welcome. The same may be said of the struggle for independence. Much of the historiography of that period is coloured by links to the nationalist movement. There has, for example, been a consistent attempt to see the trade union movement as one of the nationalist forces, whereas in fact the relationship between the unions and the political parties was generally strained. The most promising work in this field is the monograph by Henry

Meebelo. He showed courage in writing on such a sensitive topic as he was working for the research bureau of UNIP at the time.

The economy

Zambia was one of the richest African countries at independence but is currently one of the most indebted. That is beyond dispute, but the reasons for this decline are not. The economic literature on Zambia actually avoids reflection on the historical roots of this decline, which was not foreseen at independence. Independence is a useful starting point however, as a development strategy unfolded at that time and remained influential for decades. The strategy was laid down in an economic report written by a United Nations economic mission named after its chairman, Dudley Seers. The crucial problem highlighted by the report was that while a highly modern mining and urban sector had developed, most of the Zambian economy had been neglected. This wrong had to be corrected and the country was fortunate in that it had access to revenues from the mining industry to do so. In the first place the report called for a social infrastructure for healthcare and education to be created to cater for all Africans. Secondly, there was some room for urban development as there was ample scope for import substitution in industry. Previously, Zambia had merely been a market for Zimbabwean and South African industry. The biggest challenge of all, however, was seen in rural development. The rural areas had been most neglected by the colonial state. Rural development was needed to diversify the economy and free it from dependence on copper. Above all, rural-urban migration had to be stemmed. Economic prospects in the urban sector were seen as limited, and a continuing drift to town would lead to unemployment and social problems. Seers thus proposed an inter-sectoral development strategy which related mining to industry, agriculture and government services.

The mining industry had to raise the surplus for developing the other sectors. A first step towards this was the unilateral abrogation of the 'treaty' with the British South Africa Company. Secondly, the financial drain of mining revenue to Southern Rhodesia was halted when the federation was dissolved. The years immediately after independence were boom years in the copper industry. Good years for the mining companies raised the question of whether more revenue could be generated for government expenditure. The mining companies for their part were pressing for a shift in the taxation system from royalties per unit of output to taxation on profits. The latter would give them an incentive to invest. The government resisted that, as a tax on output is easier to administer and provides a secure income. The system as proposed by the companies was a licence for tax evasion, as profit depends largely on the way accounts are presented. However, in 1969 the Zambian government decided to take a fifty-one per cent interest in the copper mines in order to have a greater hold on the mining industry. This move was welcomed by one of the two big mining companies, the South African Anglo-American Corporation, and less so by the American Roan Selection Trust – part of AMAX. The latter did not resist, however. This is not surprising, as the deal was extremely advantageous for the companies. Firstly, they received generous payment for their shares. Secondly, they were retained on management contract and a large part of their income was thus secured irrespective of profitability. The benefits of the deal depended on the copper price. The higher the price, the more the benefits for the government as its income depended upon profits; the lower the price, the more the companies benefited relative to the government, as a large part of their income was independent of profit. The deal was made when copper prices were at a record level and thus seemed to benefit government. However, from the early 1970s prices have been on a downward slide and so the terms of the deal have primarily benefited the mining companies.

There is a substantial literature of good quality on the nationalization of the mines – of which Faber and Potter's work was probably the most prescient. This literature covers events up to the mid 1970s. At that time, there was a brief revival of copper prices and so the government tried to gain more control over the industry by redeeming immediately the bonds issued as part payment for its stake in the companies. This upsurge in prices was a fleeting phenomenon, however. There is a dearth of literature on the management of the mines since 1974. Further information in this regard would be useful to facilitate a satisfactory analysis of the country's economic decline in which the mines are crucial.

It is known that Zambia's competitive position deteriorated: aluminium was substituted for copper in distributing electricity; and new copper deposits were discovered elsewhere. The ore was lower grade, but it was mined in open pits rather than underground and the new mines were located nearer to sea ports. It is also known that Zambia produced less and less copper, although the growing role of cobalt, which was originally a side product, is hardly documented. Thirdly it is known that the mines became a drain on government resources instead of contributing to them. This became clear when the international financial institutions pressed the Zambian government to privatize the mines in the mid 1990s. The need to restructure public finance was the main drive behind this. If the mines were privatized, then the financial drain would be halted. Besides that, private ownership was expected to revitalize the mines and bring in better management. The effectiveness of privatization depends thus upon the degree to which the decline in the sector is caused by poor management or not.

There was no immediate great interest in buying the mines – a reflection partly of the diminished competitive position of Zambian copper. It was also a wasting asset. Many of the ore bodies were exhausted; most of the mines were underground and this meant their exploitation was much more labour intensive and costly than open pit mining; the mines were run down and needed much investment. There was a keen interest only in the old slag heaps – from which copper can be separated at little cost with modern technology – and the establishment of a new big open pit mine, Konkola Deep. A large part of existing operations will be shut down after privatization. Even if the production and profitability of the mines recover however, the government will not receive much tax revenue from the sector: the new investors have a twenty-year tax holiday. Income tax from the employees – who are few because of mechanization – and auxiliary industries will be the only profit accruing to government. The government will, however, have a burden from the mines as well: it took over the debts incurred at privatization.

The industrial sector grew fast in Zambia during the first decade after independence. Virtually the whole of Zambia's industrial sector was in European hands and it was part of the Southern African economic system at independence. It is therefore not surprising that the government moved in to industrialize for nationalistic reasons. In the late 1960s, the government took controlling interests in most existing industries and set up numerous government-owned industries in areas into which private capital did not want to move – some examples of the latter being a fertilizer factory in Kafue or a copper cable manufacturer on the Copperbelt. These industrial and trade interests were consolidated in a parastatal holding company, INDECO. Industrialization seemed well-founded in this first decade. Zambian industry had also a captive home market as the South African grip on Zambia's markets diminished because less was imported from there for political reasons

Zambia became dependent, however, upon long overland import routes as it cut ties with South Africa and was therefore an expensive producer. Import substitution, in Zambia as elsewhere, did not lead to less dependency. This was a hotly debated issue, and the exchange between Robin Fincham and Ann Seidman about the degree of autonomous development in Zambia's industrialization is still worth reading. Events rather than arguments showed the true situation, however. When foreign exchange became scarce, industrial development appeared to be import dependent to a large degree, and capacity utilization decreased enormously. This sealed the fate of many Zambian industries because profitability had always been problematic in the parastatal sector and now plummeted disastrously. Given this lack of competitiveness, it is not surprising that Zambian industry was later severely hit by import liberalization and a free floating of the exchange rate. Under a liberal and open trade regime, the scope for industrialization is limited in a landlocked country with few forward and backward linkages. The older industries, such as cement and beer, supplying a relatively stable and sizeable home market, survived privatization best.

It is obvious from the entries in this bibliography that the rural sector attracted more attention than any other economic sector. The general tenor in these publications is pessimistic: urban bias in policy making and investment is the most common explanation for stagnation in the rural sector; and urban bias is also considered the cause for the unabated drift to the cities. This argument is usually made in terms which compare town and country, but this comparison may obscure important dynamics in the rural sector.

It especially obscures the fact that there has been massive investment in the rural areas. Immediately after independence, government services were spread over the country. For example, each district has at least one secondary school. Tarred roads were built to each provincial capital and even beyond. Several massive agricultural credit programmes were launched. The government created a marketing structure penetrating deep into the rural areas through its parastatal, NAMBOARD. There was thus a transfer of resources from the urban to the rural sector, backed up by extensive institution building. These new institutions were often not effective – resources disappeared through these organizations instead of their generating productive activity – but they were not consistently parasitic.

It would thus be wrong to see rural Zambia as merely dormant and stagnating in the years since independence. From the late 1970s in particular, the government spread more and more programmes over the country to provide credit for input packages, an extension effort was made and produce was bought. In the 1980s, this resulted in a dramatic expansion of the area under maize, the staple food, in outlying areas of Zambia. The creation of this boom depended on subsidized fertilizer, subsidized transport and subsidized marketing. The staple food was thus sold far below cost price on the urban markets. It has therefore been constructed as a subsidy for urban consumers, but it drove rural production in the first place. When Zambia was faced by conditionality in obtaining further financial assistance in the 1980s, the foreign donor community was pressing for abolition of the system. They argued that it was a wasteful drain on the government budget and that it was inefficient to grow maize – a low-value bulk commodity – far away from where it was consumed in urban areas. One option was to raise food prices, but this has led several times to serious unrest. When a food price rise led once more to unrest on the Copperbelt in 1987, Zambia decided to go its own way and broke with the Structural Adjustment Programme which had been agreed with the IMF. This episode has generated many entries in this bibliography despite the fact that it seems now to be of primarily historical interest. A new government came to power in 1991 and dismantled the old regime's system of subsidies, credit and marketing. No urban protests followed and the drain on government finances was ended. Rural Zambia has thus not been merely stagnating in the past decades. Government policies have been effected much more than is often assumed. To recapitulate: there have been transfers from the mining sector to the rural areas. In the first decade after independence this was mostly in the form of infrastructure. Later subsidies to the rural sector mainly took the form of credit packages, inputs, extension and marketing, thus driving the maize boom in the 1980s. That maize boom was the result of a policy emanating from the Seers report. It was proposed at that time that African smallholders should produce what large-scale commercial farmers were producing, namely hybrid maize, to feed Zambia's urban population. During the 1980s, commercial farmers moved into different crops: cattle ranching increased in volume; there was much more irrigation introduced than before – for example on winter wheat; horticulture and flowers for export to Europe became a viable business. Maize, the staple food, was then grown by smallholders and not by peasant farmers. There was nevertheless a crucial difference from the envisaged policy. The maize boom was driven by transfers, which no longer came from the mining sector but from foreign financial assistance and especially foreign borrowing. To see Zambia's rural policies as an unmitigated failure, however, distorts the situation.

It may also be mistaken to see policy making as determining what actually happens in rural Zambia. There is a considerable body of literature – especially that following in the tradition of Norman Long's work in Serenje – which stresses farm dynamics and processes from below in explaining rural change. The literature on ox-drawn ploughing is illustrative. The assumption that rural Zambia was economically stagnant in the colonial period overlooks such grassroots initiatives. This perspective makes important regional differences also more intelligible. In Luapula Province, fish has for decades been a source of income; Mwase Lundazi in Eastern Province was producing for the market as far back as the 1950s. It may well be that government policies after independence – which did not recognize such differences – affected rural economies for the worse as a result. For example, as Achim van Oppen has shown, there was a substantial trade in cassava from North Western Province to the Mongu plain. When maize at highly subsidized prices became available, this trade collapsed.

The debate on Zambian rural development is characterized by ambiguity and paradox. Scant attention is paid, for example, to erratic time series of agricultural production. Zambia even has to import maize in some years. The trend of production is upwards, however, remaining just below the rate of population growth. Time series also therefore do not show an unambiguous stagnation of rural production. Finally, the rural sector has responded ambiguously to liberalization. There are some quite spectacular growth areas, notably in tobacco and cotton. The immediate explanation seems to be that multinationals set up an infrastructure of credit, inputs, extension and marketing for those crops. Food marketing, particularly of maize, is the most problematic area after liberalization. It may be that a return to state support or regulated supporting arrangements will occur.

Our knowledge of the policy orientations in various periods is much clearer than our knowledge of what actually happened in the economy. Zambia started out in 1964 from the premise that the state should complement private initiatives in the economy rather than replace them. In the 1970s and early 1980s the state became more and more interventionist. This was a self-defeating development as this state involvement was increasingly financed from foreign loans, and loan servicing would one day prove to be a problem. Zambia acquired relatively easy access to loans by playing East against West and by pointing to its stance in the fight against apartheid. Political rather than economic criteria established Zambia's creditworthiness. When majority rule established itself in Southern Africa and the cold war ended, Zambia's indebtedness became a stark fact. Zambia became dependent upon the international financial institutions.

These, as well as the foreign aid donor community, pressed more and more for a reduced role on the part of the state and for market liberalization. Internal resistance against *dirigisme* grew as well, and this was an essential part of the struggle for a return to multipartyism. The donor community therefore welcomed into power the new government, which unreservedly supported liberalization.

Economic reform along those lines has taken root in Zambia, and a return to state involvement and regulation as in the first decades after independence is highly unlikely. Economic reform has not had the expected effects, however. Robust growth has not returned to the economy and macroeconomic stabilization appears to be elusive: the exchange rate continues to fall and inflation remains high. The donor community sees the explanation for that in the size of the public sector: Zambia cannot afford such a large public sector. Whether the country would benefit from further reduction of public expenditure is, however, contentious. Zambia developed its educational and health services impressively in the first decade after independence. These have now deteriorated, and it is questionable whether benefits would accrue from further expenditure cuts. The continuing demand for reduction of public expenditure and its deflationary effects may actually be an impediment to growth.

Public expenditure in Zambia cannot be looked at in isolation from its crippling debt. A large part of Zambia's public expenditure goes towards debt servicing. Debt cancellation and public sector reform are now the main themes in the policy dialogue between donors and the Zambian government, the issue being whether debts can be cancelled on condition that Zambia pursues policies enhancing growth and alleviating poverty.

Politics

Zambia's recent political history tends to be subdivided into three periods, designated as republics. The first republic lasted from 1964 to 1973, when Zambia was a multiparty state in which UNIP under Kenneth Kaunda was the dominant force. The African National Congress (ANC) was in opposition, but its support was primarily regional. Its leader, Harry Nkumbula, originated from Southern Province and there the party was strong. The second republic lasted from 1973 to 1991 when Zambia was a one-party state, whose slogan was: One Zambia-One Nation; One Nation-One Party; One Party-Kaunda. The third republic has lasted from 1991 to the present day. Multipartyism has been reintroduced, but one party is dominant again: the Movement for Multi-party Democracy (MMD). Its leader, Frederick Chiluba, is at present serving his second term as president. Opposition in this dominant party system remains primarily regional. UNIP, as the main opposition party, finds its support in the east.

The continuities in Zambian politics are obvious. Single party dominance as well as a presidential system persist under all circumstances. It may be helpful in this introduction to stress the variations more. The interest in studying Zambian politics has been very uneven over time and the periodization above may help the user to place the relevance of reading. The first republic is well described in empirical terms: more as contemporary history than through theorizing. The second republic is far less well described. The later period in particular, from 1985 to 1991, is poorly documented. This was also the time when neo-marxism flourished in the study of African politics. Since the reintroduction of multipartyism, Zambia has been seen as a trailblazer in democratization. This and human rights are now the main themes.

Zambia's constitution at independence provided for a president, but gave ultimate power to parliament. Zambian parliaments have in practice, however, never taken the power given to them in the constitution. A presidential system – where most power resides in the executive – dominated UNIP as a party as well as the government in power after independence. In the first republic, the locus of political struggle was not in government, nor in parliament, but in the political party. These struggles reached a climax at the UNIP party conference of 1967. The dividing lines within the party at that time, however, were not along ideological or policy lines, but in terms of the region from which politicians originated, expressed mainly in language groups. Zambia is divided into four broad language groups: Bemba, which is spoken in Northern, Luapula Province, the

Copperbelt and the northern part of Central Province; Nyanja, which is spoken in Eastern Province and Lusaka Province; Tonga, which is spoken in Southern Province and the bordering part of Central Province; and Lozi, which is spoken in Western Province, together with the Lunda related languages of North Western Province. The struggle within UNIP about the power of regions in the various parts of Zambia was related to organizational issues. The question was whether leadership posts should be distributed on a regionally balanced basis or whether areas in which the party was strong should receive equal representation. The latter position would have implied a dominance of the Bemba-speaking regions. Kaunda resisted that and has always used the argument of tribal balancing.

Opposition within the party remained, however, and was increasingly considered to be associated with Simon Kapwepwe. He was a boyhood friend of Kaunda and was long seen as the definite number two in the party. In 1971 Kapwepwe broke with UNIP and formed the United Progressive Party (UPP). The formation of the UPP cannot be reduced exclusively to Bemba sentiments, despite the fact that Kapwepwe was seen as the leader of the Bemba faction. The economic situation was his main stated reason for breaking with UNIP. He foresaw the consequences of the falling copper price and argued that Zambia should react to that problem with austerity measures. Kapwepwe also argued that Zambia could not afford – for financial reasons – the confrontational policies in Southern Africa. Lastly he argued that UNIP had lost its identity as a democratic organization open to the grassroots and was in the hands of political opportunists instead.

Kaunda (UNIP) reacted to this with repression. Numerous people were put in detention and the UPP became a proscribed party. The special branch's grip on society became clear and ever after remained an essential element of Kaunda's rule. Kaunda, however, is an enigmatic politician and was not unambiguously repressive. He came to an agreement with the leader of the opposition, Harry Nkumbula, rather than imposing directly a one-party state. Almost all detainees were released after that. Elections that offered a degree of choice were organized. The voter could vote 'no' to the single presidential candidate and could choose between a number of parliamentary candidates on the same party ticket. If one was a party member, one could participate in the internal selection of those candidates.

The one-party state was welcomed and was not unpopular in the early days. The main reason was that it ended intimidation by vigilantes of both parties, which had been a problem especially in the poorer urban areas. Kaunda co-opted opposition leaders to a very great degree. He created space for this in a central committee of the party equal in status to the cabinet. High political office was thus extended, and vested interests in positions created loyalty. This was obvious when Kaunda dismissed people from leadership at short notice, as he regularly did. People thus turned into great loyalists if they were allowed to return. A spectacular return was that of Nalumina Mundia who resisted the one-party system for a long time and became a cabinet minister after being released from detention. Kaunda did not succeed in bringing Kapwepwe back to the fold, however. After being released from jail, Kapwepwe stayed quiet at first. He was readmitted to UNIP in 1978, but he did not react with loyalty. On the contrary, he challenged Kaunda for the leadership of the party. That was unacceptable to Kaunda.

This is indicative of one issue that Kaunda could not quell. When the one-party state was established, there was not much resistance to it. There was, however, a clear demand for rotation of leadership. There was a virtually unanimous demand for the limitation of presidential leadership to two five-year terms. Kaunda rejected this. Resistance against Kaunda increased also because he created more and more positions of influence for his children. It looked as if Zambia would be ruled by a dynasty, and this was resented.

The opposition to one-partyism came primarily from the educated stratum of society in forums such as the Economics Club of Lusaka or the Law Society of Zambia. In Zambia, the single party never managed to establish as hegemonic a position as in other countries. There was, for example, a broad protest from the churches against the gradual acceptance of marxist doctrines by UNIP. The most powerful institution to resist appeared to be the trade union movement. Opposition was, therefore, found at the grassroots too, but popular opposition could also take less focused and more widespread forms, which were manifested especially in riots against food price rises. The military in Zambia never managed to stage a successful coup, but there were quite a number of coups aborted at the last moment.

The opposition to the one-party state did not stem only from democratic concerns, however. The 1980s was also a period of horrifying economic decline. Kaunda and UNIP were held responsible for that, especially as they were seen as more concerned with securing wealth through their own positions than with the well being of the country. The political elite awarded themselves massive loans on which they defaulted with impunity.

In 1990 a number of developments came together: a coup was staged but failed; there was student unrest; and there were riots to protest against rising food prices. The party and Kaunda seemed to have lost legitimacy. It was also at this time that two trade unionists suggested a referendum on the one-party state for that same reason. The referendum was never held, as the outcome was obvious. The Movement for Multiparty Democracy turned itself into a political party. It won convincingly the multiparty elections of 1991 as well as those of 1996. The considerable literature on those elections need not be summarized here. One thing often not sufficiently noted should be mentioned though. Frederick Chiluba, the trade unionist who became the leader of the MMD, was not originally a prominent member of the party. His rise to power came at the first convention where he had an overwhelming success in the elections for leadership against three competitors.

This illuminates an important aspect of politics in the third republic. Chiluba was surrounded by people who had presidential ambitions themselves but who lacked Chiluba's grassroots support. Thus the only way to challenge Chiluba was by forming another party. This was an important mechanism behind the numerous schisms in MMD during the first five years of rule. One of the parties emerging from such a split – the National Party – was even nicknamed the party of aspiring presidents. A leadership challenge was never the stated reason for resignation from MMD, of course. Corruption and heavy-handed leadership within MMD were the most common complaints. Rival parties tended to dissolve in internal conflicts. Non-governmental organizations (NGOs) tend to be more vital and vocal political actors in Zambia than political parties. Their leadership is usually highly educated, but often lacking in grassroots support.

Another challenge to MMD came from the defeated party, UNIP, under the leadership of Kaunda. Kaunda seemed to have accepted defeat in 1991, and he announced his retirement from party leadership. He obviously regretted that decision and heavy-handedly manipulated a return to the command of UNIP. He challenged the legitimacy of MMD rule and demanded immediate elections. In reply, MMD adopted a constitutional clause, which disqualified Kaunda from standing for election. The clause required that both parents of a candidate should be born in Zambia.

The 1996 elections were a litmus test for MMD. Kaunda had called for a boycott. Foreign donors had suspended aid because of concerns about the legitimacy of the elections. The constitutional clause was the major reason, but they took other opposition complaints seriously as well. Chiluba went into the election claiming that it showed Zambia to be a healthy democracy: four presidential candidates and more than 600 parliamentary candidates were competing. The outcome of the elections showed widespread grassroots support for Chiluba. He appeared even more popular in the presidential elections than his party was in the parliamentary elections. Kaunda's boycott on the other hand received hardly any support.

Chiluba and MMD, however, were not embarking on a honeymoon with the foreign donor community. Almost immediately after the elections, the government moved against the non-governmental organizations. Chiluba argued that they were foreign financed and considered it contrary to the national interest for foreigners to finance internal Zambian politics. He conveniently overlooked the fact that MMD had itself accepted foreign finance in the early days. MMD quickly lost the democratic credentials it had gained through the elections.

These events encapsulate Zambian politics in the last ten years. On the one hand, Zambia is a much more open and free country than it was –

especially compared to the last years under Kaunda – not only in terms of political freedoms, but also because of economic deregulation. All parties in Zambia have a tendency towards arbitrary use of power. The MMD government is often highhanded in dealing with opposition. The authorities display no sense of proportion when it comes to dealing with the independent press. It is inexcusable that police shot at Kenneth Kaunda and Rodger Chongwe while breaking up a political meeting. One can, however, see similarly autocratic tendencies in the opposition: there is generally no internal party bureaucracy. Electoral defeats tend not to be accepted by losers. Non-governmental organizations neglect grassroots membership, and they are often more a vehicle for personal ambition than a representation of wider interests.

Outside observers and the local community of non-governmental organizations are concerned about the threats to democracy. It is regularly argued that Zambia lacks a democratic culture. Zambia's political history shows the opposite, however. The one-party state never quelled all forums of opposition. Political parties and leaders have to gain legitimacy and do not automatically dominate. The government may own media, but these report on the opposition and are often critical of the government's actions. Presidents regularly find themselves having to replace the editors-in-chief. In the struggle for multipartyism, the judiciary has ruled consistently in favour of democratization. The opposition's accusations against the MMD government may reflect more a vital democratic culture than a sign of democracy under threat.

International relations

Zambian politics tends to have an impact outside the domestic arena. The country's international significance was previously more pronounced than it is now, however. In the first twenty-five years after independence, Zambia played a major role in the liberation of Southern Africa. Immediately after independence in 1964, it was clear that Zambia offered a sanctuary for the liberation movements of the whole of Southern Africa. Secondly, Zambia immediately made plans to become less dependent upon communications through Southern Africa. There was a deliberate attempt to loosen the ties to the Southern African political economy, which is and was dominated by the big mining companies. A tarred road and later a railway was constructed to Dar es Salaam in Tanzania, on the east coast of Africa. The road was financed with a loan from the United States, while the People's Republic of China built the railway. This is indicative of the non-aligned approach which Kaunda followed, exploiting cold war rivalry as much as possible.

Similarly, Kaunda resorted to the widest gamut of political means: varying from supporting the armed struggle to meeting the adversaries, such as Ian Smith or John Vorster, in the midst of such struggles. Kaunda was regularly accused of compromising himself irretrievably with the white minority regime. He was especially criticized for this in the mid 1970s when a debate raged over *détente* with Southern Africa. This *détente* was supposed to be fuelled by the interests of a local emerging capital class. Kaunda's attempts to forge broad national fronts were equally severely criticized, particularly in Angola where Kaunda teamed up with South Africa to allow all three liberation movements – most notably Jonas Savimbi's UNITA – a role in the transition instead of allowing the MPLA to gain dominance backed by Russian firepower. Zambia has suffered armed incursions from the South as well as violence among guerrillas within its borders because of its stance on Southern Africa.

With the wisdom of hindsight, Kaunda did not compromise in the struggle for the liberation of Southern Africa. Zambia's contribution to the liberation of Southern Africa was vital, and especially so towards the end of the struggle in South Africa when the South African ANC lost its bases in Mozambique after the so called Nkomati agreement. Zambia was the most southern country where the ANC found a safe haven.

Kaunda's policies on Southern Africa were not always popular domestically, especially because of the economic hardships they brought, but such opposition disappeared towards the end. After majority rule came to South Africa, Zambians tended to be proud of their role in its liberation. The complete liberation of Southern Africa coincided with the end of the Kaunda period.

The new government which came to power in 1991 soon made its mark on foreign policy. It wanted clearly to signal a discontinuity. A number of measures were taken almost immediately: diplomatic ties with Israel were re-established; the Saddam Hussein Boulevard in Lusaka was renamed and the ban on Salman Rushdie's *Satanic verses* was lifted. This is indicative of a much more pro-Western and far less Third World oriented course in international relations. This also fits the MMD government's much more neo-liberal stance on economic policy. Kaunda continued to capitalize on his old contacts in opposition to the new government, notably on the long-standing and loyal relationship with Nelson Mandela of South Africa. Frederick Chiluba, his successor, rapidly gained international prestige in his second term of office, as he kept Zambia out of the wars in Angola and Congo while playing a mediating role there. The economy, however, has again reoriented itself strongly to Southern Africa. This is particularly obvious at Lusaka International Airport where the flights to Johannesburg are the most frequent and the most in demand. It is also evident in daily life. For example, South African supermarket chains have opened outlets, and Anglo-American, the biggest mining house in Southern Africa, has moved back into Zambia after privatization of the mines. International relations in

Central and Southern Africa are fluid, if not chaotic, but Zambia is more a Southern African nation than a Central African one.

Social problems, society and culture

Zambia as a nation has experienced tremendous downward mobility. This is pervasive in daily life. Whereas the period from the end of the Second World War to the mid 1970s opened up opportunities for a large number of Zambians, the period from the mid 1970s onwards has seen a dramatic diminution. It would be a distortion to consider the past decades to have brought a universal drop in living standards; some people are doing well. However, the spread of poverty has been reinforced by a dramatic decline in the government's provision of education and health services. This is accompanied by a more general sense of insecurity caused by a rising crime rate. The most pervasive corrosion of the social fabric is, nevertheless, not directly linked to economics and politics, but is expressed in the saying that there are 'too many funerals' these days. The AIDS pandemic has hit Zambia severely. HIV infection comes on top of other widespread diseases: malaria, tuberculosis and meningitis. A considerable epidemiological literature is growing on such topics, but knowledge in these fields is still emerging.

The social effects of the AIDS pandemic are gradually becoming apparent. A major consequence is the increasing number of orphans, and it is expected that children will head some families in situations where all adult relatives have died. The extended family is, however, a pervasive institution in Zambia and it is not unusual for parents not to be the biological parents. Indeed, it is difficult to understand Zambian society if one cannot reason in terms of kinship. Newcomers to the country would do well to read a little anthropology in order to understand the reason why missionaries taught about God, the brother of the mother in matrilineal societies. It is common to declare in Zambia that the extended family is rapidly losing significance. To an outsider, however, it appears to be enduring, and most strikingly so in the case of funerals. The moral obligation to attend funerals of even distant relatives is almost binding. Matters of health, fertility and death have a meaning which is often related to the almost mystic belief in the harmony of the family. The other side of this coin is a belief in the supernatural, which can distort this and which outsiders tend to label as witchcraft.

Kinship is also important in situations where different values seem to be dominant. Weddings have all the distinctly western trappings: bridal gowns, bridesmaids, wedding cakes, kitchen parties (the equivalent of hen nights) and stag nights. Yet marriage is usually the outcome of negotiations between families, in which the preferences of the partners play a role but no more than that.

Introduction

Particular societies cannot be understood without reference to their culture. Culture manifests itself in customs and norms, but is expressed also in the arts. It may be noted that that section in this bibliography is rather small. The prime reason is that the literary arts are not well developed in Zambia. Folklore may be of high quality, but it still needs to be recorded in forms that are accessible to a wider public. In the 1970s, local publishing became more significant in Zambia than before. This led to a massive production of manuscripts, but few of them were published. Their quality tends to be poor. Independence brought also opportunities for Zambian painters and sculptors. Some obtained scholarships to study in Europe or the USA and others adopted European crafts and approaches without being educated in them. A visit to the National Museum in Lusaka shows much talent, but little is recorded in publications.

The theatre has probably appealed most among the modern art forms. This may be explained by the fact that many of the older arts were rooted in performance. The arts in which Zambian people show themselves strongest are still dance and music. One might wish that more were written about these topics. Two types of dances have been written about in detail: the *makishi* in the west and the *nyau* dance in the east. Both are deeply interwoven with religious beliefs. These beliefs persist and in the minds of people are often not incompatible with the Christian beliefs that are almost universally adhered to. In addition, in the Christian churches one can find drumming, singing and dancing of very high quality. Such experiences can only be partially transmitted by the written word, but can be vital to becoming acquainted with a country. Despite its shortcomings, the hope is that this bibliography has its uses in this respect as well.

The Country and Its People

1   The peoples of Zambia.
Sally Aldridge.   London: Heinemann Educational Books; Lusaka:
NECZAM, 1978. 162p. 40 maps. bibliog.
This is a secondary school textbook, but it is a very good one. Aldridge has written an
African-centred rather than a colonial history. Newcomers to Zambia could quickly learn
a good deal about the country from this book as it is very wide ranging and includes topics
such as anthropology and geography. For example, Aldridge's illustrated explanation of
different marriage practices among patrilineal and matrilineal societies would give non-
Zambians a very good understanding of what is happening around them.

2   Zambia: between two worlds.
Marcia M. Burdette.   Boulder, Colorado: Westview Press; London:
Avebury, 1988. 210p. 3 maps. bibliog.
This is a volume in a series of profiles of African nations and will appeal to people who
want to familiarize themselves with Zambia. The book is, however, primarily a study of
the country's political economy up to 1985, although there is an introductory chapter
which is historical and geographical in nature, as well as a chapter on society and culture.
The book provides an informative overview of the main events in the economy and the
political system until that time, and it is particularly valuable in the documentation of the
economic decline of Zambia in the early 1980s. It can be read as a whole or dipped into.
The book gives a feeling for the political life of the country, for example in the neat
summing up of the careers of prominent politicians John Mwanakatwe and Simon
Kapwepwe. There are nice observations, as when the way Kaunda deals with people
around him is compared to the parable of the prodigal son. There is room for a degree of
scepticism, however, as time has moved on and changed perspectives. What has come to
light in recent years makes it even more doubtful than it was at the time whether Zambia
under Kaunda deserved its reputation as a country with a good human rights record (as
suggested on p. 108).

3   Spectrum guide to Zambia.
Compiled and edited by Camerapix.   Nairobi: Camerapix Publishers
International, 1996. 354p. 11 maps. bibliog.
The photographs in this guide are glorious and the text is also thorough. It is a travel guide
and aims at comprehensive coverage. A good amount of space is devoted to the general
background to sights and experiences. Birdwatching and wildlife are comprehensively
covered in a seventy page section on special features. The guide also contains checklists
of birds and wildlife: birdwatchers especially will be keen to start ticking! The checklists
are included in the section listing a wide range of useful addresses, which are not merely
of tourist interest: business associations, conference centres and government offices and
ministries can be found there as well. There is also a section on business in Zambia.

4   La Zambie contemporaine. (Contemporary Zambia).
Edited by Jean-Pascal Daloz, John D. Chileshe.   Paris: Editions
Karthala, 1996. 382p. 5 maps. bibliog.
This is the most recent general scholarly introduction to the country, but it is only
accessible to those who read French. The authors are all either French or Zambian, and
the book includes a general political introduction, together with a few essays on mining,
agriculture and industry, and several chapters on cultural affairs. The last two chapters are
on gender and youth. The work distinguishes itself from other general introductions to the
country by concentrating more on cultural affairs: oral tradition, languages, literature,
theatre and media. This is not surprising, as one of the editors, John Chileshe, has a
background in the study of literature. There is one regional chapter on agriculture in
Western Province. A chapter on Lusaka has the intriguing title: 'From segregation to
archipellisation'. This book is one of a series of studies sponsored by the French Ministry
of Foreign Affairs, with the aim of making the French intelligentsia more acquainted with
anglophone Africa.

5   Sambia: mit einem Anhang Fakten-Zahlen-Übersichten. (Zambia:
with a supplement of facts, numbers and overviews).
Axel Drescher.   Gotha, Germany: Justus Perthes Verlag, 1998. 199p.
22 maps. bibliog.
This is an exceptionally good introduction to Zambia, but one needs to know German to
read it. Drescher is a geographer and this discipline is particularly suitable to introduce
the many facets of a country. Drescher discusses a broad range of issues, but he is
selective. The mining industry, for example, receives little attention as compared to
agriculture. The last chapter is a superb introduction to the latter topic, written with a
thorough understanding of African – as opposed to modern commercial – agriculture. His
treatment of Lusaka's geography and problems provides another particularly good
summary of the extensive literature in this field. Drescher often uses specific cases to
illustrate general phenomena. The building of the Kariba dam is an obvious choice, but
other topics – for example, development problems in North Western Province – are rarely
treated elsewhere.

6 Zambia.

David Else. In: *Malawi, Mozambique and Zambia.* Hawthorne, Victoria, Australia: Lonely Planet, 1997, p. 247-89. 8 maps.

This provides a minimum of information on where to stay, where to eat and how to get around. The series caters especially for the backpacker. Zambia is not particularly suitable for such tourism thanks to the country's size and the fact that tourist attractions are dispersed around its periphery. It is not surprising that Zambia gets the least attention of the three countries covered. Nevertheless, worthwhile places which are not widely known are mentioned; for example the Moto Moto museum of Bemba culture in Mbala or Ngopnye Falls in Western Province. Whereas other guides talk about driving conditions, the Lonely Planet guide includes phrases such as, 'access is not easy: you have to be dropped off at...'

7 Historical dictionary of Zambia.

John J. Grotpeter, Brian V. Siegel, James R. Pletcher. Lanham, Maryland: The Scarecrow Press Inc., 1998. 2nd ed. 570p. map. bibliog.

This new edition is much more extensive than the previous one, and the coverage is much more thorough. As the title indicates, one can find a great deal of historical information in this reference work, but there is also much to be found of contemporary relevance. There is a detailed entry on the politician Frederick Chiluba, for example. It contains essential linguistic information, including an explanation of such prefixes as 'ma-' and 'ci-', as well as an explanation of crucial anthropological terms like 'clan' and 'matrilineal descent'. There is a chronology of important events to refer back to when placing particular episodes in history. The elaborate bibliography contains references to obscure publications which may be highly significant for people working on precise details of Zambian issues.

8 Tales of Zambia.

D. Hobson. London: The Zambia Society Trust, 1996. 224p.

Hobson describes himself as a 'scribbler in the margins of history', and it is therefore not surprising that this book is, above all, entertaining. It contains eighty-six short chapters that deal with subjects such as the moment of arrival of independence, the history of the 'castle' in Lundazi, personalities such as Chirapula Stephenson and especially nature and landscape. This is an invaluable source for residents and travellers alike who want to know more about what is to seen about them in the country. The work exemplifies a balanced personal reaction to colonialism and independence in Zambia.

9 Cultures of the world: Zambia.

Timothy Holmes. Singapore: Times Books International, 1998. 128p. map.

This coffee-table book contains, besides beautiful photographs, a fair amount of text, and covers a wide range of topics. Some, such as economy and government, are to be expected in a book like this, but others – for instance, birth, childhood, marriage and death – are less commonplace in such a book. Holmes stresses rightly that funerals are very important in Zambia and illustrates this by telling us that 'every day at set hours[,] the Zambian radio broadcasts announcements of deaths calling relatives together' (p. 59).

10 Zambia.
Jaynee Lee. In: *Complete guide to walks and trails in Southern Africa*. Cape Town: Struik Publishers Limited, 1993, p. 310-20. map.

The chapter describes fourteen walking trails in Zambia. 'Trail' is perhaps the wrong word here, because it is mainly guided walking safaris in game parks that are included. The necessary contact addresses are provided; the work is of interest for a particular type of upmarket tourism.

11 Large mammals and a brave people: subsistence hunters in Zambia.
Stuart A. Marks. Seattle, Washington: University of Washington Press, 1976. 254p. 3 maps. bibliog.

The jacket of this book recommends it to the general reader as well as to pre-historians and anthropologists concerned with human evolution and hunting societies. Indeed, although this study does not ignore the modern world, it very much takes second place, as muzzle loaders made hunting in groups unnecessary, and labour migration drained the ranks of specialized guilds. The wish to document a vanishing culture pervades this book, which describes Bisa hunting in the Luangwa valley. Marks is an anthropologist and ecologist and this is made apparent by a long chapter on animal populations and their ecology in the valley that may be relevant to many readers. Wildlife enthusiasts will find much of value in this esoteric but brilliant book. Marks makes apt use of early written sources. See also: 'Profile and process: subsistence hunters in a Zambian community' by Stuart A. Marks (*Africa*, vol. 49, no. 1 [1974], p. 53-67).

12 Zambia: the Bradt travel guide.
Chris McIntyre. Chalfont St. Peter, England: Bradt Publications, 1999. 2nd ed. 406p. 38 maps.

This is by far the best travel guide to Zambia available at time of writing. This second edition is much more elaborate than the first, partly because Zambia itself has changed: there is now much more accommodation available and tourist attractions are more developed. This guide is very good on the subjects of travel within Zambia – note especially the plethora of maps – accommodation and the like. It pays attention to places which were previously out of the orbit of tourism, like the Bangweulu swamps. It has retained the distinctive human touch of the first edition, for example warning against taking lifts with drunken drivers. Contrary to general opinion, McIntyre considers Zambia a good country for hitchhiking, especially in remote areas. Hitchhikers are, however, then expected to pay like everybody else. This kind of detail is often missing from other publications.

13 National monuments of Zambia: an illustrated guide.
D.W. Phillipson, revised by N.M. Katanekwa. Livingstone, Zambia: National Monuments Commission, 1992. 4th printing. 110p. map.

This is a delightful booklet for anybody residing in or visiting Zambia. There is a commonly held view that Zambia's natural environment is monotonous, but anyone who is of this opinion should look into this beautifully illustrated listing and find, to give a few examples, the Kundalila Falls, Lunsemfwa Wonder Gorge or Nsulu Cave. These three are all in Central Province and so within the reach of urban residents. The national monuments may be subdivided into three categories: spectacular nature; places of archaeological interest; and memoirs of the modern period, from Livingstone's place of death to former president Kaunda's house in Chilenje.

14 Mosi-oa-Tunya: a handbook of the Victoria Falls region.
Edited by D.W. Phillipson. London: Longman, 1975. 222p. 9 maps. bibliog.

This is the last update of earlier collections of articles on the Falls region. It consists of papers on geology, prehistory, art and the natural environment. These scholarly articles contain much of interest to the tourist and visitor not primarily interested in white-water rafting or bungy jumping. The beautiful illustrations make browsing a pleasure.

15 Visitor's guide to Zambia: how to get there, what to see, where to stay.
Nicholas Plewman, Brendan Dooley. Halfway House, South Africa: Southern Book Publishers, 1995. 190p. map.

This very accessible guide contains essential information. Clearly written, it is of most benefit to the slightly upmarket tourist. It contains eleven route descriptions for travel by car with realistic, accurate assessments (for example: Livingstone to Mongu: potholed tar and sand road; four wheel drive preferable). Its list of places to stay is prefaced by a reminder that accommodation in Zambia covers the full spectrum, from the most luxurious to the positively penal. This guide's great appreciation for Zambia's nature and landscape is evident not only from the listing of birdwatching spots, but also from the writers' challenge to Shiva Naipaul's derogatory view of Zambia's landscape on page 56.

16 Zambia.
Chris Stuart, Tilde Stuart. In: *Guide to the Southern African game and nature reserves; South Africa, Namibia, Botswana, Zambia, Malawi, Zimbabwe.* London: New Holland Publishers Ltd., 1992, p. 316-32. 2nd ed.: revised and updated. 14 maps.

The authors provide a summary of the game management areas and national parks in Zambia. Further information is provided on the national parks in a brief and matter of fact form. While this book is popular among tourists, the information is here and there out of date and there may soon be a new edition.

17 Zambia.
Edited by Richard Vaughan with photographs by Ian Murphy. Harare: The Corporate Brochure Company, undated. 182p. map.

This is the ultimate coffee table book on Zambia: it is simply beautiful. The photographs are often spectacular and strikingly capture the atmosphere of the country. The accompanying text is helpful to anyone wanting to become acquainted with the country. It is not only a useful introductory book on Zambia, but also an excellent means by which those who have left the country can relive the past. The book has clearly been drawn up with public relations in mind, and it is therefore totally uncritical. Although the authors do not date their book, there is an edition dating from the 1970s in which former president Kaunda is quite central, and one dating from the mid 1990s in which there are no pictures with a political content.

Geography and the Environment

18   Zambia: national conservation strategy and national environmental action plan.
Lubinda Aangola, Patrick Chipungu.   In: *Strategies for sustainability; Africa.*   Edited by Adrian Wood.   London: Earthscan Publications, 1997, p. 147-70.

This is quite a formal report on policy making with respect to the environment in Zambia. Its language is technical and bureaucratic, leading to phrases such as 'task force seminars were held to review the work of the technical group'. It ends with an assessment of the strengths and weaknesses of the strategy that has been implemented. The lessons learnt may be of more interest to activists in the field than to a general audience. The paper notes as a positive outcome the emergence of a group of Zambians who are enthusiastic and dedicated to environmental causes.

19   The politics of common resource management in Zambia's Mweru-Luapula fishery.
B.H.M. Aarnink.   In: *Co-managing the commons; setting the stage in Mali and Zambia.*   Edited by Thea Hillhorst, Nettie Aarnink.   Amsterdam: Royal Tropical Institute, 1999, p. 41-63. map. bibliog.

This article has a very practical agenda: what has to be done so that some form of common management of the fishing stocks in Lake Mweru will take place? The two major issues are closing the fishing season at the time of breeding and protecting a major breeding ground. However, a host of other issues are discussed, varying from environmental abuse to the change of government in 1991. The article makes it clear that everybody is convinced that something has to be done, but that no concrete results are forthcoming. It is based on close observation and gives the impression of a close acquaintance with Zambian society.

20 Zambia.
M. Banda, G. Nyirongo. In: *The Southern African environment: profiles of the SADC countries.* Edited by S. Moyo, P. O'Keefe, M. Sill. London: Earthscan Publications, 1993, p. 272-305. 5 maps. bibliog.

This is a chapter in what is primarily a reference work on environmental issues and problems. The legal framework of the state in its dealings with the environment receives special attention. The need for more and better legislation, as well as a greater capacity for implementing that legislation, is seen as a major factor in the management of the environment. Besides being a reference text, the chapter is also useful as an introduction to such issues. The authors tend, however, to gloss over moot points: their strong conviction that individualization of land tenure will automatically lead to better conservation practices is an example.

21 Is there hope for conservation in Africa?
John Cartwright. *Journal of Modern African Studies*, vol. 29, no. 3 (1991), p. 355-71.

This article compares wildlife policies in Zambia and Cameroon. The pages on Zambia (p. 360-64) give an impressionistic account of the situation on the eve of multipartyism. It is striking that former president Kaunda's name is usually associated with conservation and that his successor, Chiluba, did not build up any record in that regard.

22 Miombo ecology and management: an introduction.
Emmanuel N. Chidumayo. London: Intermediate Technology Publications, 1997. 166p. 9 maps. bibliog.

The *miombo* – or brachystegia – woodlands are the most common vegetative cover in Zambia, but are diminishing as wood is used for fuel and land is cleared for other purposes. The people living in and near them also use them intensively. This is a technical book, written from the viewpoint of a forester who wants to harvest. This conclusion, based on extensive research, may give an idea of what the book is all about: 'cutting in September and October probably results in the most vigorous and productive coppice in Zambian Miombo woodland' (p. 131). The fire resistance of *miombo* woodland intrigues many laymen, who may therefore be interested in the chapter devoted to fire.

23 School/community links in environmental education: a review of the factors of success in the chongololo clubs of Zambia.
Bruce K. Downie. Washington, DC: Environment Education and Communication; Academy for Educational Development, 1999. 98p.

The *chongololo* clubs were initially set up in the 1970s at schools to propagate the conservation of wildlife. Nowadays they concern themselves with much wider environmental issues. This evaluation of these clubs was carried out by an American consultancy firm for USAID. It compares schools with and schools without *chongololo* clubs in Mfuwe (near Luangwa national park); Choma district in Southern Province; and in the cities of Kitwe and Lusaka. It is generally positive in tone. One comment relating to Mfuwe states that students generally demonstrate a good understanding of the links between various environmental factors: for example, between tree cutting and erosion, or the effects of wildlife depletion on tourism revenue.

24 Bureaucrats and the environment in Africa: the politics of structural choice in a one-party state.

Clark G. Gibson. *Comparative Politics*, vol. 31, no. 3 (1999), p. 273-95.

This study is situated in the late Kaunda period. Kaunda's personality and his position with respect to wildlife conservation plays a major role in the article. Two cases of wildlife conservation programmes, both in the Luangwa valley, form its core. One initiative originated from within the government bureaucracy – the establishment of a game management command – but sought to escape political influence. The other – the Luangwa Intensive Resources Development Project – originated from a group led by Europeans who sought Kaunda's patronage. The result is a lively inside view into the politics and administration of conservation in Zambia. If one is primarily interested in that subject, then it may be worthwhile to read through the rather pretentious theory which builds on the question of political choice in the context of a non-industrialized, non-democratic, one-party state.

25 Politicians and poachers; the political economy of wildlife policy in Africa.

Clark G. Gibson. Cambridge, England: Cambridge University Press, 1999. 244p. bibliog.

Zambian wildlife conservation in the 1980s figures prominently in this book, which uses the Zambian material as a point of comparison with Kenya and Zimbabwe. Drawing on the Zambian material, Gibson seeks to make points which have a much wider significance than for Zambia alone. In a chapter called 'The political logic of poaching in one-party states', for example, he writes that 'the restrictive wildlife laws enabled the incumbent UNIP government to use wildlife as a resource in patronage politics'. People who are predominantly interested in Zambia will find in chapters four and five a detailed description of the Luangwa Integrated Rural Development Program (Lirdep) and the Administrative Management Design for Game Management Areas (ADMADE). In chapter five Gibson looks in detail at the impact of these institutions at local level.

26 Monitoring illegal wildlife use and law enforcement in African savannah rangelands.

Hugo Jachmann. Lusaka: Wildlife Resource Monitoring Unit, 1998. 123p. bibliog.

This is a technical book which analyses, for example, the incentive structure of income for game scouts so that they will not be tempted by poachers; the effectiveness of conventional patrols by scouts as compared to concentrating on investigations, and so on. It also contains a great deal of merely factual information – for example, on the number of illegally killed elephants found by game scouts, or the number of elephants killed in the period of legal culling (1967-72). Anybody who has visited a game park will be impressed by the fragility of such wilderness landscapes. This book is therefore important reading for anybody interested in game conservation and well worth browsing through for anybody interested in Zambia.

27 **Aerial sample survey of the central Luangwa valley; animal abundance, trends and distribution.**
Hugo Jachmann, C.M. Phiri. Lusaka: Wildlife Resource Monitoring Unit, 1999. 74p. 9 maps. bibliog.

Potential readers may be frightened by the statistical sophistication of this paper, but one can find in it what the title promises. Actually it gives more, as it reviews all aerial surveys of wildlife from 1993 onwards. It not only gives the numbers and trends in decline or growth of animal populations, but explains these trends as well. The park saw, for instance, explosive growth in a thriving hyena population as illegal hunters left elephant carcasses after taking the tusks. The hyenas are now in decline as the poaching of elephants has subsided.

28 **Recent population movements in Zambia: some aspects of the 1969 census.**
Mary Elizabeth Jackman. Manchester, England: Manchester University Press, 1973. 66p. 8 maps. bibliog.

This reworked master's thesis in geography at the University of Zambia provides a competent reading and interpretation of the 1969 census. It is well worth noting because relatively little use is made of census material in the study of Zambian society and migration is essential to understanding of this subject. One would have expected the lifting of colonial controls over migration, which tended to stimulate the migration of single males, to lead to more females leaving for urban areas. The opposite was the case: the male to female ratio actually declined in many districts after independence.

29 **A social geography of Zambia: a survey of population patterns in a developing country.**
George Kay. London: University of London Press, 1967. 157p. 4 maps. bibliog.

This book is written from an outdated perspective in which urbanization is seen almost as an aberration in African society. It is of course also based on outdated census data. However, George Kay is still a very talented geographer. Given the controversy about Kaunda's Malawian origins, it is interesting to see on page 60 a concentration of Zambians born outside Zambia living along the Malawian border. Similarly it is worth noting that Western Province (Barotseland) had the lowest incidence of taxable male absentees in 1962. That situation changed drastically later. This geography is therefore a valuable historical source, useful for a wider audience than geographers only: one can, for example, use the aerial photograph of Cairo Road, Lusaka, to note the huge changes between then and now.

30 **Dambos: a study in morphodynamic activity on the plateau regions of Zambia.**
Rudiger Mäckel. *Catena*, vol. 1 (1974), p. 327-65. map. bibliog.

Mäckel is a physical geographer who has written extensively on wetlands and marshy areas in Zambia. This article deals with a striking element in the Zambian landscape – the dambo. Dambos are shallow depressions in the headward zone of rivers, without a marked stream channel. They are seasonally waterlogged and grass-covered. Most of Mäckel's work is published in German, but *Catena* is a German journal which publishes articles in English as well. Anyone who has an interest in physical geography and reads German will find it very worthwhile to consult more work by Mäckel.

31 The imperial lion: human dimensions of wildlife management in Central Africa.
Stuart A. Marks. Boulder, Colorado: Westview Press, 1984. 196p. 5 maps. bibliog.

This book is not primarily directed at scholars – although it may also prove rewarding for them – but at a wider community which includes developers and wildlife administrators. It deals with the insights for the practical management of wildlife which resulted from Marks' anthropological and ecological research. His main message is that environmental management should not start from the assumption that a natural state has to be maintained, but rather that change and human presence has to be accommodated.

32 Early warning on agricultural production with satellite data and simulation models in Zambia.
M. Meneti, J. Huygen, S. Azzali, J.A.A. Berkhout. In: *Satellite remote sensing for agricultural projects.* Edited by J.P. Gastellu-Etchegorry. Washington, DC: The World Bank, 1990, p. 187-207.

This paper is written by bureaucratic specialists and their writing is difficult to paraphrase or summarize. The paper deals with the MARS project, which links geographical information systems, data base management systems, crop growth simulation models and the routine functioning of an early warning system designed to detect famine. So far, that is comprehensible, but phrases such as 'MARS hardware and software configuration has to accommodate the Zambian CFEWU procedures' (p. 196) demand a command of specialist vocabulary. Remote sensing data are, however, more and more used in geography and increasingly in the study of Zambian agriculture, and this article may be helpful to guide and initiate those who are sceptical as to the quality of the data.

33 Regeneration process of the miombo woodland at abandoned citemene fields of Northern Zambia.
Shuichi Oyama. African Study Monographs; the Center for African Area Studies, Kyoto University, vol. 17, no. 3 (1996), p. 101-16. 2 maps.

This is a technical article on a subject of importance to many people in Zambia. The viability of *citemene* agriculture depends upon the time needed for vegetation to regenerate. The article gives a detailed description of the *citemene* system. The conclusion is that a fallow period of up to sixteen years is needed for regeneration in the tree cutting areas and more than fifty years in the more intensively farmed garden areas. The Bemba (one of the main peoples of Zambia) can sustainably utilize the *miombo* or brachystegia woodlands or forests while producing a certain level of food before regeneration. This article provides important material for discussion among environmental specialists and important issues for the general public to note.

34 **The Zambezi teak forests; proceedings of the first international conference on the teak forests of Southern Africa held in Livingstone, Zambia, March 1984.**
Edited by G.D. Piearce. Ndola, Zambia: Government of the Republic of Zambia, 1986. 535p. 3 maps.
Many people who look at the map of Zambia are intrigued by the railway's small branch line which goes to Mulobezi. It was laid because of the teak forests there – teak forests that are an essential part of a quite specific environment. These conference papers, many of which will only be of interest to specialist foresters, give exhaustive information on them. It is also true to say, though, that any prospective visitor to the forests will benefit, for example, from the paper on the geography of Zambezi teak by Dennis Huckabey.

35 **The ecology of the Gwembe Tonga.**
Thayer Scudder. Manchester, England: Manchester University Press, 1962. 247p. map. bibliog.
This is a companion volume by a geographer to Colson's anthropological study of the Gwembe Tonga (see item nos. 197, 199). It provides an extremely detailed description of the interaction between Tonga society and the natural environment. The longest chapter (100 pages in length) is devoted to agriculture. A separate chapter on famine is particularly worthwhile. The study is a trailblazer which preceded present day concerns with ecology and the local knowledge of African farmers. It deals, however, with an ecosystem that has disappeared under the waters behind the Kariba dam and, as such, has limited contemporary relevance. The book would be more accessible if an explicit system ordered the variety of rich material.

36 **The district map: an episode in British colonial cartography.**
Jeffrey C. Stone. *Cartographic Journal, Journal of the British Cartographic Society*, vol. 19, no. 2 (1982), p. 104-12. 2 maps.
The emphasis here is on the early history of map-making in Zambia, investigating who made the maps and what means were used. An example of the latter suggests a degree of technical complexity: 'The cyclometer was evidently frequently employed by touring officers and indeed it could be indented for from Government Stores' (p. 108).

37 **The compilation map: a technique for topographic mapping by British colonial survey.**
Jeffrey C. Stone. *Cartographic Journal, Journal of the British Cartographic Society*, vol. 21, no. 2 (1984), p. 121-29. map.
The topic here is map-making in the early decades of Zambia's colonization. The type of map created was then the so-called compilation map: 'Survey departments were often unable to carry out the work necessary for topographic maps which could satisfy their standards. As a stop gap measure they drew upon whatever data was available' (p. 121). These maps bore the imprint of the director of surveys, but their content was not under his control as he merely brought various sources together.

38 **The soils, vegetation and agricultural systems of North Western Rhodesia.**
C.G. Trapnell, J. Clothier.   Bristol, England: Radcliffe Press for the Ministry of Agriculture, Food and Fisheries, 1937. Reprinted, 1996. 96p. 3 maps.
The soils, vegetation and agriculture of North Eastern Rhodesia: a report of the ecological survey.
C.G. Trapnell.   Bristol, England: Radcliffe Press for the Ministry of Agriculture, Food and Fisheries, 1943. Reprinted, 1996. 146p.
These reports were originally published in 1937 and 1943, based on ecological survey work carried out in the 1930s. The brilliant inspiration for these surveys was to classify land on the basis of the vegetation observed in it. In this way, the type of soil in a particular area was deduced from the trees and other vegetation found there. This was then intimately related to local agricultural practices. It is telling that these reports were republished in the 1990s. Much has been written about Zambian agriculture over the past few decades which could have benefited from these reports or which may even, in the light of them, be doubtful if not wrong. They are not easy to read and digest, but even casual readers will be gripped by the ideas presented in them and will look at the Zambian landscape with different eyes.

39 **Ecology and history: the example of eastern Zambia.**
Leroy Vail.   *Journal of Southern African Studies*, vol. 3, no. 2 (1977), p. 129-56.
This is an influential article because it was the first attempt to look at ecological deterioration as a function of the impact of capitalism and imperialism. According to Vail, fear, greed and ignorance on the part of the colonial government, in conjunction with the growing impact of South African imperialism, led to erosion, disease and depopulation. The spread of the tsetse fly is central to this story. The article is impressively documented. It is, however, worthwhile to read this article in conjunction with John McCracken's criticisms in 'Colonialism, capitalism and ecological crisis in Malawi; a reassessment', in: *Conservation in Africa: people, policies and practices*, edited by M. Anderson, R. Grove (Cambridge, England: Cambridge University Press, 1987, p. 63-74).

40 **Resource atlas of Zambia.**
B.M. Willet, D. Gaylard.   Lusaka: NECZAM, 1985. 97p. maps.
This is a school atlas of Zambia containing only maps. The first fifteen pages are devoted specifically to Zambian geography and are useful as an introduction to the country, especially on basic data such as population distribution and rainfall.

41 **Lusaka and its environs: a geographical study of a planned capital city in tropical Africa.**
Edited by Geoff Williams.   Lusaka: Zambia Geographical Association Handbook Series no. 9, 1986. 331p. maps. bibliog.
A geographical perspective can be all-encompassing and that is the case with this book. The range of subjects covered can be illustrated from a selection of perhaps unexpected ones. To give some examples: in the first part of the book – called 'the scene' – there is a chapter on prehistoric settlement in the Lusaka area; in the second part – 'the city' –

there is one on water supply, sewage and drainage, and in the third part – 'the region' – there is one on land tenure. The book can be used in many ways. The individual chapters give specialist knowledge, but the book is also a reference work, containing the most up-to-date knowledge, at the time of publication, of Lusaka and Zambian urbanization in general. Above all, it is a delightful book for everybody, including the casual tourist, to browse through and pick up much worthwhile information. A comparison of the historical photographs with the present situation will be especially pleasing to everybody who knows Lusaka.

42 Development and ecology in the lower Kafue basin in the nineteen seventies.
Edited by Geoffrey J. Williams, Geoffrey H. Howard. Lusaka: University of Zambia, 1977. 99p. 10 maps.

When hydroelectric dams were built in the Kafue there was a strong feeling that the mistakes of Kariba should not be repeated. Therefore in 1967 an interdisciplinary Kafue Basin Research Committee was set up. This is a collection of papers mainly from geographers, but covering a wide range of topics. It is not surprising to find a contribution by Leo van den Berg on industrialization in the area, as part of the development was the emergence of Kafue town as an industrial centre. However, there are also papers on the threat of development – for example, on the ethology of the Kafue Lechwe (a semi-aquatic antelope unique to the area) by Richard Schuster. A paper by Dorothy Lehmann on the Batwa, the people who may have been the original inhabitants, also brings to light aspects that may not be seen by developers.

Geology

43 Geologie en mijnbouw. (Geology and mining).
Edited by D.R. de Vletter, S. Dijkstra, J.W. ter Bruggen. *Journal of the Royal Geological and Mining Society of the Netherlands*, Zambia issue, vol. 51, no. 3 (1972), p. 265-365.

Many of the articles in this issue are only wholly accessible to mining specialists, but some can be understood more widely, especially those which deal more with the management aspects of the mining industry. Much of that material is of course dated.

44 List of publications 1999/2000; geological survey department.
Geological Survey Department. Lusaka: Government of the Republic of Zambia, The Director, Geological Survey Department.

Because of the mining sector, geology is obviously an important topic in Zambia. It is, however, difficult for lay people to penetrate. Professionals may benefit from this publication which is electronically available. Contact: email GSD@ZAMNET.ZM.

45 Proceedings of the 1995 international conference on industrial minerals: investment opportunities in Southern Africa held on the 7-9th of June 1995 in Lusaka.
Edited by S.H. Mambwe, S. Simukanga, O.N. Sikazwe, F. Kamuna. South Africa: Council for Geoscience. 374p.

These proceedings contain eighteen papers on Zambian subjects. The focus here is on mineral deposits and not the metals copper, cobalt, zinc and lead. Topics mentioned include lime, acid, sands and gravel, carbonate rocks, etc. The stress is on the economic use of these in industry and agriculture. There is a final section on project finance, which is purely economic. This book is aimed at a specialist audience.

46   The geology of the Northern Rhodesian Copperbelt.
Edited by F. Mendelsohn.   London: Macdonald, 1961. 523p.
11 maps. bibliog.

The jacket of the book states that 'The Zambian Copperbelt and the allied deposits in neighbouring Zaire's Katanga province form one of the world's greatest metallogenic regions. This book is the first comprehensive account of the Copperbelt to be published'. Some parts, however, seem to be wider in content, such as a paragraph on the structural framework of Northern Rhodesia. The editor was chief geologist with Roan Antelope and the contributors are all from within the mining industry. This is a book for specialists who understand terms such as 'the stratigram and memorphism of the Mvua system'. A wider audience may, however, be interested in the brief history of the various mines in the Copperbelt contained in an appendix.

Travel and Travellers' Accounts

47 Big game hunting in Central Africa.
James Dunbar Bruton. London: Andrew Melrose, 1912. 339p. map.
The book by the big game hunter is a genre that flourished in Zambia. This is an early
example, which illustrates the limitations and possible uses of this literature. People who
have an affinity with hunting and enjoy tall stories will enjoy these tales. Such books also
have an historic value as they are sources for the contemporary state of wildlife. This
early example is particularly apt for such purposes. Although the hunting also takes place
in Southern Rhodesia, the greater part of the action is in Northern Rhodesia.

48 David Livingstone: letters and documents 1841-1872. The
Zambian collection at the Livingstone Museum: containing a
wealth of restored, previously unknown or unpublished texts.
Edited by Timothy Holmes. London: James Currey, 1990. 202p.
2 maps.
This is quite a diverse collection of letters and documents authored by David Livingstone.
The only direct link to Zambia is that these papers were found in the National Museum
in Livingstone. They are thus late discoveries. It is probably a good collection for the
general reader who has some knowledge of the subject to dip in to. This is made easy
through short biographically-based chapters.

49 Travels north of the Zambezi, 1885-6.
Emil Holub, translated by Christa Johns. Edited by Ladislav Holy.
Manchester, England: Manchester University Press, 1975. 317p. map.
bibliog.
Holub was a Czech explorer who was greatly influenced by David Livingstone. He was
a medical doctor with a wide interest in history, archaeology and geography. He travelled
through what is now called the Tonga-Ila area, starting in Livingstone and ending in
Namwala. He also made a rather short excursion up along the Zambezi. Relations
between the Lozi and the Tonga speaking peoples are a major focus in the book. Overall,

although it may be of interest as an historical source, this is primarily a travel journal centred on the experiences of Holub and his party.

50 Livingstone's private journals, 1851-1853.
David Livingstone.   Edited with an introduction by I. Schapera.
London: Chatto & Windus, 1960. 341p. 3 maps. bibliog.

Among Livingstone's writings, these are the journals which most specifically concern themselves with areas in Zambia. They record two journeys, both of which involved a visit to the Makololo, then in control of Barotseland. During the first one, Livingstone discovered the Upper Zambezi at Sesheke. In the second journey, he ventured outside the Makololo capital into Barotseland proper.

51 Livingstone's African journal, 1853-1856.
David Livingstone.   Edited with an introduction by I. Schapera.
London: Chatto & Windus, 1963. 2 vols. 3 maps. bibliog.

Towards the end of his life, Livingstone was preoccupied with finding the source of the Nile as well as with traversing the African continent. This journal documents one of his last expeditions from Luanda in present day Angola on the west coast to Quelimane in Mozambique on the east coast. Again, the Makololo in Barotseland are the lynchpin in this journal.

52 Zambezi: journey of a river.
Michael Main.   Halfway House, South Africa: Southern Book
Publishers, 1990. 313p. 3 maps.

This is a very useful travel book. Following the Zambezi, one passes through many areas of scientific interest. There are many archaeological sites in the area; wildlife is abundant in certain places; one passes through the kingdom of Barotseland; and one meets the engineering feats of enormous dams such as Kariba. Main has a gift for popularizing scientific insights and this book is therefore highly recommended to people who, though not scientists, are intrigued by many other publications in this bibliography that are too technical and less accessible than Main's. His treatment of the social sciences may, however, sometimes raise eyebrows. For example, in his chapter on Kariba, Colson and Scudder's work (see item nos. 35, 197, 199, 691) on the relocation of the Valley (Gwembe) Tonga is not mentioned.

53 David Livingstone: the dark interior.
Oliver Rainsford.   London: John Murray, 1978. 332p. 5 maps.
bibliog.

The territory of what is now Zambia played an important part in Livingstone's travels. He travelled there extensively and died in Chitambo, Serenje district. There was a spate of biographies of Livingstone in the 1970s. This particular biography suggests that Livingstone has to be understood as a manic-depressive, but that is not why it is included here. That reason is more mundane: it is easier to extract the parts in Livingstone's life which are relevant to Zambia from this than from other biographies. The reasons are threefold: it is written engagingly; the narrative has a clear chronology; and, maybe most importantly, it has a set of clear maps indicating Livingstone's travels. Using these, anyone interested to find out more can then turn easily to the relevant parts in Livingstone's own writings.

Flora and Fauna

54 The mammals of Zambia.

W.F.H. Ansell.   Chilanga, Zambia: National Parks and Wildlife
Service, 1978. 119p. 205 maps.

This is an update of *Mammals of Northern Rhodesia* by the same author. It contains no
illustrations and lists the mammals alphabetically using Latin names, although vernacular
names are mentioned in the commentary. It is thus clear that this is primarily a book for
the professional biologist. Its main purpose is to document taxonomy and distribution.
Despite this, amateur wildlife enthusiasts may benefit for example from the careful
recording of sightings.

55 A field guide to Zambian birds not found in Southern Africa.

Dylan R. Aspinwall, Carl Beel.   Lusaka: Zambian Ornithological
Society, 1998. 106p. 2 major maps and 1 for each entry.

Most birdwatchers in Zambia use books about birds in Southern Africa, but this book is
specifically about birds found in Zambia and not elsewhere in Southern Africa. It
provides therefore an introduction in which Zambian bird habitats are described.
Thereafter the species are identified with colour plates by Gabriel Ellison. Each entry is
accompanied by a small map of Zambia in which the areas where the bird has occurred
are pinpointed. This book is a must for any avid birdwatcher.

56 Common birds of Zambia.

Dylan Aspinwall, Grace Conacher, Jim Grant, Terry Taylor.   Lusaka:
Zambian Ornithological Society, 1990. 92p. map.

This booklet gives a checklist of birds arranged by their common name, and each species
is represented by a colour plate by Gabriel Ellison. It mentions status (distribution),
identification, habitat, habits and voice. In addition it contains an introduction about birds
and birdwatching. As the blurb on the back page says, this work fulfils the need for a
popular but scientifically accurate book on Zambian birds. That need was perceived in the
1989 International Common Bird Survey in which Zambia came second in the world in
terms of the number of participants involved.

57 A guide to the common wild flowers of Zambia and neighbouring regions.

Doreen Bolnick.   Lusaka: Macmillan Publishers (Zambia) Ltd, 1995. 74p. bibliog.

The book contains thirty-two beautiful plates of drawings. The flowers depicted are classified and described in blocks of text. The descriptions mention the distribution of the flowers not only in Zambia, but also in neighbouring regions. The introduction gives a classification of Zambia's various natural environments which is useful to anybody who wants to develop an eye for the country's landscape. This is of course a reference book, but it is also nice to browse through for people who have only a limited interest in botany.

58 Kakuli; a story about wild animals, their struggle to survive and the people who live among them.

Norman Carr.   Harare: CBC Publishing, 1996. 175p. map.

Kakuli, a word which means 'a buffalo which has left the main herd and lives on its own', is Carr's nickname. Carr has spent his working life in the Luangwa valley where he started as an elephant hunter in 1939; became a game ranger there when conservation issues came to the fore; and then became a pioneer in the tourist business. This book can be regarded as his testament. It offers a mixture of personal reminiscences and anecdotes; much information about the wildlife found in the valley; and discussion of ecological issues such as the impact of tourism, fire or the culling of elephants. It is entertaining and extremely informative for people who are not biologists or conservationists but who have become fascinated by Zambia's wildlife.

59 Agroforestry extension manual for Northern Zambia.

Henry Chilufya, Bo Tengnäs.   Nairobi: Regional Soils Conservation Unit; Lusaka: Government of the Republic of Zambia, Ministry of the Environment and Natural Resources, Forest Department. 248p. 3 maps. bibliog.

This book is didactic in nature – and many of the illustrations particularly so – as it is aimed at the extension worker. For this very reason, however, it is also accessible to the layman who wants to gain a greater appreciation of the Zambian forests and landscape. It contains descriptions of the main ecological areas in the country and discusses the commonest trees in each area; the trees that it is recommended to leave standing; and advice for new plantings. The second half of the book lists the most important indigenous and exotic trees in Zambia. There is much to be gained from this book for a wide range of people.

60 Useful trees of Zambia for the agriculturist.

F.B. Fanshawe.   Lusaka: Government of the Republic of Zambia, Ministry of Lands and Natural Resources, 1972. 126p.

Over fifty trees are described under four headings: fruit trees, fodder trees, timber trees and trees of ecological significance. The book contains information of a botanical nature on habitat, distribution and identification, for which purpose it is illustrated with line drawings. The stress is on usefulness however. Here are some extracts: on *Hexalobus monopetalus* or the *mpundu* tree: 'the fruits are edible, pleasantly acid, rather like a satsuma plum. They make excellent jam' (p. 39); in contrast, on the *Parkia Filicoida Oliv*:

'The bark is used locally as a fish poison with a stupefying action' (p. 43). The book is aimed at people involved in forestry and agriculture, but in his introduction the director of agriculture envisages a wider audience: 'Most of our schoolgoing youngsters are missing this knowledge'.

61 A guide to common wild mammals of Zambia.
Richard Jeffery, Robert Monro, Leo O'Keeffe. Lusaka: Wildlife Conservation Society of Zambia, 1991. 62p. map.

This is an everyman's reference guide to wildlife in the game parks. It not only covers the big mammals, which are the main attraction for many, but pays attention all species, from rodents to elephants. Each entry is subdivided into identification, distribution and habits. The colour plates by Gabriel Ellison are most informative. The entries are particularly instructive and give a good background to species likely to be seen. The enthusiasm of the authors shines through their comments. One example is their description of the innocent looking honey badger: 'Aggressive creatures, who have sharp teeth and claws, muscles well developed for digging, an extremely tough skin and the ability to give off a most unpleasant smell' (p. 30).

62 Natural resources handbook: the fish and fisheries of Zambia.
Edited by T.E. Mortimer. Lusaka: Government of the Republic of Zambia, 1965. 98p. 6 maps. bibliog.

The title speaks for itself. The emphasis in this publication is, however, more on fisheries than on fish, so the technology and economics of fisheries get most attention. This handbook contains a detailed description of the main fishing grounds in Zambia.

63 The fate of the Nile crocodile in the African waterways.
Mwelwa Musambachime. *African Affairs*, vol. 86, no. 343 (1987), p. 197-209.

Musambachime does not think that the bad reputation of the crocodile is deserved. He gives an historical account of attitudes towards the crocodile here. There are several references to the Luapula river in Zambia in this article.

64 An introduction to Zambia's wild mushrooms and how to use them.
G.D. Piearce. Ndola: Forestry Department, [n.d.]. 28p.

As the first lines of this book say, the rainy season in Zambia brings delicious mushrooms. The danger, of course, lies in eating poisonous ones. This pamphlet makes it possible to classify them, and it gives vernacular names also. The book gives advice about when to cook them and how; for example, chantarelles are edible, common and delicious.

65 A guide to the insects of Zambia.
Elliot Pinhey, Ian Loe. Lusaka: Anglo-American Corporation (Central Africa), 1973. 38p.

One cannot but be impressed by Zambia's insects if one sits outside near a lamp during the rainy season. This book may satisfy further curiosity. A general section on the structure, life cycles and habits of insects is followed by a short description of each family of insects in its natural surroundings. The illustrations are not only clear, but also beautiful.

66   A guide to the butterflies of Zambia.
Elliot Pinhey, Ian Loe.   Lusaka: Anglo-American Corporation (Central Africa), 1977. 106p. bibliog.

Even a casual visitor will notice that there are many exquisite butterflies in Zambia. This book may kindle interest further. It is full of beautiful illustrations which introduce 135 of the 700 known species in Zambia. An introductory section gives general details of butterflies and their main features. The book also contains a list of the major museum collections of African butterflies.

67   A guide to the reptiles, amphibians and fishes of Zambia.
Malumo P.M. Simbotwe, Raphael Mubamba.   Lusaka: Wildlife Conservation Society of Zambia, 1993. 89p. map.

This book is aimed at a wide public and provides a species-by-species account of reptiles, amphibians and fish, beautifully illustrated with clear colour plates by Gabriel Ellison. Visitors to Zambia tend to have only big mammals in mind when they think about wildlife there, but even the most cursory of visitors will see ample numbers of lizards. This booklet is thus particularly suitable to enrich the experience of nature in Zambia. The species' names could inspire a poet: electric catfish, blotched wolf snake or Sundevall's writhing skink.

68   Common trees, shrubs, grasses of the Luangwa valley.
P.P. Smith.   Zennor, St. Ives, England: The Tendrine Press, 1995. 50p.

Although the title refers to the botany of the Luangwa Valley, this book is also useful in other parts of Zambia. It covers a wide range of species, from the giant baobab to wild rice. It is ordered on the basis of Latin names, but the English and vernacular names are also given. It pays special attention to the ways in which the plants are used by wildlife for food, nesting, etc., and is informative in a broad sense. For example, one can read that it was Livingstone who suggested the very old age of baobabs – 40,000 years – but that later scientific judgement proved him wrong.

69   Know your trees; some of the common trees found in Zambia.
A.E.G. Storrs.   Ndola, Zambia: Government of the Republic of Zambia, Forest Department, 1979. Reprinted by Regional Soil Conservation Unit, Nairobi, 1995. 380p.

The word 'some' in the title is a misnomer, as there are many trees described in this book. The descriptions are also elaborate, mentioning bark, leaves and fruits; regional distribution; and uses. The book covers both indigenous and introduced trees. Each species is illustrated with several photographs of pertinent aspects of their appearance. The extremely detailed nature of this book may be illustrated by the following quotation about the *mukwa* tree, much sought after by carpenters: 'Fragrant yellow or orange pea-flowers appear in hairy sprays from August to October, and are succeeded by the distinctive round bristly pods which are surrounded by a stiff papery wing' (p. 180). The uses suggested for the trees are various: poisoning, cure of venereal disease, toothbrushes, etc.

70 More about trees (a sequel to 'know your trees'). Interesting facts and uses of some common Zambian trees; including a selection of honey recipes.
A.E.G. Storrs.   Ndola, Zambia: Government of the Republic of Zambia, Forest Department, 1982. 127p.

The title of this book speaks for itself. Whereas the author's previous book was first and foremost that of a botanist or forester writing for people with a similar interest, this book is that of a forestry extensionist talking about the role of trees within human existence. It contains therefore also a considerable section on starting a plantation. It is not merely utilitarian however, but has also a section on trees in history such as the 'slave' tree in Ndola, and a section on 'weeping' trees to which magical properties are ascribed.

71 Field guide to important arable weeds of Zambia.
Richard Vernon.   Chilanga, Zambia: Government of the Republic of Zambia, Department of Agriculture, Mount Makulu Research Station, 1983. 115p.

This book is primarily meant for agricultural/botanical purposes and its handy format fits easily into a pocket. It is, however, also widely used outside agriculture by people who are simply interested in nature. A delightful book, it describes fifty-three different weeds illustrated with good photographs. Plants are identified by their Latin names, but common and vernacular names are given as well. Each entry mentions identification; similar weeds; distribution; importance; and uses. Uses can vary from nutritional or medicinal qualities to, for example, stuffing pillows. The book is, therefore, of very wide interest. Some people may find it interesting to be able to recognize the seedlings of *Hibiscus cannabinus*, and it may be useful to know that the cultivated Capetown Gooseberry resembles the poisonous Black Nightshade.

72 Forest flora of Northern Rhodesia.
F. White.   London: Oxford University Press, 1962. 455p. bibliog.

This is a book for the professional botanist. It is the culmination of more than thirty years' work by the botanical section of the Forestry Department of the University of Oxford and contains descriptions of 1,525 indigenous and exotic species found in Zambia. The illustrations are helpful for identification in the field. The information provided includes distribution, ecology, flowering and fruiting time, and vernacular names.

Prehistory and Archaeology

73 Man on the Kafue: the archaeology and history of the Itezhi-tezhi area of Zambia.
Robin Derricourt. London: Ethnographica, 1985. 252p. 4 maps. bibliog.

The area where this archaeological research was carried out is now flooded because of the construction of a hydro-electric dam. River sites are the most promising locations for such research, as the remains of earliest habitation are usually to be found there. This is a beautifully produced volume which contains copious information. Although it is primarily aimed at the professional archaeologist, as is usually the case in archaeological studies, it is precisely for this reason that the book is recommended. Its bibliography is the most up-to-date list of the considerable volume of writings by archaeologists who have worked in Zambia, including Desmond Clark, Joseph Vogel and Brian Fagan.

74 A short history of Zambia from the earliest times until A.D. 1900.
Edited by Brian M. Fagan. London: Oxford University Press, 1970. 165p. 19 maps. bibliog.

This book attempts to bring together what was known about pre-colonial Zambia at the time of writing. This was not without political significance: colonization by the British is only a small period in this view of history. Writings on Zambia's history originated in two separate institutes. The Rhodes-Livingstone Institute saw the emergence of writing on recent history stressing African initiative. At the National Museum in Livingstone, attention was paid to the pre-colonial period using archaeology as a source of information. Anybody interested in the earliest human remains found in Zambia (Broken Hill Man), rock paintings or pottery shards will find this book rewarding. It is much more accessible than most purely archaeological publications.

75 Prehistoric rock paintings and engravings of Zambia.

D.W. Phillipson. Livingstone, Zambia: Livingstone Museum, 1972. 70p. map.

The prime usefulness of this exhibition catalogue is that it gives details of all the sites where rock paintings have been identified. The introduction is mainly archaeological in nature and is followed by many photographs illustrating the most intriguing and beautiful figures. This is a publication for the lover of art as well as for the archaeologist.

History

General

76 A history of Zambia.
Andrew D. Roberts. London: Heinemann, 1976. 288p. 10 maps.
bibliog.
This history covers an enormous time span from prehistory to well after independence
(1974). Half of the book deals with pre-colonial history and predates therefore the
formation of Zambia as a political entity. Thus, Roberts speaks of a history 'in Zambia'.
The ecological setting and the changes therein resulting from the development of
technology and trade receive special attention. This history is rich in detail and precisely
written. For that reason it is useful as a work of reference. It also reads well as a narrative,
and a sophisticated vision of the development of Zambia is – almost surreptitiously –
conveyed, for example in this sentence: 'Company rule was essentially an instrument of
economic exploitation, but this of course was nothing new to the peoples of Northern
Rhodesia' (p. 179).

Pre-colonial

77 Kazembe and the Portuguese.
Ian Cunnison. *Journal of African History*, vol. 2, no. 1 (1961),
p. 61-76. map.
The Portuguese sent three expeditions in the period 1798-1832 to create links between
their possessions on the west and east coasts of Africa. In between lay two powerful
African kingdoms, one of which was a branch of the Lunda ruled by Kazembe. This
historical episode, in which the Portuguese failed to establish satisfactory contacts with
Kazembe is the subject of this work. The article gives a good feel not only for Kazembe's

skill in controlling the Portuguese attempts at influence, but also for the blundering on the part of the would-be colonizers. As Cunnison explains: 'The Portuguese were at the mercy of Kazembe not only because of their lack of goods, but also because of the division in their ranks and the unreliability of their carriers' (p. 69).

78 Zambia before 1890; aspects of pre-colonial history.
H.W. Langworthy. London: Longman, 1972. 138p. 5 maps. bibliog.

This book's clarity of style makes it a good introduction for the outsider to the essential features of pre-colonial history in Zambia: the patterns of migration; the rise and fall of centralized political structures; and the developing contacts with the outside world through trade, including the slave-trade, and missionary contacts. The book is also useful for those who are interested in particular regional histories, as most of the pre-colonial centralized states have individual chapters devoted to them.

79 Bulozi under the Luyana kings: political evolution and state formation in pre-colonial Zambia.
Mutumba Mainga. London: Longman, 1973. 277p. 5 maps. bibliog.

Pre-colonial history relying largely on oral sources can easily become more a matter of conjecture than evidence. There was earlier and more intensive contact between Barotseland and people who used writing than in other parts of Zambia, so this history of Barotseland in the 19th century can have recourse not only to oral sources, but also to others. Nevertheless, a strength of this book is the way in which Mutumba Mainga manages to convey a sense of mystery as to what happened to the rulers of Barotseland during that period. It is a story of state formation; the take-over of the Lozi state by the Makololo immigrants; the restoration of the Lozi state; and finally the European contacts. This book tells a very bloody story well, but it demands much of the reader to enter the mental universe of the protagonists. It is rewarding, however, to be introduced to a land where 'kings and chiefs succeed each other here like shadows, they are never allowed to grow old' (p. 105) by the first Lozi writing about the Lozi. That was in 1885, just before the successful restoration of the Lozi kingdom under the long-term reign of the Litunga chief Lewanika.

80 History and tradition in East Central Africa through the eyes of the Northern Rhodesian Cewa.
Max G. Marwick. *Journal of African History*, vol. 4, no. 1 (1963), p. 71-86. 2 maps.

The Cewa of Zambia are part of a much wider group of Nyanja-speaking people inhabiting Zambia, Malawi and Mozambique. This article attempts to reconstruct the processes of state formation that took place among them in pre-colonial times. The title of the article suggests that oral history is the main source, but the work is based primarily on the reports of early travellers. If one is intrigued by the question of why there are different Cewa chieftainships like Undi and Mwase, then this article will clarify the point.

81 The Ubutwa society in eastern Shaba and north east Zambia to 1920.
Mwelwa C. Musambachime. *The International Journal of African Historical Studies*, vol. 27, no. 1 (1994), p. 77-101. map.

The Ubutwa society seems to be an African equivalent of the present-day phenomenon of Rotary and Lions clubs, and especially Freemasonry. Musambachime talks indeed about lodges and initiation when he describes the organizational structure. Much about the Ubutwa society was in the open, notably the identity of its leaders, but nothing of what happened within the society was supposed to be revealed outside. It was an intra-ethnic (Bemba) organization which covered a huge area. After colonization it declined and faded into oblivion. Musambachime sees its demise as a result mainly of the opposition of missionaries. The grounds for this opposition were, however, vague. The decline was also reinforced by the emergence of labour migration, education and the massive recruitment of Bemba to fight in the First World War.

82 Chiefs of rain; chiefs of ruling: a reinterpretation of pre-colonial (Tonga) social and political structure.
Dan O'Brien. *Africa*, vol. 53, no. 4 (1983), p. 23-42. map. bibliog.

This article, based on oral testimony, is a study of headman Monze's arrest in 1904 because of his illegal collection of taxes. The basic issue involved was whether the Monze area was under the Lozi chief Lewanika or not. O'Brien uses the case to argue that the Tonga held authority over wider areas than Elizabeth Colson suggests. Colson argued that the idea of a Tonga tribe is for the most part a colonial construction. See especially E. Colson, 'Contemporary tribes and the development of nationalism', in *Essays on the problem of tribe* (Seattle: University of Washington Press, 1968).

83 The hidden hippopotamus: reappraisal in African history: the early colonial experience in Western Zambia.
Gwyn Prins. Cambridge, England: Cambridge University Press, 1980. 319p. 5 maps. bibliog.

This may be called a post-modernist book written before the term was current. It mainly deals with interpretations of Lozi society. There are of course several authoritative ones, such as Gluckman (see item no. 206), Mainga (see item no. 79), Caplan (see item no. 156). There are also more early written sources here than elsewhere, as there was a relatively good amount of early contacts with Europeans. Prins rejects the primacy of narrative and orders history around themes and symbols. As a result, the text is often difficult to access if one is not very familiar with the topic. This difficulty is reinforced by the seeming triviality of much of the information. Prins also often seems more preoccupied with himself than with the Lozi. However, there are parts where such problems disappear and where Prins appears able to write evocative history with much empathy. The conclusion is an example of this and it may be paradoxical, but advisable, to read that conclusion first.

84 **Terms of trade and terms of trust; the history and contexts of pre-colonial market production around the Upper Zambezi and Kasai.**
Achim von Oppen. Munster and Hamburg, Germany: Lit Verlag, 1993. 473p. 3 maps. bibliog.

North Western Zambia became a marginal area after the development of the copper mines gave rise to the incorporation of the various Zambian geographical areas in international exchange networks. At the end of the 19th century the situation was very different, however. This book is mainly an analysis of pre-colonial trade in this area, which was then a gateway for trading routes between the coast and the interior. Van Oppen starts with the slave trade, which was succeeded by a trade in ivory and beeswax, and subsequently followed by the period designated as the 'rubber delirium'. This incorporation in wider networks is complemented by detailed descriptions of the domestic and household economy in which cassava played a major role. The result is an extremely vivid description of a buoyant pre-colonial economy in an area which was later considered to be a backwater. This is not merely an historical account of a pre-colonial economy, but also has relevance for wider insights into the way economic relations are embedded in social relations situated in particular ecologies. The book therefore has two specific audiences: specialists in regional history and those interested in von Oppen's more general perspective on economic life in pre-colonial Zambia; but by browsing, the general reader may also find many interesting items. The author is not a great stylist or raconteur, but the book is rich in anecdotes. The chapter on intoxicants may be a stimulating beginning.

Colonial

85 **Alcohol, racial segregation and popular politics in Northern Rhodesia.**
Charles Ambler. *Journal of African History*, vol. 31, no. 2 (1990), p. 295-313.

The main focus of this article is on a series of protests and boycotts against municipal beerhalls. The colonial government's legislation with respect to alcohol was racist: access to European style drinks was not allowed and the sale of local opaque beers was regulated. The article weaves together in a complex pattern moral stands against drinking; nationalist agitation; the illicit sale of drinks and – not to be forgotten – drinking habits. To give an example: 'most whites remained adamantly opposed to African consumption of hard liquor' (p. 302). Discriminatory liquor legislation remained in force until the very eve of independence. The article ends with the observation that the consumption of all sorts of beer increased dramatically after independence.

86 **Guardians in their time; experiences of Zambians under colonial rule, 1890-1964.**
Edited by Samuel N. Chipungu. London and Basingstoke, England: Macmillan, 1992. 223p.

This collection of essays by Zambian authors who were at one time attached to the history department of the University of Zambia is primarily a search for African identity under colonialism. The book is most successful when it deals with groups who are in the shadows of history, for example the paid Native Authority employees (Boma class) or African intellectuals like the Bible translator, Paul Bwembiyo Mushindo. Africans are seen as actors who reacted creatively to colonialism, although this was often interpreted as subversion in the colonial context. The prohibition on hunting, for example, forced Africans into poaching. The search for identity is also evident in the critical reaction to the expatriate scholarship which has dominated the study of Zambia.

87 **The political economy of rural development in colonial Zambia: the case of the Ushi-Kabende 1947-1953.**
Kusum Datta. *The International Journal of African Historical Studies*, vol. 21, no. 2 (1988), p. 249-73.

Ushi-Kabende is an area in the southern part of what is now Mansa district, Luapula. The article documents and analyses early colonial development efforts after the end of the Second World War. Its major thesis is that the colonial state had to contend with many conflicting forces there and could not unambiguously impose its will. At the centre, its powers were curtailed by settler influence. At the grass roots, conservation measures were resisted and the new nationalist forces – the African National Congress – found a fertile ground on which to campaign. 'When even police-action failed to make people buy fishing licences and observe conservation rules, the colonial state gave in to many of the popular demands by the end of 1953' (p. 270).

88 **Agricultural improvement and political protest on the Tonga Plateau, Northern Rhodesia.**
Mac Dixon-Fyle. *Journal of African History*, vol. 18, no. 4 (1977), p. 579-96. map.

This article describes lucidly quite a complicated situation. More land was alienated to white farmers in Zambia's Southern Province than elsewhere. This understandably led to animosity, but at the same time African farmers started to compete. They also produced successfully for the market, and this competition became embedded in a discourse on conservation. The African producers resorted to monocropping, which led to soil erosion. This led to a call to limit African production. Most of the article deals with the Improved Farmers Scheme in which agricultural extension, marketing (dis-)incentives and conservation concerns came together. Conservation measures were resented, however. The article goes on subtly to describe the interactions between these 'improved' farmers, the mass of the Tonga population, nationalist politicians and the chiefs/native authorities. This is not only rich history, but also essential reading to obtain insight into emergent nationalism in Zambia.

89 Revival and rebellion in colonial central Africa.
Karen E. Fields.   Princeton, New Jersey: Princeton University Press, 1985. 323p. 2 maps.

The subject of this book is the rise, spread and taming of the millenarian beliefs of the Jehovah's Witnesses in Central Africa, covering Malawi as well as Zambia. The interaction between Witnesses, chiefs, missions and the colonial government is the main subject of this book, and the author sees the movement in the first place as one which subverted the colonial order. Tomo Nyirenda, the child of God (*mwana lesa*) whose witch-finding efforts led to many deaths in 1925, takes centre stage in the book. Karen Fields regularly paints with big brush strokes on a broad canvas, and the narrative strives to infer broader implications for social science. These ambitions do not always enhance readability, but there are interesting matters dealt with in this book, such as the role of European Watchtower missionaries who, on the one hand, fiercely protected their fellow believers against the state and, on the other hand, were keen to be as law-abiding as possible. The material presented suggests a movement full of ambivalences and ambiguities.

90 A history of Northern Rhodesia: early days to 1953.
L.H. Gann.   London: Chatto & Windus, 1964. 478p. 3 maps. bibliog.

The culmination of this book is the formation of the Federation of Rhodesia and Nyasaland, and it is therefore not surprising that the book deals predominantly with settler history. In Gann's view, colonization was facilitated by prestige, personal honesty and technical skill rather than military might. It would be regrettable, however, if the book were to be dismissed for its political perspective. It is extremely informative and gives, for example, detailed descriptions of the formation of the copper industry and the planning of Lusaka as a new capital. The material on African society is presented in a slanted way, but it contains useful information, for instance, on the Jehovah's Witnesses and African agriculture. It is rich in anecdotes on, for example, the Northern Rhodesian settlers' refusal to allow the immigration of Jews from Germany in 1939 for fear, among other things, of diluting the British stock in the country.

91 Zambia 1890-1964; the colonial period.
R. Hall.   London: Longman, 1976. 225p. map. bibliog.

This is a slightly reworked edition of Hall's introductory text on Zambia which was for a long time the most popular such text. This edition is a companion volume to Langworthy's on pre-colonial Zambia (see item no. 78). It starts with Rhodes and in the last chapter emphasizes the transfer of mineral rights to Zambia's independence, indicating Hall's sharp eye for the relevance of economic conditions. In between there is a history of colonialism in Zambia and the rise and victory of nationalism. The book reads well, as would be expected from a journalist, but much of the detail presented may have seemed more telling in 1965 (when Chapters 1 to 5 of this book were published as Chapters 3 to 7 of Richard Hall's *Zambia*, London: Pall Mall Press, 1965) than it is now.

92 The beginnings of Nyasaland and North Eastern Rhodesia, 1859-95.
A.J. Hanna.   Oxford: Clarendon Press, 1969. 281p. 2 maps. bibliog.

This record of early British activity in the region is of limited usefulness. It deals much more extensively with present-day Malawi than with present-day Zambia. It is quite a dated kind of history writing because the African side of this history is secondary to the European actors. It is typical of the book that the author thanks the British South Africa Company profusely for access to files. Inasmuch as the book thus presents one particular point of view, it is informative. It is also useful for readers searching for sources on that period.

93 The tobacco industry in Northern Rhodesia 1912-1938.
Ackson Kanduza. *International Journal of African Historical Studies*, vol. 16, no. 2 (1983), p. 201-31.

Tobacco was for a time the main export crop of the territory and considered crucial to its future before its importance was eclipsed by copper. Northern Rhodesia was also overtaken by Southern Rhodesia and Nyasaland, mainly because the latter were more successful in penetrating foreign markets. Kanduza discusses the rise and fall of this crop – which was mainly grown in the Chipata area – in the context of marketing arrangements, government intervention, struggle for labour and competition between settlers and indigenous producers. The article is imbued with the neo-marxist underdevelopment perspective which was current at the time of publication. It does not really succeed and comes across as dated, but the many details in this long article continue to make it of interest to readers with a specialist interest.

94 The impact of the great depression on Northern Rhodesia.
M.H.Y. Kaniki. *Transafrican Journal of History*, vol. 24 (1995), p. 131-51.

This article attempts to reassess the way in which Northern Rhodesia was hit by the depression. It is more a collection of facts that build up an impression than the presentation of a tight and coherent argument. Some facts are worthwhile: areas which were furthest away from centres of capitalist expansion were often the hardest hit as they relied more than others on wage labour. Kaniki singles out the cattle owners in Namwala as particularly affected, as they were struck by epidemic outbreaks of cattle diseases as well. The effects of the depression also lasted longer here than elsewhere, although one may dispute the contention that by 1936 the worst effects were over. The most puzzling omission in this article is a discussion of the copper mines during the depression.

95 Reaction to colonialism: a prelude to the politics of independence in Northern Zambia 1839-1939.
Henry S. Meebelo. Manchester, England: Manchester University Press, 1971. 304p. map. bibliog.

This is an example of conscientious writing of history in which nuance is more important than the bold thesis. The first two chapters record colonialization in Northern Zambia, while subsequent chapters analyse the awakening of African political consciousness in colonial society. The book deals with the Jehovah's Witnesses, traditional authorities and welfare associations. Meebelo does not project into them nationalist sentiments which are not there – he points out, for example, the internecine nature of quarrels over chieftainship – but argues that these movements and institutions were partly inspired by the genuine grievances associated with living in a colonial society. A good impression of the nature of this book can be formed by reading the quotation on the attitude of the natives on pages 241-42.

96 Cutting down trees: women, nutrition and agricultural change in the Northern Province of Zambia 1920-1986.
Henrietta Moore, Megan Vaughan. *African Affairs*, vol. 86, no. 345 (1984), p. 523-40.
This article contains ideas which were later elaborated in the book of the same title, but this is written more from a development perspective. It draws attention to the incidence of malnutrition due to the intensification of women's labour among households of cash cropping families. The article therefore stresses the need for the analysis of development in the area to shift away from concentrating on *chitemene* and male absenteeism.

97 The impact of rumour: the case of the banyama (vampire men) scare in Northern Rhodesia, 1930-1964.
Mwelwa C. Musambachime. *The International Journal of African Historical Studies*, vol. 21, no. 2 (1988), p. 201-17.
The *banyama* (vampire men) scare, which started about 1930 and continued until independence, spread from northern Zambia along the line of the railway to the south. It is, however, an even more amorphous belief system than Musambachime's dating suggests. He begins his account at the end of World War One, and its end at independence seems only arbitrary. The *banyama* scare manifests itself with more or less strength in certain periods. It reached a high point in the Luapula Valley in 1945, and Africans who joined the Capricorn Society in the 1950s in Lusaka were also accused. Selling blood and organs to Europeans is a common theme. Musambachime is a sceptic who sees no more evidence than rumour. There is no proof that *banyama* were real people, nor could it be established that people were caught by *banyama*.

98 The history of Zambian colonial education: a post structuralist approach.
Dan O'Brien. In: *Post-colonialism – culture and identity in Africa*. Edited by D. Pal Ahluwalia, Paul Nursey-Bray. Commack, New York: Nova Science Publishers, 1997, p. 199-219.
This is an exercise in post-modernist discourse analysis. It is, however, less heavy on theoretical pretensions than may seem at first sight and contains a useful summary of the debates on African education at the beginning of the 20th century. The discourse within government mainly focused on whether education would leave Africans in their proper place and whether education for Africans should be adaptive (with a strong stress on vocational training). Within the mission, the debate was on the priority of spreading the gospel relative to education. The end result was that the missionaries 'were running the schools for the government, not being helped by the government to run their own schools'; by 1931 all missionary societies had begun to accept that.

99 Land alienation and agrarian conflict in colonial Zambia.
Robin Palmer. In: *Imperialism, colonialism and hunger: East and Central Africa*. Edited by Robert I. Rotberg. Lexington, Massachusetts: Lexington Books, 1983, p. 89-113. map.
This article is short, considering the topic it covers. It deals more with colonial policy-making in respect of land than with the conflict and resistance that the title suggests. Its conclusions are bold and summarize the article well: 'through a series of decisions and

indecisions, a thoroughly incompetent settler-agricultural community was allowed to take root in Northern Rhodesia to the detriment of African farmers'. The article is, however, quite mute on what happened in African areas.

100   The Capricorn Africa society revisited: the impact of liberalism in Zambia's colonial history, 1949-1963.
Bizeck Jube Phiri.   *International Journal of African Historical Studies*, vol. 24, no. 1 (1991), p. 65-85.
The Capricorn Society was initiated by white people who were liberals in the context of colonial society. They saw the need to co-opt Africans into government, and the most radical among them envisioned a gradual transition to majority rule. They hoped that non-racial political parties would emerge on such a platform. A prominent black member in Zambia was the trade union leader, Lawrence Katilungu. Capricorn may have seemed a road to influence, but it definitely was not a road to popularity. Despite the fact that Capricorn was considered to be dead as a dodo by 1959, Phiri maintains that liberalism has been influential in Zambia's political development.

101   'Making Northern Rhodesia imperial' – variations on a royal theme 1924-1938.
Terence Ranger.   *African Affairs*, vol. 79, no. 316 (1980), p. 349-75.
Ranger is a most original historian and here this is even more evident than usual. His point of departure is the wish to understand why Africans acquiesced in colonial rule rather than protest against it. In a fashion reminiscent of the high Toryism of a philosopher like Edmund Burke, Ranger analyses how reference to, and the presence of, royalty bound the subjects to the empire. The visit of the Prince of Wales to Northern Rhodesia in 1925 is the central element in this article. It also describes Sir Herbert Stanley, the first governor after the territory had become a proper colony, as a master in creating symbolic universes of an imperial nature. It is not surprising that the Lozi people, who after all also had a kingdom, were most charmed by it all and that this culminated in the presence of their chief, the Litunga, at the coronation in 1937. The article evokes a rich, symbolic world.

102   Black heart; Gore-Browne and the politics of multiracial Zambia.
Robert I. Rotberg.   Berkeley, California: University of California Press, 1977. 359p. 2 maps. bibliog.
Stewart Gore-Brown was a central figure in colonial politics in Northern Rhodesia. This book has a preface by Kenneth Kaunda, who praises him as one of the rare white men siding with the nationalists. From this book, however, he appears more as a High Tory: an aristocrat who was concerned with the fate of the masses, prepared to adapt to changing times and imbued with a consensus ideal. This book is not only about politics. It is also about his attempt to run a feudal estate in Mpika (Shiwa Ngandu); his personal love life also plays a crucial role. *Black heart* is worthwhile not only for the specialist historian but also for anyone interested in fame, fortune and love. This book is simply a good read.

103 Struggles in southern Africa for survival and equality.
Harold Jack Simons. Basingstoke, England: Macmillan, 1997.
240p. bibliog.

This book contains only one chapter specifically devoted to Zambia: 'The colonial conquest of Zambia' (p. 43-80). While it does not contain strikingly new insights or material, many people may find it a worthwhile read because of the man who wrote it. Jack Simons was an important figure in the South African ANC and South African Communist Party and spent a long time in exile in Lusaka, where he was a professor of sociology at the University of Zambia from 1967 to 1975.

104 War propaganda during the Second World War in Northern Rhodesia.
Rosaleen Smyth. *African Affairs*, vol. 83, no. 332 (1984), p. 345-458.

The Second World War necessitated an effort to win the hearts and minds of the empire's African subjects. This article discusses the use of films and especially the government publication *Mutende* in this effort. Africans co-operated in the war effort, but at the same time the propaganda campaign offered opportunities to raise nationalist aspirations, which centred on resistance to the proposed federation of Rhodesia and Nyasaland. Governor Maybin's fear, expressed in 1939, that the new information office might 'unsettle the natives', proved justified.

105 A guide to the administrative boundaries of Northern Rhodesia.
Jeffrey C. Stone. Aberdeen, Scotland: Department of Geography, University of Aberdeen, 1979. 92p. 9 major and many other minor maps.

This is a labour of love and primarily a specialist geographical publication. Stone gives a very precise account of the changes in boundaries of districts and sub-districts in the country. It is also worthwhile for people who, although not specialist geographers, have a detailed knowledge of particular areas. Stone's remarks evoke historical realities about places. For example: health is a recurrent issue in deciding where to live.

106 Saving settlers: maize control in Northern Rhodesia.
Kenneth P. Vickery. *Journal of Southern African Studies*, vol. 11, no. 2 (1985), p. 212-35.

The heart of this article is a discussion on the controls over maize marketing which were imposed as a response to the onset of the great depression of the 1930s. The white farming community in the south of the country needed the copper mines as their market. With the coming of the depression, that market was dented to say the least. Besides, everyone conceded that the Africans sooner or later would take over the market, with or without control. When control was established after 1935, African production shot up. The article is highly readable, even for non-specialists: Vickery reproduces the discourse in colonial society engagingly and presents the burgeoning of Tonga agriculture as well. The case of maize in Southern Province during the 1930s deserves study by anyone interested in agricultural marketing. Events described here are the basis for the theory of the normal surplus as developed by the agronomist, William Allan (see entry no. 628), which regrettably is not mentioned here.

107 **Justice, women, and the social order in Abercorn, Northeastern Rhodesia, 1897-1903.**
Marcia Wright. In: *African women and the law: historical perspectives.* Edited by Margaret Hay, Marcia Wright. Boston, Massachusetts: Boston University, papers on Africa VII, 1982, p. 33-51.
The north-eastern part of Zambia changed in the period described here from a centre of vibrant trade routes into a peripheral area where labour migration became dominant. Pawning and enslavement of women was common at the beginning of the period. The article deals with the administration's responses and relies primarily on two record books kept by H.C. Marshall who 'picked up the threads of authority as the first colonial magistrate' (p. 35). The article is very specific in character and describes a rather unusual situation: its wider relevance is therefore limited.

108 **Strategies of slaves and women: life-stories from East/Central Africa.**
Marcia Wright. New York: Lynn Barber Press; London: James Currey, 1993. 238p. 2 maps. bibliog.
Marcia Wright is a specialist in the history of the so-called 'corridor people' in the area between Lake Tanganyika and Lake Malawi. In the second half of the 19th century the area was in turmoil as western colonization was gradually establishing itself. Wright tries to bring this period to life in this collection of six life histories – dealing with five women and one man – which depict, in particular, how slavery as a form of consciousness disappeared. The coming of British rule meant some kind of freedom for many people. All the characters here ended up in a Christian community with a strong anti-slavery ideology. This book complements Wright's other short articles on the subject. The administration of Hugh Marshall, the first colonial magistrate, is also important here.

109 **The spectre of a second Chilembwe: government, missions and social control in wartime Northern Rhodesia, 1914-18.**
Edmund Yorke. *Journal of African History*, vol. 31, no. 3 (1990), p. 373-93. map.
The Chilembwe rising in Malawi took place in 1915, during the First World War, and coincided with a general feeling of insecurity in Northern Rhodesia. The administration was stretched because of wartime labour demands. In the missions, the war effort meant that less European supervision was available. The missions flourished under African leadership, however. This leadership was therefore distrusted by the colonial authorities, which imprisoned some of the individuals involved. Towards the end of the war a new spectre – Watchtower (Jehovah's Witnesses) – arose, which attracted a striking number of teachers from the former Livingstonia mission station. The colonial government did not notice that there were genuine grievances during the war. This article gives a detailed description of a relatively little-known part of Zambian history.

Federation

110 **Unholy wedlock: the failure of the Central African Federation.**
Harry Franklin. London: Allen & Unwin, 1963. 240p. map.
The Federation of the Rhodesias and Nyasaland has not yet found its historian. Thus this book, an insider's memoir, is still useful for people who want to read about the topic. Franklin had a long career in the Northern Rhodesian civil service and thereafter as a politician. This is mainly a political history, and Franklin's sentiments are clear: colonial rule was trusteeship and did not bring in apartheid as, in his view, the Federation did.

111 **The two nations: aspects of the development of race relations in the Rhodesias and Nyasaland.**
John Richard Gray. London: Oxford University Press, 1960. 373p. 3 maps. bibliog.
This book used to be cited quite often but has now become dated. The book's subject is the development of race relations in the three territories up to 1953. It gives the reasons why federation was a problematic issue, but does not discuss federation itself. Some chapters are subdivided into parts referring to the three territories, so it is quite easy to access what has been written on the future Zambia. It is, however, history writing which stresses European viewpoints and policy documents rather than African initiatives from below. It is a source to be used together with others and gives an insight into the mind of people whose attitude to colonialism was, in Gray's opinion, reasonably liberal.

112 **The economics of federation and dissolution in Central Africa.**
Arthur Hazlewood. In: *African integration and disintegration.*
Edited by Arthur Hazlewood. London: Oxford University Press, 1967, p. 185-251.
This is the best literature on the federal experience currently available. Hazlewood's conclusion is clear: 'The Federal arrangements engineered a massive financial redistribution from Northern Rhodesia to Southern Rhodesia and Nyasaland' (p. 249). He gives convincing evidence that federation did not have the economic benefits it is assumed to have had. GDP rose faster before federation than after 1953. The article is, however, richer than these bald conclusions suggest. It reveals, for example, that African wages and salaries rose faster (eighty-four per cent) than those of non-Africans (thirty-four per cent) in the period 1954-63. In Northern Rhodesia the situation was even more stark: African wages and salaries rose by 205 per cent as compared to a twenty-five per cent rise for non-Africans. This has not been noticed in writings on African nationalism, but it is obviously significant.

113 **The federation of Rhodesia and Nyasaland.**
Herbert J. Spiro. In: *Why federations fail: an enquiry into the requisites for successful federation.* Edited by Thomas M. Franck.
New York: New York University Press; London: University of London Press, 1968, p. 37-90. bibliog.
This analysis of the federation period is primarily political, paying much attention to the legal arguments. The conclusion is simple: federation failed because it never solved the

crucial issue of race relations in Southern Rhodesia. Spiro underplays the economic factor and quotes Kamuzu Banda who said, 'Our people are not like pigs who want food, we want food and freedom'. Still there are surprising elements in this article: Spiro argues that in the period of federation, considerable discriminatory legislation in Southern Rhodesia was eliminated and discriminatory practices were marginally improved.

114 Welensky's 4000 days; the life and death of the Federation of Rhodesia and Nyasaland.
Sir Roy Welensky. London: Collins, 1964. 383p. map.

Welensky was an ex-boxing champion, ex-railwayman and ex-union organizer who became prime minister of the Central African Federation. He could be seen at many independence celebrations as guest of honour in independent Zambia. As he writes in this book: 'Considering that when I was a lad I swam bare-arsed with the piccanins, I think I can say I know something about Africans' (p. 13). The book is mainly interesting for people who have an historical interest in federation and the struggle for independence.

Nationalism

115 The origins of nationalism in east and central Africa: the Zambian case.
Ian Henderson. *Journal of African History*, vol. 11, no. 4 (1970), p. 591-603.

This article offers little information that cannot be found elsewhere. It is in the first place a programmatic article outlining a research agenda which Henderson regrettably did not fulfil. Its enduring importance, however, lies in the questions that it asks. According to Henderson, the origins of Zambian nationalism lie primarily on the Copperbelt. He goes on to pose 'the whole question of differential politicization in Zambia and specifically the question of why the peoples of Northern, Luapula and Southern province became early supporters of the nationalist movement in the 1950s' (p. 600).

116 Kenneth Kaunda of Zambia: the times and the man.
Fergus Macpherson. London: Oxford University Press, 1974. 478p. map. bibliog.

This book resembles a hagiography, because in it Kaunda can do no wrong. It covers only the period up to independence and therefore gives a picture of the politician Kaunda untainted by the dirty hands of power. It is useful, however, as a source on the history of the independence struggle where there are many blank spots, because it contains many details which may take on a wider significance. The relationships between unions and political parties – UNIP in particular – is one area about which we know little, but which is an important structural feature of Zambian politics. It is interesting to note that Chisata – a pro-UNIP trade unionist – declared in 1962 that the mineworkers' union could not afford a strike after Kaunda had called for a mass miners' strike (p. 368). The book also gives a good feel for Kaunda's capacity to establish friendships and to project an impression of sincere religiosity. An example can be found in his friendship with John Papworth who put him up when Kaunda was down and out in London (p. 239).

117 Zambia; the politics of independence 1957-1964.
David C. Mulford. London: Oxford University Press, 1967. 362p. bibliog.

It is no exaggeration to describe this book as encyclopaedic. It gives an extremely detailed account of the political process which led to independence. The tension in the African National Congress leading to the formation of the United National Independence Party is the starting point of the book, while the victory of Kaunda's UNIP forms the end. Mulford also writes elaborately about European politics, however. This work will be read by few from cover to cover, but browsing or following key terms in the index can be very worthwhile. Mulford's judgements – although clearly biased towards Kaunda – are careful and may shed light on many murky matters mentioned elsewhere. The Katanga dimension in the independence struggle is a case in point.

118 Rural political protest: the 1953 disturbances in Meru-Luapula.
Mwelwa C. Musambachime. *International Journal of African Historical Studies*, vol. 20, no. 3 (1987), p. 437-53.

This article is as much of interest to people interested in fishing and fish conservation as to those who are interested in the history of nationalism. It provides a detailed description of African protest against restrictions on fishing imposed in the name of conservation of fish stocks. These protests fused with emerging nationalist politics. The colonial government reacted by relying more on chiefs to get their message across, but in so doing the chiefs lost credibility. The article is also valuable because it sketches the under-researched area of the interaction between Luapula Province and the Belgian Congo.

119 Dauti Yamba's contribution to the rise and growth of nationalism in Zambia 1941-1964.
Mwelwa C. Musambachime. *African Affairs*, vol. 90, no. 359 (1991), p. 259-81.

This informative article is an attempt to rehabilitate Dauti Yamba who, according to Musambachime, is a forgotten pioneer of African nationalism. One reason for this neglect is that Yamba was a member of the Federal parliament for nine years. This was widely felt to be an unforgivable compromise with colonialism and racism. The article challenges this perspective on his personality and demands credit be given for his radicalism as well as for his pioneering work in many fields. The article contains little known but interesting facts. For example, Yamba stood on an African National Congress ticket opposite Simon Kapwepwe in the 1962 elections, but he came out of retirement to join Kapwepwe when the latter formed the United Progressive Party in 1971.

120 The rise of nationalism in Central Africa: the making of Malawi and Zambia, 1873-1964.
Robert I. Rotberg. Cambridge, Massachusetts: Harvard University Press, 1965. 360p. 4 maps. bibliog.

This book is a history of the rise of African anti-colonial protest in a broad sense – including religious independence and labour unrest – in Malawi and Zambia. The

Zambian material, however, is presented mostly in separate chapters and sections. The perspective from which it is written may be considered to be history hijacked by nationalism. It does not read easily, but does contain much valuable information. It is especially useful as a reference source on the major personalities involved. A typical example is the entries in the register on the white engineer, Zukas, who was detained and deported by the colonial government in 1952 and later played a prominent role in the Movement for Multiparty Democracy.

121 An episode from the independence struggle in Zambia: a case study from Mwase Lundazi.
Jan Kees van Donge. *African Affairs*, vol. 84, no. 335 (1985), p. 265-77.

The major part of this article is a detailed description of the conflicts in Mwase Lundazi in the east of the country during the independence struggle. These were conflicts among Africans rather than confrontations with the European rulers. The conflicts cannot be reduced to a particular pattern of class conflict. The nationalist movement was at the grassroots in Lundazi a fluid coalition of people from diverse origins. The article maintains that such a fluid coalition characterized the nationalist movement as a whole as well.

122 An old nationalist in new nationalist times: Donald Siwale and the state in Zambia: 1948-1963.
Marcia Wright. *Journal of Southern African Studies*, vol. 23, no. 2 (1997), p. 339-53.

Siwale's career spanned a long period in which he moved from being a mission teacher before 1914 to membership of the African Representative Council in the early 1950s. He is chiefly to be identified with an early form of nationalism, although in 1948 he became a member of the African National Congress. Siwale objected to the formation of the Central African Federation, but he lost empathy with the popular protests emerging after the war, especially protests about fishing rights in Lake Mweru. The article is not only relevant for those interested in early nationalism, but also highly informative on tribal politics in Namwanga in the far north of the country.

Anthropology

123 Anthropology and colonial rule: the case of Godfrey Wilson and the Rhodes-Livingstone Institute, Northern Rhodesia.
Richard Brown. In: *Anthropology and the colonial encounter.*
Edited by Talal Assad. London: Ithaca Press, 1973, p. 173-97.

This is a moving piece of intellectual history, which gives a deep insight into colonial society. Godfrey Wilson was the first director of the Rhodes-Livingstone Institute from which emanated much research that influenced the whole field of anthropology. Anthropology had previously been associated with studying isolated traditional societies, and Wilson's innovation was to divert its attention to urban situations and modern industry. This aroused great resistance in the colonial administration, but Wilson found a place in Kabwe where the general manager 'laughed at the nervousness of the Copperbelt authorities' (p. 191). Wilson had to resign, however, after accusations of fomenting African discontent and died a few years later. His essay on detribalization – now we might call it urbanization – is not inspiring for the present day reader, but was highly influential in creating a view of Africans as contemporaries rather than of being historically backward. The urbanized African is not a social anomaly, but an urban dweller like any other.

124 Passages in the life of a white anthropologist: Max Gluckman in Northern Rhodesia.

Richard Brown. *Journal of African History*, vol. 20, no. 2 (1979), p. 219-34. map.

This is a delightful article. It gives a vision of Gluckman which is different from the received wisdom: he was, it is claimed, not the revolutionary radical often depicted. Godfrey Wilson defended him by saying that his political views – for example, the suggestion that Soviet collective farms could be an example to Africa – are largely a pose. Brown shows that Gluckman was – without espousing white supremacy – actually close to the colonial state. The article makes most imaginative use of the archives of the Rhodes-Livingstone Institute. Yet it is of interest to a wider public than merely those interested in the colonial state or the history of anthropology: its human interest may appeal to all. For example, while proceeding to his fieldwork by barge on the Zambezi, Gluckman accidentally shot a Lozi royal councillor (*induna*). For lesser spirits than him, that would have been the end of the fieldwork.

125 Chisungu. A girl's initiation ceremony among the Bemba of Zambia.

Audrey I. Richards with an introduction by Jean La Fontaine. London: Routledge, 1992. 224p. map. bibliog.

Although this book did not first appear until 1956, it is based on fieldwork undertaken in 1931. It may thus be that Audrey Richardson had difficulty in formulating what she knew about initiation, and this is understandable as the book crosses further into another cultural world than most anthropology. The book is a detailed chronological description of the ritual, placed against a cultural setting and interpreted in terms of its effects. The introduction by Jean La Fontaine is helpful for people who are not familiar with the importance of kinship in Zambia. When the anthropologist Han Seur (see item no. 692) carried out research in Serenje among the Bemba-related Lala, he gave them translated extracts of anthropological texts to read. This book struck the strongest chord with them.

126 Special issue on the Rhodes-Livingstone Institute.

African Social Research, no. 24 (1977), p. 259-344.

This issue is indispensable for anyone interested in the history of anthropology in Zambia. It contains reminiscences of all the research directors of the institute. Monica Wilson takes the place of Godfrey Wilson, her deceased husband, who was the first director, while Audrey Richards writes about the prehistory of the institute. It is especially interesting to see the tensions which existed between the colonial system and the anthropologists – tensions exemplified by, for example, this comment from the *Central*

African Post on participant observation, which, according to them, went too far: 'There is no need to adorn oneself with feathers to watch the behaviour of Red Indians' (p. 318).

127 The spirit and the drum; a memoir of Africa.
Edith Turner. Tucson, Arizona: The University of Arizona Press, 1987. 164p.

This is a personal memoir of the time Edith Turner spent with her husband Victor in Zambia's North Western Province in the early 1950s. The book offers a personal description of the religious world with which they came into contact. Anthropologists may be interested in her personal account of female initiation, which was of course closed to her husband. Besides that there are the usual memoirs of living in Africa: the encounter with the rancher, who is considered racist; an incident where two immaculately dressed mission boys pull the travellers' car out of the river; the fact that living in a thin umbrella tent is uncomfortable in the cold season of July. Victor Turner's monographs (see item nos. 224, 310, 311), however, may be more absorbing than this book, which was written for a wider audience.

Education

128 The influence of Livingstonia mission upon the formation of welfare associations in Zambia 1912-31.
David J. Cook. In: *Themes in the Christian history of Central Africa.* Edited by T.O. Ranger, John Weller. London: Heinemann Educational Books, 1975, p. 14-30.

In this article, Cook opens up perspectives on proto-nationalism by examining the careers and influences of the early products of education at Livingstonia mission in Northern Malawi. The men from Livingstonia mission station moved from positions as mission teachers into positions as clerks and shop assistants throughout Central Africa. Their place in society was based upon their education, and Cook portrays them as rivals for influence with the Watchtower creed (Jehovah's Witnesses), which rejected education. Compared with the rest of African society, therefore, the Welfare Associations were elite groupings which, although proto-nationalist, were quite law-abiding. The position of the chairman of the Broken Hill Welfare Association, George Nyirenda, is typical: in 1930 he was employed as a police interpreter and was chosen as chairman for that reason, as misuse of power by the police was one of the chief problems of life in the compound. Not only does this article provide a lively evocation of an important episode in early nationalist – or rather emancipatory – black consciousness, but the wealth of detail also makes it an important source for further research.

129 The origins of secondary education in Zambia.
Trevor Coombe. *African Social Research*, (1967-68), no. 3, p. 174-205; no. 4, p. 283-315; no. 5, p. 365-405.

The subtitle of these three articles is 'anatomy of a decision' and their subject is policy making. Although African demand for secondary education is mentioned, this decision making is described as operating primarily within a European-dominated bureaucracy. The case begins in the early 1930s with the Currie report advocating secondary education for Africans, and it ends in 1938 with the opening of Munali, the first secondary school for Africans. Coombe's work is important if one is to understand the reasons why Zambia entered independence with as few educated Africans as it did, but otherwise it is primarily of interest to historians.

130 Protestant mission education in Zambia, 1880-1954.
John P. Ragsdale. Cranbury, New Jersey: Associated University Presses, 1986. 190p. bibliog.

The author was born of missionary parents and spent five years teaching in Zambia. Missionary relations with government constitute the major thread organizing the story. It would be a mistake to concentrate on the formal, rather dry nature of this history. It includes, for example, the plea by a missionary in 1940 to ban employment of mission-trained teachers in government: 'any time they leave or are dismissed from mission service they will in all probability be able to drop in a far more lucrative position in government service' (p. 141). A final chapter sums up the book and also gives the personal insights of the author on the future: mission education should be unashamedly elitist – no comprehensive primary education, but a sector of high quality education at all levels: elementary, secondary and tertiary. Missions should preferably specialize in higher and specialized education.

131 Educational development in Northern Rhodesia, 1883-1945.
Peter Dormond Snelson. Lusaka: NECZAM, 1974. 342p. map.

This is an historical narrative with little interpretation. As education originated in Zambia in the various mission stations, it is not surprising that this book is also relevant to missionary history in Zambia. Snelson pays attention to such relatively little-described missions as the Seventh Day Adventists and the Plymouth Brethren. It is also not surprising that the relations between missions and government play an important part in this history. The government clung to a policy to spread primary education as widely as possible, to the neglect of secondary and tertiary education. The miserliness of the government is also a recurrent theme, but such miserliness could also be found in missions. At the beginning of the last century, teachers in the Dutch Reformed Missions received no salary for their first six months, as they were on probation. Afterwards, they earned less than the going rate for a dishwasher.

Labour, mining and urban

132 Labour, race and colonial rule: the Copperbelt from 1924 to independence.
Elena L. Berger. Oxford: Clarendon Press, 1974. 257p. 3 maps. bibliog.

This is a very detailed study of industrial relations in the copper mining industry from 1924 until just after independence. It is based primarily on archival research. Whereas in most studies prime attention is given to the 1935 strike of African mineworkers, in the register to this book there are only four entries for the 1935 strike as opposed to ten for the 1956 strike. The focus in this book is primarily on the relations between white and black trade unionism and on the question of whether African advancement was the primary issue in relations between workers and management rather than overall pay-rises for Africans. The book gives the impression of being an exhaustive study, but it has to be read with care in terms of the selection of facts presented. Nonetheless, it contains much interesting information, such as the account of the success of William Comrie – a Scottish trade unionist, seconded by the British government to Zambia in 1947 – in organizing African workers in the mines.

133 The locus of reproduction: women's labour in the Zambian Copperbelt, 1927-1953.
George Chauncey Jr. *Journal of Southern African Studies*, vol. 7, no. 2 (1981), p. 135-65.

This is an iconoclastic article. It takes issue with the thesis that circulatory migration of men in the reproductive age group permitted 'super exploitation' instead of allowing workers to settle in town with their family. Chauncey argues that the mines considered it to be in their interest to have women on the Copperbelt. For example, the Roan Antelope mine at Luanshya, which most actively and successfully encouraged the presence of women, established a system of agricultural plots (2,000 by 1935) on otherwise unused company land where wives could grow produce. Chauncey provides ample evidence that women played a far greater role on the Copperbelt than the generally accepted perspective assumes. This article is a major contribution to the debate on the relations between mines, government, rural authorities, miners and women. Alas it has largely escaped notice; this is regrettable as it is full of the spice of life: sex and beer instead of discussion of the articulation of modes of production.

134 The Northern Rhodesian Copperbelt: 1899-1962.
Francis L. Coleman. Manchester, England: Manchester University Press, 1971. 205p. 2 maps. bibliog.

This book is not only a history, but also an introduction to copper mining, presented in order to be accessible to people who are ignorant about mining, although, for example, the detailed instructions to prevent flooding on pages 122-23 will be beyond most readers. It will, however, give a feeling of what is and was involved in extracting ore.

135 Farm labour, agrarian capital and the state in colonial Zambia: the African Labour Corps, 1942-1952.
Kusum Datta. *Journal of Southern African Studies*, vol. 14, no. 3 (1988), p. 371-92.

Labour history in Zambia has understandably concentrated on the Copperbelt. Here Datta draws the reader's attention to workers who have not figured so much in the historiography of Zambia: farm labourers. The African Labour Corps was established to mobilize labour for the war effort and continued after the war was over in order to supply a burgeoning white commercial farming sector. The article is rich in informative detail: it states, for example, that the number of white farms doubled in Lusaka in the period 1946 to 1950. It gives the story of a clumsy attempt to mobilize labour in which coercion was always at least in the background. Although it is framed in a neo-marxist analysis, this is first and foremost a story well told rather than an academic tract. Besides being a story of callousness, it is also a story of total incomprehension of Africans on the part of some Europeans, who could not understand why Africans preferred working for a contractor rather than working for the African Labour Corps 'with infinitely more attractive conditions'.

136 Early African leadership: the Copperbelt disturbances of 1935 and 1940.
Ian Henderson. *Journal of Southern African Studies*, vol. 2, no. 1 (1975), p. 83-98.

The main point made here is that the labour movement, rather than the elite-dominated welfare societies, was the main focus of anti-colonial protest: the miners were 'rapidly armed with the knowledge that they could do white work'. This is a sensitively written article, which carefully unravels the major elements in these industrial confrontations. Henderson pays attention to clerks, Mbeni dance societies and the Jehovah's Witnesses as elements in the 1935 strike, while in 1940 he says one can speak much more of a proletarian consciousness. The position and image of the Bemba are outlined without digressing into racial stereotypes: 'The Luapulans and the Bemba of Chitimukulu had worked in the Katanga mines in large numbers from 1910 onwards, and had experienced the somewhat more liberal attitude towards colour bar restrictions'. Henderson wrote several articles on labour and politics on the Copperbelt which are mentioned in the annotation.

137 Strategy and transaction in an African factory: African workers and Indian management in a Zambian town.
Bruce Kapferer. Manchester, England: Manchester University Press, 1972. 366p. map. bibliog.

This book strongly emphasizes theory: patterns and structure of interaction and leadership are major concerns. If one penetrates this jargon, then one has access to an extremely detailed and vividly described snapshot of life in Kabwe in the mid 1960s. Narrated events which culminate in a strike form an important part of the book's structure. Despite its obvious intention of presenting more than a bare account of what happened in an Indian clothing factory in Kabwe, the book leaves only a fragmentary impression.

138 African proletarians and colonial capitalism: the origins, growth and struggles of the Zambian labour movement to 1964.
Henry S. Meebelo.   Lusaka: Kenneth Kaunda Foundation, 1986.
560p. bibliog.

This work could well be described as encyclopaedic. Unlike much of the literature on Zambian trade unionism it does not restrict itself to, or concentrate unduly on, the mineworkers. It provides, therefore, for example information about the Zambesi Sawmills strike of 1943 as well as about the less studied mineworkers' strikes, such as the eight week strike of 1955. Meebelo has found sources which are not used elsewhere, such as the personal archive of Simon Zukas or the oral testimony of Michael Sata. Sata, a prominent minister in the recent MMD government, appears here as a trade unionist in 1964. Meebelo's name is associated with the research bureau of UNIP, but this has not led to a partisan rendering of the antagonism between the nationalist and labour movements in the run up to independence. His account there is so subtle that it defies summary.

139 The 'politics of trypanosomiasis' revisited: labour mobilisation and labour migration in colonial Zambia: the Robert William Company in Lubemba 1901-1911.
Thandekile Ruth Mason Mvusi.   *Transafrican Journal of History*,
vol. 23 (1994), p. 43-68. map.

The Robert William Company was a labour recruiter in what was at the time called North Eastern Rhodesia or Lubemba for the mines in Katanga. The border between North Eastern Rhodesia and the Belgian Congo was actually closed in order to control sleeping sickness. Nevertheless, Robert William was quite successful in recruiting labour. According to Mvusi this should not be explained as a voluntary drive towards wage labour; rather, one must consider the complex pressures – especially the regulations against *chitemene* and tax collection – leading to labour migration. The administration in Lubemba created the necessity to earn money without providing the opportunity to do so. This article is to be recommended to anybody who likes to read colourful and forgotten history. In addition, links between Luapula Province and the other side of the river have not lost relevance, as the controversies surrounding Frederick Chiluba illustrate.

140 Class and gender on the Copperbelt; women in Northern Rhodesian copper mining communities 1926-1964.
Jane L. Parpart.   In: *Women and class in Africa.*   Edited by Claire Robertson, Iris Berger.   New York: African Publishing Co., 1986, p. 161-78.

The central question in this essay is whether women's status was primarily determined by class position or whether there was an overarching women's solidarity. The conclusion arrived at is that both models hold true. The article contains informative material from interviews, for example on the difficult lives of women married to administrative staff. Their husbands had organized in a separate union and they were often ostracized by the wives of members of the mineworkers' union. The information is more impressionistic than systematic but to some people information about bead gambling among women on the Copperbelt may be very relevant.

141 The household and the mineshaft: gender and class struggles on the Zambian Copperbelt 1926-64.
Jane L. Parpart. *Journal of Southern African Studies*, vol. 13, no. 1 (1986-87), p. 36-56.

In her introduction, Jane Parpart praises Chauncey's article on women on the Copperbelt (see item no. 133). She goes further, however, than merely pointing to an active presence of females in the growth of these mining towns. The article aims to refute the contention that women tend to be a restraining force in collective action. Women's presence, according to her, has exacerbated tensions with capital and a propensity for collective action. It increased pressure on wages, with many of the workers' demands being made in terms of family needs and expectations. Parpart's conclusion is that, 'We need to know more about the various factors affecting decisions whether to suspend gender struggles for class struggles'.

142 'Where is your mother?': gender, urban marriage, and colonial discourse on the Zambian Copperbelt, 1924-1945.
Jane L. Parpart. *The International Journal of African Historical Studies*, vol. 27, no. 2 (1994), p. 241-71.

This article can best be described as an analysis of the discourse on African marriage in urban settings. It discusses the views of authorities as well as that of the people. Respectability as well as more mundane concerns shaped these views. For example, a Chingola district officer noted that women are not slow to take advantage of a sex ratio of two males to one woman. Powerful voices speaking on the promiscuity of women and the obtaining of marriage certificates emerged from sides as diverse as the new African elite, the mission church and the government. Again, material interests played a role. The mining companies started to provide housing for married miners and that required such a certificate. This article may be too impressionistic in nature for some readers, but it will appeal to a wider audience than professional historians.

143 Black mineworkers in Central Africa; industrial strategies and the evolution of an African proletariat in the Copperbelt 1911-41.
Charles Perrings. London: Heinemann, 1979. 302p. bibliog.

The title of this book is a misnomer in that it provides at least as much, if not more, information on the development of the copper mining sector in Katanga, Congo, than on the Zambian Copperbelt. The divergent development in these geographically adjoined territories is at the heart of the book. This aspect is exemplified by the following: 'The mining companies in Northern Rhodesia never had as much room for manoeuvre as the UMHK [Union Minière du Haut Katanga – Mining Union of Upper Katanga] – given the comparative inflexibility of underground as opposed to open pit techniques etc.' Perrings has a neo-marxist approach which bears fruit here in that he pays much more attention to the technology of mining and its implications for labour than is the case with other historical literature. He also consulted company archives more extensively than others did. The book ends with a discussion of the 1935 and 1940 strikes.

144 Colonial urban policy and planning in Northern Rhodesia and its legacy.
Carol Rakodi. *Third World Planning Review*, vol. 8, no. 3 (1986), p. 93-217. 5 maps.

This article deals mainly with the history of town planning in Lusaka. It describes Lusaka's genesis as an urban centre due to the establishment there of a school for the Afrikaner community. After it was chosen as a capital city, town planning became important and this article relates the subsequent development of Lusaka to its changing role in the political and economic environment. It therefore provides perspectives not easily found elsewhere: whereas in 1946 there were only a few owner occupiers and two thirds of all European households lived rent free, that had changed to twenty-five per cent owner occupiers in 1956. This documents the growth of a settler community in the days of federation. The legacy of colonial policies are not surprising: a segregated city in which housing tended to be provided by the employer. The article does not show much original research, but the notes introduce the grey literature on this subject.

145 Notes towards a financial history of copper mining in Northern Rhodesia.
Andrew D. Roberts. *Canadian Journal of African Studies*, vol. 16, no. 2 (1982), p. 347-59.

This is firstly a polemical plea for further research, but it must be borne in mind that the plea was made at a time when neo-marxism saw the uncovering of patterns of exploitation as central. Roberts pleads for a perspective in which there is more empathy with the entrepreneur. He urges that, 'the industry, like most mining enterprises be viewed as long-term speculation in which the assessment of performance and profits is necessarily a complex task. Such a study calls for competence' which the author does not possess (p. 347). The article does not merely make a theoretical point, however. It is full of factual information which has not crystallized in a clear perspective. Roberts' conclusion – that after independence the main leakage of copper profits abroad had ended – is contentious.

146 The development of an African working class culture on the Rhodesian Copperbelt.
Owen B. Sichone. In: *Domination and resistance.* Edited by Daniel Miller, Michael Rowlands, Christopher Tilly. London: Unwin Hyman, 1989, p. 290-99.

This is a short and rather general introduction to the major themes which urban life introduced to the cultural anthropology of the area. In Sichone's view, anthropology may have found it difficult to place African society in its proper historical context, because anthropology 'belonged to the colonial superstructure' (p. 297). Urban culture in colonial society was, however, neither traditional nor European but unique in its own right. This presents more a point of view than new insights in studies of urban Zambia.

147 **Bomas, missions and mines; the making of centres on the Zambian Copperbelt.**
Brian Siegel. *African Studies Review*, vol. 31, no. 3 (1988), p. 61-85.

This is a contribution to a special issue on development and small towns in Africa. The designation of small towns may, however, be doubted in the case of the Zambian Copperbelt. In addition, as it provides detailed information about the origins of towns, this is primarily an historical rather than a development oriented article. Its main focus, however, is on the marginalization of the Lamba, the original inhabitants of the Copperbelt. Colonial towns are in the main seen as parasitic centres intimately linked to rural stagnation.

148 **The Rhodesia Railways African strike of 1945. Part I: a narrative account. Part II: cause, consequences and significance.**
Ken P. Vickery. Part I, *Journal of Southern African Studies*, vol. 24, no. 3 (1998), p. 545-61. Part II, *Journal of Southern African Studies*, vol. 25, no. 1 (1999), p. 49-73.

The strike here described broke out in Bulawayo, Southern Rhodesia, but it also spread to one town in Northern Rhodesia, Kabwe (Broken Hill). The strike also spread to the lead and zinc mine there, and the government feared that the white railway workers would also become involved. Although Vickery notes some sympathetic mutterings from Welensky, the white union leader, that did not happen. The second part of the article outlines how differences between Northern and Southern Rhodesia played a role in the way in which the strike unfolded. At the end of the article, Vickery stresses the changing times: Welensky went to London after the strike to urge assistance for Africans forming trade unions. The Labour government reacted by dispatching the Scottish trade unionist, William Comrie, to Northern Rhodesia in 1947 (see also item no. 132).

Law

149 **Making customary law: men, women and courts in colonial Northern Rhodesia.**
Martin Chanock. In: *African women and the law: historical perspectives*. Edited by Margaret Hay, Marcia Wright. Boston, Massachusetts: Boston University, Papers on Africa VII, 1982, p. 53-68.

This article synthesizes in a nutshell the main theoretical point of Chanock's monograph: that the colonial courts system created law rather than codifying or finding existing law. This is demonstrated with court cases from various parts of Zambia. The use of actual cases illustrates theoretical points in a vivid way – one example is this rhetorical question of a magistrate in a case where a widow refused to be inherited by a male relative of her deceased husband: 'Must we allow her to abuse the freedom so given to her?'

150 Law, custom and social order; the colonial experience in Malawi and Zambia.
Martin Chanock. Cambridge, England: Cambridge University Press, 1985. 271p. bibliog.
Chanock's book makes theoretical points through detailed analysis of court records. Customary law in the colonial period was not 'the dead hand of tradition, but it represented the responses of living interests to new developments' (p. 237). Customary law may be depicted as traditional and likely to be superseded by those in 'development work', but such dismissal does no justice to the nature of that law. Channock argues this through a painstaking analysis of empirical material. Because the records in Zambia were fuller than those in Malawi, Zambia figures prominently in this book, although it focuses mainly upon Malawi. The book covers the whole gamut of topics that came before the courts in colonial times. However, it is of special interest to those interested in the laws on marriage and the family. The finding of precedents in the law is primarily seen there – as elsewhere in the book – as serving particular interests rather than as a neutral application of rules.

151 The articulation of separate legal spheres.
Sally Engle Merry. In: *African women and the law: historical perspectives*. Edited by Margaret Hay, Marcia Wright. Boston, Massachusetts: Boston University, Papers on Africa VII, 1982, p. 68-90.
This article has a lengthy theoretical introduction, but from page 77 onwards it gives a good overview of the legal systems at work under colonial rule. Merry's theoretical perspective is that of legal pluralism and she therefore describes various legal spheres. This article could be useful as an introduction to this vast subject, which was relevant to much of colonial society.

Regional

152 Politics in a changing society; the political history of the Fort Jameson Ngoni.
J.A. Barnes. London: Oxford University Press, 1954. 220p. 4 maps. bibliog.
Barnes was one of the famous anthropologists at the Rhodes-Livingstone Institute, but this book is first and foremost an historical monograph in which invasion and migration are the great themes. The Ngoni groups are offshoots of the Zulu empire in what is nowadays South Africa. They crossed the Zambezi in 1842 – dated from a solar eclipse – and became marauders through what is now Eastern Zambia and Malawi. In their turn they were subjugated by the British colonizers. This is an early example of history writing 'from below': migrations are not depicted primarily as the outcome of decisions by leaders. Barnes stresses the decentralized nature of Ngoni migration. People who were subjugated were as a rule assimilated in the Ngoni state. Barnes labels this process the

'snowball state'. The book is worth reading because of its vision of African history as a continual process of change and migration.

153 The politics of change in a Zambian community.
George C. Bond. Chicago: University of Chicago Press, 1976. 178p. bibliog.

This may be one of the most underrated studies in the extensive anthropological literature on Zambia. It provides an interesting bridge between the wide anthropological literature before independence, which paid scant attention to politics, and the political science literature of the post-independence period, which was not informed by anthropological insights. It deals with Uyombe, a little-known community in north eastern Zambia where the research was carried out between 1963 and 1965. It describes UNIP as the organization of the new men – influenced by migration and education. The nationalist struggle intermeshed with the politics of chieftainship carried out in the idiom of kinship. On a return visit in 1975, Bond found a resurgence of chieftainship (see also: 'New coalitions and traditional chiefship in Northern Zambia; the politics of local government in Uyombe', by George Clement Bond. *Africa*, vol. 45, no. 4 [1975], p. 438-61).

154 'Veni, vidi, vici?'; reassessing the Ila syphilis epidemic.
Brian Callahan. *Journal of Southern African Studies*, vol. 23, no. 3 (1997), p. 421-44.

The quotation in the title of this article is from the Namwala district commissioner in 1958 at the end of a successful campaign against syphilis. Callahan doubts whether syphilis was as serious a problem as it was said to be. Its assumed prevalence may stem from the missionary anthropologists, Dale and Smith, who were preoccupied with loose sexual morals among the Ila people. They may have mistaken yaws for syphilis, while the low birth rate reported among the Ila may have result from misinterpretation of the statistics. The reliability of the census may have been overestimated and not have taken migration sufficiently into account. The anomaly to be explained is why the Ila embraced the campaign against syphilis if it was not the problem it was said to be. Among the explanations may be the rewards for chiefs seen to be embracing a colonial programme; furthermore, the detection of syphilis cases was a powerful argument in litigation strategies concerning adultery. Finally, the Ila associated the campaign more with enhancing fertility than with combating disease. The article is not only an exercise in epidemiology, but may give important insights into Ila society.

155 Barotseland: the secessionist challenge to Zambia.
Gerald L Caplan. *Journal of Modern African Studies*, vol. 6, no. 3 (1968), p. 343-60. map.

The return of multiparty politics in the early 1990s gave rise to a revival of sub-nationalist sentiments in Barotseland. This very readable article has therefore regained actuality. It gives an historical overview of the origins of the claims for a special status; the association of the Lozi elite with federalism in the 1950s; the revival of the campaign for a special status on the eve of independence; and the relations of the Lozi elite with the white minority regimes in Southern Africa. It ends with a description of the UNIP victory and the ascendance of Zambian nationalists of Lozi descent such as the Wina brothers.

156 The elites of Barotseland; 1878-1969.
Gerald L. Caplan. Berkeley, California; Los Angeles: University of
California Press, 1970. 270p. 2 maps. bibliog.

This is a history of the contacts between the elites of Barotseland, which was and is a
highly stratified society, and the agents of western imperialism: the explorers, the
missionaries, the British South Africa Company, the colonial government and finally the
government of independent Zambia. It is a highly readable account which has been
criticized for being superficial, but it gives a succinct introduction to the problems
surrounding Barotseland. It is a pleasure to be initiated into the significance of famous
Lozi names such as Yeta, Lewanika or Winawina. With sub-nationalism again strong in
the area, it may be enlightening to read how the Zambian nationalists won
overwhelmingly in Barotseland in 1964, struggling against both white domination and
'crumbling, anachronistic feudalism' (p. 199).

157 The history and cultural life of the Mbunda speaking peoples.
Cheke Cultural Writers Association. Edited and prefaced by
Dr Robert Papstein. Lusaka: The Zambian Journal of History,
1994. 176p. map. bibliog.

This is – to my knowledge – the only published part of a nationwide oral history project.
The home of the Mbunda people is in Zambezi in North Western Province. This history,
however, claims that the whole of Western Zambia, a good part of Angola and part of
Namibia belong to the Mbunda. The Cheke Writers Association claims to descend from
the Mbunda Tribal Association founded in 1956. The political nature of these documents
is thus obvious and is also the subject of an article by Papstein (see item no. 215). This
text is difficult for outsiders to interpret as it assumes extensive knowledge on the part of
the reader. A good historical commentary is helpful in these cases.

158 Slaves, commoners and landlords in Bulozi c.1875 to 1906.
W. Gervase Clarence-Smith. *Journal of African History*, vol. 20,
no. 2 (1979), p. 219-34. map.

This is an iconoclastic article, which criticizes the voluminous literature on Barotseland,
and especially the image portrayed by the anthropologist Gluckman (see item no. 124).
The latter portrayed pre-colonial Barotseland as an Arcadia, while Clarence-Smith
depicts a heavily stratified society, in which a minority dominated access to natural
resources. Surplus was accumulated and far less redistributed than Gluckman would have
us believe. Most damning is Clarence-Smith's accusation that 'Much of the existing
literature obscures and even denies the harsh conditions of slave life in Bulozi' (p. 228).

**159 Your friend Lewanika; the life and times of Lubosi Lewanika,
Litunga of Barotseland, 1841-1916.**
Gervas Clay. London: Chatto & Windus, 1968. 192p. 3 maps.
bibliog.

Lubosi Lewanika was the undisputed Litunga (superior chief) of Barotseland from 1885
until 1916. He had emerged as victor after the defeat of the Kololo and the restoration of
the Lozi kingdom and was Litunga when Barotseland came into the European sphere of
influence. This book is much more a history of the contacts between Europeans and the
Lozi court than, as the title suggests, a biography of Lewanika. The author was a colonial

administrator in Barotseland and the contacts between Europeans and the Barotse were clearly his primary interest. A juicy titbit can be found in relation to Lewanika's visit to England to attend the coronation of Edward VII. Lewanika did not fear meeting the king: 'When we kings get together we always find plenty to talk about' (p. 124).

160 On the threshold of Central Africa; a record of twenty years' pioneering among the Barotse of the Upper Zambezi.
François Coillard. London: Frank Cass, 1971. 3rd ed. 647p. map.

The relationships, especially the friendships, of the French Protestant missionary Coillard with the Lozi establishment have been chronicled extensively elsewhere. This is a photographic reprint of the first edition of the journal which Coillard kept, first published in 1897. Coillard presents it modestly as a collection of scattered leaves and not a systematic history of the Barotse mission, nor of his missionary career. It is therefore of interest to a rather limited audience: professional historians and amateur historians who like to read the mostly mundane, daily impressions of a missionary at the end of the last century. It is engagingly written, however, and thus accessible to a wide audience.

161 The history of Nampeyo.
Elizabeth Colson. Lusaka: Kenneth Kaunda Foundation, 1991. 76p. 2 maps. bibliog.

Nampeyo is the village in which Colson did most of her fieldwork. This book is unusual among her publications, as it was written at the request of the people she studied. They wanted to preserve their history and Colson went through her notes to collate them into this short book. It provides an oral history of some events with a wider significance, especially the Ndebele raids in pre-colonial times. Most of the history focuses rather narrowly on the Chona chieftaincy, but gems of information can also be found: we are informed that Chief Chona left to work in a Southern Rhodesian mine immediately after marriage; and that he reports that, 'One day a European slapped me – it was because of a bad omen (*malweza*) because my wife at the village was sleeping with other men' (p. 36).

162 Reflections on economic and social change among the Plateau Tonga of Northern Rhodesia c. 1890-1935.
Mac Dixon-Fyle. *International Journal of African History*, vol. 16, no. 3 (1983), p. 423-39. map.

Dixon-Fyle calls his article 'reflections', and that is apt. His central concern is the adaptation of the Tonga to the social order of the 20th century. Southern Province is unusual within Zambia in that respect, as the Tonga developed into a population which produced a cash crop. There was labour migration, for example after the onset of the great depression in the 1930s, but it was never as dominant as elsewhere. The author sketches in particular the position of the *mulimi simpindi*, the indigenous large-scale cultivator class. This was never a large class however, and it remained well integrated in wider Tonga society rather than revolutionizing it. The article is broader than this topic only and draws on an impressive array of sources. It is particularly useful as an introduction to Southern Province as it presents the major themes that dominated its development.

163 Trade and politics in Barotseland during the Kololo period.
Eric Flint. *Journal of African History*, vol. 11, no. 1 (1970),
p. 71-86. 2 maps.

Trade in Barotseland changed drastically in the middle of the 19th century, shifting from slaves to ivory; and the arrival of Livingstone coincided with the wish of the Kololo – the invaders from the south who had subjugated the Lozi – to undertake long distance trade themselves. The article is mainly based on a reading of Livingstone's journals to document the effect of a rapid development of long distance power. Trade had important consequences for the distribution of power: it undercut the power of chiefs and brought forth a new type of leader.

164 Colonial policies and the reconstruction of canals in Bulozi, 1925-1964.
Sitwala Mutonga. *Transafrican Journal of History*, vol. 23 (1994), p. 184-95.

The thesis that the intricate agricultural system of the Lozi was undermined by labour migration is well known, especially as tribute labour no longer maintained the canal system. This article draws attention to the fact that the colonial government was well aware of this, tried after 1945 to revive the canal system, and also had an eye for the value of indigenous Lozi agriculture, all of which led to a revival of agriculture. This article is short – no more than six pages deal with the period after 1945 – but its importance is great for the discussion on local agricultural systems and colonial interventions.

165 Land, labour and diet in Northern Rhodesia.
Audrey I. Richards. London: Oxford University Press, 1939. 415p.
3 maps.

This classic study of the Bemba may be difficult to read even for the aficionado of detailed anthropological description. It is extremely detailed, and details given are not ascribed as much meaning as in other anthropological monographs. The reason is that Richards' extraordinarily rich research material is not structured by her research findings but by a preconceived idea. Therefore the structure of the argument often seems tortuous. The book is a continuation of a student thesis in which Richards tried to prove that hunger was the chief determinant of human relationships. However, if one takes the trouble to immerse oneself in this book, then one gets a penetrating insight into the way in which matrilineal descent functions, the material foundations – agriculture – of Bemba society, the effects of labour migration in Bembaland, and so on. For anyone with no anthropological background who wants to become familiar with Bemba culture, it may be best to browse through this book, using entries from the index.

166 A history of the Bemba: political growth and change in North-Eastern Zambia before 1900.
Andrew D. Roberts. London: Longman, 1973. 420p. 18 maps.
bibliog.

This massive historical study starts with the legend of the Bemba migration into Northern Zambia and ends with the coming of colonialism. The Bemba developed a more cohesive and powerful political organization than most other peoples of the Central African savannah. The role of chieftainship in keeping the state together as well as relations with both tributary/neighbouring groups and traders are central in this book. A concluding chapter considers the Bemba state in a comparative context. This work of great scholarship is primarily a book for specialists, but readers who are interested in the Bemba can benefit greatly from browsing. As Roberts says: 'Amidst the upheavals of the twentieth century, the Bemba have retained a sense of corporate continuity and communal pride through the survival of their political structure: a living testimony to their imperial past'.

167   The agricultural history of Barotseland, 1840-1964.

Laurel van Horn.   In: *The roots of rural poverty: in Central and Southern Africa.*   Edited by Robin Palmer, Neil Parsons.   London: Heinemann, 1977, p. 144-71. map.

This reader was very influential at the time it first appeared. It applied to Zambia the idea that rural poverty is caused by the demands of modern capitalism. Barotseland was an obvious choice to illustrate this, as it had already been explained by Gluckman in those terms. Van Horn discusses detailed issues such as the collapse of 1915 to 1916 due to cattle disease. Although the labour drain and patterns of exploitation play a major role, it is not a doctrinaire application of neo-marxism. She has an eye for the role of natural disasters, peasant initiatives into markets and the need for labour to be imported in order to maintain the Lozi system.

168   Black and white in southern Zambia: the Tonga plateau economy and British imperialism, 1890-1939.

Kenneth P. Vickery.   Westport, Connecticut: Greenwood Press, 1986. 243p. 4 maps. bibliog.

The considerable scholarly attention devoted to Zambia's Southern Province can be explained by that province's unusual nature: it was the only area in Zambia where settler farmers were dominant and it is also the area where a cash cropping peasantry emerged early. These issues are the main themes of this book also. It is not easy to summarize because it is in the first place a chronological narrative with comments on general theoretical perspectives on colonization based on the empirical material. The European side of the story gets somewhat more attention here than in other works. It is also a good read, with many juicy observations: W.F. Bruce Miller, an English settler in Choma, reported that there was little interaction between Afrikaners and English settlers. He was however worried about the affection of his son for an Afrikaner girl: '[He is] determined to marry the dirty slut' (p. 92). Vickery concludes that there was therefore some interaction. Anybody interested in studying cattle among the Tonga – a crucial subject in the area – would do well to read Chief Mapanza's comment, made in 1913, on page 153. Vickery makes exceptionally good use of sources.

Religion

169 Sectarian allegiance and political authority: the Watchtower Society in Zambia, 1907-35.
J.M. Assimeng. *Journal of Modern African Studies*, vol. 8, no. 1 (1970), p. 97-112.

The title of this article suggests an historical narrative, but that is not to be found here. The article is a series of observations and conjectures about the relationships between the Jehovah's Witnesses and authority. On page 103 there is a useful summing up of four types of conflicts with authority in which they were involved. According to Assimeng, Zambia had a higher percentage of Witnesses in 1968 than any other country in the world: one per cent of the population. He contrasts the rural character of the movement in Zambia to its urban nature in Ghana. He explains the Witnesses' clashes with the government of independent Zambia as resulting from nationalism which had, for purposes of solidarity, been raised to a religion.

170 Towards church union in Zambia: a study of missionary co-operation and church union efforts in Central Africa.
Peter Bolink. Franeker, The Netherlands: T. Wever, 1967. 430p. 4 maps. bibliog.

Some Protestant mission churches united in 1965 in the United Church of Zambia. The title of this book suggests that this is the only topic covered, but it is only one aspect of this study, which is a comprehensive and detailed history of the Protestant missions in Central Africa. It is extremely detailed and sources are well accounted for, which makes it difficult for the layman to read. However, it is useful as a work of reference for a wide public and should be consulted by anybody interested in the Protestant missions in Zambia.

171 Bemba chiefs and Catholic missions.
Brian Garvey. *Journal of African History*, vol. 18, no. 3 (1977), p. 411-26. map.

Garvey worked out the themes in this article in his later monograph (see item no. 172). His limited concern here is to explain the decline of chiefly power in Bembaland, and he sees the main explanation in the interaction with missionaries. Whereas the missionaries through their catechists maintained a chain of preaching and prayer throughout the area, the chiefs had the greatest difficulty in maintaining a major role in religious life. Furthermore, the Catholic missionaries had no rivals in Bembaland and therefore did not have to woo traditional authority to offset the influence of other missions.

172 Bembaland church: religious and social change in South-central Africa 1891-1964.
Brian Garvey. Leiden, The Netherlands: E.J. Brill, 1997. 217p. bibliog.

This work is primarily historical rather than, as the title suggests, sociological. It also deals more with the earlier periods up to 1945 than with the post-war period. However, the last chapter pays attention to the reactions of the Catholic Church to the schism of Emilio

Mulolani; to the Lumpa church of Alice Lenshina; and to the independence movement. It is also the story of the commitment of a particular religious order, the White Fathers, to Bemba rural society. The order made a definite decision not to get involved with Bemba society on the Copperbelt. Garvey is not a particularly imaginative historian or gifted storyteller, and therefore the book is mainly of interest to specialized audiences. The browser can, however, find interesting insights, for example: 'Up to this time [1931] there had been little attempt by the White Father mission to impose models of European pious society on the nascent churches' (p. 52). This may be a reflection of the greater tolerance for, and understanding of, local society by the White Fathers as compared to other orders, as they were a society specifically founded for mission in Africa.

173 Alice Lenshina's anti-witchcraft church.
Hans-Jurgen Gerschat. *Africana Marburgensia*, vol. 17, special issue (1998), p. 36-46.

This short sketch of the Lumpa church is useful, as Gerschat brings together material from diverse and somewhat obscure sources. Most notable is his reference to the hymns of the church collected by P. Louis Oger, a White Father missionary. The sketch portrays the church emphatically as a Christian, Puritan church which took on a neglected evil: witchcraft.

174 Women's revolt: the Lumpa church of Lenshina Mulenga in the 1950s.
Hugo Hinfelaar. *Journal of Religion in Africa*, vol. 21, (1991), p. 99-129.

The ideas in this article were later more extensively discussed in a book (see item no. 292). Hinfelaar's contribution to the study of the Lenshina movement is his attention to texts, notably the hymns which were sung in church. He denies that there was a millenarian element inherent in Lenshina's teaching. In his view, they had a much richer and positive side derived from Bemba ideas. According to Hinfelaar, women had a special role as mediators of religious experiences, and this notion was adapted creatively and innovatively to the Christian message.

175 A time to mourn: a personal account of the 1964 Lumpa church revolt in Zambia.
John Hudson. Lusaka: Bookworld Publishers, 1999. 147p.

Up to now there has been no account from within the administration of the Lenshina rising, and this book is therefore particularly welcome. It highlights facts which are either not mentioned or which are given a subordinate role in other accounts – for example, that Simon Kapwepwe as well as Kenneth Kaunda went on reconciliation missions to Chinsali in 1963. An astounding newly revealed fact is that soldiers of the Northern Rhodesian Regiment rebelled: officers commented that, 'The men won't move ... They feel they are on the wrong side' (p. 111). This was a reaction after a patrol in Lundazi where they visited a Lumpa settlement 'some days after riots ... inhabitants had been massacred by UNIP supporters with particular mutilations and torture' (p. 111).

176 'All good men'; the development of Lubwa mission, Chinsali, Zambia.
Arie N. Ipenburg. Frankfurt am Main, Germany: Peter Lang, 1991. 345p. 3 maps. bibliog.

Lubwa mission in Northern Zambia is more than just a mission station. David Kaunda, the father of Kenneth, came to preach there in the early 1900s. The register of this book shows many entries under the names of David, Kenneth and Robert Kaunda. The latter became prominent in the Lumpa church which violently confronted the state – under the leadership of his brother Kenneth – around the time of independence. Ipenburg writes a very conscientious, albeit somewhat conventional, history of a mission station which was involved in the most intricate and complicated conflicts in Zambia. It is no wonder that this book is full of revealing and intriguing facts. One example is this comment on the Roman Catholic competitors for souls in 1925: 'the only way to meet the Roman menace is to give people God's word and the surest way to get it to them is through the village schools' (p. 77). Such remarks make the title look ironic, which it is not meant to be. This book is valuable for a much wider audience that just those interested in mission history. Those primarily interested in the origins of nationalism; or in eschatological independent churches, and above all those who want to get a feel for the intensely religious nature of Zambian society will find this book useful.

177 The Monze rain-festival: the history of change in a religious cult in Zambia.
Dan O'Brien, Carolyn O'Brien. *The International Journal of African Historical Studies*, vol. 29, no. 3 (1996), p. 519-43.

This analysis of the Monze rain festival in Southern Province aims to prove that the rain shrine at Monze provided a unifying force for local people. Therefore, the view of the Tonga as an acephalous society without much cohesion has to be reconsidered or qualified. It describes the history of the cult and discusses the songs and ritual of the Monze rain festival (*lwiindi*). According to the authors, the Tonga would have developed into a unitary political entity if the colonial state had not fragmented them. There is thus a rather crude evolutionist thesis in this informative article.

178 Missionaries and miners; a history of the beginning of the Catholic church in Zambia with particular reference to the Copperbelt.
Michael O'Shea, SMA. Ndola, Zambia: Mission Press, 1986. 376p. 11 maps. bibliog.

Father O'Shea is from Ireland, and he has the Irish gift for storytelling. As is common in storytelling, the subject is where the story leads you. The heart of this story is the establishment of the Franciscan Conventual Fathers' mission on the Copperbelt during the 1930s. However, the book is also a history of the origin of Roman Catholic missions in the whole country, and a very good introduction to the history of the mining industry in Zambia. The book does not, however, come across as disjointed. A good storyteller keeps the attention of his audience, and the book is filled with anecdotes, colourful individuals and the like. In his introduction, the author says that 'even the scholar' may benefit from reading his book. There are, however, many less interesting, less well-documented books written by so-called scholars.

179 The Lumpa church of Alice Lenshina.

Andrew D. Roberts.   In: *Protest and power in black Africa.*
Edited by Robert I. Rotberg, Ali Mazrui.   New York: Oxford
University Press, 1970, p. 513-71.

This is a masterful piece of contemporary history. As Roberts stresses, the Lenshina church is of special interest as its growth coincided with the development of a successful nationalist movement. In 1964, the church came into an apocalyptic confrontation with the government which was just coming under nationalist control. Any attempt to summarize this article will fail as it is so carefully crafted. Whatever is published on the Lenshina movement after this adds little to the story, and in its empathy with the protagonists this study is unsurpassed.

180 Christian missionaries and the creation of Northern Rhodesia 1880-1924.

Robert I. Rotberg.   Princeton, New Jersey: Princeton University
Press, 1965 . 240p. map. bibliog.

This is not a particularly penetrating study of early missionary endeavour. It is impressionistic rather than systematic and, for reference purposes, Rotberg's book on nationalism (see item no. 120) is much better. Its appendices on sources, and especially the biographical sketches, may, however, be of value to people interested in the subject.

181 Christians of the Copperbelt: the growth of the church in Northern Rhodesia.

John V. Taylor, Dorothy Lehmann.   London: SCM Press, 1961.
308p. map. bibliog.

This book was radical at its time of writing. It addresses missionary activity in a cultural melting pot instead of a supposedly traditional society. It also deals with political questions, especially the issue of federation. Thirdly, it pays attention to independent churches. It is now an historical document showing how Christians thought at that time, but it is still often quoted. It reads well, and anybody who knows the Copperbelt will, on reading it, see how life has changed there.

182 The influence on national affairs of Alston May, bishop of Northern Rhodesia, 1914-40.

John Weller.   In: *Themes in the Christian history of Central Africa.*
Edited by T.O. Ranger, John Weller.   London: Heinemann
Educational Books, 1975, p. 195-213.

The career of Alston May is a vehicle for Weller to defend the position of missionary influence in Northern Rhodesia as giving a voice to the voiceless, with whom May was in close touch according to Weller. He depicts May as a man with a gift of friendship who not only moved politically as the member of a team with fellow missionaries, but also had the ability to establish good relationships with the administration. He had the advantage that he shared his background with many of the latter.

183 **Some developments in Bemba religious history.**
Douglas Werner. *Journal of Religion in Africa*, vol. 4, fasc. 1
(1971/72), p. 1-24. 3 maps.
Pre-colonial history is often quite open to speculation as there are few written sources.
This article uses linguistic evidence in combination with oral traditions in order to
describe how religion fitted into the process of centralization in the Bemba royal ancestral
cult, and explores the relationship between the ancestral cult surrounding the Bemba
chiefs (*bena ngandu*) and beliefs in nature spirits (*ngulu*).

184 **Vampire priests of central Africa: African debates about labour
and religion in colonial northern Zambia.**
Luise White. *Comparative Studies in Society and History*, vol. 35,
no. 4 (1993), p. 746-72.
White's main subject is *banyama* (vampires) stories about Africans employed by
Europeans who are supposed to have the intention of drinking the Africans' blood. The
article concentrates on accusations against the White Fathers in this regard, but also deals
with such accusations against, for example, Orne Gilman: 'the latter was a white store
manager; shadowy even by the standards of white settlers in Northern Rhodesia'. These
accusations are set within the labour and racial relations of the time. The article depicts
very well the atmosphere in northern Zambia in the 1930s. It may be, however, that the
theoretical constructs which see vampire accusations as debating the merits of modernity
may be far-fetched for some.

185 **Tsetse visions: narratives of blood and bugs in colonial Northern
Rhodesia 1931-9.**
Luise White. *Journal of African History*, vol. 36, no. 2 (1995),
p. 219-45.
The author states clearly that the article is about 'the mosaic of colonial beliefs, African
and European, the supposedly superstitious and the supposedly scientific, about sleeping
sickness control'. The setting is Zambia's Northern Province – Bembaland – before the
Second World War. White combines in one analysis the vampire beliefs of local societies
and the understanding of the tsetse fly among European administrators. The link between
these apparently disparate concerns is the subject of blood. She writes more, however,
about ecological understanding in the broadest sense and that includes, for example, big
game hunting and *citemene* agriculture. It is fortunate that she talks about a mosaic of
belief, because the article reads as a collection of fragments. These can be entertaining in
themselves, but the pattern in the fragments is not always clear.

Colonial Memoirs and Nostalgia

186 The diary of a district officer.
Kenneth Bradley.   London: Macmillan, 1966. 4th ed. 192p. map.

Bradley spent his whole career in the colonial civil service and sixteen years of those in Zambia. This book is a diary which he kept as a touring district commissioner in what is now Eastern Province. It is of historical interest, but suffused by paternalism. For example, he praises indirect rule: 'The Chief is being taught to rule again and it is my job to guide him' (p. 35). This book will be especially appreciated by those who are nostalgic for the time when population was scarce, when wildlife, especially in the Luangwa valley, was abundant and when a social order of district commissioner, chiefs and messengers seemed unassailable.

187 For the president's eyes only; the story of John Brumer, agent extraordinary.
Roy Christie.   Johannesburg: Hugh Keartland Publishers, 1971. 183p.

John Brumer claims to have formed the Zambian secret service after independence. He gained the confidence of Kaunda while in the pay of Rhodesian intelligence. The gullible Kaunda was not the prime enemy of Rhodesian intelligence in the mid-1960s. The British security apparatus, however, was, and they exposed Brumer to the Zambians. This did not spoil his good relationship with Kaunda, who is, in this book, forever an idealistic gentleman. Kaunda engineered an honourable escape for Brumer, which was not noticed. In fact, at the same time as Brumer made his escape, Kaunda entertained the parents of Mrs Brumer. The book is not particularly informative despite its name dropping. It is of significance as a testimony of the culture among Southern African whites at the time: they were in their own eyes immeasurably more clever than Africans while living life to the full, hunting, drinking and so on. It is colonial nostalgia of a dubious kind.

188 Nswana – the heir; the life and times of Charles Fisher: a surgeon in Central Africa.
Monica Fisher. Ndola, Zambia: Mission Press, 1991. 246p.

Charles Fisher's life provides a glimpse of colonial society from the missionary side. He was born into the Kalene mission of the Plymouth Brethren in North Western Province and, although he worked there in the beginning of his career, this was too confined an environment for him. Extensive travel for research purposes in the then Belgian Congo certainly broadened his mind. He moved to work in the mines' medical services on the Copperbelt. He was a pioneer administrator in the medical profession in Zambia and founded, for example, Medic Air, the flying doctor service. This is an interesting book for anybody who likes to read about eventful lives in the colonial period. It is, however, also an important political source on European politics before independence. Fisher was close to Gore-Brown and associated his name with the Capricorn Society, which supported African advancement in a colonial context.

189 The flag-wagger.
Harry Franklin. Preface by Elspeth Huxley. London: Shepheard-Walwyn, 1974. 204p.

Huxley's preface is a defence of the colonial civil service: 'a corps of amateurs. They ran the world's largest empire on very little money, loving their work despite considerable drawbacks and finding out many things as they went along'. Franklin's view of himself fits this description. This is a book for people who like to read about a sudden stop to shoot a leopard in a tree on the way to a first posting in Serenje; who like to read about the time when the noise in Lusaka came primarily from the shrinking and expanding of corrugated iron; or who like to read about the invention of the saucepan special, a radio which Africans could afford. Franklin was also a journalist: the book reads extremely well.

190 The Africa house; the true story of an English gentleman and his African dream.
Christina Lamb. London: Penguin Books, 2000. 349p. 4 maps. bibliog.

The house in question is Shiwa Ngandu in Mpika, and the gentleman is Stewart Gore-Brown. His life is filled with romanticism, romance, tragedy and politics and is therefore a marvellous topic for a journalist who writes for a wide public. Christina Lamb's portrayal of Gore-Brown as a High Tory – not her words, but he was a man who considered himself aristocratic; had a paternalistic concern for the poor; and bridged political opposites – is apt. It is a book which can essentially be characterized as 'faction', and some of the fictionalized bits are overdone: 'As the vicar spread some earth on the coffin... a choked sob came from somewhere deep within the girl reminding Gore-Brown of a wounded Hartebeest on some of his hunts' (p. 123).

191   In witch-bound Africa; an account of the primitive Kaonde tribe and their beliefs.
Frank H. Melland.   London: Frank Cass & Co., 1967. 316p. 3 maps.

This book, first published in 1923, studies the people in North Western Province – the Ba Kaonde mentioned in the title as well as the Alunda and the Andembu. It is therefore to be recommended to anyone interested in the anthropology of these peoples. Melland was a district administrator in Kasempa district for eleven years of his long colonial career. In that capacity, he was an amateur anthropologist who collected also the insights of other amateur anthropologists. The book contains an elaborate description of life in the area at the beginning of the 20th century. It gives a comprehensive overview of life in these societies at that time, but stresses particularly religious and belief systems. Although the book is clearly a product of its time and regularly patronizing in tone, it would be wrong to be deterred by that, as it chronicles the fascinating encounter of a human being with a culture which is totally different from his own. Above all, he takes the people whom he meets seriously. The book is of course nowadays an historical record as well. As such it is not only informative on the local population but also pertinent for those readers interested in colonial nostalgia.

192   So this was Lusaakas.
Richard Sampson.   Lusaka: Multimedia Publications, 1971. 2nd ed. 197p. bibliog.

Sampson was a long-standing mayor of Lusaka in the 1950s, and he dedicates his book to all the races who helped build it. He remains a man of his era, however: this is a colonial history of Lusaka and it is filled with nostalgia for the pioneering times. It is thus of limited use in getting to know the place, and indeed it becomes more interesting once one knows the city well. Studying the pictures is a good way to approach this book, as they give informative comparisons of parts of the city centre in different times.

193   African sunset.
Robin Short.   London: Johnson Publications Ltd, 1973. 279p. 2 maps.

These are the memoirs of an unapologetic colonial civil servant who considers the way independence was granted – if not independence itself – a fatal historical error. His dedication to the district messengers of Northern Rhodesia, and the caption under a picture that says: 'Progress: The new bridge at Lundazi built in 1962', are typical of this book. Short served mostly in North Western Province, but there is a brief period covered in the east, when he was posted to Lundazi. The work also gives a striking impression of life on the Copperbelt in 1955. The book is – in my experience – a very good historical source, which gives important names that have faded into obscurity. Short is partisan but accurate. He also gives a good idea of the nature of colonial administration as a light administration, stressing regularly how far away the police and other forces of law and order were from the spots he had to administer. Finally, it is a good read for anybody interested in colonial nostalgia.

194 Jungle pathfinder: a biography of Chirapula Stephenson.
Kathaleen Stevens Rukavina. London: Hutchinson, 1951. 252p.

Stephenson was a legendary explorer, adventurer, pioneer and servant of the British South Africa Company. The notable aspect of his life is that he went native and married two African women. This biography is a hagiography and talks with relish about how a jungle man could make money out of native trade, native recruiting and guiding travellers to the Congo. It illustrates how imperialism opened opportunities for spectacular careers and the possibility of living in the interstices of society. Stephenson retired to Stonehenge amidst his African servants. There is a good discussion of Stephenson in Karen Tranberg Hansen's book on domestic service in Zambia (see item no. 717).

195 Tambalika: perspectives on a colonial magistrate in Central Africa.
Marcia Wright. *African Affairs*, vol. 85, no. 338 (1986), p. 13-23.

Tambalika was the nickname of the first administrator of Abercorn, later Mbala, on the border with Tanganyika. His real name was Hugh Marshall and the article mentions that he acquired his local reputation through his mediation in internal political struggles among so-called 'corridor' people, especially the Lungu. The relevance for African history is limited, but this article will be considered valuable by readers of colonial nostalgia – one example of such nostalgia is the description of Tambalika's lifestyle on pages 20-21.

Nationalities, Minorities and Peoples

196 Mutomboka ceremony and the Lunda-Kazembe dynasty.
Munone Chinyane, Chiloya J. Chiudla.   Lusaka: Kenneth Kaunda
Foundation, 1989. 130p. bibliog.

Since democratization there has been a revival of sub-nationalism leading to a
mushrooming of ethnic societies and sentiments in Africa. Within Zambia this has always
been strong among the Lozi, but the Luapula Lunda were among the first ethnic groups
to join them. They attach great importance to their annual festival, the *mutomboka*. This
ceremony commemorates the crossing of the Luapula: 'During the inter tribal wars, the
Lunda won many victories and naturally that called for merry making and great
excitement' (p. 34). The possible sectionalist feelings that this may arouse are obvious.
The book is characterized by many eulogies and praise songs to the Mwate Kazembe, the
chief.

197 Social organization of the Gwembe Tonga.
Elizabeth Colson.   Manchester, England: Manchester University
Press, 1960. 233p. map. bibliog.

The Gwembe (or Valley) Tonga were resettled after the construction of the Kariba dam,
when the valley in which they lived was flooded. Colson was asked to study the Gwembe
Tonga before they moved. She had previously studied the Plateau Tonga, but the social
structure of the Valley Tonga differs significantly. Although the latter also keep cattle,
their social organization is much more structured on the neighbourhood or locality.
Matrilineage is the dominant structure in local organization. Residence is, however, not
strictly tied to matrilineal descent, although in each neighbourhood one or two lineages
take precedence over others, as these are believed to be the first settlers in the area. The
Valley Tonga, like the Plateau Tonga, are a highly segmented or acephalous society. In
this case also, Colson sees indigenous religious beliefs as the crucial entrance to an
understanding of Tonga society. Chapter V, 'The cult of the shades', dealing with
inheritance and authority, is the kernel of the book. Colson emphasizes too the harsh life
in the valley where crop failures have been common. Local people frequently have to
resort to begging: 'Valley Tonga are expert in exerting pressure, as anyone who has been
subject to their begging has to admit' (p. 53).

198 The Plateau Tonga of Northern Rhodesia; social and religious studies.
Elizabeth Colson. Manchester, England: Manchester University Press, 1962. 237p. map. bibliog.
This collection of seven previously published articles may well be considered as Colson's most outstanding work. Its guiding theme is the non-centralized character of Tonga society whose diffused nature is reinforced by the tracing of descent in the matrilineal line combined with virilocal residence: the women move on marriage to the man's place of habitation. Cattle are central in Tonga society, but here also dispersal is characteristic of herding arrangements and kraal formation. Nevertheless, it is also an integrated society, and Colson brings out the importance of local religious beliefs in combination with kinship claims to illustrate this.

199 The social consequences of resettlement: the impact of the Kariba resettlement upon the Gwembe Tonga.
Elizabeth Colson. Manchester, England: Manchester University Press, 1971. 277p. map. bibliog.
This is the sequel to Colson's study of the Gwembe Tonga before resettlement. It is a much more impressionistic book, which lacks the coherence found in most of her other work. It should be noted, however, by those who are interested in the effects of relocating people for development purposes. There are a few sections which describe futile and tragic armed resistance to the move. The discussion of the role of political parties is relevant for studying the rise of nationalism.

200 Seven tribes of British Central Africa.
Edited by Elizabeth Colson, Max Gluckman. Manchester, England: Manchester University Press, 1949. Reprinted with corrections, 1959. 409p. 6 maps. bibliog.
This book was originally published in 1949 and presented the initial results of fieldwork by a generation of gifted anthropologists who worked in Zambia and neighbouring countries. It offers incisive and clear chapters on the following Zambian people: the Lozi by Gluckman; the Plateau Tonga by Colson; the Bemba by Audrey Richards; the Fort Jameson Ngoni by Barnes. Although these chapters were written a long time ago, the book is still recommended reading for anyone who wants to understand the terms in which people express their world view – especially through kinship – in the relevant parts of Zambia. As introductory readings in the anthropology of the area they are still highly relevant, if not unsurpassed.

201 The Luapula peoples of Northern Rhodesia; custom and history in tribal politics.
Ian Cunnison. Manchester, England: Manchester University Press, 1959. 258p. 4 maps. bibliog.
This is a relatively neglected volume compared to the monographs originating from the Rhodes-Livingstone Institute, which are classics in anthropology. This neglect is regrettable, because the book offers perspectives on the study of Zambian society which foreshadow later approaches. The Luapula valley is depicted as an area where waves of immigrants have settled and in which there is an active creation of identities using

elements of lineage, clan and tribe. The immigration of the Lunda meant that a form of centralized authority was established, embedded in a distinction between commoners and aristocrats. Another relatively fixed element in this society is the tracing of descent through the mother's line. It is rewarding to compare what is later written on Luapula society with what Cunnsion says, as large disparities appear. This is especially true of a comparison with the work of Poewe (see item nos. 216, 686).

202 The Indian minority of Zambia, Rhodesia and Malawi.
Floyd Dotson, Lillian O. Dotson.   New Haven, Connecticut: Yale University Press, 1968. 444p. map. bibliog.

As is the case with Europeans, the Asian inhabitants of Zambia have received little attention from social scientists. This study is therefore mentioned here, despite the fact that it is unsatisfactory. The story is not Zambia-centred and is dated because the research was carried out in the early 1960s. It is mainly qualitative research that may best be called impressionistic, and this leads to heavy-handed judgements: 'The operative assumption with respect to African servants is that they are intrinsically uninteresting' (p. 281); or 'The predominant tendency towards Asian-African offspring is clear: rejection' (p. 283). If these sentiments were general and absolute, then it would be difficult to explain how Asian communities manage to interact with the societies of which they have now for a long time been part. The situation must surely be more complicated than the Dotsons suggest.

203 The clans of the Bemba and of some neighbouring tribes.
Joseph Melville Doucette.   Kasama, Zambia: Malole Parish, 1994. 157p.

This book updates and codifies further what is known about Bemba clans among the White Fathers, who have had a long association with Northern Province. The book opens with a quite sharp disagreement with Andrew Roberts (see item no. 166), the major historian of the Bemba, as he belittled the importance of clans. This book lists all the clans known; states the villages where they are found; and considers opposite or joking clans (so called because interaction between clans is often ritualized in the form of one clan making fun at the expense of the other), relations with the paramount chief (Chitimukulo) and the history or myth of the founding of the clan. The last chapters deal with Chitimukulo's court and the role of the clans therein. The very last chapter outlines a missionary reaction to Bemba culture.

204 The role of cattle in the Ila economy; a conflict of views on the uses of cattle by the Ila of Namwala.
Robin J. Fielder.   *African Social Research*, no. 15 (1973), p. 327-61. map. bibliog.

As is often the case with rich fieldwork, it is difficult to summarize this article, which takes issue with the view that the Ila are holding on to their cattle for a number of traditionalistic reasons and that a commercialization of their herds is called for. It gives impressive factual insight into the cattle population, herding and ownership. Much of the article may be summed up in the sentence: 'An Ila's three quarter century experience of colonial commerce has made him wary of being given short-term value for long-term loss, and of exchanging productive capital for depreciable consumables' (p. 355). The article is economistic in nature, however, and Fielder even argues that funeral slaughter is more economical than regular slaughter for sale.

205 The judicial process among the Barotse of Northern Rhodesia.
Max Gluckman. Manchester, England: Manchester University Press, 1955. 368p. map. bibliog.

Gluckman wrote extensively about the Lozi and about African law, and this book is the *magnum opus* among those writings. It is a monograph focusing fairly narrowly on the Lozi, and as such primarily to be recommended to those who have an immediate interest in the Lozi. If an introduction to the wider spectrum of people in western Zambia is needed, it may be better to turn to other writings, including Gluckman's. His book *The economy of the Barotse plain* (see item no. 206) would be a better source in such a case. This monograph, however, is also a treatise on the anthropology of law, in which Gluckman searches for the universals in legal systems. He argues that law is not a prerogative of Western societies and he outlines sharply in Lozi society the idea of the reasonable man, which, according to him, is prominent in all legal systems. Above all, however, it is a celebration of anthropological observation. The patience and sustained attention required to read through the case material in this book will be richly rewarded.

206 The economy of the Barotse plain.
Max Gluckman. Manchester, England: Manchester University Press, 1968. 132p. 2 maps. bibliog.

Gluckman declares in his introduction to the 1968 edition that the vision of the Barotse plain as presented in this book is outdated. When Gluckman visited the Barotse flood plain for the first time in 1940, he found a land of plenitude. It was also described as such by David Livingstone about a century earlier. In 1965, Gluckman found a famine area dependent upon remittances from wage labour. Such themes were, however, also important in the 1940 version of the study. The influence of the money economy is shown to destroy a stable society and a prospering economy in tune with its environment. Gluckman's approach later fitted into what was more generally known as the development of underdevelopment (dependency theory). The book is not merely a delicate description of a vanished world however. It provides much information surrounding transhumance in the Lozi plain, and the relationship between the plain and its borders, which makes present day life in that part of Zambia intelligible.

207 White mine workers in Northern Rhodesia, 1959-60.
J.F. Holleman, S. Biesheuvel. Leiden, The Netherlands; Cambridge, England: African Studies Centre, 1973. 135p.

The expatriate white tribe in Zambia has received little attention from anthropologists. This is a rare study of white mine workers on the Copperbelt and in Kabwe (the former Broken Hill). Among the topics discussed are: club life and attempts to stabilize the white workforce through home ownership. Their observation of egalitarian tendencies in white communities, because they worked, lived and entertained so closely together, is striking. This study was undertaken in the last stages of colonialism, and African advancement is therefore a big issue. An attitude scale revealed that fifty per cent of all white employees would not tolerate African advancement to the point where it would involve social contact.

208 Settlement patterns and rural development; a human geographical study of the Kaonde, Kasempa district, Zambia.
Dirk Jaeger. Amsterdam: Royal Institute for the Tropics, 1981.
382p. 16 maps. bibliog.

This voluminous work is useful for those who want to know more about the Kaonde. The first hundred pages of this geographical study are historical and anthropological in nature. This part concludes that it is 'against the background of this spatially fluid situation that, especially since independence, rural development is being stimulated' (p. 106). The rest of the book deals with agriculture, rural development and especially with settlement schemes initiated in Kasempa. Jaeger advocates the singling out of a progressive elite and concurs with the strategy of 'advancing spontaneous growth tendencies exhibited by progressive individuals' (p. 323). Such a strategy was not fashionable at that time when the poor were being specifically targeted and rural transformation was being tackled on a broad front.

209 Kuomboka; a living traditional culture among the Malozi people of Zambia.
Likand Kalaluka. Lusaka: NECZAM, 1979. 110p. map.

This is an introduction to the essential offices and ceremony of the Lozi people. It describes not only the ritual of the movement from the plain to the edge of the plain, but also the offices of Litunga (superior chief) and Ngambele (chairman of the council). The Lozi are an intensely political group in Zambia and this is obvious here as well: 'On the surface, *kuomboka* looks prosperous and enthusiastically dedicated to continuing values, to social success', but there is also 'a fear of innovation and experimentation and a prudent disinclination to question too deeply the culture's past and present' (p. 89). Kalaluka laments the lack of economic progress that the traditional leadership should have brought to Western Province (Barotseland).

210 Ngoni nc'wala ceremony.
M.B. Lukhero. Lusaka: Zambia Education Publishing House,
1992. Revised edition. 54p. bibliog.

The *nc'wala* ceremony is a Zulu first-fruits ceremony, revived among the Zambian-based Ngoni people who split off originally from the Zulu empire. The author started his career as a research assistant at the Rhodes-Livingstone Institute and therefore draws heavily on the work of Barnes (see item no. 152). The work is primarily a history of the Ngoni rather than a pamphlet on the ceremony. It illustrates well the paradoxical nature of these ethnic (sub-nationalist) revivals: 'Although the people are highly excited and ready to fight, their main interest is in unity, peace and prosperity in their daily lives' (p. 47). Among the songs sung at the ceremony is one which states that, 'In Zambia we all know there is only one Kaunda' (p. 49).

211 Zion in Africa; the Jews of Zambia.
Hugh Macmillan, Frank Shapiro. London: I.B. Tauris, 1999. 342p.
map. bibliog.

This book, a labour of love to remember a remarkably colourful community, is brought to life in narrative that is primarily structured around individuals whose positions in society are placed against the background of rapid economic development and some of the most traumatic events in European history: the developments in Russia and Germany in the

20th century. It is of course a history of a religious community – the Ndola and Mufulira *shuls* (religious schools) were the last to be sold, in the 1990s – but it is also a history of entrepreneurship and of the political ambiguity inherent in being a Jew in a racist society. It is a good book to browse through, especially for someone well acquainted with Zambia. Its answer to the question as to what connections Nadine Gordimer and Joe Slovo have with Zambia should interest a wide audience.

212　**Race, colour and class in Southern Africa; a study of the**
　　　***coloured* question in the context of an analysis of the colonial and**
　　　white settler racial ideology and African nationalism in twentieth
　　　century Zimbabwe, Zambia and Malawi.
　　　Ibbo Mandaza.　Harare: SAPES Books, 1997. 838p. map. bibliog.
This massive tome is fortunately clearly subdivided into chapters dealing with the various territories. The subject leads into a swamp of race-related arguments, as the question of whether one belonged to European or African society was a vexed one with great consequences for privileges enjoyed. Mandaza has a clear eye for the absurdities of racism: 'The search for a definition of *native* occupied the best legal minds in the colonial office and settler establishment before its futility was realized'. The mixed race community in Zambia turned unequivocally to the nationalist movement. It produced people like Henry Charles Thornicroft, Aaron Milner and J. Adamson, who occupied leading government positions after independence.

213　**Bemba myth and ritual. The impact of literacy on oral culture.**
　　　Kevin B. Maxwell.　New York: Peter Lang Publishing, 1983. 197p.
　　　bibliog.
The author is a theologian, and religion is the main focus of this book; this is true to a greater extent than suggested in the title. It is in the first place a discussion of notions of Bemba thought and identity as described by other authors. A major part of the book discusses for example *chisungu*, the initiation ritual for females, which is described so well by Audrey Richards (see item no. 125). This is not to dismiss the author's inside knowledge of society: not only is the book based on more than fifty hours' recorded interviews – deposited in the UNZA library – but the author also acknowledges instruction by prominent politician Simon Kapwepwe at the latter's home. Nevertheless, it is probably of more interest to philosophers and theologians than to people who want to become acquainted with the Bemba.

214　**Thwarted development: a case study of economic change in the**
　　　Kabwe rural district of Zambia, 1902-70.
　　　Maud Muntemba.　In: *The roots of rural poverty: in Central and*
　　　Southern Africa.　Edited by Robin Palmer, Neil Parsons.　London:
　　　Heinemann, 1977, p. 345-65. map.
This paper deals with the Lenje, who live between Lusaka and Kabwe. As is to be expected, in this article Muntemba describes a relatively well-adapted society before colonization which is destabilized by labour migration and land alienation. She describes peasant initiatives, but these were 'thwarted' as peasant agriculture was subordinate to the interests of mining and farming capitalist interests. This article is worth noting, however, not only because of its ideological stance, but also because it describes a little-known area.

215 From ethnic identity to tribalism: the Upper Zambezi region of Zambia.
Robert Papstein.   In: *The creation of tribalism in Southern Africa.*
Edited by L. Vail.   London: James Currey; Berkeley, California;
Los Angeles: University of California Press, 1989, p. 372-95.
The heart of this article is a local history project in which an area called Chavuma is
central. It is in dispute between groups who identify themselves either as Luvale or
Lunda. In addition there have been Lozi claims on the area. Papstein stresses the close
relationships between these groups and how the creation of a local history by local
intellectuals played a central role in the emergence of this tribalism in the context of a
nation state. Papstein also outlines his personal involvement through his activity as
historian in this conflict.

216 Religion, kinship, and economy in Luapula, Zambia.
Karla Poewe.   Lewiston, New York: The Edwin Mellen Press,
1989. 265p. 4 maps. bibliog.
Kinship provides the background against which Poewe discusses kinship and religion.
She depicts a radically matrilocal kinship system, which may not be convincing to
everybody. The fundamental proposition of the book is that 'it is problematic
for matrilineally related Zambians to coordinate family or other labour, to plan future
investment and to overcome productive individualism' (p. 2). She describes how
Jehovah's Witnesses and Seventh Day Adventists overcome such problems in an overall
intensely religious environment. Her description of the economy of the area contains
valuable data on fisheries, the economic mainstay of the area she studied. Conflicts
between the state and small capitalists, as well as problems surrounding inheritance in a
matrilineal society, dominate her study of the economy. The data on the economy may
not be as well structured as they might be, but the book gives a good feel for economic
life in that part of Zambia at the time.

**217 Continuity and change in the Gwembe Tonga family and their
relevance to demography's nucleation thesis.**
Neil Price, Neil Thomas.   *Africa*, vol. 69, no. 4 (1999), p. 510-35.
bibliog.
The authors' prime concern is to make a theoretical point. They challenge an evolutionary
view of kinship and marriage that will lead to the nuclear family. This article is based on
research findings from the Gwembe Tonga, which have been and are extensively studied
by Colson and Scudder (see item nos. 35, 197, 199, 321, 691, 750). Price and Thomas
argue that there are many changes in the structure of marriage and kinship among the
Gwembe Tonga, but that this does not lead to the emergence of nuclear families.
Matrilineage remains predominant. Because Tonga society is not characterized by
unambiguous social structures, many interpretations of a given situation are possible. The
research is also quite impressionistic.

218 **Magic, divination and witchcraft among the Barotse of Northern Rhodesia.**
Barrie Reynolds. London: Chatto & Windus, 1963. 181p. 2 maps.
Reynolds's speciality is the collection and precise documentation of material artefacts and stories around them. The artefacts – well illustrated – form the main part of the book. Reynolds treats stories about spirits, divination, etc. in the same way. One chapter deserves special attention: his description of the Twelve Society is post-modern before its time. This society was adept at mingling old and new and elements from the Lunda Luvale with Lozi beliefs. Nowadays its founders would be called *bricoleurs.*

219 **History of the Tonga chiefs and their people in the Monze district of Zambia.**
Santosh C. Saha. New York: Peter Land, 1994. 125p. map. bibliog.
This simple monograph has little to offer readers who are looking for sophisticated anthropological analyses, but it contains useful information about Monze district: a list of the Tonga chiefs and their historical claims, and a list of the missions with the story of how they were founded there.

220 **The 'wild' and 'lazy' Lamba: ethnic stereotypes on the Central African Copperbelt.**
Brian Siegel. In: *The creation of tribalism in Southern Africa.*
Edited by L. Vail. London: James Currey; Berkeley, California; Los Angeles: University of California Press, 1989, p. 350-71.
The Lamba are the original inhabitants of the Copperbelt, which has long been swamped by immigrants attracted by the mining industry. The Lamba have been marginalized in this process, and Siegel documents the negative stereotype of them that has emerged as a result. Special attention is paid to the role of Lamba women who were quick to take advantage of the shortage of men in towns.

221 **National commitment among local elites in Western Zambia.**
Philip Silverman. *Journal of Modern African Studies,* vol. 22, no. 1 (1984), p. 153-62.
This modest article contains interesting fieldwork in the form of a survey carried out during 1966 to 1967 in Barotseland, which is an important centre for sub-nationalism in Zambia. Silverman's concern is to examine to what extent the Senanga district elite has ideas that are Zambian (i.e., national), and to what extent they have specific Lozi ideas. The question then is whether these ideas clash with each other. The main finding is that many respondents could quite easily integrate commitments to both tribal and national institutions. The findings could be a source of inspiration for contemporary research. It would be interesting to see whether present day district elites can precisely mention the name and position of as many as three national leaders.

222 Change in an African village; Kefa speaks.
Else Skjønsberg.   West Hartford, Connecticut: Kumerian Press,
1989. 271p. map. bibliog.

This is a detailed monograph of a Chewa village close to Chipata, the provincial capital
of Eastern Province. Kefa is the name of the village, and the title indicates how the author
tries to sketch life in the village through the words of the villagers themselves. The map
of the village and the list of the villagers at the beginning of the book help to form an
image of the wide panorama covered. At the time of the study, the author was employed
as a sociologist in a development project, for which she carried out a time allocation
study, which may be of interests to students of women in development. This monograph,
however, is not coloured by development concerns. On the contrary, it gives primarily an
impression of village life with the touch of reality observed. It is therefore highly
accessible to laymen, but professional sociologists may feel the lack of general themes
which could have given more meaning to the data presented.

223 Shimunenga and the traditional culture of the Baila.
Tobias W.C. Sumaili.   Lusaka: Zambia Educational Publishing,
1994. 20p.

This is one of several publications resulting from the ethnic revival and growing sub-
nationalism in Zambia. *Shimunenga*, the annual ritual of the Ila people concentrated in
Namwala, celebrates a battle fought to find good pasture for their cattle. This booklet
describes the ceremony and reproduces songs, costumes and artefacts used. There is also
a section on games which comes across as wholesome among the quite narrow ethnic
sentiments that such ceremonies entail.

**224 Schism and continuity in an African society; a study of Ndembu
village life.**
Victor W. Turner.   Manchester, England: Manchester University
Press, 1957. 348p. 6 maps. bibliog.

There is a thin dividing line between art and anthropological 'thick' description. Turner
was probably the most artistic among the great anthropologists who worked during the
late colonial era in Zambia. This is his first book and more conventional than his later
ones. His subject is the central cultural ideal in Ndembu society of splitting off with a
group of people and starting one's own village. The failure of the central character,
Sandombu, to do so is a theme that runs through the book. This figure of Sandombu, the
childless, hard working, marginal man is movingly portrayed. The particular situation is
explained as resulting from contradictory elements in the kinship structure. This makes
the book eminently suitable for a reader who wants to become familiar with reasoning in
terms of kinship. It not only introduces a variety of thinking in terms of kinship but also
elucidates the point that kinship systems are not at all as neatly coherent as either insiders
or some anthropologists like to suggest.

225 **The unit of study and the interpretation of ethnicity; studying the Nkoya of Western Zambia.**
Wim M.J. van Binsbergen. *Journal of Southern African Studies*, vol. 8, no. 1 (1981), p. 82-94.

The main thrust of this article is that the researcher has to move away from the tribal model imposed by anthropology on the study of Zambian societies. Van Binsbergen's evidence for the predominance of the concept of tribe as an analytical unit in the ethnography of Zambia can be challenged. The article concentrates somewhat on other scholars and the author himself. If one penetrates the self-centred concerns in this article, one finds interesting information on Nkoya identity, especially in relation to the neighbouring Lozi.

226 **Tears of rain; ethnicity and history in Central Western Zambia.**
Wim van Binsbergen. London; New York: Kegan Paul International, 1992. 495p. bibliog.

The Nkoya people in Western Zambia like to differentiate themselves from the centralized Lozi group who are their neighbours. It is therefore not surprising that a Nkoya intellectual like the Revd Johasaphat Malasha Shimunika wrote a history of the Nkoya asserting that their particular identity is an outcome of many influences: mythical material found widely in the region, the Bible and a Nkoya history document by a colonial civil servant. Van Binsbergen's voluminous work is a commentary on Shimunika's text, showing that ethnic identity is here, as elsewhere, a social construction and not a primordial sentiment. This is not easily gleaned, however, from the poorly organized and wide ranging theoretical speculations which make up this book. Van Binsbergen has written elaborately about the Nkoya and all his writing offers much theoretical construction – which may be of more value to some than to others – as compared to actual information on the Nkoya. The book's bibliography provides access to his scattered work.

227 **Nkoya royal chiefs and the Kazanga cultural association.**
Wim van Binsbergen. In: *African chieftainship in a new socio-political landscape.* Edited by E. Adriaan B. van Rouveroy van Nieuwaal, Rijk van Dijk. Hamburg, Germany: Lit Verlag, 1999, p. 97-135. bibliog.

Van Binsbergen has written prolifically about the Nkoya. His bibliography gives an overview of most of his publications on them since he published *Tears of rain* in 1992. This is more to be recommended than many of his other publications as it is relatively more accessible. It has fewer theoretical pretensions and Van Binsbergon writes less about himself than is often the case. The empirical material presented is, as usual, more impressionistic than the result of methodical fieldwork, but these impressions and anecdotes are about significant themes in the study of sub-nationalism in contemporary Zambia, and especially Western Province: fear of dominance by the neighbouring Lozi state; the cultural or ethnic revival of recent years (the *Kazanga* cultural association); and the shift of power from UNIP to MMD in the context of democratization. This is an informative article about chieftainship and the way it has evolved in modern times.

228 **Tribal cohesion in a money economy: a study of the Mambwe people of Northern Rhodesia.**
William Watson.   Manchester, England: Manchester University Press, 1958. 246p. bibliog.

This book is a classic in anthropology in its own right, but it is and remains particularly relevant for understanding rural Zambia. Watson's detailed ethnography of Mambwe society in 1952 disputed the argument that labour migration to urban areas undermines the rural, agricultural economy. The language which he uses may be outdated, as in the following example: 'Mambwe participation in industry has not led to a breakdown in tribal life' (p. 225); however, the observation has not lost any of its relevance. He explains this in part by comparing the Mambwe with the Bemba. The former are virilocal and the latter uxorilocal and therefore residential patterns among the Mambwe are more stable. It would be wrong, however, to see this monograph as one-tracked, defending a thesis. It is also a holistic description of Mambwe society as Watson found it. Watson also had a more than usually keen eye for kinship in action: the practice as distinct from the theory.

229 **Likumi lya mize and other Luvale traditional ceremonies.**
Patrick Wele.   Lusaka: Zambia Educational Publishing House, 1993. 132p. bibliog.

This book is more elaborate in its description of rituals – especially boys' and girls' initiation – than most other ethnic revivalist publications. It is also the most political such book. Wele describes himself on the cover as an 'avowed Luvale traditionalist whose enthusiasm never wavers' and writes in his preface about a 'time of great personal embitterment'. The background to this is rooted in bitter struggles over land. The book not only documents the revival of the ceremony and the establishment of an ethnic society, but is part of a bitter dispute with neighbouring groups, which has been documented by Robert Papstein (see item no. 215). Development plays almost as big a role in this book as tradition, as shown by the following: 'Backed by his civil service experience Senior Chief Dungu (V) scored numerous successes during his reign' (p. 77).

230 **The Manchester School in south central Africa.**
Richard P. Werbner.   *Annual Review of Anthropology*, vol. 13 (1984), p. 157-85. bibliog.

The group of anthropologists who worked at the Rhodes-Livingstone Institute in Lusaka are often referred to as the Manchester School as Max Gluckman – the influential second director – later occupied the chair of anthropology there. Werbner writes for insiders in this article and keeps his arguments on a general theoretical plane. The article's bibliography is especially useful for people who want to orientate themselves broadly in the ethnographic literature on Zambia. His judgements are contentious, however. He hardly refers to the empirical material in the books he reviews, and it is a moot point whether one can discuss their theoretical insights without referring to that material. His judgement that Long's work can be recast in marxist language is difficult to accord with Long's subtle debate with the marxist dependency school in the 1970s.

231 An outline of Luvale social and political organisation.
Charles M.N. White. Manchester, England: Manchester University
Press, 1960. 51p. bibliog.

This is the only entry by Charles White in this bibliography, but it should be stressed that
White has published much on all aspects of the Luvale. His anthropological work is that
of a craftsman: it provides precise information about people who live differently from
ourselves. The problem is that his work is Luvale-specific and not of much interest to a
wider audience. He lacks the artistry – the probing of aspects of the human condition in
general – to be found among the other anthropologists of the Rhodes-Livingstone
Institute.

**232 Masks and transformation among the Chewa of Eastern
Zambia.**
Kenji Yoshida. *Senri Ethnological Studies*, no. 31 (1992), p. 203-
73. map. bibliog.

The objects of study here are the semi-secret masked *nyau* dance groups characteristic of
Chewa society. Yoshida provides a very detailed description of masks, dances and the
social occasions when dances will be performed. Central in his discussion are three kinds
of transformation: masking, spirit possession and sorcery. These are quite different realms
and he provides a comparative matrix to point this out. For example, the animals that
appear in *nyau* are harmless and edible, while the animals into which sorcerers turn are
mainly dangerous animals that eat humans. An abstract cannot do justice to the wealth of
information and insight in this paper, which is all the more exceptional as *nyau* societies
are for a large part secret.

Languages

General

233 Zambian languages: orthography approved by the Ministry of Education.
Edited by S.S. Chimuka.   Lusaka: NECZAM, 1977. 128p.

This book presents the official standardization of spelling in Zambia's main languages, showing also the forms which are no longer recommended.

234 Migration and language change: the interaction of town and country.
Mubanga E. Kashoki.   In: *Town and country in Central and East Africa*.   Edited by David Parkin.   London: Oxford University Press, 1975, p. 228-50.

This article documents loan words adopted into the Cibemba language as a result of the interaction of the Bemba-speaking people with the rest of the world because of migration. To give one interesting example: *kaffir* as an Afrikaans invective for a black person became *kaafula* in Cibemba and acquired the meaning of 'country bumpkin'. This article was somewhat ahead of its time, as nowadays borrowing (*bricolage*) is seen as an elementary human activity in this post-modern age.

235 The factor of language in Zambia.
Mubanga E. Kashoki.   Lusaka: Kenneth Kaunda Foundation, 1990. 164p. bibliog.

Kashoki has written prolifically about language in Zambia, and many of his contributions are to be found in this book. He has written about language from a political, from an educational and from a sociological point of view. The book is comprised of these three parts. Whereas the first two parts may be somewhat too prescriptive, the third part about urbanization and language use contains much information that gives penetrating insights on much wider aspects of Zambian life than language alone. On pages 116-23, Kashoki presents a tabular overview of the proportion of Zambians who claim particular languages as their mother tongue and the proportion of Zambians who claim to speak those languages. The dominant role of Cibemba is most striking there.

236 Lozi names in language and culture.
Mukumbuta Lisimba. Libreville: International Bureau for Bantu Civilisations, 2000. 320p.

This book consists of a general introduction, which tries to situate the meaning of language in Lozi culture, and a discussion of names as these appear in praise songs, proverbs, etc. It is both a linguistic and an anthropological work because it looks at language in social situations. It may be helpful for people who are learning the Lozi language, as a large vocabulary would be easily picked up by reading this book.

237 Languages in Zambia.
Edited by Sirarpi Ohanessian, Mubanga E. Kashoki. London: International African Institute, 1978. 461p. 8 maps. bibliog.

This massive study is one among several sponsored by the Ford Foundation. To understand the concern of the study, it is helpful to keep in mind that it was undertaken at a time when English-language teaching was introduced throughout the Zambian educational system (see the contribution by Bryson McAdam). This led to a concern for the future of Zambian languages. The book is subdivided into three parts. The first of these is an overview of and a comparison between Zambian languages. Then the subject turns to the use of Zambian languages in particular contexts. Graham Mytton describes, for example, the use of language in the media. The third part focuses on the role of language in education. The book is undoubtedly a product of its time, but that does not mean that it is dated. Anybody who is interested in Zambian languages should read the first three chapters (by Kashoki, Mann and Lehmann).

238 Studies in Zambian languages.
Edited by Yasuteshi Yukaka. Tokyo: Institute for the Study of Languages and Cultures of Asia and Africa, 1987. 478p.

This is a book for and by linguists. All but one of the papers – written by a mixed group of Japanese and Zambian scholars – are on the tonality of various Zambian languages from the west or south of the country. The first few pages are generally accessible to laymen and contain interesting information. One example is the fact that present-day Silozi is a form of Sikololo, the language of the invaders who were subsequently overthrown. A conqueror's language was thus kept although the conqueror was repelled.

Bemba

239 A Chibemba note book.
T.S.L. Fox-Pitt.   Cape Town: Longman, 1961. 2nd ed. 58p.

Fox-Pitt was a colonial civil servant who sympathized with the nationalists. It is not surprising that he had an interest in the language of the Bemba people, among whom he lived.

240 Bemba pocket dictionary; Bemba-English and English-Bemba.
E. Hoch.   Lusaka: NECZAM, 1974. 138p.

Bemba is the most widely spoken language in Zambia. This small dictionary is useful for beginners.

241 Lessons in Chibemba: being one hundred easy graded lessons, based on the grammar of Rev. Father Schoeffer.
William Lammond.   Kawambwa, Zambia: Mbereshi Press, 1949. 2nd ed. 160p.

The approach to language teaching in this work may appear outdated, but it is a system that conveys the basic structure of the language.

242 English-Bemba phrase book.
London: Macmillan, 1959. 3rd ed. 53p.

This book was originally prepared for Silozi and adapted for Bemba.

243 An elementary grammar of Cibemba.
G.W. Sims.   Fort Roseberry (Mansa), Zambia: Mansa Mission, Christian Missions in Many Lands, 1959. 227p.

It is interesting to note that, in keeping with a long tradition, this grammar was published by a missionary society. Bemba is, of course, the most widely spoken language in Zambia.

244 A Bemba grammar.
J. van Sambeek.   Cape Town: Longmans, Green, 1955. 117p.

This is a useful book for beginners in Bemba.

245 Bemba English dictionary.
The White Fathers.   Chilubula, Zambia: The White Fathers, 1947. 1505p.

Missionaries were at the forefront of the study of African languages. The White Fathers worked mainly among the Bemba-speaking people.

Chokwe

246 Chokwe-English, English-Chokwe dictionary and grammar lessons.
Malcolm Brooks McJannet.   Vila Lusu, Angola: Missão de Biula, 1949. 91p.
The Chokwe live near the Angolan border, so it is not surprising that this book was published in Angola.

Ila

247 Ila made easy: part 1, twenty-four graduated lessons, forty-seven exercises and key; part 2, phrases for all occasions, vocabulary and useful words.
Edwin William Smith.   London: W.A. Hammond, 1914. 96p.
The Ila language is quite similar to the Tonga language. Again, this book was compiled by a missionary.

248 A handbook of the Ila language (commonly called the Sukulumbwe) spoken in North Western Rhodesia, South Central Africa: comprising grammar exercises, specimens of Ila tales and vocabularies.
Edwin William Smith.   Ridgewood, New Jersey: Gregg Press, 1964. 488p.
This handbook was actually composed in the early part of the 20th century. Smith, a missionary, also wrote an early ethnography of the Ila together with Andrew Murray Dale.

Kaonde

249 A short introductory dictionary to the Kaonde language, with English-Kaonde appendix.
R.E. Broughall Woods.   London: Religious Tract Society, 1924. 234p.
This dictionary is one of the many published by missionary societies in the languages of the peoples among whom they preached – in this case the Kaonde of North Western Zambia.

250 Kaonde notebook, with an elementary grammar of the language.
J.L. Wright, N. Kamukwamba. London: Longmans Green, 1958.
60p.
The Kaonde language is spoken in North Western Zambia.

Lala

251 Lala-Lamba-Wisa and English, English and Lala-Lamba-Wisa dictionary.
Arthur Cornwallis Madan. Oxford: Clarendon Press, 1913. 328p.
This covers the languages spoken in a band from the Copperbelt (Lamba) through Mkushi and Serenje (Lala) into Mpika (Bisa, sometimes called Wisa). These languages are variations of Cibemba.

Lamba

252 Textbook of Lamba grammar.
Clement Martyn Doke. Johannesburg: Witwatersrand University Press, 1938. 484p.
Lamba is spoken on the Copperbelt. Brian Siegel's articles (see item nos. 147 and 220) make interesting reading on the Lamba people and their fate in urbanized Zambia.

253 An English-Lamba vocabulary.
Clement Martyn Doke. Johannesburg: Witwatersrand University Press, 1965. 2nd ed. 179p.
Lamba is the language spoken by the original inhabitants of the Copperbelt. Doke also wrote a minor ethnography of the Lamba people.

Lozi

254 An English-Lozi vocabulary.
J.P. Burger. Sefula, Zambia: Paris Missionary Society, 1960. 171p.
Lozi is the language of the people of Barotseland in Western Province. It is related to
South African languages such as Sotho.

255 Dictionary of the Lozi language, vol. 1 Lozi-English.
A. Jalla. London: United Society for Christian Literature, 1936.
393p.
Barotseland (Western Province) is the home of the Lozi language. This publication again
is of missionary origin.

256 Introduction to Silozi grammar.
M.W. Mwisiya. Lusaka: NECZAM, 1977. 168p.
This work is one of the newer language courses available.

257 English-Silozi dictionary.
Owen O'Sullivan. Lusaka: Zambia Educational Publishing House,
1993. 362p.
Dictionaries are still being produced, but this time the source is educational rather than
missionary.

Lunda

258 English-Lunda (Ndembu) abridged dictionary, with Lunda-
English basic vocabulary.
M.K. Fisher. Lusaka: Zambia Publications Bureau, 1967. 164p.
Lunda is a language spoken in North Western Zambia.

259 A Lunda-English vocabulary.
Charles Matthew Newton White. London: University of London
Press, 1957. 80p.
Charles White, an anthropologist, was a meticulous craftsman so it is not surprising to see
that he produced this thorough dictionary of the Lunda language.

Luvale

260 Luvale notebook: based on the Chibemba notebook by Commander T.S.L. Fox-Pitt.
James C. Chijavata. London: Longman, 1958. 39p.
Luvale is one of the languages spoken in North Western Zambia.

261 A grammar of Luvale.
A.E. Horton. Johannesburg: Witwatersrand Press, 1949. 221p.
The Luvale people live in the Upper Zambezi region in North Western Zambia.

262 A dictionary of Luvale.
Introduced by A.E. Horton. No publisher, no place, 1975. Revised edition. 487p.
It is strange that no publisher is indicated for this extensive dictionary.

263 English/Luvale dictionary.
No author, no publisher, no place, 1978. 285p.
This dictionary may seem elusive but has been seen by the compiler. It probably originates from the Plymouth Brethren missions in North Western Province.

264 A Luvale-English phrase book.
Charles Matthew Newton White. London: W. Heinemann, 1955. 39p.
Charles White was a member of the Rhodes-Livingstone Institute who carried out extensive anthropological studies on the Luvale (see item no. 231).

Mambwe

265 Cimambwe grammar.
Lusaka: Northern Rhodesia and Nyasaland Publications Bureau, 1962. 54p.
The Mambwe live in the corridor between Lake Malawi and Lake Tanganyika. Although they are a distinct group, Bemba is also widely spoken there.

266 **Mambwe-English dictionary.**
Andrzej Halemba. Ndola, Zambia: Franciscan Mission Press, 1994.
984p.
It is interesting to note that the missionary societies are still involved in producing dictionaries of the regional languages in Zambia.

Nsenga

267 **Chisenga handbook; a manual of the Nsenga language, spoken in the protectorate of Northern Rhodesia.**
A. Sydney B. Ranger. London: Sheldon Press, 1928. 337p.
The Nsenga live in Petauke district. Although they consider themselves a distinct group, they also speak Chinyanja.

Nyanja (including Chichewa)

268 **Dictionary of the Nyanja language, being the encyclopaedic dictionary of the Mang'anja language.**
David Clement Rufelle Scott. Edited and enlarged by the Revd Alexander Hetherwick. London: United Society for Christian Literature, Lutterworth Press, 1929. 612p.
This dictionary is still the standard work on the Nyanja language.

269 **Chinyanja basic course.**
United States Foreign Service Institute. Edited by Earl W. Stevick, Linda Hollander. Washington, DC: United States Department of State, 1965. 107p.
A set of tapes that can be used in a language laboratory comes with this Chinyanja course.

270 **The student's English Chichewa dictionary.**
Zambezi Mission Inc. Blantyre, Malawi: Christian Literature Association in Malawi, 1986. 173p.
The term Chinyanja – literally the language spoken by the lake – is used in Zambia to designate the dominant language in eastern Zambia and in Lusaka. After independence the term Chichewa – harking back to the idea of a Chewa empire – became common in Malawi. Chinyanja is more a *lingua franca* and relatively liberal in its grammatical

structure, while Chichewa is a precise and more formal language. There is, however, substantial overlap between them.

271 Chichewa intensive course.
N. Salaun. Lusaka: Teresianum Press, 1993. 3rd ed. 147p.

This is much the most commonly used book in learning Chichewa or Chinyanja. It is also useful for people who want to have an idea of how Bantu languages are constructed (mainly using prefixes and suffixes) rather aiming to master a language. It has also been published without date and author by Likuni Mission Press, Lilongwe in Malawi.

Soli

272 Notes on the grammar of the Soli.
Bernardus Isak Christiaan van Eeden.   Cape Town: National Press, 1936. 51p.

The Soli live towards the east and the southeast of Lusaka.

Tonga

273 Tonga grammar.
A. Collins.   Lusaka, NECZAM, 1975. 182p.

Citonga is the language spoken in Southern Province. Earlier editions of this work were published in London by Longman.

274 A practical introduction to Tonga.
Cecil Robert Hopgood.   Lusaka: Zambia Educational Publishing House, 1992. 320p.

Earlier editions of this work were published by Longman, Green and Company.

275 Citonga course.
Francis Keenan, S.J.   Monze, Zambia: Kisito Pastoral Centre, not dated. 126p.

This is another example of a language tutor produced by a missionary society.

276 Citonga notebook: based on the Chibemba notebook by Commander T.S.L. Fox-Pitt.
L. Nkazi. London: Longman, 1957. 48p.
Commander Fox-Pitt's approach was obviously found useful in language tutoring.

277 Chitonga-English phrasebook.
John Thompson. Lusaka: Teresianum Press, 1980. Revised edition. 97p.
This is a more modern phrasebook than some of the others cited here.

278 An English vernacular dictionary of the Bantu Botatwe dialects of Northern Rhodesia.
J. Torrend. Mariannhill, South Africa: Mariannhill Mission Press, 1931. 649p.
Bantu Botatwe means literally 'three peoples' and is sometimes used to refer to the Tonga, Ila and Lenje, whose languages are broadly similar.

Tumbuka

279 Tumbuka-Tonga English dictionary.
William V. Turner. Blantyre, Malawi: Hetherwick Press, 1952. 284p.
People who live on the shores of Lake Malawi around Nkhata Bay are also called Tonga, but are very different from the people who live in southern Zambia bearing that name. Tumbuka is the language most commonly spoken in northern Malawi as well as in north-eastern Zambia.

Religion

280 'Open the wombs!': the symbolic politics of modern Ngoni witchfinding.
Mark Auslander.   In: *Modernity and its malcontents: ritual and power in postcolonial Africa.*   Chicago: University of Chicago Press, 1993, p. 167-92. bibliog.
For a year, Auslander followed the witch finder, Black Moses, who operated among the Ngoni in Eastern Zambia. Young males were predominant in Black Moses' following, and his attacks were mostly directed against women and older people. If the cleansing was completed then the villagers would be capable of 'making money'. This is an engagingly written account of a phenomenon which is common in Zambia and rural Africa in general. The bibliography mentions significant earlier reports on witchfinding movements. This is more recent than other writings, and Auslander firmly locates the movement in the time when the study took place (1988), when the Ngoni had to grapple with an explanation for economic failure. These links with a particular time may seem farfetched to some, but this article is influential and much cited.

281 A prophecy that failed: the Lumpa church of Uyombe.
George C. Bond.   In: *African Christianity; patterns of religious continuity.*   Edited by George Bond, Walton Johnson, Sheila S. Walker.   New York: Academic Press, 1979, p. 137-60.
This is a modest contribution on a topic about which too little is known. Bond undertook research among the Yombe – a branch of the Tumbuka – in northern Lundazi in 1964-65. He knew Lumpa congregations there and visited individuals in detention as well. The Lumpa uprising coincided with the coming of independence. Bond maintains, however, that the church was neither anti-European nor anti-colonial, albeit that in 1964 it was against any external authority whatever. Bond stresses also that Lumpa drew adherents from among the poorest in society, while UNIP attracted the educated. This article conveys a vivid impression of the time and expresses interesting opinions, but it is not a systematic account of the history and structure of the church.

282 Conversion and Jesuit schooling in Zambia.
Brendan P. Carmody, S.J. Leiden, The Netherlands: E.J. Brill,
1992. 179p. 3 maps.
The title of the book may suggest more spiritual content than it actually contains. The
question of how to retain a Catholic identity and zeal in the face of pressures for high
quality manpower, concern for social justice and increasing government influence on
schooling is a major theme, but the monograph is primarily a history of schools
management at Chikuni mission in Southern Province in rapidly changing environments.
Elite education is a preoccupation which suffuses the book. Carmody provides interesting
insights into the relationship with the nationalist movement and may be an interesting
source in that respect. Mainze Chona, the prominent UNIP politician, was one of their
pupils who spoke warmly about the place: 'they needed the colonial government for
security and assistance but whenever I went to Chikuni they were sympathetic to my
cause' (p. 90). The book gives insights into the life of the missionaries – French, Polish,
Irish – paying much attention to leading personalities. On the whole the book will portray
a recognizable world to those who have some inside knowledge of Zambian education,
but to others it will often seem like reporting from a rather alien world. The bibliography
mentions several articles by Carmody which deal with this same subject matter in
condensed form. See also 'Conversion and schooling at Chikuni 1905-1930' by Brendan
Carmody (*Africa*, vol. 58, no. 2 [1988], p. 193-210).

**283 Church and state in Africa: the case of the African Methodist
Episcopal Church.**
David J. Cook. In: *Christianity in independent Africa*. Edited by
E. Fasholi Luke, R. Gray, A. Hastings, G. Tasu. London: Rex
Collings, 1978, p. 285-303.
This article predates the book by Walton Johnson on the AME (see item no. 294),
although it refers to Johnson's PhD thesis. The slightly different perspective in this article
should be noted, however. Cook throws a much sharper light on the rift between the AME
and the nationalists. Kenneth Kaunda, for example, was a member of this black American
church, but after 1958 the church tried to keep politics out. Its membership included
believers from two bitterly opposed parties and so it became non-political to save itself
from schisms and rifts. This article provides many insights – not only with respect to the
AME – into the relationships between religion and nationalism.

**284 Independent churches and independent states: Jehovah's
Witnesses in East and Central Africa.**
Sholto Cross. In: *Christianity in independent Africa*. Edited by
E. Fasholi Luke, R. Gray, A. Hastings, G. Tasu. London: Rex
Collings, 1978, p. 304-15.
This article provides little factual information about this fascinating subject. The few facts
that it mentions whet the appetite of the reader: for example, one-quarter of all Jehovah's
Witnesses in Zambia live in Luapula Province. Instead, the author provides long and
general reflections on the clashes between states in the area and Jehovah's Witnesses.
Cross's PhD on the Jehovah's Witnesses, *The Watchtower movement in South Central
Africa, 1908-1945* (Oxford, 1973), is reputed to be a significant work on the subject. He
also wrote a biographical sketch of Jeremiah Gondwe, an independent church leader
within the movement.

285 **The Korsten basketmakers; a study of the Masowe apostles, an indigenous African religious movement.**
Clive M. Dillon-Malone. Lusaka: Institute for African Studies, 1978. 169p. 4 maps. bibliog.

Johane Masowe considered himself to be an incarnation of John the Baptist and started preaching in Mashonaland – in what was then Southern Rhodesia – in the early 1930s. His church expanded when he moved to Matabeleland and then to the town of Korsten in South Africa. He and his followers were deported from there as illegal immigrants as a consequence of a slum clearance project by the apartheid government in the early 1960s. They did not want to resettle in Southern Rhodesia, but asked the newly independent Zambian government for permission to settle in Lusaka. There was already a community of apostles of Zimbabwean origin in Zambia. They made their headquarters, after permission was granted, in the Marrapodi area of Lusaka. The name of Korsten basketmakers is derived from the way in which they made their living in Korsten. Johane gave the general instruction that hands should always be busy, therefore directing members towards manual work, of which basket making is one example. In the early 1970s they became dominant in the taxi business of Lusaka and miraculously kept old Peugeot estates on the road for that purpose. Dillon-Malone's monograph is filled with fascinating information, not only with respect to their belief system, but also of a more sociological nature – for example, about their relationships with governments, the congregations of sisters in the church, conflicts and splits after the death of Johane, etc. The book is often tantalizing, creating a desire for more information and explanation. Standard sociological interpretations seem inadequate to explain the emergence and flourishing of a group like this one.

286 **The 'Mutumwa' churches of Zambia: an indigenous African religious healing movement.**
Clive Dillon-Malone. *Journal of Religion in Africa*, vol. 14, fasc. 3 (1983), p. 204-22.

Dillon-Malone draws attention to this fluid body of church communities which had its origin in Isoka district in north eastern Zambia but which has spread among the Bemba-, Nyanja- and Tonga-speaking peoples of Zambia. He describes the Mutumwa churches as first and foremost healing communities, but those seeking treatment are more numerous than full members and form a continuously shifting population. He describes their belief systems as full of ambiguity towards European as well as African medicine, but he sees them firmly as Christian churches despite their syncretism of spirit beliefs and preoccupation with witchcraft. The churches originated as witch-finder movements. Dillon-Malone calls for attention to be paid to the positive aspects of holistic healing in a culturally determined context, which is at the centre of Mutumwa medico-religious practices.

287 **The Mutumwa church of Peter Mulenga Part I.**
Clive Dillon-Malone. *Journal of Religion in Africa*, vol. 15, fasc. 2 (1985), p. 122-41.

The Mutumwa churches are characterized by many splits and factions. One such split-off group is concentrated in Southern Zambia under the leadership of Peter Mulenga. He established his headquarters in Mtendere township in Lusaka in 1977. Mulenga's conversion and an interpretation of his account of conversion is the chief subject of the article. Dillon-Malone describes this Christian experience as creatively fused with Bemba concepts and symbols. A spirit world fitted in a dualism of good and evil is central in the latter.

288 The Mutumwa church of Peter Mulenga Part II.
Clive Dillon-Malone. *Journal of Religion in Africa*, vol. 17, fasc. 1 (1987), p. 2-13.

Ritual which is firmly set in the context of healing is the main subject of this article. Dillon-Malone uses medical terms such as 'diagnostic procedures' and 'aetiology' in his analysis. Spirit possession is the main theme, and the world of spirits is seen as extending into the modern world. Modern spirits, in contrast to the traditional ones, are seen as merely destructive and have to be driven out. A comparative reference is made to the healing activities of Archbishop Milingo in the conclusion.

289 Zambia.
Paul Gifford. In: *African Christianity: its public role*. London: Hurst & Company, 1998, p. 181-245. map. bibliog.

Paul Gifford has a clear eye for the importance of religious discourse in Zambian society. He considers Zambia to be a unique environment for Christianity, as the religion never had to be on the defensive there. On the contrary, Zambia's culture – and especially politics – is suffused with Christianity. A major theme of this colourful and vividly written chapter is the comparison between the way Christianity was warped in Zambian society in the Kaunda years and the way it developed after Chiluba took over. At that point, an evangelical brand of Christianity became dominant and Chiluba created great controversy by declaring Zambia a Christian nation. Another major theme is the relationship between missionaries and local churches. Zambia was part of settler colonial Africa and therefore race relations played a major role. Gifford writes very soon after the events described: some judgements may seem rash and could have benefited from more reflection. The religious and the political scene are both also in constant flux, and that makes it difficult to come to accurate judgements: for example, the evangelistic preacher Nevers Mumba is no longer the MMD stalwart portrayed by Gifford, but considers himself persecuted by that government.

290 John Lester Membe.
Adrian Hastings. In: *Themes in the Christian history of Central Africa*. Edited by T.O. Ranger, John Weller. London: Heinemann Educational Books, 1975, p. 175-95.

This is, in the main, a life history of Membe told in his own words. John Lester Membe was one of the prominent leaders in the African Methodist Episcopal Church in its heyday. His most prominent period was his time as AME pastor in Abercorn from 1933 to 1944. Membe's life offers rich insights into the history of Christianity in Zambia through his association with the missions of Lubwa and Livingstonia. Membe exemplified the AME as a church where people with limited education could develop great influence as well as a church which – although embodying the values of the emancipation of black people – was ultimately non-political in nature.

291 **Christian missions in Africa: a social geographical study of the impact of their activities.**
Reinhard Henkel.   Berlin: Dietrich Reimer Verlag, 1989. 236p. 46 maps. bibliog.

The discipline of geography can synthesize much knowledge using a spatial perspective. That is the case here in this book which is almost encyclopaedic in character. It begins with an historical chapter and thereafter the spatial distribution of the major churches in Zambia – including the evangelical and independent churches – is analysed. Special attention is paid to education and health and their spatial impact. The penultimate chapter consists of five case studies, taken from all over Zambia, concentrating on the economic impact of the churches. In one of these, set in the Nsanye area in Eastern Province, the case is based on survey material. This book defies summary and it is only possible to give an impression of what can be gleaned from it. Among its contents are information about the Plymouth Brethren (Christian Mission in Many Lands), who are active in North Western Province and about whom literature is scarce; and details of how the relationships between education and religious groups – usually assumed to be strong – appear to be weak in the Nyanja area.

292 **Bemba speaking women of Zambia in a century of religious change (1892-1992).**
Hugo F. Hinfelaar.   Leiden, The Netherlands: E.J. Brill, 1994. 224p. bibliog.

The crucial part of this book consists of two chapters on local African churches. The chapter on the Lumpa church of Alice Lenshina contains an elaborate analysis of the hymnbook compiled by Robert Kaunda (the brother of Kenneth). According to Hinfelaar, Lenshina restored women's religious role as intercessors. The second important chapter is on the Church of the Sacred Heart, founded by Emilio Mulolani. While Lenshina was related to the Protestant missionary effort at Lubwa, the Church of the Sacred Heart was an offshoot of the Catholic mission. Mulolani too 'enhanced the religious importance of women as the medium of union with the Divine'. Hinfelaar traces in these cosmologies standards of an older generation of proto-Bantu origin, which was still very much alive in rural northern Zambia. The book's main concerns are with cosmologies and the missionary effort rather than with the sociological, historical or economic aspects of religion. A fundamental observation by Hinfelaar is that women form the bedrock of faithful church attendance.

293 **Lubwa: the Presbyterian mission and the Eastern Bemba.**
Arie N. Ipenburg.   Lusaka: Historical Association of Zambia-Multimedia Zambia, 1984. 53p. map. bibliog.

This pamphlet introduces all the themes which Ipenburg later worked out in his monumental monograph (see item no. 176) on Lubwa: the racial situation, the competition with the Roman Catholic White Fathers, the Lumpa church, etc. It makes this material accessible to a wider public, which can also benefit from his carefully stated views on colonialism and racism. For example, Ipenburg stresses that Africans – David Kaunda and Ellen Nyirenda – opened the mission rather than Europeans. His argument that Alice Lenshina's ability to attract followers was boosted by nationalism's loss of credibility in the eyes of the villagers (caused by its failure to stop federation) is also worth more credit than it has been given.

294 Worship and freedom: a black American church in Zambia.
Walton R. Johnson. London: International African Institute, 1977.
152p. 3 maps. bibliog.
This modest book offers rich insights from an insider's viewpoint. The author comes from
a family belonging to the African Methodist Episcopal Church (AME) in the United
States, and his work is the result of fieldwork as a participant observer – a fellow believer
in the AME church – in Zambia during 1967 to 1970. Johnson offers detailed descriptions
and sociological analysis of life in an AME congregation, known as a circuit. This is,
however, as much a work of political history as of the sociology of religion. Although it
is connected to the United States, AME developed almost wholly in Africa as a result of
African initiative. It was definitely proto-nationalist in nature, and a considerable number
of nationalist politicians were members at one time. The church remained aloof from
nationalist politics, however, and it became more and more the province of the less
educated, eventually losing its vanguard role.

295 The Africanization of a mission church: the African Methodist
Episcopal Church in Zambia.
Walton Johnson. In: *African Christianity; patterns of religious*
continuity. Edited by George Bond, Walton Johnson, Sheila S.
Walker. New York: Academic Press, 1979, p. 89-106. bibliog.
This article is principally a summary of the larger monograph by Johnson on AME, which
was originally an Afro-American church. The article gives a history of the development
of the church and describes its structural features. Above all, it aims to provide an analysis
of the growth and decline of the church. The author even talks about: 'The church's
demise and failure of the present Zambian elite to belong to it' (p. 106). Things were
different in the past, when it was embraced by the African elite and close to the nationalist
cause. Johnson's work is important to note, not only for students of religion, but maybe
even more so for students of the origin of nationalism.

296 The politics of therapeutic ngoma: the Zionist churches in urban
Zambia.
Cor Jonker. In: T*he quest for fruition through ngoma.* Edited by
Rijk van Dijk, Ria Reis, Marja Spierenburg. Oxford: James Currey,
2000, p. 117-33. bibliog.
This is primarily a descriptive article, which discusses, mostly in general terms, the so-
called *mdzimu* (spirit) churches. This form of religion has a strong healing component.
The portrait of Mr Mazyopa, the archbishop of the Zion spirit church, is worth noting. The
characterization of the social background of these churches is generally interesting: while
the leaders are male, the overwhelming majority of the membership is female, and
whereas the men's concerns straddle politics, the women are apolitical. The churches are
rooted among the very poor in the informal sector.

297 The conversion experience: the apostles of John Maranke.
Bennetta Jules-Rosette. *Journal of Religion in Africa,* vol. 7,
fasc. 2 (1975), p. 132-75.
The topic of this article is the phenomenon of religious conversion, and Jules-Rosette
argues that this is more an ongoing process than a sudden event as is usually assumed.

The article gives her own experience as a convert to the apostles of John Maranke. The fact that this process involved a good deal of travelling between Lumumbashi and Lusaka gives a fascinating insight into the international nature of this independent church. Jules-Rosette had scruples about some practices of the church, such as the requirement that she should kneel before all male church members. Apart from being a treatise on the nature of conversion, for many people this will be simply a good read.

298 **Prophecy and leadership in the Maranke church: a case study of continuity and change.**
Bennetta Jules-Rosette. In: *African Christianity; patterns of religious continuity.* Edited by George Bond, Walton Johnson, Sheila S. Walker. New York: Academic Press, 1979, p. 89-106.
Jules-Rosette has written elaborately about her rich fieldwork in the Marrapodi area in Lusaka. The Apostolic Church of John Maranke was dominant there, and this article gives a supremely accessible account of the history and nature of this church. Central in this article is a threat of secession, which the church attempts to resolve through visionary solutions. These threats become more and more potent as the church grows: it was originally a Zimbabwean church but spread into Zaire, Mozambique and other neighbouring countries. This clear and colourful article is an excellent introduction for readers who want to familiarize themselves with African independent churches.

299 **Constructing local worlds: spirit possession in the Gwembe valley, Zambia.**
Ute Luig. In: *Spirit possession; modernity and power in Africa.* Edited by Heike Behrend, Ute Luig. Oxford: James Currey, 1999, p. 124-42. bibliog.
The Gwembe valley continues to attract anthropologists building on the foundations laid by Colson and Scudder (see item nos. 35, 197, 199, 321, 691, 750). This article concerns mainly Masabe spirits, which are associated with healing and empowerment. They are distinguished from spirits associated with rain shrines, territorial claims and personal ancestor spirits. The spirit world among the Gwembe Tonga is delineated against the background of social change, most notably the forced removal of the Gwembe Tonga from the Zambezi valley. The article contains many general statements, which are not necessarily informative. Nevertheless, there are interesting anecdotes here: for example, in the 1950s, spirits such as guitar, ma-dance and cilimba (accordion) emerged.

300 **Sorcery in its social setting; a study of the Northern Rhodesian Chewa.**
M.G. Marwick. Manchester, England: Manchester University Press, 1965. 339p. 6 maps. bibliog.
Sorcery and witchcraft pervade life in Zambia. This book is on the one hand a classic, thorough anthropological monograph and on the other hand a study of witchcraft and sorcery. As a study of the Chewa it provides an excellent introduction to thinking in matrilineal terms. Marwick also explains excellently the joking relationships and avoidance behaviour embedded in this kinship structure which can baffle the outsider. A main thesis of Marwick is that witchcraft accusations are especially frequent among matrilineal relatives in relationships where conflict is not ideologically recognized. The notion of occult power is embedded in a view of Chewa norms. Chapter eight, 'Sorcery

as a moral force', may be a good starting point for becoming acquainted with an African definition of good behaviour and how this relates to witchcraft accusations.

301 The world in between.
Emmanuel Milingo. Edited with an introduction, commentary and epilogue by Mona Macmillan. London: C. Hurst, 1984. 137p.

This is a collection of abstracts from the writings of this former Roman Catholic archbishop of Lusaka who incorporated African elements of healing into his ministry. They will not be particularly interesting to people who do not share religious experiences, but the comments of Mona Macmillan may explain the issues to a much wider public.

302 'On the side of the robbed'; R.J.B. Moore, missionary on the Copperbelt 1933-1941.
Sean Morrow. Journal of Religion in Africa, vol. 19, fasc. 3 (1989), p. 244-64.

Sean Morrow brings to light a most unusual person in colonial Copperbelt society. Moore was a pioneer of the missionary effort in urban settings. From this position he – this 'shy and undiplomatic' person – came into conflict with virtually the whole white community and especially mine and government officials. The main reason was his defence of the position of striking mineworkers. After his expulsion from the Copperbelt, he turned towards anthropology and wrote – according to Morrow – 'one of the most penetrating analyses of the Copperbelt in his time'.

303 Blood on their hands.
Kampambana Mulenga. Lusaka: Zambia Educational Publishing House, 1998. 255p.

This book should be read by anybody interested not only in the Lumpa church, but in independent churches generally. It is the first publication by a Zambian on the topic, and the book is dedicated to Mulenga's aunt who died together with other followers of Alice Lenshina. It is the most elaborate description of the history of the Lumpa church, and the only one which gives detailed information on what happened to the followers of Lenshina after the uprising. The author is openly partisan. UNIP was the violent party and should have left the Lumpas alone. Lenshina is credited with much good work: 'she eradicated witchcraft in the areas where the church had influence' (p. 177). Mulenga has a formidable historical imagination which sometimes carries him too far – for example in his description of dissident politician Simon Kapwepwe's apocryphal visit to Lenshina to ask for her support in the possible contest for UNIP leadership in 1978. Independent churches tend to attract the non-educated, and they have mostly been described by Europeans. In this book, a Zambian intellectual writes sympathetically about an independent church, and that makes it worth close attention.

304 The life of a Zambian evangelist.
Paul Bwembya Mushindo. Lusaka: University of Zambia; Institute for African Studies, 1973. 60p.

The life of Mushindo as an African intellectual has recently been the subject of scholarly interest in the work of Ackson Kanduza. It is, however, also rewarding to read Mushindo in his own words. This is a most tragic account of his work in which his relationship with the intensely racist missionary Robert MacMinn plays a central role: 'he loved me as one can love his or her best tool, which is useful to his or her work' (p. 49). Yet Mushindo remained loyal to the Presbyterian Church. The note on Mushindo by the – definitely not racist – missionary Fergus Macpherson, which precedes the memoirs, is also very worthwhile.

305 The Mwena Lesa movement of 1925.
Terence Ranger. In: *Themes in the Christian history of Central Africa*. Edited by T.O. Ranger, John Weller. London: Heinemann Educational Books, 1975, p. 14-30.

This brilliant article offers the most complete description available of this dramatic episode in Zambian history. Ranger describes the position of a northern Malawian, Tomo Nyirenda, in Lala society, Serenje district, and tells how he amalgamated Christianity with Lala beliefs. Ranger's thesis is that Nyirenda's activities have to be situated in a void of missionary activity and tries to see a humanity which may be obscured by the lethal elements, witch killings, of the episode. The article is of much wider relevance than the immediate as it gives deep and empathetic insights into the millenarian beliefs which have been so common in Zambia's religious development.

306 Passing on the rites of passage: girls' initiation rites in the context of an urban Catholic community on the Zambian Copperbelt.
Thera Rasing. Aldershot, England: Avebury, 1995. 112p.

The main part of this short book is a long chapter which provides a detailed description of an initiation rite as performed in the context of a Roman Catholic parish in Luangwa township near Kitwe on the Copperbelt. The Catholic Church these days embraces the concept of enculturation and tries to incorporate such rites in the Church instead of condemning them, as used to be the practice.

307 From independence to multiparty democracy in Zambia; a personal view from inside the church.
Foston Dziko Sakala. In: *Peacemaking and democratisation in Africa; theoretical perspectives and church initiatives*. Edited by Hizkias Assefa, George Wachira. Nairobi: East African Educational Publishers, 1996, p. 117-30. bibliog.

This article is primarily important as an historical source. Reverend Sakala came to prominence during the campaign for multiparty elections as chairman of the Zambian Election Monitoring Co-ordinating Committee (ZEMCO). On behalf of the churches – who had been organized in ZEMCO – he had regular contact with Kaunda at the time about which he writes here. The article covers a much longer period however, and Sakala describes earlier involvement of the churches in politics. It is not comprehensive, but it is important to note, for example, the letter by church leaders on *Marxism, humanism and Christianity*. The church leaders were then (1979) concerned about a drift to godless scientific socialism.

308 The healing ministry of Archbishop Milingo of Zambia.
Gerrie ter Haar. London: C. Hurst & Co., 1992. 286p. bibliog.

In the 1970s and early 1980s, Archbishop Milingo developed a healing ministry near Lusaka, supported by a religious order of sisters. His syncretism of African belief systems brought him into conflict with the church hierarchy and the end result was a posting to Rome. Ter Haar places Milingo's work in the context of Zambian politics and society, but the book remains visibly a theologian's work. An interesting aspect of Milingo's ministry was his appeal to the Zambian elite. An analysis of their letters to him reveals their struggles with evils such as corruption. The findings from the letters have also been separately published: 'Spirit possession and healing in modern Zambia' by Gerrie ter Haar, Stephen Ellis. (*African Affairs*, vol. 87, no. 347, [1988], p. 185-206).

309 Experiencing ritual; a new interpretation of African healing.
Edith Turner, William Blodgett, Singleton Kahona, Fideli Benwa.
Philadelphia, Pennsylvania: University of Philadelphia Press, 1992.
239p. bibliog.

Edith Turner was not merely the wife of Victor Turner, but also an anthropologist in her own right. She returned to the Ndembu people with an assistant in 1985 after a decade's absence. This resulted in these observations of the *ihamba* ritual, which was still being performed at that time. This is striking as it is linked to hunting, and game has decreased considerably in rural Zambia. The comparisons between the early 1950s and 1985 are most valuable for further analysis. The book, paradoxically, probably also offers a more perceptive insight into her life there in the 1950s than her personal memoir (see item no. 127). The main theoretical concern is the question of whether one can study ritual without immersing oneself in it and becoming part of the shared group feeling. This concern plays, however, a remarkably minor role in the whole of the book.

310 The forest of symbols: aspects of Ndembu ritual.
Victor Turner. Ithaca, New York: Cornell University Press, 1966.
405p.

Turner published in this book a disparate collection of essays on themes relating to the indigenous religious life of the Ndembu in North Western Province. This particular sub-group of the Lunda is, however, often seen in a comparative perspective, drawing on sources from all over Africa. It provides a good introduction to African religious world views in general. Many of the chapters are written in an engaging manner and that is especially the case in Turner's famous piece on 'Muchona the Hornet, interpreter of religion', which is also a story of friendship across cultures. Other essays are less personal and some are mainly ethnographic inventories, of interest only to specialists in the field of African explanations of misfortune; disease; colour symbolism; ritual, etc.

311 The drums of affliction; a study of the religious processes among the Ndembu of Zambia.
V.W. Turner. Oxford: The Clarendon Press, 1968. 326p. 3 maps.
bibliog.

This is arguably the best monograph which has ever been written about healing in an African society. The main part of the book consists of a description and analysis of healing rituals. These are interpreted in cultural and sociological terms. However, the book is not a mere anthropological treatise. Turner brings the characters he studied more vividly to life than is usual. Witness these remarks about Kamahasanyani, a central character: 'he was aware of the liaison between Jackson and his wife, but he did not come to blows with the adulterer' (p. 149)...; 'he appeared to have passive homosexual tendencies' (p. 192). These latter are seen in relation to an unusually close affiliation to his patrilinear relatives in a matrilineal society. The interpretation of religious symbolism in social contexts through the detailed description of actors becomes here a form of art.

312 The possession of the dispossessed; songs as history among Tumbuka women.

Leroy Vail. In: *Power and the praise poem: Southern African voices in history.* Edited by Leroy Vail, Landeg White. Charlottesville, Virginia: University of Virginia Press; London: James Currey, 1991, p. 231-78.

The *vimbuza* is a disease which overwhelmingly affects women and which can be cured by a healing dance ceremony. The phenomenon is a combination of indigenous healing and religion; art in the form of singing and dancing as well as entertainment. The *vimbuza* is embedded in the culture of the Tumbuka, a group which is mainly found in northern Malawi but also in north eastern Zambia. They also have a considerable urban presence. A large part of the research for this article was undertaken in Zambia. Vail interprets the cult and its associated songs from a gender perspective and what may be termed a sub-nationalist point of view. Relationships between Tumbuka and Ngoni and the changing position of women as a consequence of labour migration as well as the rise of polygyny are seen as central. The article is worthwhile not only as a case study but also as an approach to popular culture in Zambia, even if one finds the conclusions far fetched: *vimbuza* provides women 'with an interpretation of history based on the ethical truths perceived as existing in the matrilineal system before 1856' (p. 270).

313 An African church in transition from missionary dependence to mutuality in mission: a case study on the Roman Catholic Church in Zambia.

Frans J. Verstraelen. Tilburg, The Netherlands: Interuniversity Institute for Missiological and Ecumenical Research, 1975. 2 vols. 2 maps. bibliog.

At its time of publication, this was probably seen as an innovative study, but it is now more dated than a more conventional narrative would have been. It is sociological research – undertaken among Zambian laity and expatriate missionaries in the dioceses of Lusaka and Chipata – into issues which became highly salient after political independence. This event put Africanization of the church centre stage, and that meant a drive towards more self-financing of the Roman Catholic Church in Zambia and the recruitment of a local instead of an expatriate clergy. There is a concluding chapter summing up the findings of the study. There is also an informative chapter on the members and structure of the Catholic Church in Zambia. It may be rewarding to those interested in this subject to look out for the forthcoming history of the Catholic Church in Zambia to be written under the guidance of Hugo Hinfelaar.

**314 From Dutch mission church to Reformed Church in Zambia;
the scope for African leadership and initiative in the history of a
Zambian mission church.**
Gerdien Verstraelen Gilhuis. Franeker, The Netherlands: T. Wever,
1982. 366p. 2 maps. bibliog.

This history of the missionary endeavours of a South African Afrikaner mission church
(Dutch Reformed Church) in the eastern part of Zambia is encyclopaedic in nature. It is
therefore mainly useful for people who have specialized interests in this subject.
Nevertheless, it may for example be worthwhile to be able to place the name Hofmeyer
– which is also a place in Petauke district – if one gets to know Eastern Province. The
major theme of the book is naturally the relationships between the parent church and its
missionary offshoot. The issue of race is in the background throughout: 'African
evangelists were preaching at the farms of Afrikaner Boers. We, however, did not know
the Boer and his Christianity; they were just praying for themselves, one of them said'
(p. 210). Changes resulted not only from political developments, but also from new
theological insights developed in related churches in the Netherlands. The book is
pervaded by a sense of empathy with the missionary effort, despite its critical stance on
many issues.

**315 The effects of a religious mission on rural development: a case
study in Lwawu, Northwest Province, Zambia.**
Lee E. Weissling. *Canadian Journal of African Studies*, vol. 24,
no. 1 (1990), p. 75-97. 2 maps. bibliog.

This is primarily a geographer's paper on the spatial effects of this Roman Catholic
mission, established in 1955. The mission is seen as too successful as a development
agent, since it attracts hundreds of migrants because of the services it provides. The
presence of the mission is central to the survival strategies of the local population because
of the opportunities it affords. Weissling considers these as including – paradoxically –
resorting to hopelessness and deviant behaviour. The article is above all a snapshot of
rural life around a mission station in 1985.

**316 Mainstream Christianity to 1980 in Malawi, Zambia and
Zimbabwe.**
John Weller, Jane Linden. Gweru, Zimbabwe: Mambo Press, 1984.
225p. 3 maps. bibliog.

This book is primarily written as a textbook for theological education and therefore
stresses elementary matters in an accessible way. The emphasis is on facts rather than
interpretation. The major chapters are neatly divided into Malawian, Zimbabwean and
Zambian sections. The last chapter is devoted to the churches and national affairs, but it
ends with the remark that: 'With the achievement of independence under President
Kaunda, the influence of Christianity upon national affairs entered a new phase, and one
that lies outside the scope of the present study' (p. 199). That may be disappointing for
some.

317 Some spirits heal, others only dance: a journey into human selfhood in an African village.

Roy Willis. Oxford: Berg, 1999. 220p. 2 maps. bibliog.

This book is about spirits, healing, sorcerers, herbalists and related matters among the Lungu, one of the groups inhabiting the corridor between Lake Tanganyika and Lake Malawi. The book deals mainly with the Zambian side, located near the town of Mbala. It would be tempting to say that this book is about the supernatural among the Lungu, but that would be completely against its spirit, which considers such phenomena as real. The author participates in the rituals and is inspired by the later work of Victor Turner (see item nos. 310, 311) on the assimilation of the self in the communities. For some, this will be a gem of a book that goes inside what we experience as supernatural. For others, it will lack objectivity. A large part of the book is written as a diary in which interpretation and structuring of events seem to be secondary to conveying the experience.

318 Cosmologies in turmoil: witchfinding and AIDS in Chiawa, Zambia.

C. Bawa Yamba. *Africa*, vol. 67, no. 2 (1997), p. 200-24.

The African belief in witchcraft has to do with explaining misfortune, and the AIDS pandemic provides a lot of misfortune to be explained. It is therefore not surprising that deaths from AIDS provide a fertile ground for witchfinders. The particular value of this article is in the gruesome detail with which it depicts the plight of people under accusation. The battle between Chaka the witchfinder and Peter Katiyo who said 'Help us fight AIDS, but not witchcraft' is breathtaking reading for everyone. Although Katiyo started out by claiming the irrelevance of witchcraft, he was forced by sheer social pressure to admit to being a witch. The research was carried out as part of an AIDS prevention programme.

Urban Development, Poverty and Social Problems

319 Evaluation of sites and services projects; the experience from Lusaka, Zambia.
Michael Bamberger, Bishwapura Sanyal, Nelson Valverde.
Washington, DC: The World Bank, 1982. 201p. map. bibliog.

The title of this publication may be misleading because it deals with the squatter upgrading programme in Lusaka rather than sites and services as such. It was a World Bank financed programme, and this is an evaluation by the World Bank. It starts from a remarkable political assumption: 'The guiding policy of the local party organisation was to obtain as many services as possible for the squatter areas from a reluctant administration' (p. 7). Much of this evaluation is technical in nature, covering, for example, physical design and administrative arrangements. Another focus is cost recovery and affordability, and in these sections there is valuable information on income distribution in Lusaka, which is of wide interest and could be used in designing new research.

320 An assessment of the structures and dimensions of mutual aid among the urban poor: the case of Lusaka and Kafue districts.
W. Chama, L.K. Mwape. Lusaka: Study Fund Committee of the World Bank Social Recovery Project, 1998. 103p. 2 maps. bibliog.

This is one of a long series of studies, of variable quality, commissioned by the Study Fund of the World Bank. This particular one is highly salient to concerns in the 1990s. Informal networks of social security are sought as the state no longer provides social safety nets. The research reports on the results of a questionnaire and gives a number of case studies that profile the poor. This study is worth noting as it is so highly topical, but the findings are often self-evident.

321 For prayer and profit; the ritual, economic and social importance of beer in Gwembe district, Zambia 1950-82.

Elizabeth Colson, Thayer Scudder. Stanford, California: Stanford University Press, 1988. 147p. bibliog.

The title of this monograph speaks for itself and the essence of the authors' message is contained in this sentence: 'Although the time devoted to drinking increased from the 1960s on and had become what we regarded as excessive by 1980, drinking in the 1980s was rarely associated with what people thought of as creative work, either ritual or otherwise' (p. 101). One of the chapters is aptly called 'The rising tide of beer', and the change of beer into a commodity rather than something embedded in the social and cultural life of the village is the major theme of the book.

322 A concrete response to poverty; rethinking approaches to urban poverty and infrastructure: a Zambian case study.

Hilary Cottam. *IDS Bulletin*, vol. 28, no. 2 (1997), p. 68-76.

Some readers may wonder where the concrete material is in this short article which is mainly theoretical in nature. This theoretical perspective is formulated in sentences like: 'the majority [of the urban population] are without services to be rehabilitated, but [approaches] remain within the Fordist blueprint mould'. A Japanese collusion between JAIKA and Mitsubishi was observed by the author to be a significant impediment to the localized differential investment proposed for low-income areas by NGOs and the World Bank. The exemplary nature of the latter's effort results in a case study of a water supply project of about one page in length.

323 Urban microfarming in central southern Africa: a case study of Lusaka.

A.W. Drescher. *African Urban Quarterly*, vol. 11, no. 2/3 (1996), p. 229-48. 2 maps. bibliog.

Drescher carried out a survey in 1992/93 to study small-scale farming in urban Lusaka. This article is a very detailed presentation of this research, which led to interesting observations. Microfarming does not appear to be a viable survival strategy for the poor, because access to water and land is lowest in high-density, low-income compounds in Lusaka. People have therefore to go quite a distance to farm, and theft – which was reported as an issue by nearly forty per cent of the respondents – is increasingly becoming a problem in this situation.

324 Scenes from African urban life; collected Copperbelt essays.

A.L. Epstein. Edinburgh: Edinburgh University Press, 1992. 233p. map. bibliog.

This is a collection of previously published essays with an introduction reflecting on Epstein's Copperbelt research. Courts, trade unions, language and the Jehovah's Witnesses are among the topics covered. Epstein's writing is so subtle that it is difficult to convey a proper idea of these papers. His originality may be clear in the title of his concluding chapter: 'Response to social crisis: aspects of oral aggression in Central Africa'. The bibliography gives good access to other work on the Copperbelt by Epstein.

325 Mobile workers, modernist narratives: a critique of the historiography of transition on the Zambian Copperbelt.
James Ferguson. Part One, *Journal of Southern African Studies*, vol. 16, no. 3 (1990), p. 385-412. Part Two, *Journal of Southern African Studies*, vol. 16, no. 4 (1990), p. 603-21.

This is primarily an extensive literature review debating theoretical issues, although the author presents these articles as the result of a one-year period of fieldwork in Kitwe. According to Ferguson, there is unwarranted stereotyping in models of urban society – and especially of urban-rural relationships – in Zambia. He maintains that there was much more stability in urban society in earlier times, when circulatory migration between urban and rural society was thought to be the norm. Rural-urban links have become, however, much more important in recent times since a model of urban stabilization has become central in sociological models. He argues against a dualistic and evolutionist picture of the Zambian working class. Postmodernism's phrase that 'the grand narratives have broken down' comes to mind while reading Ferguson: there is not one narrative of urban Zambia, but many, which reflect a multitude of actors' strategies. His work has been challenged by Hugh Macmillan (see item nos. 340, 341). There is, however, a very strong reason to draw attention to these articles, irrespective of the quality of Ferguson's arguments. The annotation is a good guide to the literature on urbanization in Zambia because Ferguson reviews a mass of relevant literature.

326 Modernist narratives, conventional wisdoms, and colonial liberalism: reply to a straw man.
James Ferguson. *Journal of Southern African Studies*, vol. 20, no. 4 (1993), p. 633-40.

Ferguson replies here to Macmillan's contentions (see item nos. 327, 340, 341) that he has created a debate where none existed. Ferguson concludes: 'Apparently I made it all up; it is all just a figment of my imagination'. The thrust of the article is that there is actually a straw man in this debate, but that it is Macmillan himself.

327 Urban trends on the Zambian Copperbelt: a short bibliographical note.
James Ferguson. *Journal of Southern African Studies*, vol. 22, no. 2 (1996), p. 313.

Ferguson points to empirical evidence from the 1990 census and Moore and Vaughan's monograph (see item no. 676) in this final rejoinder to Macmillan (see item nos. 326, 340, 341).

328 Expectations of modernity: myths and meanings of urban life on the Zambian Copperbelt.
James Ferguson. Berkeley, California; Los Angeles: University of California Press, 1999. 326p. 3 maps. bibliog.

Ferguson's articles on the historiography of the Copperbelt and his fascinating debate with Macmillan (see item nos. 326, 327, 340, 341) created high expectations for the monograph that was to follow. In this monograph he publishes his fieldwork which was only in the background in the previous work. From page 123 onwards, in four chapters illustrated with thirteen cases, numerous newspaper articles, letters, etc., he discusses urban life on the Copperbelt in the late 1980s. Two chapters, on the rural connections (back to the land) and on family life (domesticity), are closely related to behaviour. The other two – using jargon such as 'cosmopolitan style' and 'global disconnect' – are especially influenced by postmodernism, paying attention to language, signs and culture. The monograph tends to be more the momentary presentation of social life rather than direct observation of behaviour over time. This work is highly recommended to anybody who is interested in the study of urban life in Zambia – Ferguson brings together much literature here – and to people who want to get a feel for everyday life on the Copperbelt. It is, however, especially recommended for people who like to disagree with authors: Ferguson has a definite and idiosyncratic vision.

329 Situation analysis of children and women in Zambia.

Government of the Republic of Zambia, United Nations Children's Fund. Lusaka: Government of the Republic of Zambia, United Nations Children's Fund Programming Committee, 1986. 163p. 4 maps.

This report deals with poverty, an issue that has become more and more prominent in development policy. It also contains much information which is not immediately related to the theme of poverty. For example, it includes an overview of the mass media in Zambia and of the need for intersectoral co-ordination in nutrition policies. There is no poverty survey of the type that became common in the 1990s using a poverty datum line. However, the work does contain a comprehensive overview of the data on social indicators – health and education – for this period.

330 Lusaka's squatters: past and present.

Karen Tranberg Hansen. *African Studies Review*, vol. 25, no. 2 (1982), p. 117-36.

This is very much a period piece, as is evident from the first sentence: 'Between 1967 and 1970 the number of squatter settlements in Zambia's capital, Lusaka, increased from 9-32, accounting for more than one third of the city's population.' The article is an impressionistic account of attempts to come to grips with this spurt of urbanization. It also gives a useful periodization of African urbanization in Zambia. The introduction of the idea of squatter upgrading is discussed and the role of the political party, UNIP, in governing the squatter areas is described.

331 Negotiating sex and gender in Urban Zambia.

Karen Tranberg Hansen. *Journal of Southern African Studies*, vol. 10, no. 2 (1984), p. 219-38.

This article is mainly descriptive. It gives impressions rather than analysing patterns of social behaviour. It sketches how women struggle for a niche in urban society in a context of poverty; subordination to men in household and conjugal affairs; and – especially in the past – discriminatory government attitudes and government regulation. Much of the article is general in nature and based on secondary sources, although the author presents it as the result of fieldwork carried out in 1971/72 and in 1981. The annotation refers to earlier publications based on the 1971/72 fieldwork.

332 Keeping House in Lusaka.
Karen Tranberg Hansen. New York: Columbia University Press,
1997. 228p. 5 maps. bibliog.

This is a sociological study of Mtendere in Lusaka. Mtendere is described by Hansen's informants as 'the nicest of Lusaka's compounds'. It is thus a study of the respectable side of the poorer parts of Lusaka. The monograph is the outcome of research which covered a time span of about twenty years and seeks to give an all encompassing view of life in the area. Hansen's main interest, however, is gender relations and their effect on livelihoods, in which the informal sector plays a major role. Her conclusion here is unconventional and merits attention: activity should not be confused with prosperity when analysing this sector. The book is stronger in those sections where she gives vivid close observations of everyday life. Political scientists can also profit from this book because of the key part played by the party UNIP in organizing life in the compound. The bibliography mentions many articles by Hansen based on the material in this book.

333 Second-hand clothing encounters in Zambia; global discourses.
Karen Tranberg Hansen. *Africa*, vol. 69, no. 3 (1999), p. 343-66.

This is the last in a series of articles which Hansen published on the second-hand clothes trade in Zambia. This trade has indeed become a striking feature of life since Zambia became an open economy. The author rightly starts from the assumption that people in Zambia are particular about dress. Most of the article consists of impressions and opinions about taste in dress. 'Foreignness' is a quality particularly appreciated. Zambians nowadays distrust neatly ironed second hand clothes as they may be even third hand, sold by a Zambian. The theme is further explored in item no. 334.

334 Salaula; the world of second hand clothing and Zambia.
Karen Tranberg Hansen. Chicago: The University of Chicago
Press, 2000. 298p. 3 maps. bibliog.

Hansen published several articles on the surge in trade in second-hand clothes from the developed world in Zambia during the1990s. These articles built extensive theoretical constructs on a limited base of observation. This book is different and has a much more solid empirical base. It contains information on the trade in second-hand clothes worldwide, the emergence of the trade in Zambia in the wake of economic liberalization and, most significantly, a discussion of the meaning of dress in Zambia's recent history. She discusses the short-lived fad of traditional dress for men around independence; and the meaning of wearing *chitenge* cloth, miniskirts, etc. Her starting point is that dress is highly valued in Zambia, where it is often embedded in a complicated social code. The book will appeal to a wide public as the subject is intertwined with such significant events as the rise and fall of import-substituting textile industry; economic liberalization and democratization, etc. Above all, the book is rich in illustrative examples. For instance, the way Zambians experiment with clothing is illustrated by one man 'who wore what looked like a hospital orderly's white uniform topped by a pink peignoir. Another young man dressed proudly in a church elder's purple gown' (p. 200).

335 **Symbols of change: urban transition in a Zambian community.**
Bennetta Jules-Rosette. Norwood, New Jersey: Ablex Publishing
Corporation, 1981. 225p. map. bibliog.

Jules-Rosette has made an extensive study of one of the relatively early unofficial
settlements in Lusaka: Marrapodi. She has published extensively, and the bibliography
offers useful references. This book integrates her material on religion, healing, small-
scale entrepreneurship and the emerging community of artists in Marrapodi. The general
theme is a defence of neighbourhoods like Marrapodi, which are often derogatorily
referred to as 'squatter-compounds'. Whereas town planners and administrators see
disorganization, she points to the developing communities which represent an adaptation
to urban life. Characteristic of Marrapodi is the striking presence of the apostles,
followers of Johannes Masowe and of John Maranke. Both are originally Shona
(identified with Zimbabwe) churches. Jules-Rosette has a clear eye for the complexities
in social life: one example is the way she treats a mutual singing slanging match between
the two religious groups as an example of ceremonial ecumenism.

336 **Self help housing and national housing policy in Zambia.**
B.A. Kasongo. *Vierteljahresberichte; Probleme der*
Entwicklungsländer, no. 82 (1980), p. 365-75. 2 maps.

This reads as a civil servant's article. It mentions the various elements of Zambia's
housing policy since independence, the difficulties encountered in site and service
schemes, slum clearance, etc., but opts for a middle-of-the-road position, a combination
of various approaches. The article contains an extensive description – with drawings – of
a self-help housing scheme in Kabwe.

337 **An analysis of the policy towards squatters in Kitwe, Zambia.**
B. Anthony Kasongo, A. Graham Tipple. *Third World Planning*
Review, vol. 12, no. 2 (1990), p. 147-67. 2 maps.

Both authors of this article worked for Kitwe City Council. This is thus an inside account
of the evolution of housing policies in Kitwe. They distinguish three periods: first there
is a policy of resettlement and clearance (1966-71); thereafter, co-operation with squatters
and upgrading becomes the policy (1972-76); resettlement and removal reappear after
that date. The cut-off date of their observations is in the mid-1980s. The article provides
quite detailed information on the situation in Kitwe, but it can be read profitably by
people who have a wider interest in the subject. The authors identify, for example on
page 155, 'a common stumbling block in resettlement proposals ... councillors who
represent the mixture of informal sector residents and squatters tend not to champion the
squatters' causes'.

338 **Shacks and mansions: an analysis of the integrated housing**
policy in Zambia.
Stefanie Knauder. Lusaka: Multimedia Publications, 1982. 167p.
5 maps. bibliog.

This book has two noteworthy parts. The description of five different urban areas gives a
good introduction to the nature of Zambian towns and can also be useful to the
unorthodox tourist who may decide to visit the Kafue estate in Kafue town, or old
Kabwata in Lusaka. The other part will appeal to a smaller audience and reports on a
survey regarding attitudes to, and integration of, various income groups in urban

neighbourhoods. Segregation along racial lines was often transformed after independence into segregation along lines of income and class. The background to this survey is a policy of integrated housing, intended to counter segregation, which is fundamental in the origins of town planning in Zambia.

339 Situation analysis of orphans in Zambia; volume 5 draft summary report.
Mark Loudon. Lusaka: Government of the Republic of Zambia, 1999. 37p.

This study records what is known of the uncharted but important phenomenon of orphans in Zambia. The severity of the AIDS pandemic has led to situations where one speaks of child-headed households. That was not found in this study to be a major problem, but orphans are mostly found in poor or very poor households. Poverty is the issue that intermeshes sharply with the problem of orphans. However, as most children in Zambia live in poor or very poor households, the study suggests that it is the issue of poverty that needs to be tackled rather than the issue of orphans as a separate group. This is, however, primarily a policy document stating what has to be done, and factual information is provided to support that rather than in its own right.

340 The historiography of transition on the Zambian Copperbelt – another view.
Hugh Macmillan. *Journal of Southern African Studies*, vol. 19, no. 4 (1993), p. 681-713.

This article represents the beginning of a polemic exchange between Macmillan and Ferguson (see item nos. 326, 327, 341) on the way in which urbanization on the Zambian Copperbelt has been portrayed. Macmillan disputes Ferguson's demographic interpretations: his reading of the available literature as well as his interpretations of policy. There has been, according to Macmillan, very little evidence to counter the supposition that rural-urban links are implicit in a modernist narrative. He accuses Ferguson of perpetuating an image of towns as being somehow alien and hostile.

341 More thoughts on the historiography of transition on the Zambian Copperbelt.
Hugh Macmillan. *Journal of Southern African Studies*, vol. 22, no. 2 (1996), p. 309-12.

Oddly enough, this short article may be a good starting point to study the debate between Macmillan and Ferguson (see item nos. 326, 327, 340), because Macmillan succinctly sums up in four points the areas of difference between them. The article again disputes the reading of literature dating from colonial times. Macmillan stresses that the anthropologists working in the Rhodes-Livingstone Institute in particular, but also others in colonial Northern Rhodesia, did not have a bias against Africans in cities. The anthropologist Gluckman is central in this debate. Similarly, Macmillan maintains that there is increasingly a stable urban population in Zambia's towns.

342   Rural-urban migration and urbanisation in Zambia during the colonial and post-colonial periods.
Nsolo J. Mijere, Alifeyao Chilivumbo.   In: *Population growth and environmental degradation in Southern Africa.*   Edited by Ezekile Kalipeni.   Boulder, Colorado: Lynne Rienner, 1994, p. 147-79. bibliog.

Zambia is, by African standards, a highly urbanized country, and it is difficult to provide new insights on the nature of rural-urban migration as so much has already been said about it. There is, however, a great lack of relatively recent material on the subject. This article contains highly relevant analyses of the 1969 to 1980 census period. One most interesting finding among many is that in that period the secondary cities, such as provincial capitals, grew at a much faster rate than the Copperbelt and Lusaka. The graphical material in the paper makes the findings easy to access.

343   The kalela dance: aspects of social relationships among urban Africans in Northern Rhodesia.
J. Clyde Mitchell.   Manchester, England: Manchester University Press, 1956. 52p.

This classic of urban anthropology is deceptive in its simplicity. It is one of the first descriptions of urban African culture and describes the dancing teams, the song, the origin of the kalela, etc., but it is above all a sociological paper, which documents how urban Africans use elements from the tribes or backgrounds from which they come to create an urban life view. It is typical for the dance to incorporate, besides 'tribal' elements, mockery of the way of life of Europeans.

344   Social networks in urban situations: analyses of personal relationships in Central African towns.
Edited by J. Clyde Mitchell.   Manchester, England: Manchester University Press, 1969. 378p. bibliog.

This is primarily a book on the methodology for analysing society in networks. The illustrations, however, are all drawn from Zambian urban situations, mostly on the Copperbelt. Some cases are more colourful than others; A. L. Epstein's analysis of gossip about adultery is strongly recommended. Peter Harries-Jones' description of the importance of home-boy ties in urban situations has not lost any of its relevance, and his description of shifting loyalties in urban life on the eve of independence is from time to time gripping. The petrol bombing described on pages 324-25 illustrates how the political and non-political aspects of these changing loyalties cannot be separated. The book provides good reading for a wide public, although it seems to be directed primarily at sociologists.

345   Cities, society and social perception: a central African perspective.
J. Clyde Mitchell.   Oxford: Clarendon Press, 1987. 336p. 6 maps. bibliog.

The foreword by Bruce Kapferer opens with the statement that 'Clyde Mitchell is the leading figure in the study of African urbanisation'. This is undoubtedly the case, and his theorizing was built upon empirical observation which was mostly undertaken on the

Zambian Copperbelt. Most of the empirical material in this book was collected before 1964, and Mitchell attempts to collate here much material published in different forms elsewhere. The major themes are perceptions of urban life; social ranking; and regionalism/ethnicity. People who want to research urban Zambia will find here inspiring ideas and angles of observation. However, this is a book primarily directed at professional sociologists who are not necessarily interested in Zambia.

346 Confronting crisis in Chawama, Lusaka, Zambia.
Caroline Moser, Jeremy Holland. Washington, DC: World Bank, Urban Management Programme, 1997. 125p. bibliog. (Vol. 4 of *Household reponses to poverty and vulnerability*).

The particular value of this research report is in its comparison of the situation in 1978 (based on material collected by Carol Rakodi) with that collected in a survey in 1992. Chawama is considered poorer than Lusaka as a whole or urban Zambia generally, with fifty-five per cent of the population being considered poor. The situation of the poor is approached from many angles: household composition; inequalities within households; income and employment; and, maybe the most crucial variable, housing. Despite a division between renters and nonrenters, housing remains the most important asset, especially as a means to reduce vulnerability. Reports like these are written in a bureaucratic style, subdividing in paragraphs rather than constructing a narrative. Similarly, readers are offered executive summaries as a shortcut to content. The wealth of information in this report is to be found in the main text, however, and in the numerous tables, although it may take considerable effort to reach it.

347 Zambia: urbanization and training for settlement improvement.
Elipidius Mpolokoso. In: *Urban innovation abroad: problem cities in search of solutions.* Edited by Thomas L. Blair. New York: Plenum Press, 1984, p. 128-38. bibliog.

Mpolokoso had at the time of writing just left the National Housing Authority to take up a job in adult education at Mindolo Ecumenical Centre. Concerns about housing are expressed in this short article, which is more informative about the National Housing Authority than about education in Zambia.

348 Urban-rural migration of Zambian retirees; re-adjustment and contribution to rural development.
Lawrence Mukuka. Lusaka: World Bank Social Recovery Project, 1997.

This survey, carried out in Lusaka, gives food for thought. Retirement, for many Zambians, appears to mean downward mobility and not the serene evening of one's life. Re-settling in rural areas may be desirable, but in practice few people follow this course. The majority retire in urban areas and forty per cent of those who originally intended to retire to rural areas have had to change their mind. Retirement to a farming existence requires capital, but the state retirement package is not sufficient for that. The general opinion is that it is much easier to secure income in urban areas, but fewer than half of those who retired in Lusaka were financially balanced or secure. Many of them were destitute and had nobody to look after them.

349 Urbanization and the organization of self-help housing in Lusaka.
Steve S. Mulenga, Annie M. Mubanga. *Vierteljahresberichte; Probleme der Entwicklungsländer*, no. 82 (1980), p. 393-401. bibliog.
This article is noteworthy because of its brief description of the Lusaka Housing Project Unit, which was set up with a World Bank loan in the 1970s to upgrade squatter settlements.

350 Planned spontaneous settlements: the importance of site and service projects in Lusaka.
Goodwin Nyau. *Vierteljahresberichte; Probleme der Entwicklungsländer*, no. 82 (1980), p. 375-93. map. bibliog.
This overview and discussion of Zambia's housing policy is colourful and combative. It contains references to the differences in traditional housing in various areas of Zambia as well as to Livingstone and Rhodes. Nyau defends site and service schemes against the complaint that these are ugly: 'Aesthetic judgement is simply a matter of taste and usually is dominated by middle class values' (p. 384). The article also contains much interesting information presented in the form of statistical tables.

351 Rural-urban migration in Zambia and migrant ties to home villages.
Mitsuo Ogura. *Developing Economies*, vol. 29, no. 2 (1991), p. 145-65. map.
The article starts with a brief general overview of migration and reports on a survey – undertaken in 1987 and 1989 – among inhabitants of Mufulira, a town in the Copperbelt, and Lusaka. The main conclusion is that present day migrants are far from circular migrants (that is, likely to return to their point of origin), but have firm roots in towns and live there for long periods of time. That does not mean that links with the villages from which they originate are unimportant. Even second-generation migrants retain close links to their village. The ideal of retirement to one's village is virtually universal.

352 The evolving phenomena of migration and urbanisation in Central Africa: a Zambian case.
Patrick O. Ohadike. In: *Town and country in Central and East Africa*. Edited by David Parkin. London: Oxford University Press, 1975, p. 126-45.
Ohadike conducted a survey in Lusaka during the years 1968 to 1969 in order to document the migration into the city. The results portray an extraordinary city: one that grew by twenty per cent in one year and in which 88.5 per cent of the established resident population was under fifteen years of age, and that changed from a city rooted in the east of the country to a city which drew migrants from all over the country.

353 Work attitudes and life goals of Zambian youth.
Kwaku Osei-Hwedie. *Journal of Social Development in Africa*,
vol. 6, no. 1 (1991), p. 63-73.

This survey among more than 1,100 young people (between ten and thirty-three years old) focuses on occupational preferences and life goals. An overwhelming majority of the respondents believed that personal abilities and good education lead to success in life as opposed to factors like family position (25.1 per cent) or witchcraft and medicines (9.8 per cent). Everyday experience of life in Zambia suggests different belief systems to many people.

354 The management of squatter upgrading: a case study of organisation, procedures and participation.
David Pasteur. Farnborough, England: Saxon House, 1979. 232p.
3 maps. bibliog.

There is no shortage of literature on squatter upgrading in Lusaka. This book distinguishes itself among such literature in its elaborate and detailed description of administrative procedure. It also bears the hallmark of documenting planning in action, as the study was carried out in 1977 while the programme was being implemented. Numerous administrative documents are reproduced as annexes. A telling example among these is a summary of administrative problems raised at a George Planning Workshop in January 1977.

355 Lusaka: management and institution building for squatter upgrading.
David Pasteur. In: *Urban innovation abroad: problem cities in search of solutions*. Edited by Thomas L. Blair. New York: Plenum Press, 1984, p. 112-27. bibliog.

This is a quite formal description of administrative structures and processes in Lusaka City Council's housing project unit as it grew during the 1970s. Pasteur argues strongly that its success is partly due to its loose relationship to the council. The bibliography is useful as it points the way towards several evaluation studies of squatter upgrading projects in the grey literature.

356 Urban food subsidies in the context of adjustment: the case of Zambia.
Richard Pearce. *Food Policy*, vol. 16, no. 6 (1991), p. 436-51.

In his first note, the author mentions earlier versions of the material presented here. There is also a later version of this evaluation of food subsidies administered by a coupon system (see item no. 585). It is interesting to note that in this earlier article he sees no possibility of reverting to the situation as it was before the introduction of food subsidies through coupons. This does not, however, remove his scepticism about targeting, and he stresses the need to have much better administrative capacity to apply such a scheme at all. The most vulnerable among the urban poor, he maintains, have not benefited.

357 The plight of street children in Zambia.
Jonathan Phiri. *African Insight*, vol. 26, no. 3 (1996), p. 276-82.
map.

The whole of this particular issue of the journal is devoted to street children in various African countries. This article has a clear structure: description, explanation and prevention. Most of the research material on which it is based dates from 1991, and the situation may have changed for the worse as the causes mentioned – population growth, AIDS and economic hardship – have spread. Phiri mentions the figure of 35,000 *mishanga* boys (a widely applied term which originally meant sellers of one cigarette at a time) and considers 350,000 children to be at risk. Surprisingly, many of the street children still have links to a house where they sleep. The distinguishing characteristic is that they make their living in the streets. This article reveals the type of poverty one finds in Zambia.

358 Upgrading in Chawama, Lusaka: displacement or differentiation?
Carol Rakodi. *Urban Studies*, vol. 25, no. 4 (1988), p. 319-33.

This is a highly recommended article for those interested in illegal or spontaneous (squatter) settlements in Zambia's cities. In the 1970s the policy towards such areas changed from considering them as blights which had to be removed to attempting to upgrade conditions there. This evaluation of one of these projects in Lusaka is particularly clearly structured around the main question that divided those concerned with improving the plight of the poor. Did upgrading mean that poor people were displaced from the area, as they could not raise the necessary money for improvements or for the service charges after improvements? Or did it imply the creation of a privileged class of house-owners who could then exploit others? The answer, according to Rakodi, is that there was displacement as people opted out because of resettlement cost, but it did not signify the emergence of more significant capitalist interests in housing markets.

359 Urban agriculture; research questions and Zambian evidence.
Carol Rakodi. *Journal of Modern African Studies*, vol. 26, no. 3 (1988), p. 495-515.

Urban agriculture has generally not been recognized as such, but has tended to be seen as an aberration on the urban landscape and penalized by administrators. This article argues that town planners should pay more attention to this sector, which is especially important for women and the poor. Rakodi stresses the need for more research before administrative action. The review of what has been ascertained about urban agriculture as part of the extensive research effort on illegal, spontaneous or squatter settlements in urban Zambia brings to light much that can be classified as 'grey' literature. The annotation of this article is therefore valuable for people who have a broader interest in urban studies than this particular topic.

360 Who gets what, where and how: a critical look at the housing policies in Zambia.
Biswapriya Sanyal. *Development and Change*, vol. 12, no. 3 (1981), p. 409-40.

The World Bank sponsored the research for this article, which has its origins in an early case of conditionality. An IMF loan was given in the mid 1970s on condition that Zambia should review its subsidies on housing. The study found, not surprisingly, that distribution of housing subsidies was extremely skewed: the higher people were in government employment, the bigger the subsidies on their housing. People at the lower levels got relatively little, and a large proportion of people were left out altogether. This documentation of an extremely regressive aspect of income inequalities in Zambia may have lost some of its validity during later periods of adjustment, but is still well worth noting.

361 George – the development of a squatter settlement in Lusaka, Zambia.

Ann Schlyter, Thomas Schlyter. Gävle, Sweden: The National Swedish Institute for Building Research, 1979. 256p. 9 maps. bibliog.

This is an exhaustive survey of a squatter area in Lusaka, carried out in three stages: 1969, 1973 and 1977. It is first and foremost a report written by town-planners/architects, which provides extremely detailed descriptions of the use of space and the construction of buildings. Intriguing facts are revealed. For example, in 1969 less than half of households had a table, while in 1977 nearly three out of four had one. Such observations give a tangible insight into the lives of poor people in Lusaka. The authors also pay ample attention to social and economic factors. An observation like the following has resonance with a wide audience: 'A myth, very hard to kill, about squatter areas is that they house a lot of unemployed. But in reality unemployment is very evenly distributed throughout Lusaka' (p. 33). The numerous photographs give an excellent idea of urban life in such areas and are informative for anybody who expects to come into contact with life in an area like George.

362 Upgrading reconsidered – the George studies in retrospect.

Ann Schlyter. Gävle, Sweden: The National Swedish Institute for Building Research, 1984. 114p. map. bibliog.

This is a logical follow up on the previous work undertaken by the author in George (see item no. 361). Most of the information presented comes from a follow up visit in 1982 and documents the changes brought about by a World Bank financed upgrading programme. This report is, however, above all a polemical review of what has been written about squatter upgrading, especially from a neo-marxist perspective of class differentiation. Schlyter's main conclusion is based on the actors' perspective: 'None of the groups in power was found to have had any special interest in the project, and no group other than the target group seems to have received any kinds of benefits' (p. 93). The drawings in the report are highly evocative and will spur people to read this closely argued book.

363 Recycled inequalities; youth and gender in George compound, Zambia.

Ann Schlyter. Uppsala, Sweden: Nordic Africa Institute, 1999. 135p. bibliog.

Anne Schlyter observed life in George compound over a period of more than thirty years and this is by far the most pessimistic of her publications. Whereas before she could feel a pioneering, independent and hopeful spirit in George, the picture she presents here is primarily one of alienated youth. For example: the party youth (associated with UNIP) used to be a source of moral order, but this had probably disappeared as far back as the late 1980s. As is found in other studies, homeowners do not sell their houses, but more people are renting, and multiple occupancy of the same space has increased. Poverty, youth and gender are the main themes and are treated with unsparing pessimism: Schlyter writes, for instance, that, 'violence towards young unmarried women in households was common and it was the brothers, cousins and uncles who battered, not the fathers' (p. 125).

364 From self-help housing to sustainable development; capitalist development and urban planning in Lusaka, Zambia.
John Tait.   Aldershot, England: Avebury, 1997. 377p. 6 maps. bibliog.

This book consists of three parts and only the second two are specific to Zambia. The first 150 pages are of a theoretical and general nature. Thereafter, Tait discusses the evolution of Zambian housing policies against the background of the country's historical development; in the third part he discusses the results of surveys undertaken in 1989 – updated on a return visit in 1995 – of two low-cost housing areas in Lusaka: Kalingalinga and Kanyama. The former benefited from a German-financed upgrading scheme, while the latter did not. As is to be expected in a marxist framework, Tait's concern is with the poor, and he considers urban upgrading schemes in Lusaka exemplary in the sense that they control upward filtering of housing stock and contain the emergence of a housing market (commodification). As other literature substantiates, people will let houses in urban Zambia, but they will be very reluctant to sell them. The survey results offer much more than that, however, and give penetrating insights into economic life in such areas. The book contains a virtually exhaustive overview of the relevant literature, and the bibliography therefore offers a good point of entry to the subject of housing and physical planning in Zambia.

365 Anticipating urban growth in Africa: land use and values in the rurban fringe of Lusaka, Zambia.
Leo M. van den Berg.   Lusaka: Zambian Geographical Association, 1984. 166p. 27 maps.

This book is organized around a theory of land values which will be of interest to few users of this bibliography but, while it is primarily a study of the growth of Lusaka, on reading it one gets a feel for the history of street names and neighbourhoods that are well known in Lusaka. Kabulonga, Twin Palm and Emmasdale all appear to be named after farms. The term 'rurban' denotes the mixture of urban and rural which is found on the edges of many urban areas, but more in Lusaka than elsewhere. The maps and aerial photographs are interpreted in an exemplary way and invite comparison with the actual situation as it is now.

366 Urban squatters: problem or solution.
Jaap van Velsen. In: *Town and country in Central and East Africa*.
Edited by David Parkin. London: Oxford University Press, 1975,
p. 294-307.
This is a wonderful article, which combines indignation with the sensible application of
the findings of social science research to a policy question. Van Velsen takes issue with
the common stereotype that the areas designated as squatter areas in urban centres contain
the loafers and the unemployed. Indeed, he objects to the use of these as synonyms. On
the contrary, the inhabitants of these areas are usually in employment and provide
essential services for the cities without receiving services in return.

Women

367 Gender and ngoma: the power of drums in Eastern Zambia.
Annette Drews. In: *The quest for fruition through ngoma.* Edited by Rijk van Dijk, Ria Reis, Marja Spierenburg. Oxford: James Currey Ltd, 2000, p. 39-61. bibliog.

The subject of this article is a female initiation ceremony, *chinamwali*, among the Kunda in Eastern Zambia. It is also structured as a healing ritual in the context of menstruation. Most of the article concerns a specific case: the *chinamwali* of Lucy. This event was a Christianized version of the initiation ceremony. Part of the occasion is the enactment of a sketch – entitled 'Smarty and the Fool' – in which the initiate is supposed to play the fool: 'Through the identification with the ridiculed fool, the initiate feels the shame put on such behaviour by the community' (p. 48). Drews' main concern is to show how gender identities are forged through such rituals. Initiates should be able 'to handle any man'.

368 Women and politics in Zambia: what difference has democracy made?
Anne E. Ferguson with Beatrice Liatto-Katundu. *African Rural and Urban Studies*, vol. 1, no. 2 (1994), p. 11-31. bibliog.

This is very much work in progress, but worthy of note nonetheless. The women's wings of political parties may be on the decline since the re-introduction of multipartyism, but, while the 1991 changes may have marginalized women as there were no longer reserved political positions for them, they also afforded professional and wealthy women new opportunities to become active through non-governmental organizations (NGOs). It has been argued that – as homemakers – women especially feel the brunt of structural adjustment. However, in this paper much support among women for economic reform is noted.

369   Who is losing out? Structural adjustment, gender and the agricultural sector in Zambia.
Gisela Geisler.   *Journal of Modern African Studies*, vol. 30, no. 1 (1992), p. 113-39.
A shift away from the growing of hybrid maize is the central subject of this article. The main reasons for the shift are mismanagement of agricultural marketing in the Kaunda period and the collapse of large parts of the marketing system after liberalization. Geisler notes the marginalization of small farmers in Zambia as a result. The article speculates on how a switch to other crops may influence decision making and power within the household. The article was written before the full impact of liberalization in the Chiluba period was felt and may therefore be dated. The author herself admits that, 'It remains to be seen how further liberalization will actually benefit the majority of the peasants'.

370   New women of Lusaka.
Ilsa M. Glazer Schuster.   Palo Alto, California: Mayfield Publishing Company, 1979. 209p. 3 maps. bibliog.
This book tends to polarize reaction. People consider it either a raw but true picture of a group of women in Lusaka during the seventies (for example, Professor A.E. Epstein in his foreword), or an offending caricature (for example, Luise White, who wrote on Nairobi prostitutes). The reason for this is the overwhelming place given to sex in these women's lives and the emphasis placed on the way in which they are imprisoned in oppressive relationships. For example, it is claimed that if a woman lacks the courage, social skill and good judgement of character to refuse a man's demand for sexual intercourse, the pattern of exploitation, self interest and lack of trust will exist from the first moment a couple decides to marry (pages 89 and 133). The book lacks a precise scholarly frame and is often suggestively written. Despite that, there are less spectacular impressions and observations which are worth noting. For example, the authorities claim that women invite rape by their dress and by being out at night. In official discourse, the moral danger is not seen as coming from males in high places, while these play an essential role in Glazer Schuster's account. See also 'Perspectives in development: the problem of nurses and nursing in Zambia' by the same author (*Journal of Development Studies*, vol. 17, no. 3 [1981], p. 77-97).

371   Alcohol and politics in urban Zambia: the intersection of gender and class.
Ilsa M. Glazer.   In: *African feminism: the politics of survival in Sub-Saharan Africa.*   Edited by Gwendolyn Mikell.   Philadelphia: University of Pennsylvania Press, 1997, p. 142-58. bibliog.
Beer is a vital ingredient in Zambian social life, and therefore this article is highly topical. It contains general observations about beer, urban life, class distinctions and, above all, gender relations, but it is not a detailed, disciplined ethnography. It is, rather, a useful introduction to the social rules surrounding beer. For that reason, it is particularly useful for new researchers, but it also gives an orientation to anybody about to venture into urban Zambia. The article is entertaining: for example it reveals that one kind of particularly strong beer is called '*kantankamaninueko*' meaning 'go and stagger somewhere far'. Glazer maintains that the return of multipartyism was accompanied by a lower consumption of government brew.

372 **Marriage and medicine: women's search for love and luck.**
Bonnie B. Keller. *African Social Research*, no. 26 (1978),
p. 489-505. bibliog.
Marriage by elopement.
Bonnie B. Keller. *African Social Research*, no. 27 (1979),
p. 565-85. bibliog.

Both these articles are based on research in Mazabuka, a town some 125 km south of
Lusaka. The first article describes how women resort to magical substances in order to
influence their vulnerable position with respect to men. Bonnie Keller found less concrete
evidence that women use medicines to threaten a man's virility. The article on marriage
by elopement is also based on research in Mazabuka, where Keller studied fifty local
court cases. She argues that elopement – setting up house without negotiations between
the families – is a recent phenomenon, which is sometimes encouraged by the parents.
She depicts quite a complicated set of games surrounding this phenomenon.

373 **Woman know your place; the patriarchal message in Zambian
popular song.**
Edited by Sara Longwe, Roy Clarke. Lusaka: Zambian Association
for Research and Development (ZARD), 1998. 269p.

Most of this book is composed of song texts in various Zambian languages and their
English translation. They cover subjects which give an inside view of relations between
the sexes in Zambia. The scope of topics they cover is large: staying in the village while
the husband is in town; the unexpected wife in town; the child of Indian-African descent;
drinking husbands; and so on. Some typical song lines are, 'Let me finish building my
house in Lusaka'; 'Don't ask me for marriage in this *kachasu* [locally distilled liquor]
house'; 'Why did he propose to me when he had a wife at home?'. An analysis of the
content and context precedes the texts of the songs.

374 **Social and physical living conditions of nannies in high cost
residential areas of Lusaka, Zambia.**
Mubiana Macwang'i. In: *Gender research on urbanization,
planning, housing and everyday life.* Edited by Sylvia Sithole
Fundire, Agnes Zhou, Anita Carlsson, Anne Schlyter. Harare:
Zimbabwe Women's Resource Centre and Network, 1995, p. 185-95.

This minor paper deserves attention because of the originality of its subject. It offers a
number of research findings which bring out the plight of women employed as nannies:
'The majority (seventy-nine per cent) share a sleeping room with two or more people,
often children, and sometimes they have to give up their shared space for visitors'
(p. 191).

375 Women and the state: Zambia's development policies and their impact on women.

Monica L. Munachonga. In: *Women and the state in Africa.* Edited by Jane L. Parpart, Kathleen A. Staudt. Boulder, Colorado: Lynne Reiner Publishers, 1989, p. 130-43. bibliog.

This article will not be of much relevance outside the circle of those who have an exhaustive interest in Zambian gender issues. Certain aspects of it are worth noting, however. It contains informative material on the distribution of top government and party posts by sex (1974 to 1983) which indicates that women's participation there was minimal. It also documents some rather early feminist activism in Zambia in the form of the Women's League.

376 Women and development in Zambia.

Monica Munachonga. In: *Women and development in Africa.* Edited by Jane L. Parpart. Lanham, Maryland: University Press of America, 1989, p. 279-313. bibliog.

The title of this article is misleading. The kernel of the paper is research carried out into changes in the meaning of marriage since independence. The article gives a good overview of the relevant legislation. The research tries to understand how people decide on either a European-style wedding, governed by codified law (before the ordinance) or a 'traditional' marriage which is far less governed by written law. It documents telling pronouncements such as the opinion of a magistrate that widows who are plundered by their late husband's relatives have themselves to blame, because they have forsaken their 'traditional' duties. Another important finding is that virtually all couples who marry before the ordinance fulfil also customary obligations at the time of marriage.

377 Women as food producers and suppliers in the twentieth century.

Shimwaayi Muntemba. *Development Dialogue,* nos. 1-2 (1982), p. 29-50.

The Zambian case is only introduced in this article from page 37 onwards. Then follows a bird's eye historical overview from the pre-colonial situation to the neo-colonial situation, 1964 to 1981. The general conclusion is that the position of women has deteriorated and the author deduces from this conclusions for policy: 'Women must be conscientized to challenge the sexual division of labour' (p. 48). Perhaps the most interesting information is to be found on page 45, where Muntemba argues strongly that land shortage is a problem in Zambia for women. This runs contrary to the persistent opinion that there is plenty of land in Zambia.

378 Women and AIDS in rural Africa.

Genevieve Mwale, Philip Burnard. Aldershot, England: Avebury, 1992. 127p. bibliog.

The fourth chapter of this work, 'The women's views', is the longest at forty pages. The book is more a collection of opinions than a placing of AIDS in the worldviews characteristic of the society under study. The remarks quoted are sometimes too gratuitous. For example, it is claimed that formerly, 'after the initiation ceremony the young girls were not promiscuous at all...now the children don't listen, that is why the

AIDS number is rising' (p. 78). It is, of course, a sentiment of every generation that formerly people were more moral.

379 Listening to the girl child. Voices for change and redress in primary education in Zambia.
Dickson Mwansa. Lusaka: Government of the Republic of Zambia, Ministry of Education and UNICEF, 1995. 43p. bibliog.

This research was commissioned to obtain an insight into the differing expectations applying to girls as compared to boys in education. This report consists therefore mainly of opinions which are related to attitudes. It contains important sections on teenage pregnancies, sexual abuse and initiation rites. The primary recommendation of the report is for sex education. The bibliography gives a good first access to the substantial grey literature on gender in Zambia.

380 Globalisation and the making of consumers: Zambian kitchen parties.
Thera Rasing.   In: *Modernity on a shoestring: dimensions of globalisation, consumption and development in Africa and beyond.* Edited by Richard Fardon, Wim van Binsbergen, Rijk van Dijk. Leiden, The Netherlands: EIDOS; African Studies Centre; London: Centre of African Studies London, 1999, p. 227-45. bibliog.

Kitchen parties are part of the wedding ceremony mainly among urban and upper class Zambians. They are the female equivalent of the stag night, which in Zambia is also rooted in practices of local societies. The article contains a short, detailed ethnographic account of kitchen parties (p. 228-30), and the rest of the article consists mainly of interpretations and theoretical reflections.

381 Responsible men and provocative women: an analysis of gendered domestic homicide in Zambia.
Darlene Rude.   *Journal of Southern African Studies*, vol. 25, no. 1 (1999), p. 7-29.

This horrifying, richly documented article deals with the dark side of Zambian social life. The YWCA in Lusaka kept a 'Femicide Register' to document gendered domestic homicide in Zambia. The period covered in this study extends from the late 1980s to 1996. The article is based on 150 cases, most of which (125) were garnered from the press. This is not an exhaustive examination: some 350 cases were on the register. Domestic violence appears to be perpetrated by men of all ages and social classes, from all parts of Zambia. The victims are mostly women of childbearing age. Newspaper accounts tend to be silent on the position of the victim: she is barely mentioned, while the judiciary tends, according to the newspaper accounts, to assume that the men were provoked.

382 Women householders and housing strategies; the case of George, Zambia.
Ann Schlyter. Gävle, Sweden: The National Swedish Institute for Building Research, 1988. 156p. 2 maps. bibliog.

Schlyter's work on George compound (see item nos. 361, 362, 363) always had a gender aspect. This particular work is the product of a follow-up study to George in 1985 which was part of a wider research project into the position of women in urban Southern Africa. It is as much to be recommended as her other work. In addition, here, one gets a feeling of 'hands-on' observation, despite the use of the bureaucratic paragraphing format. The wealth of detail makes it difficult to distil her work, but Schlyter's observation, that women in George were all convinced to stay in town as they had nothing to go back to, illustrates the rich insights to be found here. Women in employment, who had a relatively high income, preferred to rent, while the low-income and illiterate women were desperate for a place of their own. This runs counter to a considerable number of commonly held beliefs about housing.

383 Beyond inequalities; women in Zambia.
Mercy Siame, Nakatiwa Mulukita, Sara Longwe, Roy Clarke. Lusaka: Zambia Association for Research and Development (ZARD), 1998. 104p. bibliog.

In this publication, ZARD presents a situation analysis of the position of women in Zambia. Gender gaps in education, market participation, division of labour and earnings, school enrolments, education, etc., are elaborately documented. There is also a large section devoted to kinship and the nature of marriage in Zambia. This very readable report is, above all, informative. This is not a bland book, however, as all four authors have outspoken views: 'In effect, men are licenced as sexual predators'. The situation analysis results in policy recommendations after a review of current policies.

384 Documenting women's views through participatory research: diaries of daily activities in rural Zambia.
Else Skjønsberg. In: *Women wielding the hoe; lessons from rural Africa for feminist theory and development practice.* Edited by Deborah Fahy Bryceson. Oxford: Berg Publishers, 1995, p. 225-37.

This is primarily a methodological article advocating time allocating studies among rural women through participatory research. The research is situated in a village in Eastern Province, but a precise location is not given; nor is there an ethnic identification of the village. The article is more to be read for the casual insight and revealing remarks than for its substantive content. The interesting sections refer more to what is being researched than to research methods. This quote from a female informant is particularly salient to the study of sexuality in Africa: 'So when a man and a woman meet in the bush and that is what they do when they want to love each other, or the woman needs the man's money, they take care that nobody sees them. They don't want to trouble their friends'.

Health

385 A study of maternal mortality at the University Teaching Hospital, Lusaka, Zambia: the emergence of tuberculosis as a major non-obstetric cause of maternal death.
Yusuf Ahmed, P. Mwaba, C. Chintu, J.M. Grange, A. Ustianowski, A. Zumla. *International Journal of Tuberculosis and Lung Disease*, vol. 33, no. 8 (1999), p. 675-80.

This article focuses on three important aspects of health in Zambia: maternal mortality, tuberculosis and AIDS. Its findings are that maternal mortality has increased eightfold in the past two decades, but that this is due to a large extent to non-obstetric causes (fifty-eight per cent of the cases), especially tuberculosis and respiratory diseases. AIDS was closely related to the latter. In the case of tuberculosis, ninety-two per cent of the patients were HIV positive.

386 The referral process and urban health care in sub-Saharan Africa: the case of Lusaka, Zambia.
Sarah Atkinson, A. Ngwengwe, M. Macwang'I, T.J. Ngulube, T. Harpham, A. O'Connell. *Social Science and Medicine*, vol. 49, no. 1 (1999), p. 27-38.

A good referral system, which ensures that only the most serious patients are seen at the higher-level hospitals, is an effective way to decongest the health service. This research – carried out in Lusaka – showed that people bypassed the lower levels because they expected the main hospital to be better supplied with drugs and to be cheaper. It appeared that few patients were given enough information about their diagnosis to make it clear whether or not they should be referred. Other findings were incidental to this research, but revealing for the social context of medical care. The most striking result was the degree of unmet need for health services and the large number of individuals who were self-medicating due to lack of money rather than the minor nature of their illness.

387 A systematic approach to the development of a rational malaria treatment policy in Zambia.
L.M. Barat, B. Himonga, S. Nkunika, M. Ettling, T.K. Ruebush, W. Kapelwa, P.B. Boland. *Tropical Medicine and International Health*, vol. 3, no. 7 (1998), p. 535-42.

Malaria is one of the major causes of death in Zambia. This is a technical article on malaria resistance to drugs. Chloroquine, it is reported, appears to have lost its efficacy and alternative treatment is proposed. The nature of this article – covering, as it does, malaria treatment for the whole of Zambia – may give non-medical people a good introduction to the subject.

388 Severe anaemia in Zambian children with *Plasmodium falciparum* malaria.
G. Biemba, D. Dolmans, P.E. Thuma, G. Weiss, V.R. Gordeuk. *Tropical Medicine and International Health*, vol. 5 no. 1 (2000), p. 9-16.

Malaria is especially dangerous for children, and cerebral malaria is considered more dangerous than other forms. This study compares children with anaemia caused by malaria and children with cerebral malaria. The case fatality rate of severe malarial anaemia was about half that of cerebral malaria but, because severe malarial anaemia was more common, these two forms of complicated malaria were implicated in similar numbers of in-hospital paediatric deaths.

389 Seizures in rural Zambia.
G.L. Birbeck. *Epilepsia*, vol. 41, no. 3 (2000), p. 277-81.

Seizures, fits, spells and fainting were common in a population of patients who were admitted to Chikankata hospital in rural Zambia. Epilepsy, it appeared, was being underreported, underrecognized, and undertreated. Epilepsy patients received treatment primarily from traditional healers; only thirty-one per cent reported ever receiving anti-epileptic drugs. Among those who had received such treatment, drugs were frequently underdosed. This article raises important issues about the efficacy of 'traditional healers' versus modern medicine.

390 Coping with cost recovery; a study of the social impact and responses to cost recovery in basic services (health and education) in poor communities in Zambia.
David Booth, John Milimo, Ginny Bond, Silverio Chimuka, Mulako Nabanda, Kwibisa Liywalii, Monde Mwalusi, Mulako Mwnyamwale, Edward Mwanza, Lizzie Peme, Agatha Zulu. Stockholm: Swedish International Development Co-operation Agency, 1995/96. 122p. map. bibliog.

This report is the product of rapid interactive social research on the following sites: Litoya and Mongu in Western Province; Jumbe in Eastern Province; Chiawa in Lusaka Province (rural); Twapia in Ndola (urban). The research is policy-oriented, but it contains insights of wider significance. The authors' findings on the heterogeneity of the wealthy and the poor within these communities (based on wealth ranking) are especially significant.

Communities are all too often merely designated as either poor or rich. The writers' general conclusion is that, in a context of declining use of public facilities as the quality of services deteriorates, there will be further decline because of the introduction of user charges.

391 Caring for people with HIV in Zambia: are traditional healers and formal health workers willing to work together?
A. Burnett, R. Baggaley, M. Ndovi-MacMillan, J. Sulwe, B. Hang'omba, J. Bennett. *AIDS Care*, vol. 11, no. 4 (1999), p. 481-91.

Traditional healers and workers in the formal health sector were brought together for this article to see how much knowledge they had about AIDS, how they were treating AIDS patients, and how far they could co-operate in treatment and care. The results showed serious misunderstandings. Twenty healers (fifty-one per cent) and four formal health workers (fifteen per cent) claimed a cure existed for AIDS. The majority of traditional healers interviewed claimed difficulties in discussing a diagnosis of HIV directly with patients, mainly due to fear of the patient becoming depressed and suicidal. Formal health workers said that it was difficult for them as well, but less so than for traditional healers. There was a widespread desire for co-operation among the two groups. The suggestion was made that condoms should be distributed through traditional healers.

392 Health-seeking behaviour of patients with sexually transmitted diseases in Zambia.
E. Faxelid, B.M. Ahlberg, J. Ndulo, I. Krantz. *East African Medical Journal*, vol. 75, no. 4 (1998), p. 232-36.

The aim of this paper is to describe health-seeking behaviour, the period with symptoms and sexual activity during the symptom period among patients attending the public health sector for treatment of a sexually transmitted disease (STD). The article reports the result of a survey carried out among young people who came to health centres in both an urban and a rural environment. The study was conducted at two urban health centres and at one rural mission hospital during four months in 1994 and 1995. Sixty per cent of the patients in the urban setting and fifty per cent in the rural setting had taken some kind of medicine before they came to the clinic. Market places, other clinics and doctors, friends and relatives were common treatment sources. Ten per cent of patients had received medicine from a traditional healer. The patients had mostly experienced STD symptoms for one to two weeks before coming to the clinic for treatment. One finding of this study is particularly striking in the light of the AIDS pandemic: sex during periods while STD symptoms are exhibited is common.

393 The patients of traditional doctors in Lusaka.
Joyce Leeson, Ronald Frankenberg. *African Social Research*, no. 23 (1977), p. 217-34.

This was quite an innovative piece of research at the time, and it deserves attention now that healing has become a major subject for anthropologists. The authors compare the patients who visited a Western-trained private doctor with patients of *ng'angas* (traditional doctors). Differences between the two groups of patients cannot be explained by payment for treatment as medical care was on a private basis in both instances. Both require payment and that factor is thus excluded. Both doctors have different caseloads, with cases dealing with mental health problems (absent in the surgery of the Western-trained doctor) and infertility prominent in the case of the *ng'anga*. The authors' main characterization of the *ng'anga*'s patients deserves to be taken into consideration in present-day studies of the subject: they tend to have chronic problems and to have first sought help in the modern sector; they are thus survivors who have not immediately been felled by the disease.

394 Health partnerships in Zambia.
John T. Milimo. *IDS Bulletin*, vol. 31, no. 1 (2000), p. 43-48.
This is a succinct description of the organizational structure of health care in Zambia after the attempt to decentralize. The neighbourhood committee is seen as the cornerstone for participation and, according to Milimo, it has rapidly gained trust among the poor.

395 Report of a joint evaluation of primary health care in the Republic of Zambia.
Ministry of Health of the Government of Zambia; World Health Organization; United Nations Children's Fund. Lusaka: Ministry of Health of the Government of Zambia; World Health Organization; United Nations Children's Fund, 1984. 124p. map.
This evaluation concerns itself specifically with the evaluation of programmes intended to deal with maternal and child health, malaria, sexually transmitted diseases, etc. It contains therefore a substantial amount of valuable epidemiological data. Administrative and management factors dominate the recommendations, however: the first main recommendation is for further decentralization.

396 Deliberations of the committee selected to study the World Bank's recommendations in draft report no. 4715-ZA on population, health and nutrition.
National Commission for Development Planning. Lusaka: National Commission for Development Planning, 1984. 91p.
This report refers to the World Bank study mentioned in item no. 400. It has the blandness which tends to characterize writing by bureaucrats. To give one example, 'It was recommended that the relationships between the demographic characteristics and development should be determined, or establish relationships between socio-economic factors and institutional arrangements and processes etc.' (p. 83). It is nonetheless worth noting for two reasons: firstly, the discussion on population growth and a national population policy; secondly, the discussion on user charges, as financing the health service remains a crucial issue.

397 Child growth and duration of breast feeding in urban Zambia.
N.H. Ng'andu, T.E. Watts. *Journal of Epidemiology and Community Health*, vol. 44, no. 4 (1990), p. 281-85.
Malnutrition is one of the main causes of child mortality in Zambia. This article reports on a survey of a sample of 438 children in Lusaka on the effects of breastfeeding practices on child growth. The findings suggest that, in this community, duration of breastfeeding is strongly associated with the linear (i.e., uninterrupted and gradual) growth of children, and the association changes with the infant's age. The beneficial effects of breastfeeding

disappeared after two years. One strong risk factor suspected to be responsible for the poor growth performance of children in this study is the low nutritional quality of the weaning foods which are used to supplement breast milk during the lengthy weaning period.

398 A study of the factors associated with maternal mortality in Zambia.
Buloti G. Nsemukila (principal investigator). Lusaka: Government of the Republic of Zambia: Ministry of Health and UNFPA. 185p. bibliog. 2 maps.

This study is of course primarily of interest to health personnel. However, maternal mortality is also used as a prime indicator of poverty. This study refers extensively to social status, which is also measured by more indirect means such as the source of water supply or toilet facilities. It is not surprising that the lower the socio-economic status, the higher the maternal mortality. Health professionals will be challenged to explain why most of the maternal mortality is after labour (60.7 per cent) and why almost half of it occurs in a health institution (49.6 per cent). The geographical spread is puzzling: why is the situation in Eastern Province so much worse than elsewhere? There is a last chapter on socio-cultural beliefs in which much use has been made of focus group research: in this context, marital infidelity is seen as a major cause of difficulties in labour and maternal mortality.

399 An assessment of the nutrition situation in Zambia for planning nutrition interventions.
Linda M. Perez. Eschborn, West Germany: German Agency for Technical Cooperation (GTZ), 1984. 105p. bibliog.

This is the first volume of a report commissioned by the GTZ to make proposals for a project in nutrition. The second volume is only of interest to specialist administrators, but this volume contains much information. It gives a comprehensive overview of government interventions and programmes in the field. However, its special value lies in the attention it pays to poverty, which is nowadays a major focus for policy making. It tabulates many health indicators classified by province and records major differences. For example: Luapula Province scores 185 on an index which takes Zambia as 100. Southern Province in contrast scores 68.6. The last part of the report is a detailed discussion of the situation in Luapula. These data have to be treated with some caution, as within quite small areas in Zambia there can be huge variations in this respect.

400 Zambia: population, health and nutrition sector review.
Population, Health and Nutrition Department of the World Bank. Washington, DC: Population, Health and Nutrition Department of the World Bank, 1984. 88p.

This is a policy document in which most of the problems that plagued the Zambian health service in preceding decades were identified. It is therefore useful reading as a background to later reforms in the sector. For example, it singles out centralization as a major problem, and in the 1990s decentralization was the major stated element of Zambia's health policy. It may be a sobering thought that decentralization of primary health care was already a stated policy as early as 1981. The section on nutrition stresses in particular links with agricultural policies. The policy analysis in the paper stresses mostly management and administration – this is also reflected in the statistical tables.

401 Evaluation of primary health care in the republic of Zambia.
Kåre Tønnesen. Lusaka: Ministry of Health; Government of the Republic of Zambia, 1986. 80p. map.

This evaluation gives remarkable insights into the deficiencies of the health service at its lowest levels. For example forty-three per cent of refrigerators in health service facilities were not working and eighteen per cent of those working were at the wrong temperature. Twenty per cent of trained community health workers had dropped out. Only sixty per cent of community health workers gave a satisfactory reply to a question on the dosage of malaria medication. The report ends with a list of the recommendations from the 1984 evaluation, indicating to what degree they had been implemented.

402 The professionalisation of indigenous medicine; a comparative study of Ghana and Zambia.
Patrick A. Twumasi, Dennis Michael Warren. In: *The professionalisation of African medicine*. Edited by Murray Last, Gordon Chavunduka. Manchester, England: Manchester University Press, 1986, p. 117-37. bibliog.

Pages 125-32 of this article are specifically devoted to Zambia and contain references to documents which are rarely discussed. One is the Witchcraft Ordinance of 1967 and the second is the report of the traditional healers' conference in Mulungushi hall of 1977, organized by the Ministry of Health. Both try to distinguish good from bad doctors.

403 User fees: what did the health reforms in Zambia achieve?
Sjaak van der Geest, Mubiana Macwang'i, Jolly Kamwanga, Dennis Mulikelela, Arthur Mazimba, Mundia Mwangelwa. *Health Policy and Planning*, vol. 15, no. 1 (2000), p. 59-66.

This article reports on qualitative research carried out in Lusaka and in Western Province as to the effects of health sector reforms in Zambia. The general tenor is pessimistic, but it is difficult to summarize the diversity of opinions reported here. For example, it is stated that the availability of drugs rather than more preventive health concerns was still the acid test by which the health system was judged. People did not object to paying user fees as such, but did object if it did not make a difference to the quality of service rendered.

404 Attitudes to 'kaponya mafumo': the terminators of pregnancy in urban Zambia.
D. Webb. *Health Policy and Planning*, vol. 15, no. 2 (2000), p. 186-93.

This study was carried out among adolescents in urban Zambia, among whom pregnancies were said to be a common occurrence. An estimated two-thirds of unwanted pregnancies ended in unsafe abortions. The abortions were mostly carried out by the girl herself or with the assistance of other non-medical personnel. Formal health institutions were avoided because of the lack of privacy and confidentiality. An overdose of chloroquine was by far the most widely used way to abort. The decision on whether to abort or not was primarily determined by the reaction of the boyfriend: his willingness to accept not only paternity, but also the associated financial implications.

405 Endemic malaria, malnutrition and child deaths.
Robert W. Wenlock. *Food Policy*, vol. 6, no. 2 (1981), p. 105-13. 2 maps.

Wenlock reports on a nationwide survey, the aim of which was to determine the relative importance of malnutrition and malaria in child mortality. He argues that it may be better to target malaria rather than nutrition to reduce child mortality. One of the arguments is that, as malaria reduces the food intake, the nutritional status of the sufferer often becomes critical as a result of malaria rather than through other causes.

Politics

406 Unions, parties and political development: a study of mineworkers in Zambia.
Robert H. Bates. New Haven, Connecticut: Yale University Press, 1971. 291p. bibliog.

As far back as the 1950s, Epstein saw the nationalist party and the trade unions as rival organizations on the Copperbelt. Their rivalry is the main theme in this book, which documents how this fight for a legitimate sphere of influence continued after independence. The party in government claims to represent national interests, which clash with the interests of the mineworkers represented by the unions; the latter are depicted by the government as partial. Much of the debate centres on wages and is now outdated, but this book is extremely valuable in documenting the tensions between unions and the nationalist party. More than wage policy was at stake: the struggle was also about the question of whether an independent entity – apart from a political party – could legitimately exist. Chapter 7, 'The Union and the Party', can be especially recommended as it deals specifically with that issue. The trade union movement appears to be a force which is difficult to contain in Zambian society, and it is not surprising that a trade unionist – the MMD president, Chiluba – played a major role in bringing down the one-party state. The conflict may be less visible since 1991, but it probably still exists. The book is a pleasure to read: Bates obviously knew many people in the populations studied here, and he writes engagingly about them.

407 The rise of the Zambian capitalist class in the 1970s.
Carolyn L. Baylies, Morris Szeftel. *Journal of Southern African Studies*, vol. 7, no. 2 (1981), p. 135-65.

The rise of a new Zambian owning class is a theme that diffuses the work of Baylies and Szeftel. In this article they bring together their insights gained in several research contexts. Their main thesis is that the beneficiaries of new avenues of wealth were not the existing petty bourgeoisie, but rather the incumbents of high political office or high salaried positions. Although they stress the importance of politics for capital formation, they do not argue that there is an unambiguous overlap between ownership of capital and political position. The article would be improved if they had brought out explicitly the speculative nature of many of their theses. Evidence exists that those in high positions in the state attempt to accumulate capital, but the question arises as to whether this attempt is successful. Owning land, for example, is one thing, but productive farming is another matter.

408   The rise and fall of multi-party politics in Zambia.
Carolyn Baylies, Morris Szeftel.   *Review of African Political Economy*, no. 54, (July 1992), p. 75-92.
This article is an account of the reintroduction of multipartyism in Africa from a neo-marxist perspective. It stresses in its analysis the groups involved in the protest against one-partyism and UNIP and their economic roots. For example, a broad national consensus legitimized the place of prominent bourgeois figures in the party's leadership. The nature of Zambia's underdevelopment and its relationship with international capital is a constant factor in the background of their analysis. The article ends with a gloomy prediction: MMD seems set to reproduce rather than replace UNIP. The article notes the low turnout in comparison with earlier elections, a concern which was again important in the 1996 elections.

409   The 1996 Zambian elections: still awaiting democratic consolidation.
Carolyn Baylies, Morris Szeftel.   *Review of African Political Economy*, vol. 24, no. 71 (1997), p. 113-28.
This is a mainly descriptive article about the elections, including an overview of election results, in the context of events preceding the elections and the immediate aftermath. The authors' conclusion is that these elections should have been a triumph for the MMD government. Instead the Chiluba government found itself at loggerheads with the opposition and the foreign donor community, which disputed its democratic credentials. The article is sympathetic to the opposition and the imposition of conditions by donors.

410   Democratization and the 1991 elections in Zambia.
Carolyn Baylies, Morris Szeftel.   In: *Voting for democracy: watershed elections in contemporary Anglophone Africa.*   Edited by John Daneel, Roger Southall, Morris Szeftel.   Aldershot, England: Ashgate Publishing Ltd, 1999, p. 83-110. bibliog.
Although the title does not suggest it, the 1996 elections are also discussed in this article. It is something of a latecomer among the several articles on Zambian elections. Szeftel and Baylies have written several of these, and their main concerns here also are class formation and political apathy. As regards the former, their belief that unionists and local capitalists were the main beneficiaries in the one-party state but nevertheless turned against it, is intriguing and contentious. They accept rather uncritically Derrick Chitala's estimation that levels of the disenfranchised – mainly youth – were as high as fifty per cent. Chitala, a relatively young opposition politician, can be considered partial. However, the authors conclude that, 'democracy and elections are something that have happened to someone else as far as a large part of the population is concerned' (p. 101).

411 Observing multiparty elections in Africa: lessons from Zambia.
Eric Bjornlund, Michael Bratton, Clark Gibson. *African Affairs*,
vol. 91, no. 364 (1992), p. 405-33.

The authors were observers at the 1991 general elections, which reintroduced multiparty politics. Their article documents the issues involved in observing and monitoring the elections. It deals especially with the technicalities of organizing and observing the elections and brings out well some contentious issues. It stresses the complementary nature of international observation to the local political process and notes, for example, the significance of constitutional bodies such as the courts, electoral commission, etc., in the transformation. It provides detailed information on inadequate voter registration, an issue which also played a major role in the 1996 elections.

412 The local politics of rural development; peasant and party-state in Zambia.
Michael Bratton. Hanover, New Hampshire: University Press of
New England, 1980. 334p. 6 maps. bibliog.

This is a detailed study of rural grass-roots politics in the 1970s, the heyday of the one-party state. UNIP always claimed to be a one-party participatory democracy, and the participatory organs at the grass roots – Village and Ward Committees – are central in this study. The study focuses on Kasama district, and two villages which were involved in government sponsored regrouping schemes are described in detail. According to Bratton, the party had atrophied since independence, but the participatory organs, especially at ward level, were more institutionalized than they may have seemed at the time; this argument is summarized on pages 272-74. Class consciousness has not entered these political arenas to any significant extent, despite growing inequalities, and patron-client relationships dominate. This book is of interest to political scientists who will, for example, find a detailed description of village leadership (p. 81-92). It is also of interest to a wider audience wishing to form a general impression of grass-roots politics in Zambia.

413 Economic crisis and political realignment in Zambia.
Michael Bratton. In: *Economic change and political liberalization
in Sub-Saharan Africa*. Edited by Jennifer A. Widner. Baltimore,
Maryland: The John Hopkins University Press, 1994, p. 101-28.

The main point made by Bratton is that patronage politics runs out of steam when there are no resources to redistribute. He stresses the economic content of MMD opposition to UNIP and brings out the liberal anti-state interventionist nature of MMD's programme. The electorate, however, laid the blame for the poor economic situation on corrupt leadership rather than ill advised economic policies. The article ends on a cautionary note that the victory of MMD does not necessarily mean an end to patronage politics.

414 Political participation in a new democracy: institutional considerations from Zambia.
Michael Bratton. *Comparative Political Studies*, vol. 32, no. 5
(1999), p. 549-88.

The thesis developed in this article is that democratic consolidation is best conceived as a process of reciprocal co-determination between institution building and cultural change.

This may be opaque language for many, but there are also more transparent conclusions in this article, which emanates from survey research carried out in 1993. The most notable finding is that respondents on different income levels were generally likely to display similar levels of political participation. This finding is contrary to the usual situation where the wealthy account for a disproportionate amount of political participation.

415 A focus group assessment of political attitudes in Zambia.
Michael Bratton, Beatrice Liatto-Katundu. *African Affairs*, vol. 93, no. 373 (1994), p. 535-65.

This article represents an attempt to use intensive structured discussion to identify the political attitudes of ordinary people towards politics after democratization. The main conclusion is that the political culture of single party rule has inculcated habits of obedience and dependence that have an inertia of their own. On the other hand, the authors note that the moderate levels of political trust which they found can be healthy in a democracy. Interesting insights are revealed in a short section on economic policy matters. Respondents had only speculative ideas about where government got its money, stating, for example, that, 'we think it comes from overseas'.

416 A first look at second elections in Africa, with illustrations from Zambia.
Michael Bratton, Dan Posner. In: *State conflict and democracy in Africa*. Edited by Richard Joseph. Boulder, Colorado: Lynn Rienner, 1999, p. 377-409.

The starting point of the authors is the question of whether the second set of elections after democratization will show the fragility of democracy or a deepening of the democratic process. They give an overview of the Zambian 1996 elections against this background and their conclusions are ambivalent: 'At the end of 1996, democracy was barely surviving in Zambia and its future did not look promising' (p. 403). But they also write that, 'With few exceptions, second elections (Zambia's included) also confirm that polling procedures and vote counting are not the principal sources of electoral malpractice in Zambia' (p. 404).

417 The politics of poverty and the poverty of politics in Zambia's third republic.
Peter Burnell. *Third World Quarterly*, vol. 16, no. 4 (1995), p. 675-91.

This is a wide ranging essay which displays a high level of generality. It is therefore difficult to summarize. Some quotations may convey its nature: 'The poor are a large but widely distributed and variegated group', therefore they are 'vulnerable to sectional and provincial politicking' (p. 681); or, 'The classical liberal argument that individual freedom is the wellspring of progress in society is well understood by President Chiluba' (p. 684).

418 The significance of the December 1998 local elections in Zambia and their aftermath.

Peter Burnell. *Journal of Commonwealth and Comparative Politics*, vol. 38, no. 1 (2000), p. 1-20.

Zambia has already held two local government elections since 1991. This is remarkable as democratization at the central level in Africa is not automatically followed by democratization at the local level. Therefore this article is a useful study. It gives the election results (MMD won overwhelmingly) and discusses the major themes surrounding the election: opposition parties and NGOs did not declare it free and fair. Burnell gives quite a balanced judgement and offers political speculation, especially about the succession of Chiluba. Burnell did not discuss what may be the most important event in these local elections: Kaunda's speech in Luanshya where he built up considerable sympathy among miners and ex-miners who were disgruntled about privatization. This was followed by a visit by Chiluba, who was barracked by the crowds. MMD won all the seats in Luanshya.

419 The 1978 Zambian elections.

Bornwell Chikulo. In: *The evolving structure of Zambian society.* Edited by Robin Fincham, John Markakis. Edinburgh: Centre of African Studies, 1980, p. 96-120.

Chikulo has produced a series of minor but informative articles on Zambian elections, for example in works edited by Turok (see item no. 596) or by Sichone and Chikulo himself (see item no. 469). The reason for singling out this article is that he was one of the few people who wrote on Zambian elections when the one-party state seemed to be ensconced without challenge. Electoral politics was seen as uninteresting at that time. For example, in presidential elections there was only one candidate and the choice was limited to voting for (yes) or against (no) the single candidate. It is, however, important to note, for example, the increase in the 'no' vote. Chinsali, Kaunda's home district, produced the following result: 50.9 per cent 'yes' and 49.1 per cent 'no'. Of course, this was also the election in which Kaunda's former ally Simon Kapwepwe, also from Chinsali, was barred from standing.

420 Alderman Safeli Hanock Chileshe: a tribute to the man, his life and history.

Jonathan H. Chileshe. Ndola: Mission Press, 1998. 191p.

Chileshe wrote this tribute to his elder brother who had been the first black mayor of Lusaka. It is interesting reading for sociologists as it gives an insight into the first beginnings of a Zambian middle class. Safeli Chileshe's wife, Martha, also receives ample attention, especially in her role as patron of the Zambian Girl Guides. There is a photograph of Martha and the girl guides with Kaunda in the book, yet there is no prominent picture of Chileshe himself with Kaunda. The book is often wordy and vague, and especially so when controversial political matters are at stake. According to this book, Safeli Chileshe was present at preparatory meetings to launch MMD. There are, however, no other records of this fact.

421 Democracy: the challenge of change.
Frederick J.T. Chiluba.   Lusaka: Multimedia Publications, 1995.
164p. bibliog.

After his accession to the presidency, Chiluba undertook a rapid academic career. Unlike many other African heads of state, he did not go for the doctor *honoris causa* title, but submitted a thesis which raised him straight from secondary school to masters' level. This is a shortened version of the thesis and contains little that is new, but it is often significant to see the elements he stresses in recent Zambian history. For example, he sees external factors as more important than academic observers do, and he singles out British Prime Minister Mrs Thatcher's considerable service to the cause of democratization in Africa. Another example: Chiluba has not struck observers as being among the initiators of the MMD, while he himself argues that this was in fact the case.

422 The downfall of President Kaunda.
Beatwell S. Chisala.   Lusaka: Co-op Printing, 1994. 382p.
map.

This is a curious, loosely structured book, which aims to portray 'a shattering account of some of the incredible events during Dr. Kaunda's 27 years of rule' (p. i) – among these, a chapter on 'My Bitter London Experience' is prominent, as well as a chapter entitled 'Special Branch'. The author is not, however, without goodwill towards Kaunda, and he presents an interpretation of political events which deserves to be noted. Chisala originates from Chinsali in Northern Province, the heartland of the Bemba-speaking people. Kaunda as well as Kapwepwe, his close collaborator in the struggle for independence, came from the same areas. When Kapwepwe broke with Kaunda in the early 1970s this therefore resulted in competition for the Bemba vote. There are few inside voices on this issue, so this book by a Bemba is therefore an important source on the politics of those times. For example, we are told that at Kapwepwe's funeral 'Relatives, friends, President Kaunda and his wife Betty, all wept uncontrollably', but, 'Kapwepwe's children stopped Kaunda from speaking at the funeral' (p. 316-17). Chisala also gives an account of the Luchembe coup in 1991.

423 Zambia's captured peasantry.
William Cowie, Jotham Momba.   In: *The politics of agriculture in tropical Africa.*   Edited by Jonathan Barker.   Beverly Hills, California: Sage Publications, 1984, p. 239-69. bibliog.

Cowie and Momba obtained their doctorate in the same year (1982) as a result of research dealing with rural Zambia. In this article, they bring their insights together in an overview of the politics of rural Zambia. The principal plank of their argument is that UNIP's urban-based origin explains its difficult relationship with the peasantry. The authors' main concern is to explain the passivity of the latter. Momba's insights are published elsewhere and the value of the article is therefore particularly in the access it gives to Cowie's far less easily available study of Kanyanja parish in Chipata.

424 The rules of the game.
Kate Crehan. In: *African democracy in the era of globalisation.*
Edited by Jonathan Hyslop. Johannesburg: Witwatersrand
University Press, 1999, p. 139-52.
The central thesis in this article is that there are two discourses in rural Zambia: one
within the world of government – the Boma – where everybody is equal before the law,
based on the notion of citizenship; the other based on the notion of kin, where people
cannot be removed from the hierarchical maps of kinship, age and gender. Crehan admits
that the empirical material is taken from her larger study (see item no. 638). The article is
worth noting because she engages in a comparative discussion of most of the recent
writing on this subject, especially in relation to the position of women's wings in political
parties.

425 Zambia: a wind of change in expenditure management.
Elizabeth Cromwell. In: *Votes and budgets: comparative studies in
accountable governance in the South.* Edited by John Healy,
William Tordoff. Basingstoke, England: Macmillan Press, 1995,
p. 153-211.
The comparison between the UNIP and MMD governments in this article will be
considered controversial by many. Most people will agree that actual resource allocation
under the UNIP government had little to do with the formal process of public expenditure
planning. The common explanation of clientalism is adduced here also. According to
Cromwell, the vulnerable in society did not benefit either. Her conclusion on the MMD
government, however, goes against many stated opinions. In her view, under the MMD,
clientalism does not have an impact on the budgeting process; the government strives to
eliminate the budget deficit and adheres to planned expenditure patterns; and the MMD
sticks to priority spending in health and education. This long article contains much
detailed information and opinion on the budgeting process against the background of
civic culture in Zambia.

426 Politics and criticism in Zambia: a review article.
Sholto Cross. *Journal of Southern African Studies,* vol. 1, no. 1
(1974), p. 109-19.
Ten years after independence, the challenge to intellectuals was how to be critical while
remaining committed to Zambian autonomy. It is telling that Cross is concerned about
Zambian humanism, the political ideology espoused by Kaunda: will it be no more than
a set of slogans that can be elevated to totalitarian status? The article is worthwhile
because the author asks central questions which have not lost relevance. For example:
how are the jealously guarded routes of access to the ear of the president structured? He
does not give an answer, nor have such questions been answered up to the present day.
The article is above all useful as a reflection of the mood of the times.

427 Politics in an urban African community.
A.L. Epstein. Manchester, England: Manchester University Press,
1958. 254p. 2 maps. bibliog.
Zambia was the scene of pioneering studies of urban life as it was simply more urbanized
than other African countries. This book is as much a description of how the town was

regarded as a study of actual social change over time. At first, authority in urban settings was seen to reside in tribal elders; then in African welfare societies; then in the trade unions; the last source of authority to appear was the nationalist party. In the tension between union and political party, Epstein outlined a trait of Zambian political life which had lost little of its actuality when Frederick Chiluba, as a trade unionist, challenged the political party – UNIP – and its leader Kaunda as the sole source of political power. Although its date of publication suggests that this is primarily an historical source, it is definitely much more than that.

428 Sisters under the skin; women and the women's league in Zambia.
Gisela Geisler. *Journal of Modern African Studies*, vol. 25, no. 1 (1987), p. 43-67.

This is a critical analysis from a feminist perspective of UNIP's women's league. UNIP's women appear primarily to be concerned with (im)morality which is seen as resulting from female misbehaviour. Tradition is for them the source of true morality and this implies subservience – if not submission – to husbands. It is therefore not surprising that the league tends to condemn abortion outright and is – although Geisler notes a small change – opposed to contraception. Attention is also paid to their conservative stance on more developmental issues. The article tends to condemn the women's league on predictable feminist grounds, where clarification as to the nature and circumstances of this worldview may be more appropriate. On the other hand there are many lively and insightful observations. This combination of condemnation and observation is clear in this characterization of most of the women's league as: 'petty traders, the backdoor sellers of scarce commodities and beer in unlicensed bars in the townships'.

429 The dynamics of the one-party state in Zambia.
Cherry Gertzell (ed.), Carolyn Baylies, Morris Szeftel. Manchester, England: Manchester University Press, 1984. 262p. 5 maps. bibliog.

The first elections held under a one-party state in 1973 form the backbone of this study. The book is composed of a general part – which does not deal exclusively with the elections – and a part which discusses the elections in three regional settings: the Copperbelt, Luapula and Western Provinces. It is primarily contemporary political history, but one contribution succeeds more than others in conveying the atmosphere of Zambia at that moment. Gertzell's chapter on dissent and authority in Zambia in the period 1973 to 1980 brings out clearly how the introduction of the one-party state did not mean an end to political opposition. Her singling out of the labour movement as a source of persistent opposition was prescient given its role in the reintroduction of multipartyism.

430 Thoughts are free: prison experience and reflections on law and politics in general.
Munyonzwe Hamalengwa. Don Mills, Canada: Africa in Canada Press, 1991. 390p.

Hamalengwa was a student leader at the University of Zambia in 1976, when the university was closed in reaction to a series of events connected with Angolan independence, starting with a demonstration in favour of the MPLA (Movement for the Popular Liberation of Angola). This was controversial, as the Zambian government was still attempting to exert its influence to bring a broad coalition – including UNITA

(National Union for the Total Independence of Angola) – to power in Angola. Student leaders were detained and Hamalengwa left the country after being released. He then created a new life for himself as a lawyer in Canada. This book is a varied collection of pieces, as the title indicates. It is valuable because of the first few chapters, which give a detailed account – including the reproduction of many original documents – of the events at that time. It gives a good insider's account of the rather crude nature of student politics at the time and the repression of which Kaunda was capable.

431 Class struggles in Zambia 1889-1989 and the fall of Kenneth Kaunda 1990-1991.
Munyonzwe Hamalengwa. Lanham, Maryland: University Press of America, 1992. 182p. bibliog.

The latter part of the title is covered in only a small part of the book, and the period before independence is also covered briefly. The major topic is the relationship between UNIP and the trade union movement, which is framed in a theoretical discussion of whether the term 'labour aristocracy' is appropriate to Zambian workers. Hamalengwa denies that this was the case. The maintenance of democracy, he claims, has been dependent on the existence of a strong, autonomous labour movement. The particular value of this book is in a quite detailed description – analysing, for example, legal instruments – of the deteriorating relationships between trade unions and government from 1970 to 1991. It has a good feel for grassroots sentiments in unions, partly uncovered through a survey. It may have its weaknesses as a political history: the possibilities of links between the trade union movement and the United Progressive Party (UPP), which was especially significant on the Copperbelt, is not explored, for example.

432 Freedom and labour: mobilisation and political control on the Zambian Copperbelt.
Peter Harries-Jones. Oxford: Basil Blackwell, 1975. 256p. map. bibliog.

Harries-Jones studied the emergence of UNIP in Luanshya in the early 1960s. This work is a beautiful evocation of the struggle for independence at the grassroots. It has a very immediate feel, for example in the account of the political involvement of Foster Mubanga – a women's league leader – in her own words. Harries-Jones writes perceptively about rumour in politics and uses the accusations against himself as an example. A strong point of the book is that it does not romanticize the independence struggle and that it is very perceptive about the conflicts which it caused in African societies. What Harries-Jones says about the trade unions is especially valuable as the tensions between unions and nationalists is a neglected area of study. Similar things can be said of the tensions between the educated and the uneducated. The idea of sponsorship is central in his theoretical analysis, which is akin to network analysis.

433 Economic crisis, civil society and democratization: the case of Zambia.
Julius O. Ihonvbere. Trenton, New Jersey: Africa World Press, 1996. 335p. bibliog.

Ihonvbere writes current history in which opinions, including his own, are central. The book pays some attention to the prelude to the movement towards multipartyism; this is followed by an elaborate description of the movement's rise and victory as well as a discussion of developments after the movement came to power. It is valuable as a source. It contains, for example, a description of the zero-option plan, allegedly adopted by UNIP to destabilize the MMD government through fomenting opposition by legal and illegal means. It also contains information on a neglected area in Zambian politics after MMD's accession to government: power struggles within MMD at provincial level. Ihonvbere's likes and dislikes are clear throughout the book. He disagrees strongly, for instance, with MMD's neo-liberal economic programme. Opinion, however, sometimes overtakes possible interpretations. This is exemplified by the great significance he attributes to Kaunda's sacking of Frederick Hapunda as Minister of Defence in June 1990 as an event in the struggle for multiparty democracy. Hapunda is singled out for thanks in his preface and may be important to Ihonvbere. I am not aware, however, that other observers have identified Hapunda as of great importance in that historical episode.

434 **How not to consolidate democracy: the experience of the Movement for Multiparty Democracy (MMD) in Zambia.**
J.O. Ihonvbere.   In: *Multiparty democracy and political change: constraints to democratization in Africa.*   Edited by J.O. Ihonvbere, John Mukum Mbaku.   Aldershot, England: Ashgate, 1998, p. 219-41.

This article contains a lively portrayal of important incidents during the first term of the MMD government. It is also an unequivocal statement of opinion: the MMD has accommodated the same phenomena 'which aided Kaunda in running down the economy and squandering possibilities for growth, development and democracy'. The explanation is sought in the lack of prerequisites for a transition to democracy.

435 **Kenneth David Kaunda: founder president of the Republic of Zambia; perspectives of his exit from office.**
Compiled and edited by Tiyaonse Chisanga Kabwe.   Harare: SAPES Books, 1997. 189p.

This is a most curious book containing messages which Kaunda received after losing the 1991 elections. These messages often praise him for the way he accepted defeat – some notable ones are from George Bush and Julius Nyerere. Others, however, speak a different language: 'It is with great sorrow that I heard the news, you do not deserve it' (Ted B. in Malta), or 'I am sorry for Zambia' (Amo Houghton in Washington). It is not surprising then to find a postscript by Kabwe suggesting that the elections of 1991 and 1996 were rigged. The book is informative for anyone interested in the Kaunda camp's thinking on recent political history.

436 **Fundamentals of Zambian humanism.**
Timothy K. Kandeke.   Lusaka: NECZAM, 1977. 249p.

The ideas embodied in Zambian humanism as expounded by Kenneth Kaunda appear now to be of mere historical significance, as they have not survived the change of government. In the 1970s and 1980s, however, ideology seemed to be of prime importance. This book is typical of attempts to connect humanism with the marxist tradition. The last chapter in this volume illustrates this particularly well. Writings of this type led to protest from the churches, which did not accept the atheistic nature of marxism.

437 Zambia: the disintegration of the nationalist coalitions in UNIP and the imposition of a one-party state, 1964-1972.
Eric M. Kashimani. *Transafrican Journal of History*, vol. 24 (1995), p. 23-70.

This long article aims to set the historical record straight, because, Kashimani claims, myths have been elevated to the status of historical facts. He refutes the allegation that there was a serious problem of ethnic strife in Zambia leading up to the one-party state. The fundamental issue in Zambian politics after independence was 'the sacrifice of internal party democracy' on the altar of personal consolidation on the part of Kaunda. As contemporary political history, the article is rather shallow, but it is rich as a statement of a Zambian intellectual on the pretensions of the one-party state. The refutation of UNIP's arguments for a one-party state from page 51 onwards is the crux of Kashimani's argument.

438 Zambia shall be free.
Kenneth Kaunda. London: Heinemann, 1962. 202p. map.

This is a ghost-written account (by Merfyn Temple) of Kaunda's political life until the Federal Review Conference in London in 1960. It portrays a rather naïve politician and, more than other writings, reveals Kaunda's spiritual, mystic and religious side.

439 Humanism in Zambia and a guide to its implementation.
Kenneth D. Kaunda. Part I: Lusaka: Zambia Information Services, 1967. 50p. Part II: Lusaka: Zambia Information Services, 1974. 131p.

Kaunda's ideology of Zambian humanism has not taken root in people's minds and is nowadays history. It is of historical interest, however, and in this context it is striking how syncretic Kaunda's ideas were. In the introduction to Part 2 he makes that obvious in his gratitude to Dr Krapf, Reverend James Oglethorpe, Reverend Dr Colin Morris and Mr John Papworth. Kaunda's humanism is a *bricolage* of Christianity, African heritage, marxism, etc. He clearly links it to policies but leaves implementation vague. From time to time the ideology comes across as naïve. In Part I, for example, 'weeding at the right time' is stated to be part of humanism. Kaunda was not at all naïve when it came to wielding power, however.

440 Zambia.
Michael Krennerich. In: *African elections, a data handbook.* Edited by Dieter Nohlen, Michael Krennerich, Bernhard Thibaut. Oxford: Oxford University Press, 1999, p. 938-62. bibliog.

This is an excellent work of reference. An introduction gives an historical overview; this is followed by a set of election statistics; and the section is concluded with an excellent bibliography. The statistics are most elaborate in the case of recent elections, but all Zambian elections since 1964 are covered.

441 **The church, labour and the press in Zambia: the role of critical observers in a one-party state.**
Gatian F. Lungu. *African Affairs*, vol. 85, no. 340 (1986), p. 385-410.

This is an important article, which documents how the one-party state in Zambia had to cope with persistent opposition. It documents an important episode, which has not been sufficiently noticed: the resistance of the churches against scientific socialism (marxism). The persistent independence of the *Times of Zambia* – even after it had moved into full state ownership – is often not sufficiently emphasized, either. The article ends with a quotation from Richard Hall, who doubts whether any political change could come from mass democratic activity. Events seem to have proven him wrong.

442 **Milk in a basket; the political-economic malaise in Zambia.**
Akashambatwa Mbikusita-Lewanika. Lusaka: Zambia Research Foundation, 1990. 181p.

Some books are relevant to note more because of the people who have written them than for what they contain. Mbikusita-Lewanika was one of the front runners in the formation of the MMD and, although he left that party, he has remained an important figure in the Zambian political system. Some parts of this book are revealing about how the politician sees himself: the pictures in which he is seen with other important people and the introduction where he sketches his biographical background. The book does not contain much relevant information on the Zambian economy, but some political opinions are worth noting. His dismissal (p. 134), for example, of the ideas behind IMF-inspired structural adjustment must almost necessarily reflect a clash with Chiluba, who championed such economic reforms.

443 **Zambia in der dritten Republik; demoktratishe Transition und politische Kontinuität; Analyse und Dokumentation.** (Zambia during the third republic; democratic transition and political continuity; analysis and documentation.)
Peter Meyns. Hamburg, Germany: Institut für Afrika-Kunde, 1995. 333p. bibliog.

Although this book is written in German, it is still worthwhile for people who do not read that language to take note of it. Indeed the first 136 pages, in which Meyns gives a political history of Zambia in the period 1989 to 1994, will not be intelligible to most users of this bibliography as it is in German. Meyns stresses that Zambian politics is particularly bound to personalities; he adheres to the common belief in the patriarchal nature of Zambian politics. The second part of the book, however, is a valuable collection of documents: manifestos, constitutions and policy statements of the various parties. It contains, for example, a reproduction of the zero-option plan to cut short the MMD's term of office through formenting civil unrest. It led Chiluba to declare a state of emergency – which MMD abhorred in Kaunda's time – and the Chaile commission's comments on drug trafficking by the Winas and Vernon Mwaanga. This is simply an important collection of documents.

444 Peasant differentiation and rural party politics in colonial Zambia.
Jotham C. Momba. *Journal of Southern African Studies*, vol. 11, no. 2 (1985), p. 281-94.

The United National Independence Party (UNIP) won a landslide victory in the independence elections. This makes one forget that the impact of nationalism in rural Zambia was uneven and that the African National Congress (ANC) retained pockets of strong support, the major one being in Southern Province from which the ANC leader, Harry Nkumbula, hailed. Momba argues in this careful analysis that regionalism and organizational factors explain these phenomena less than is usually assumed. Although he pays ample attention to Southern Province, he broadens the perspective to cover other areas: Luapula and Eastern Province. He argues that peasant differentiation – the emergence of a stratum of richer peasants – was a major factor in explaining reluctance to sympathize with the nationalist cause and loyalty to ANC. Class formation and the nationalist struggle are therefore related in that those who had gained in rural Zambia during colonialism were a conservative force.

445 The political reality of the freedom of the press in Zambia.
Robert C. Moore. Lanham, Maryland: University Press of America, 1992. 144p. bibliog.

This is the product of a Fulbright professorship in Zambia during 1990 to 1991, a period which falls between two social orders. The struggle for multi-party democracy led in Moore's words to 'new winds of fairness blowing across the land', but the book begins in the old order with a treatise on Kaunda's ideology of Zambian humanism. One can find in this book information on the organization of the Zambian press in the days of the one-party state and the changes brought by multipartyism. The verdict of the author on Zambia's press freedom is very negative. One may wonder therefore why Zambia has such readable newspapers and why Kaunda wanted to sack the editor of the *Times of Zambia* every few years.

446 Retreat from democracy in post one-party state Zambia.
Chisepo J.J. Mphaisha. *Journal of Commonwealth and Comparative Politics*, vol. 34, no. 2 (1996), p. 65-85.

The argument made here is that it is naive to equate the re-introduction of *de jure* multiparty politics with democratization. One should critically examine the new government's attitude to political opposition and look at political practices in key areas. Three such areas discussed are constitutional revision, the media and the attitude to opposition parties. Mphaisha's conclusions are pessimistic. For example, he says that Chiluba has made it very difficult for opposition parties to organize themselves effectively. Mphaisha's conclusions are rather sweeping and one may question whether a political scene like that of Zambia, which exhibits so much protest and conflict, can be characterized as an autocratic political culture.

447 The archives of Zambia's United Independence Party.
Mwelwa C. Musambachime. *History in Africa; a journal of method*, vol. 18 (1991), p. 291-96.

The archives of both the ANC and the UNIP were all entrusted to the director of UNIP's research bureau after the formation of the one-party state. Access to these files was possible, although not automatic. The situation described refers to the period of the one-party state.

448 Unrepresentative 'democracy': one-party rule in Zambia, 1973-1990.
Chiponde Mushingeh. *Transafrican Journal of History*, vol. 23 (1994), p. 117-42.

The message in this article is unequivocal: the one-party state was anything but democratic and participatory as it claimed to be. At the time when the decision to establish it was taken, less than half of the Zambian people belonged to UNIP. It did not represent popular will and was established by a tiny ruling class to consolidate its dominance. The article does not shun rhetoric or emotional statements and gives therefore an idea of the way an intellectual looks back at the experience of living in a one-party state rather than carefully building up history, verifying sources against each other. There is nevertheless some interesting information to be found here. For example, the article draws attention to the important and influential pastoral letter of the Catholic bishops of 1990 on 'Economics, politics and justice'.

449 An extraordinary life.
Vernon J. Mwaanga. Lusaka: Multimedia Publications, 1982. 307p.

Mwaanga has certainly had an extraordinary life. His career is founded on having been, even before independence, a UNIP supporter in the ANC-dominated Southern Province. After independence he became one of the great men in Zambia's foreign service, ambassador in Moscow in 1965 at the age of twenty-seven, and then Minister of Foreign Affairs. Later he became a member of UNIP's central committee and subsequently editor in chief of the *Times of Zambia*; in the mid 1970s he moved into business. The book ends there. Mwaanga emphatically says that it is not an academic book, and indeed it can be read as merely an extraordinary life. There is also no lack of human interest, as his love life is colourful to say the least. There is, however, also good source material for social scientists: the network that is revealed here is most interesting. The book carries the recommendation of Chou En-lai, the number two in Mao Tse-tung's China during the 1960s, on the back.

450 The other society; a detainee's diary.
Vernon J. Mwaanga. Lusaka: Fleetfoot Publishing, 1987. 327p.

Mwaanga was not only a high flyer under UNIP; he also founded MMD and is an important figure in that party. This book is, in his view, the foundation of that continuing career as it is meant to be an indictment of detention without trial as practised by Kaunda. On the insistence of foreign donors, Mwaanga was stripped of government positions, while remaining important in the party. The alleged reason for his demotion was drug dealing and, although Mwaanga explicitly talks about detention without trial (p. ix), he was tried on the charge of dealing in drugs (specifically Mandrax), illegal importation of motor cars and smuggling out of foreign exchange. Mwaanga was a journalist for a time, and he writes well. The book is of wider importance, however, as a source on the murky side of Zambian politics. We find Mwaanga here in the company of Princess Nakatindi, another name that appears later in connection with MMD and drug dealing; John Mwanakatwe is their lawyer and, maybe most important of all, Mwaanga was working for the Bank of Credit and Commerce International (BCCI).

451 End of Kaunda era.
John M. Mwanakatwe.   Lusaka: Multimedia Publications, 1994.
301p. bibliog.
Mwanakatwe had a long and distinguished career as a cabinet minister in UNIP
governments. From 1978 onwards, he practised as an independent lawyer, but he
remained quite central in political life. In the mid 1990s, he chaired the commission of
enquiry into constitutional revision during the first Chiluba period. Such a man has many
tales to tell. This book is written as a political history of Zambia and not as a memoir, but
it is suffused by Mwanakatwe's personal experience. It is therefore valuable, despite the
fact that is not particularly systematic and often shies away from really controversial
issues. It helps to be knowledgeable about recent Zambian history to appreciate the book.
However, the index is rich in references to important people and events. The book
provides above all good source material, a prime example of which is Mwanakatwe's
personal account of Lieutenant Mwamba Luchembe, who staged the failed 1990 coup.
The author is clearly presented in these pages as a liberal who regards human freedoms
highly.

**452 Harry Mwaanga Nkumbula: a biography of the 'old lion' of
Zambia.**
Goodwin Mwangilwa.   Lusaka: Multimedia, 1982. 157p.
This is a remarkable book, as it questions the wisdom of the one-party state at a time when
such views were not commonly expressed. The description of Nkumbula's role in the
Choma declaration, which announced this political set up in the first place is most
ambiguous. One needs to be familiar with Zambian political history to be able to grasp
the subject of this book. The ANC's links with Moise Tshombe in Katanga and with
Eastern Angola make spectacular reading. The prominent role of trade unionist Lawrence
Katilungu is also striking. Katilungu is said to have saved the ANC organizationally in
the early 1960s – he used the skills he acquired as a trade unionist – and, what is more
surprising, is that for this purpose he used money which had been given by Tshombe.

453 The Kapwepwe diaries.
Goodwin Mwangilwa.   Lusaka: Multimedia, 1986. 241p.
This is another brave attempt to draw attention to a disavowed founder of the nation at a
time when that was not politically expedient. The book was published after Simon
Kapwepwe, Kaunda's former ally and eventual rival, died and so no longer presented a
threat to Kaunda's government. It is curiously structured: part of it consists of
Kapwepwe's actual diaries, but these are not continuous. In between, there are pieces of
biography. The main interest here of course is Kapwepwe's break with UNIP and the
formation of the UPP. This book is worth reading for those interested in Zambian politics
inasmuch as it presents new insights. For instance, whereas Kapwepwe has been
portrayed as an impulsive, radical politician, the remarks he is reported to have made
about the Zambian economy when he broke with Kaunda in 1971 now appear to have
been analytical and precise. He foresaw the decline that has come about.

454 A walk in the past.

Philemon N'goma.   Lusaka: Kenneth Kaunda Foundation, 1988. 183p.

Independence in a country where there were few educated people gave the opportunity for spectacular careers like this one. N'goma originates from northern Malawi; he went to secondary school in Munali, Lusaka, then went into teaching and travelled to England on a PE training course; thereafter he moved into district administration. After independence he rose swiftly into the inner circles of State House as private secretary to Kaunda. Thereafter he enjoyed a career in diplomacy: ambassador in Peking and Rome with long interludes in the United States. He ended his career as director general of Post and Telecommunications. This amazing story is useful for historians and social scientists as it shows so clearly the networks of power in Zambia under Kaunda.

455 Participatory democracy in Zambia.

Patrick E. Ollawa.   Ilfracombe, England: Arthur H. Stockwell, 1979. 520p. 2 maps. bibliog.

Works of political science run the risk of becoming outdated unless they deal with deep underlying trends in society. This book aims towards deeper theoretical insight, but it is firmly situated in the Zambian environment of the 1970s. For example, on page 225 it is stated that, 'The introduction of the one-party state was a major breakthrough in the ideological implementation'. It contains much anecdotal material which is still instructive about the period, for example on student politics (p. 299-301). The kernel of this meandering work is, however, a questionnaire on attitudes, administered in six district towns between 1975 and 1977. Public opinion research has become more widespread since democratization and it may be worth looking at this research set in a different environment.

456 The role of ethnicity in multi-party politics in Malawi and Zambia.

Bertha Osei-Hwedie.   *Journal of Contemporary African Studies*, vol. 16, no. 2 (1998), p. 227-47.

Part of this article is – as the title indicates – devoted to Malawi. There are some general remarks on ethnicity (sub-nationalism) in politics, which show a slight but ambivalent sympathy towards regional balancing and governments of national unity. The value of the article is in titbits of information on the regional background of the Zambian leadership. The article has to be treated with caution, however. Many would not agree with the statement that Baldwin Nkumbula died in a car accident in which MMD leaders were implicated (p. 243). A detailed analysis of the 1996 elections is missing and would make the statement that MMD won these because of ethnic and regional support doubtful. In that election, MMD as a party enjoyed support throughout the country.

457 Contradiction and coalition: class fractions in Zambia, 1964-1984.

Jane L. Parpart, Timothy M. Shaw.   *Africa Today*, vol. 30, no. 3 (1983), p. 23-51.

With class analyses of Zambia now out of fashion, it may be worthwhile to read how the country was regarded in the early 1980s in terms of a neo-marxist framework. Parpart and

Shaw identify two excluded classes in Zambian society: the national bourgeoisie and the labour aristocracy who are seen as growing in self-consciousness. Indeed these were the ranks from which the MMD leadership was drawn. The article may be of interest because of its perspective on Zambian society, but it offers more a feeling of the atmosphere in those times than a systematic description of the Zambian class structure. The peasantry is not mentioned.

458 Zambia's second republic – the establishment of a one-party state.
Jan Pettman. *Journal of Modern African Studies*, vol. 12, no. 2 (1974), p. 231-44.

This is a brief narrative of events preceding and during the establishment of the one-party state. It is a useful source of information. One finds, for example, the reasons Simon Kapwepwe gave for breaking with UNIP, which are seldom mentioned. It documents well both the opposition to the one-party state and the nature of the evidence collected by the constitutional commission on the establishment of that state. The conclusions are full of nuance, but are imbued by a scepticism which may have been prescient: the 1973 elections, it is claimed, 'deprived Zambia's leaders of the positive vote of confidence which they had hoped would secure and legitimize the new political structure' (p. 234).

459 Zambia: security and conflict.
Jan Pettman. Lewes, England: Julian Friedmann Publishers, 1974. 284p. map. bibliog.

The political history of Zambia between 1964 and 1970 is well documented. This is one of several books on the topic and it focuses especially on security. The army and police are discussed in some detail on pages 105-11. The section entitled 'The coming of the second republic 1970-73' occupies only seven pages but is quite informative. This material is, however, covered more effectively in a journal article (see item no. 458) by Pettman.

460 Zambia: the myth and realities of one-party participatory democracy.
Bizeck Jube Phiri. *Geneve-Afrique*, vol. 29, no. 2 (1991), p. 11-24.

There are a number of articles in which Zambian intellectuals try to take stock of the experience of living under a one-party state. This is an early and, in some respects, a mild one, which accepts for example that the one party-state was justified in view of external enemies. Phiri also writes, however, that Kaunda had emerged as a virtual dictator by 1969. The article does not give new insights: its interest is limited to the struggle by a Zambian intellectual to come to an historically founded opinion.

461 Cautionary notes on democratisation; lessons from India and Zambia.
Vicky Randall, James R. Scarrit. *Journal of Commonwealth and Comparative Politics*, vol. 34, no. 2 (1996), p. 19-44.

This article is not based on new or original information, but is merely an attempt at interpretation. Its chief concern is theoretical, looking at conditions for and results of democratization. The authors doubt whether democratization is conducive to economic and social transformation.

462 Political competition and one-party dominance in Zambia.
Thomas Rasmussen. *Journal of Modern African Studies*, vol. 7, no. 3 (1969), p. 407-24.

Rasmussen reviews opposition to the then ruling UNIP by other political parties as well as within UNIP. The article gives a good feel for Zambian politics in the first period of multipartyism, but its special value is in the description of the formation and fate of the United Party in the period 1966-68 (p. 413-17), an episode that is hardly ever discussed. The special focus in this article is on Barotseland. The general conclusion is worth consideration: 'Democratic political competition has not so much indicated political preferences as it has created disaffection among disappointed competitors or their supporters' (p. 423).

463 Electoral systems and democratization in Southern Africa.
Andrew Reynolds. Oxford: Oxford University Press, 1999. 341p. 6 maps. bibliog.

Reynolds aims to make a theoretical point by distinguishing inclusive and exclusive political systems, arguing that the former will lead to stability and progress. Although the title suggests a concern with institutional arrangements, this distinction of political systems is based on cultural factors and ethos. The book contains a short specific description of the 1991 and 1996 Zambian elections, but broader elements of Zambian politics are discussed throughout the book. Reynolds claims that arguments that MMD is a broad coalition and therefore signifies an inclusive system are mistaken: 'As of 1998 both Zimbabwe and Zambia have to all intents and purposes lapsed back into de facto one-party states and have displayed a disturbing track record of severely restricting political and human rights' (p. 3). The book attempts to make predictions and reads like an oracle. History will decide whether this is a cool analytical judgement or a partisan misjudgement.

464 The analysis of social class, political participation and public policy in Zambia.
James R. Scarritt. *Africa Today*, vol. 30, no. 3 (1983), p. 5-22.

This article contains opinions on Zambia, but no original research. Its usefulness is as an introduction to a number of authors who wrote on this topic, as it reviews the literature produced at a time when neo-marxism was in vogue in the study of African politics.

465 President Kenneth Kaunda's annual address to the Zambian national assembly: a contextual content analysis of changing rhetoric 1965-83.
James R. Scarritt. *Journal of Modern African Studies*, vol. 25, no. 1 (1987), p. 149-57.

This is highly recommended to anybody studying the Kaunda period. It is also interesting and intriguing political science; a scholarly comparison with Chiluba would be of the greatest interest. Kaunda was an extremely verbose ruler and it was often difficult to pick out more than a few passages in his speeches that made sense to an outsider; Zambians on the other hand often considered the speeches highly relevant. This computer-based content analysis brings this aspect of Zambian politics into sharper focus. It is a significant finding that, as time passed, peace was increasingly seen as an internal problem and became more and more associated with unity. That fits with the general writing on Zambian politics, but other facts are less evident and meaningful in other writing: references to education and rural development declined considerably after the introduction of the one-party state.

466 Middle class politics in Zambia.
Ian Scott. *African Affairs*, vol. 77, no. 308 (1978), p. 321-34.

This is a valuable article as it contains more information on the formation and ultimate fate of Simon Kapwepwe's breakaway United Progress Party (UPP) than is found elsewhere. Scott argues that the episode meant the excision of the most vocal, populist elements of UNIP, and especially that section of the party which had trade-union support. The one-party state meant the triumph of middle-class politics. Political apathy was the price that had to be paid for it.

467 Political money and party organisation in Zambia.
Ian Scott. *Journal of Modern African Studies*, vol. 20, no. 3 (1982), p. 393-410.

This article is valuable because it gives an insight into some less obvious pressures in the one-party state. UNIP had difficulty financing itself, and by 1973 the party was essentially insolvent. The government rescued the party and took over control of it as well. This was formalized in the one-party state. Prior to the establishment of the one-party state, there was much political violence and intimidation, with party youths selling party cards, often forcibly, at entrances to markets, buses and the like. This ended with the introduction of the one-party state.

468 The sacred and the obscene; personal notes on political ritual, poverty and democracy in Zambia.
Owen Sichone. In: *African democracy in the era of globalisation*. Edited by Jonathan Hyslop. Johannesburg: Witwatersrand University Press, 1999, p. 152-66.

Sichone is a Zambian anthropologist who attempts here to give an insider's account of Zambian political culture. The first part of the article is a personal account of how politics was experienced during his lifetime. One can learn there for example what university students meant in Kaunda's days by PiG (the party in government) or by *gabament*, which originated as an imitation of the veteran UNIP politician Rueben Kamanga's mispronunciation of the word government. In the second part, Sichone discusses the meaning of the word 'independence', and he ends with a discussion of rituals such as Independence Day or the visits of foreign heads of state: 'Independence alas is more about missiles and the greatness they symbolize than about food and good health' (p. 164). There is also a brief comparison of Chiluba and Kaunda, which is sympathetically critical of the former.

469 Democracy in Zambia; challenges for the third republic.
Edited by Owen Sichone, Bornwell C. Chikulo. Harare: SAPES Books, 1996. 237p. bibliog.

This is a collection of articles by authors who were attached to the University of Zambia. It can best be characterized as a textbook for a university course on politics and administration in Zambia since 1991. It covers topics on democratization; public administration; industrial relations; ethnicity; and gender. The style of the articles varies from general philosophizing – 'capitalist societies are as democratic as its [sic] social movements make it' (p. 110) – to anecdote. The latter articles, however, are often informative as well: the description of the role of fear in the election campaign of 1991 (p. 27) is one instance. It is therefore a book that can profitably be browsed through. Some contributions could have been more substantial, but the book contains, here and there, information not readily obtainable elsewhere – one example is the review of labour relations in the 1980s on page 139.

470 The politics of structural adjustment in Zambia.
Neo Simutanyi. *Third World Quarterly*, vol. 17, no. 4 (1997), p. 825-39.

Simutanyi analyses in this article how interest groups were affected by and reacted to structural adjustment. His main focus is on the business class and the trade unions. The former were on the whole favourable to structural adjustment, although their attitude was sometimes equivocal. Simutanyi's depiction of trade unions as opposed to structural adjustment gives rise to a contradiction: originally the MMD government had strong links with the unions but the party was strongly in favour of liberalizing the economy. The business class has therefore, according to Simutanyi, gained power to a greater extent than the trade unions since MMD came to power. The article is made particularly valuable by its use of insider sources, especially in the trade union movement. His description of opposition by trade unions may be debatable: opposition may have been more directed against enrichment of an elite through one-partyism than against structural adjustment as such. Chiluba at any rate had already identified early on with Lech Walesa, who brought down a socialist government in Poland through trade union activism.

471 Zambia: class formation and government policy in the 1970s.
Tony Southall. *Journal of Southern African Studies*, vol. 7, no. 1 (1980), p. 91-109.

Southall has a central interest: 'The ability of the Zambian government to remain apparently stable and unchallenged by serious opposition'. This situation is perplexing as he identifies undeniable patterns of class formation since independence, and the UNIP/Kaunda government identifies more and more with the emerging upper classes. Southall describes the situation rather than giving the reason for this stability. The valuable element in this article is the author's eye for the complexities of Zambian politics. He notes, for example, that in 1978 Kaunda's rival Simon Kapwepwe turned against socialism and advocated capitalism. Kapwepwe wanted first to introduce capitalism so that there would be something to share among the people. The analytical questions raised have not lost their value, and the article provides much anecdotal evidence which is still worthy of consideration.

472 Corruption and the spoils system in Zambia.
Morris Szeftel. In: *Corruption, consequences and control*. Edited by Michael Clarke. New York: St. Martin's Press, 1983, p. 163-90.

This article is mainly a description of corruption cases which were officially documented in the late 1960s and the 1970s. The main ones are: the 1968 commission of inquiry into the affairs of Lusaka City Council; the dismissal in 1977 of the Minister of Lands because of corruption related to land registration; and the African Farming Improvement Funds scandals of 1970. The article is therefore valuable for those interested in case material, which Szeftel fits into an analysis of patronage, factionalism and the dominance of government by an emerging capitalist class. In the latter respect it adds little to his other writings.

473 Politics in Zambia.
Edited by William Tordoff. Manchester, England: Manchester University Press, 1974. 439p. 2 maps. bibliog.

The contributors, with the exception of one, Anirudha Gupta, who writes on trade unions, were at one time members of the Department of Political Science at the University of Zambia. Their work excels in solid empiricism and gives a vivid and deep insight into Zambian politics during the 1960s. The crucial event which crops up time and again is the crisis during the August 1967 UNIP General Conference, which brought sectionalist (sub-nationalist) tensions to the fore. The article by Robert Molteno on cleavage and conflict in Zambian politics evokes enduring elements in Zambian political culture and has validity even outside Zambia. The articles cover events until just after the establishment of the one-party state. This is essential reading for students of Zambian politics who have then to face the question of what was specific to the historical period and what was not.

474 Aspects of democracy and democratisation in Zambia and Botswana: exploring African political culture at the grassroots.
Wim van Binsbergen. *Journal of Contemporary African Studies*, vol. 13, no. 1 (1995), p. 3-35.

The author advocates scepticism about a universal, global image of democracy and illustrates this with the example of the reaction of the Nkoya in Kaoma district, Western Province, to political events in Zambia. According to him, the Nkoya react to political events in terms of their own ethnic (sub-nationalist revival) priorities and did quite well out of the Kaunda period: he refers to an ethnic revival and enhanced economic opportunities. Part of the Nkoya leadership – organized in a cultural association – switched their support quickly when the new government came to power. However, according to van Binsbergen, UNIP continued to attract support. The value of the article is primarily as an informed comment on reactions from the grassroots to democratization.

475 Kaunda and Chiluba: enduring patterns of political culture.
Jan Kees van Donge. In: *Democracy and political change in Sub-Saharan Africa*. Edited by John A. Wiseman. London; New York: Routledge, 1995, p. 193-220.

This article gives a chronological account of the events leading up to the 1991 elections and their aftermath. It analyses political change in the light of the assumption that relatively stable and enduring patterns – a political culture – underlie political behaviour in political systems. A notable pattern in Zambia, for example, is the attempt to form extensive coalitions which embrace as large a part of the country as possible. Paradoxically, this particular strategy is also an attempt to counter a strong tendency towards fission. Typically in this situation, when schisms occur, the group that splits tends to adopt the word 'united' or its cognates in its name – UNIP or Congress of National Unity are examples. These centrifugal tendencies put pressures on leaders to concentrate power on themselves and partially explain the persistence of the presidential system of government.

476 **Reflections on donors, opposition and popular will in the 1996 Zambian general elections.**
Jan Kees van Donge. *Journal of Modern African Studies*, vol. 36, no. 1 (1998), p. 71-99.
The general elections of 1996 were held despite Kenneth Kaunda's call for an election boycott. The reason for his action was an article in the constitution which disqualified Kaunda from standing. There was also pressure from foreign donors to drop the article. The MMD government maintained that they could not quash decisions taken by parliament, as that would mean going against popular will. The election results showed an indisputable victory for Chiluba and the MMD government. The article looks at this episode in order to disentangle the interplay between local political culture and outside forces.

477 **Zambia – no model for democracy: continuing human rights violations.**
Alex Vines. *Human Rights Watch*, vol. 10, no. 2A (1998). 57p.
Judgements on Zambia in relation to human rights have a tendency to be extreme. The title indicates a great disillusionment with democratization. The reporter, Alex Vines, portrays here a vision of Zambian politics that is especially prevalent in the community of non-governmental organizations. It is definitely not a universally held view, however.

478 **Zambia's most famous dissidents; from Mushala to Luchembe.**
Patrick Wele. Solwezi, Zambia: PMW, 1995. 208p. bibliog.
There is a rebellious streak in Zambia's political culture, and this book is an important source on this. Some names, such as Shamwana, Christon Tembo and Luchembe, are well known from coup trials. The chapter on UNZA student unrest is also no surprise, but there are other chapters that mention instances and names which are not so widely known: Chipango, Lupasa and Robbie Makayi. Makayi was the first editor of *The Weekly Post*, which played a major role in the struggle for multipartyism.

479 **The night without a president.**
Sikota Wina. Lusaka: Multimedia Publications, 1985. 91p.
This is a personal memoir of a formative event in Zambian politics. It deals with the aftermath of the Mulungushi UNIP general congress of 1967 in which tribalistic feelings flared up and smouldered on into 1968. The issue came to a head in a UNIP National Council meeting in Lusaka in February 1968. Kaunda resigned for a night at that point and subsequently came out on top of the various faction struggles taking place. This is a politician's book and that makes many of the things he says interesting. Although he eulogizes Kaunda, Wina was one of the most prominent people in the formation of the MMD in 1990. Simon Kapwepwe, Kaunda's erstwhile ally is the villain of the piece in this version: his aspiration to become president was resented by a group of non-Bemba intelligentsia (among them Sikota Wina). It is also valuable as a source of biographical material on the UNIP leaders who were then competing.

480 Corruption and inefficiency in Zambia – a survey of recent inquiries and their results.
Klaas Woldring. *Africa Today*, vol. 30, no. 3 (1983), p. 51-74.
This article covers much the same ground as a later book edited by Woldring and Chibaye (see item no. 481). It is worth noting because of the anecdotal evidence it contains – see for example the open letter which Andrew Mutemba, a writer and then High Commissioner in Nigeria, published in 1981 in the *Times of Zambia*. This represents a striking example of opposition from within the one-party state.

481 Beyond political independence; Zambia's development predicament in the 1980s.
Edited by Klaas Woldring, Chibwe Chibaye. Berlin; New York; Amsterdam: Mouton, 1984. 352p.
This is a very wide-ranging collection of papers by people who were at one time associated with the University of Zambia. Chapters cover the mining industry; the rural sector; parastatals and industry; class formation; the urban informal sector; corruption; the press; and foreign policy. It reflects a great pessimism about the country, particularly because of the way state institutions were (mis)managed. It is worth browsing through for two reasons: firstly because it gives such a clear impression of the period, and secondly because it contains many facts from newspapers, policy documents and anecdotes. Woldring's chapter on corruption is especially worthwhile; particularly informative are the nine cases of corruption which he extracted from the press. The fact that these were reported illustrates the paradoxical nature of the Kaunda government: things went wrong but remedial action was also always on the agenda.

Constitution and Legal System

482 Dispute settlement and dispute processing in Zambia: individual choice versus societal constraints.
Richard S. Canter. In: *The disputing process; law in ten societies.* Edited by L. Nader, H.F. Todd. New York: Columbia University Press, 1978, p. 247-80.

This is primarily a descriptive article on the choice of remedies – or legal arenas – at the disposal of people living in Lenje, an area near Kabwe. The people in question adhere to a matrilineal kinship ideology, but kinship patterns in practice are fluid. Dispute settlement is described more as a process, involving the mobilization of networks which differ in the various juridical arenas. The description of these various legal arenas is highly instructive and of value for people who are studying rural settings elsewhere in Zambia. The article ends with a statistical analysis of cases, in which general impressions are also mentioned. The latter tend to be particularly instructive: disputes between close relatives seem common, and this is not surprising as emotions run high on issues of inheritance of property (notably land) and offices such as chieftainships. The article is not an easy read, but it is instructive on important aspects of rural life.

483 The commonwealth and the new world order safe-guarding civil society.
Rodger M.A. Chongwe. *African Journal of International and Comparative Law*, vol. 4, no. 3 (1992), p. 962-71.

Rodger Chongwe was one of Kaunda's main opponents in the early years of the Movement for Multiparty Democracy (MMD), but in recent years, together with Kaunda, has been a bitter opponent of the MMD government. The article gives an overview of the changes that multipartyism brought, including an enlightening section on the Mvunga Constitutional Review Commission. It is, however, more noteworthy because of who wrote it and the viewpoint implied by statements such as, 'The freedom and liberty that was ushered in by the new state is being enjoyed by all Zambians without exception' (p. 969). If the commonwealth standing commission on human rights for which Chongwe pleads were set up, however, he would nowadays be a major complainant there.

484 The law of succession in Zambia: recent proposals for reform.
Simon Coldham. *Journal of African Law*, vol. 27, no. 1 (1983),
p. 162-68.

Inheritance law is a bitterly contested issue in Zambia. Feminists especially have argued
against the practice whereby the relatives of the male in many cases inherit everything.
The 1982 report on the law of succession was the first report to be published by the Law
Development Commission and it resulted in a proposed bill to change the system.
Coldham reviews this report as well as the bill and finds it wanting, despite understanding
the constraints under which the commission operated: he affirms that, 'It is difficult to
identify any determining principle running through the Bill; some of its proposals appear
unnecessarily cautious, others excessively ambitious. The case for reform is not made
out' (p. 168). This is a rich and carefully argued article, but without legal training it is
difficult to read.

**485 The wills and administration of Testate Estates Act 1980 and the
Intestate Succession Act 1989 of Zambia – statute note.**
Simon Coldham. *Journal of African Law*, vol. 33, no. 1 (1989),
p. 128-32.

This article deals with two acts in inheritance – one dealing with wills and one with
intestacy – which were passed as a result of proposals by the Law Commission. The main
thrust of these acts is that the spouse and children of the deceased become the main
beneficiaries and that the relatives of the male lose out. Zambian reforms to prevent
property grabbing from widows and children are more ambitious than reforms carried out
elsewhere in Commonwealth Africa. Coldham doubts whether reforms which make so
few concessions to gender relations in customary law will prove acceptable to the
majority of Zambian people. If they do not, then the law will, he believes, be difficult to
implement.

486 Customary marriage and the urban local courts in Zambia.
Simon Coldham. *Journal of African Law*, vol. 34, no. 1 (1990),
p. 67-75.

The topic of this paper is the anomalous position of urban courts that enforce the law on
customary grounds, despite the fact that there is no customary authority in urban areas.
Urban courts have the power to issue marriage and divorce certificates and in so doing
they lay down minimum requirements for customary marriage. In practice, this means
that urban courts develop the law, and the article documents the grounds on which they
take decisions. The article is based on a research trip undertaken in 1984.

**487 Culprits, culpability and crime: stock theft and cattle
manoeuvres among the Ila of Zambia.**
Charles R. Cutshall. *African Studies Review*, vol. 25, no. 1 (1982),
p. 1-27.

Cattle rustling is discussed here in a broad perspective which includes overt and covert
manoeuvres. The first refers to the distribution of cattle among kinsmen and client-
followers, while the second refers to outright theft. The article contains some court cases,
some historical material and some direct observations by the author. The article offers
colourful anecdotal insight rather than tightly reasoned argument. It is enlightening,

however, on the role of crime in Zambian society at the time: examples given include mob justice against a suspected rustler – fifty people kicked him to death and the police did not react; the shift from rustling by individuals to rustling by gangs; and instances of covert cattle manoeuvring as an economic levelling device in Ila society.

488 The ideas in Barotse jurisprudence.
Max Gluckman. New Haven, Connecticut; London: Yale University Press, 1965. 299p. 2 maps. bibliog.

This book is the outcome of the Storrs lectures which Gluckman delivered in 1963 at Yale University. Teachers must be accessible to their audience, and these lectures can be characterized as a comprehensive and systematic introduction to Barotse law. The book is written in plain language that reads easily. As is typical for Gluckman's writing on law, he compares the Barotse material with European law and the insights of other anthropologists. This search for universalities may be less interesting for people primarily interested in Barotseland. It does, however, provide insights which are applicable in much wider areas in Zambia. For example: 'it is the social relationships centring on property which are of interest to the people, and these social relationships define all legal and forensic duties. There are no distinctions between general kinds of rights and duties: indeed the Barotse have but one word to cover both right and duty, derived from a verb we can translate as ought' (p. 158).

489 The law of intoxication in Zambia.
John Hatchard. *Comparative and International Law Journal of Southern Africa*, vol. 15, no. 1 (1982), p. 92-101.

Zambians have a reputation for liking alcohol, and the excuse that 'I was drunk and I could not help it' is often heard. This is a learned article on the responsibility of the intoxicated offender, mainly based on English case law. It brings out points which are not clarified in Zambian law – for example, the distinction in culpability between self-induced and non self-induced intoxication.

490 Crime and penal policy in Zambia.
John Hatchard. *Journal of Modern African Studies*, vol. 23, no. 3 (1985), p. 483-507.

The statistics on reported crimes in this article show a dramatic increase since independence. Specific attention is paid to robbery, stock theft, theft of motor vehicles and corruption. Legislative, judicial and public responses to increases in these crimes are discussed. A detailed discussion is devoted to the increasing length of prison sentences. The author pleads for alternative corrective measures. The material in the article deals mainly with the 1970s however, and is therefore dated.

491 Protection of widows and administration of customary estates in Zambian courts.
Chuma N. Himonga. In: *Focus on women in Africa.* Edited by Gudrun Ludwar-Ene, Mechtild Reh. Bayreuth, Germany: Eckhad Breitinger, Bayreuth University, 1993, p. 159-97. bibliog.

This article discusses in strictly legalistic terms the position of widows (females) in cases of inheritance. It discusses the problems encountered in the protection of women in such cases mainly in administrative terms, rather than as emanating from positive law. For example, the author argues that local court judges are old men, who are neither legal professionals nor highly literate. The possibilities for the protection of women that exist in the law are thus not utilized. The Intestate Succession Act of 1989, which tends to redress problems by legislation, is merely described and not discussed. This article differs markedly in spirit and content from the writings of Simon Coldham on the same subject (see item nos. 484, 485).

492 Family and succession laws in Zambia: developments since independence.
Chuma N. Himonga. Munster, Germany: Lit Verlag, 1995. 335p. 2 maps. bibliog.

Besides giving a general overview of the legislation on inheritance and succession, this book is based on an impressive amount of case law. The essence of the author's position can be found on pages 106-09 where he offers opinions on the inadequacy of customary law in the face of modern socio-economic conditions. Law reform to remedy this has had limited effect, however. A general impression of the reasons for this can be gleaned on pages 151-56, where cases involving the operation of the Wills and Administration of Testate Estates Act are described. Few people have made use of the possibilities offered in this act; when these few wills have been challenged in court, the latter has tended to reassert customary law. This is a lawyer's book, but one which has a sharp eye for the context in which the law operates and which pays attention to enforcement problems, fear of witchcraft and the like.

493 The impact of the ombudsman institution in developing African countries.
J.K. Kampekete. *Lesotho Law Journal*, vol. 9, no. 2 (1996), p. 49-67.

This article is devoted to the ombudsman in Zambia, although the title suggests that it is much more wide-ranging. It is quite a formal paper, which alludes to problems, such as staffing difficulties, encountered in the working of the institution. Although the Zambian ombudsman had already existed for more than twenty years at the time this paper was published, the author has little to point to in terms of concrete achievements. Indeed, the institution of the ombudsman may experience a revival in the wake of foreign donors' clamour for good governance, but its impact has not been strongly felt in countries where it has existed for a long time.

494 Resilience of the status quo: the sad story of the Zambian Lands Bill, 1994.
Moses Kaunda. *Journal of African Law*, vol. 39, no. 1 (1995), p. 87-102.

The main provisions of the Lands Bill can be found in this article, but Kaunda firstly writes an ardent defence of the bill, which has been received critically; procrastination in the political process seems to have sealed its fate. Kaunda considers it a substantial benefit of the bill that it allows for the conversion of customary held land into lease land. This would encourage the mobility of land and create legal security. There are, the author concedes, valid criticisms to be made of the bill, but he sees the main obstacle in the opposition of the traditional establishment as it is supposed to erode the powers of chiefs.

495   The ombudsman in Zambia.
Robert Martin. *Journal of Modern African Studies*, vol. 15, no. 2 (1977), p. 239-59.

The concerns of this article are highly topical now that good governance is a major issue in development policy. The article not only discusses the ombudsman, but does so against the background of the independence of, and respect for, the judiciary as well as in the context of the introduction of the one-party state. An Investigator General was proposed by the Chona commission's report on the one-party state. Martin considers it a disappointing report, and analyses serious flaws in the recommendations made. Subsequently the discussion of the Commission for Investigations Act 1974 is followed with a review of its functioning in its first years. Martin is stingingly critical while remaining sympathetic to Zambia's attempts to give the citizen a check on government. For example, an amendment was passed in 1975 that gave the president the power to intervene at any time in the work of the commission.

496   Extension of powers of preventive detention to economic crimes in Zambia – a casenote.
M.L. Mbao. *Journal of African Law*, vol. 33, no. 1 (1989), p. 116-25.

The case discussed here is Rao vs. the Attorney-General and at stake is the issue of whether government has the power of preventive detention in the case of economic crimes, which were not recognized when most of the relevant legislation was drafted and passed. The Appeal Court decided that it had never been the intention of the legislators that the law should be applied to activities like trafficking in rhinoceros horns, Mandrax, etc. Ordinary criminal law should be able to take care of that. This is an interesting case as it shows judicial resistance against the encroachment on liberties in the era of the one-party state. Economic crime remains a big problem in Zambia.

497   Emergency (essential supplies and services) regulations 1988 of Zambia – statute note.
M.L. Mbao. *Journal of African Law*, vol. 33, no. 1 (1989), p. 126-28.

This note deals with a piece of opportunistic legislation against black marketeers in the days of pervasive economic controls. The central consideration in the note is whether such legislation can exist independent of the declaration of a state of emergency. It may not have lost relevance as it is politically almost impossible to declare a state of emergency under multipartyism. The president may thus be tempted to have legislation passed which does not officially lead to emergency powers, but which in fact provides similar powers.

498   Human rights and discrimination: Zambia's constitutional amendment 1996.
Melvin L.M. Mbao. *Journal of African Law*, vol. 42, no. 1 (1998), p. 1-11.

This article discusses four controversial amendments to the constitution enacted in 1996 prior to the second multiparty elections: the clause that Zambia is a Christian nation; indigenization of the presidency (the controversial anti-Kaunda clause); limitations on the tenure of office of the President; and the clause demanding that traditional authorities (chiefs) renounce office if they want to contest a political post. The author supports the limitations on tenure of office but is very critical of the other amendments. He uses arguments from international law, but the arguments made in the Zambian political arena are more telling. He refers to critical newspaper articles by prominent Zambian intellectuals like Muna Ndulo and Masuatse Phiri, but the point of view of the government is also well presented.

499 Land policy and economic development in Zambia.
Anthony C. Mulimbwa. *Lesotho Law Journal*, vol. 9, no. 2 (1996), p. 149-69.

This is primarily an informative article which outlines the changes in land law over time under the UNIP government. It goes on to discuss Land Act No. 20 of 1995 against the background of the situation as it had evolved under UNIP. The changes in the powers of the president to grant land and the creation of a Lands Tribunal which can review executive action are seen as central. Mulimbwa argues that the Land Act of 1995 must be seen in the context of a general trend towards economic liberalization, but does not discuss in detail whether or not a land market is emerging.

500 The sources of labour law and the jurisdictional limitations of the Zambian industrial relations court.
Kabenda R.K. Mushota. *Comparative and International Law Journal of Southern Africa*, vol. 14, no. 3 (1981), p. 278-99.

The point made in this article is that the industrial relations court as it was established by the Industrial Relations Act of 1971 is unconstitutional. A brief description of what the act entails is followed by an elaborate learned discussion. Zambia now has a different constitution, but the article may still have some relevance as the country does not possess a constitutional court. The issue of whether the courts may protect the constitution is therefore not beyond discussion.

501 Law and social change: a case study in the customary law of inheritance in Zambia.
Mphanza P. Mvunga. *African Social Research*, no. 28 (1979), p. 643-55.

The position of women in inheritance cases is a subject that arouses strong emotions. Mvunga presents here not an ideological but an empirical discussion of the problem. He undertook research in local courts among the patrilineal Ngoni and the matrilineal Luvale and Tonga. His conclusions are that the nuclear family is increasing in importance and that there is a tendency to take the widow into consideration in patrilineal societies, while, especially among the Tonga, definite trends towards patrilineal inheritance can be detected. Mvunga's opinions are worth noting as he later became chairman of the law commission formulating legal innovation.

502 **The 1996 Zambian constitution and the search for a durable democratic constitutional order in Africa.**
Muna Ndulo. In: *African yearbook of international law*, vol. 5.
The Hague: Kluwer Law International, 1997, p. 137-75.

Muna Ndulo reviews here the amendments made to the constitution in 1996 against the background of earlier experiences with constitutions in Zambia. His judgement is clear from the heading of the fifth chapter of his paper: 'The 1996 Constitution: Contradictions and lost opportunities'. The latter refers to the government's refusal to take up the recommendations of the so-called Mwanakatwe commission, which held hearings on the review of the constitution. Ndulo is a proponent of the view that a constitution should be a 'consensus document' and therefore deplores the fact that the 1996 document left the country divided. Furthermore, according to him, the 1996 document was the least democratic constitution since independence. It may be worthwhile to read carefully what Ndulo writes about the 1973 constitution, which included a bill of rights, albeit omitting freedom of speech, assembly and association. This paper provides good, solid ground for debate about the undemocratic nature of the various constitutions.

503 **Civil liberties cases in Zambia.**
Muna Ndulo, Kaye Turner. Oxford: The African Law Reports,
1984. 579p.

This is an important book: firstly, because it was a courageous enterprise to compile this casebook at the time of the one-party state; secondly, because it is an important source book for the political history of Zambia. Many of the cases discussed evoke important and often painful episodes in Zambia's political history: *In re* Chiluba (1981); *In re* Kapwepwe (1972); Shamwana vs. Attorney-General (1980). The cases are not, however, all political in nature but refer to other matters such as evading exchange control, deportation, etc. It is difficult to judge whether the law as documented here has become obsolete in the third republic, but that will definitely not be the case with in all fields of civil liberties covered here.

504 **Constitutional law and political change: recent developments in Zambia and in Kenya.**
J.B. Ojwang. *African Journal of International and Comparative Law*, vol. 4, no. 2 (1992), p. 325-52.

Ojwang mainly discusses the power of parliament versus the executive in both countries, especially in light of the return of multipartyism. He discusses issues such as the requirement to stand for re-election if party allegiance changes; the possibility to table a vote of no confidence in the president (which does not exist in Zambia) and suchlike. The recent changes may be an evolution in the direction of western systems, but the author concludes that the power of parliament will remain modest. Ojwang does not provide a systematic treatise; the work remains a collection of remarks and observations.

505 The power of parliament to commit persons for contempt in Zambia.
Journal of African Law, vol. 24, no. 1 (1998), p. 138.

This is a case report on M'membe and Mwape vs. The Speaker of the National Assembly and others, which was heard in March 1996. Parliament committed two journalists, M'membe and Mwape, to prison because of allegedly slanderous remarks on parliament and the Supreme Court. The High Court quashed the imprisonment and maintained the independence of the courts *vis-à-vis* parliament. The case is interesting inasmuch as it demonstrates the plurality of Zambian institutions; the presentation of it here contains many insights on the authoritarian tendencies of MMD.

Administration and Local Government

506 From vision to reality: implementing health reforms in Zambia.
Sarah Atkinson. *Journal of International Development*, vol. 9,
no. 4 (1997), p. 631-39.

The author is modest in her pretensions and states clearly that this short article deals with a policy intention rather than a reality. Atkinson's special concern is with the way in which three elements of the 1994 National Strategic Health Plan – decentralization, cost-sharing and increased popular involvement – are perceived and interpreted by the actors involved. This article may merit more attention than its limited pretensions would suggest. Reform in the Zambian health sector in the 1990s was seen within the foreign donor community as exemplary.

507 Administration for development: the effects of decentralization on district development in Zambia.
Reinhard Bodemeyer. Giessen, West Germany: Zentrum für regionale Entwicklungsforschung der Justus-Liebig Universität, 1984. 104p. 2 maps. bibliog.

This research report provides detailed information on the implementation of the 1981 administrative reforms, intended to establish integrated local government. The research was situated in Mkushi district, and Chapter V is an excellent introduction to the everyday practice of administration in rural Zambia. Bodemeyer shows that the reform did not remove the bureaucratic inertia and entropy that are endemic in Zambia's decentralized bureaucracy.

508 Improving the organisation and management of civil service training in Zambia.
C.L. Carmichael. *Public Administration and Development*, vol. 6, no. 2 (1986), p. 187-201.

Carmichael is a consultant with Peat, Marwick, Mitchell and Co. This possibly determines his perspective, which is normative: how things should be organized rather than what is actually happening is the subject of his paper. The topic of the article is mainly management development and training within the Cabinet Office and how this is, or should be, related to other government departments. Since 1991, civil service reform has become a major concern in Zambia and therefore this article is relevant. It contains, for example, some figures on the size of the public sector. These are crucial in current debates.

509 The Zambian administrative reforms: an alternative view.
Bornwell C. Chikulo. *Public Administration and Development*, vol. 1, no. 1 (1981), p. 55-65.

Decentralization of government services is a persistent issue in Zambia, and so it may be worthwhile to read this review of attempts at administrative reform from independence until the 1980 Local Government Act. Chikulo analyses these as moves in the establishment of party hegemony over the bureaucracy and not from a managerial perspective. Decentralization attempts were therefore, in his view, often attempts at centralization under party control. His quotation from Kaunda's speech establishing the District Governorship in 1967 is telling: 'the second thing that we must do is to decentralize in centralism' (p. 59). Chikulo's perspective is stimulating; the story he tells can also be read as a persistent refusal of the bureaucracy to come under party control.

510 Reorganization for local administration in Zambia: an analysis of the Local Administration Act, 1980.
Bornwell C. Chikulo. *Public Administration and Development*, vol. 5, no. 1 (1985), p. 73-81.

Chikulo presents this article as a follow-up to his 1981 article, in which he argued that administrative reform in Zambia was mainly aimed at establishing party control over the civil service. According to him, that is also the rationale for the 1980 reforms propagating integrated local government: he maintains that, 'It is now profitable to run for party office since there is a possibility of one becoming a councillor and, therefore, of receiving the appropriate allowances from the council. As a consequence there has been a marked increase in the interest shown in holding local party office since the enactment of the 1980 Act' (p. 79).

511 Economic crisis, adjustment and the effectiveness of the public sector in Zambia.
Dennis Chiwele, Christopher Colclough. In: *Constraints on the success of structural adjustment programmes in Africa*. Edited by Charles Harvey. New York: St. Martin's Press, 1996, p. 192-210. bibliog.

The delivery capacity of the Zambian public sector declined in the 1980s and 1990s because of skills erosion and a decline in earnings. Skills erosion took place for two main reasons: firstly, expatriates, who were still necessary in highly specialized professions, were no longer attracted to work in Zambia's deteriorating economic circumstances; secondly, structural adjustment required a contraction of the civil service. Vacancies were no longer automatically filled, and the contraction did not take staffing priorities into account. Extreme wage restraint due to the terms of structural adjustment led to an erosion of earnings which resulted in moonlighting, corruption and so on. The article contains valuable time series on real wages in the public sector and the value of emoluments –

especially the housing allowance – as part of salaries. The authors do not doubt the sound economic reasons for a reduction in the public sector, but this should have been accompanied by a rationalization of service delivery.

512 **Communication and ward development committees in Chipata: a Zambian case study of administrative inertia.**
Lammert de Jong, Jan Kees van Donge. *Journal of Modern African Studies*, vol. 21, no. 1 (1983), p. 141-50.
A complicated structure for participation in administration was legislated into existence during the second republic. This short article describes how, in practice, a much more simplified structure came into existence in Chipata, the capital of the Eastern Province; it explains the issues that arose in this process of participation; and finally it documents how these initiatives for participation tended to get stuck in bureaucratic inertia. New structures were created after the reintroduction of multipartyism, and the question now is whether these will suffer the same fate.

513 **Managing policy formulation and implementation in Zambia's democratic transition.**
Harry Garnett, Julie Koenen-Grant, Catherine Reilly. *Public Administration and Development*, vol. 17, no. 1 (1997), p. 77-93.
This is a mainly prescriptive article outlining a project to reform administrative procedures to improve policy making at the highest levels. There are, however, some interesting opinions on the corridors of power in Zambian politics. The authors contrast Chiluba's open style in cabinet meetings with Kaunda's 'controlled' discussion. The section on 'Outstanding issues to be addressed' discerns a generation struggle in the Zambian civil service and notes frictions between the Ministry of Finance and the newly established policy analysis and co-ordination division in the Cabinet Office.

514 **Impasse in Zambia.**
Ravi Gulhati. *Public Administration and Development*, vol. 11, no. 3 (1991), p. 239-44.
This short piece is part of a special issue on bottlenecks in development. It tries to sum up the reasons why Zambia retrogressed economically after 1964 and cites some factors which are not often mentioned, for example over-rapid Zambianization, the replacement of expatriate manpower by local personnel in the process of decolonization. The list of issues in the breakdown of negotiations between Zambia and the IMF is also clarifying and instructive.

515 **Urbanization and the government of migration; the inter-relation of urban and rural life in Zambia.**
Helmuth Heisler. London: C. Hurst & Company, 1974. 166p. bibliog.
This is a curious work. In his acknowledgements, Heisler thanks his colleagues in the civil service, and it is a civil servant's book. Its main concern is how government tried to regulate rural-urban migration and the relationships between town and countryside in various periods. At the same time it is also highly iconoclastic. For example, on page 66 the author notes that Eastern Province was relatively prosperous although the propensity

to migrate to urban areas was high, and that the situation in the west was exactly the reverse, thus undermining a widely held belief that migration undermines rural economies. It is also interesting to note that although there was prostitution in the 1940s on the Copperbelt, it was prohibitively expensive. This is indicative of the influence which women could have in a male dominated society. It is thus informative and challenging to a much larger extent than other books on urbanization in Zambia. The labour histories collected by Max Marwick which can be found at the end of the book give a feel for the realities of life for labour migrants that is not found elsewhere.

516 District administration in Zambia.
Ruud C.E. Kapteyn, Chris Emery. Lusaka: National Institute of Public Administration (NIPA), 1972. 68p. map.
The reorganization of district administration is, at time of writing, considered an urgent issue, and it has been so before. This is the main volume of a series of reports documenting case studies showing the necessity for co-ordination and integration in district administration (see also item no. 520). It has to be seen in conjunction with the 1979 proposal for integrated local government, which contains substantial extracts from this report. Related grey literature was written by Lawrence Taylor, then principal of NIPA, and Alan Simmance, who was an advisor to the Cabinet Office on public administration.

517 Administrative responsibility in a developing country: theoretical considerations and the case of Zambia.
Gatian F. Lungu. *Public Administration and Development*, vol. 3, no. 4 (1983), p. 361-71.
This article is a scathing attack on the lack of responsibility in Zambia's administrative system during the Kaunda era. The presidential system is central to Lungu's analysis and that makes the article interesting as Lungu describes the impotence of the president in a situation where he nominally has much power. The quotation on page 368 is revealing. Lungu also locates part of the problem in a distrust of educated people. The political situation may have changed, but the sentiments expressed in this article have still lost little relevance. The Zambian elite still tend to locate responsibility for maladministration in the political sphere.

518 Role ambiguity in African public management: lessons from Zambian permanent secretaries.
Gaitan F. Lungu. *Cahiers Africains d'Administration Publique / African Administrative Studies*, no. 51 (1998), p. 23-37.
This analysis of the role of the permanent secretary in the Zambian bureaucracy depicts such people as having a high status but little power. The ambiguities in their role stem firstly from their relationship with their political masters: they are supposed to be neutral technocrats but are politically appointed. Secondly, the PS is responsible to the head of the civil service as well as to his minister: is the Zambian PS a chief executive or a minister's clerk? Thirdly, the Ministry of Finance has an overriding influence in this ambiguous situation. The article is cogently argued from the rulebooks of government: General Orders and Cabinet Handbook. The article is written in the spirit of distrust of politics that can often be found in the Zambian civil service.

519 **The effects of achievement variables on styles of management in Lusaka, Zambia.**
M. Mufune. *Cahiers Africains d'Administration Publique / African Administrative Studies*, no. 35 (1990), p. 63-77.

Mufune carried out a methodologically sophisticated study of forty managers in Lusaka. He studied the effects of achievement, measured by three variables: mobility, rank and power, on three dependent variables: authoritarianism, 'rule-mindedness' and favouritism. This study is highly formal in tone and carries no local flavour at all. Nonetheless, it is worth noting the implications of the findings, which show a preoccupation with promotion and a problem of self-esteem and credibility on the part of the managers. Important clues may be gleaned from this in relation to particular Zambian management problems.

520 **Zambia's Local Administration Act, 1980: a critical appraisal of the integration objective.**
R.M. Mukwena. *Public Administration and Development*, vol. 12, no. 1 (1992), p. 237-49. bibliog.

Over ten years had elapsed at the time of writing of this article since the law aimed at achieving integrated local government had been passed, but the integration had not taken place. The article analyses what actually happened in this attempt by the single party, UNIP, to control the state more effectively at a local level. One of the examples it gives is that central government departments were still dependent on ministerial headquarters for funding; the district development plans, which were supposed to co-ordinate the local administration, had never materialized. Mukwena writes lucidly on page 244 about the demands of local party officials to be rewarded in terms of jobs and allowances as the major motive behind the administrative reorganization.

521 **Local government finance in Zambia in the third republic: future and prospects.**
Royson M. Mukwena. *Cahiers Africains d'Administration Publique / African Administrative Studies*, no. 43 (1994), p. 51-60.

The reintroduction of multipartyism in 1991 was accompanied by a new Local Government Act. Mukwena discusses the financial provisions in this act. He sympathizes with the need to broaden the resource base of the councils, but considers improving their financial management a greater priority. This article is valuable only to those with specialist interests.

522 **Party and local government in Zambian decentralized planning, 1964-85.**
Bonard L. Mwape. In: *Decentralizing for participatory planning?* Edited by Peter de Valk, Kadmiel Wekwete. Aldershot, England: Avebury, 1990, p. 176-92.

Mwape gives an historical overview in which he argues that a prefectorial system has been maintained throughout the period considered. The article may be useful for those dealing with decentralization in Zambia in that it gives a more elaborate description of the ideal envisaged in the 1980 Act.

523 Recruiting for decentralised local government system in Zambia.
B.L. Mwape. *Cahiers Africains d'Administration Publique /
African Administrative Studies*, no. 37 (1992), p. 37-45.
There have been several attempts in Zambia to decentralize and reinvigorate local
government. This short article looks at the complications in recruitment surrounding these
attempts. It is worth noting for those involved in decentralization, which became
fashionable again in the 1990s.

524 Decentralization and the role of district and provincial planning.
D. Noppen. In: *Decentralizing for participatory planning?* Edited
by Peter de Valk, Kadmiel Wekwete. Aldershot, England: Avebury,
1990, p. 192-206.
The focus of this paper is on civil servant planning units, which were seen as instrumental
in bringing about integrated local government as envisaged in the 1980 Act. This
overlooked the possible role of the province, and the article documents how the province
has become more important over time. The first sentence of the article states that it takes
more than policy statements to make policies work. The lack and poor implementation of
policies is the theme of the article: district planners were posted to few districts; the
provincial planning units operated in isolation instead of as co-ordinating mechanisms,
and so on.

**525 Recent reforms in policy coordination in Zambia: inter
ministerial committee of officials (IMCOs).**
Siazongo D. Siakalenge. *Cahiers Africains d'Administration
Publique / African Administrative Studies*, no. 49 (1997), p. 129-32.
This is a short, technocratic and bureaucratic explanation of the restructuring of the
Zambian cabinet office in 1993. It is worth attention from people who will come into
contact with policy making in Zambia.

526 Administration in Zambia.
Edited by William Tordoff. Manchester, England: Manchester
University Press, 1980. 306p. map. bibliog.
This is a volume of contributions by members of the University of Zambia staff, most of
them from the Department of Political Science. Tordoff is always primarily concerned
with contemporary history and this volume follows up where his previous volume,
Politics in Zambia (see item no. 473), left off. During the 1970s, the one-party state was
in place; a large part of the economy was under state control; and the bureaucracy was
about to develop. It is not surprising that two of the contributions – by Sheridan Johns and
George Simwinga – deal with the parastatal sector and state enterprises, and three are on
rural administration and development. The material presented here may be dated –
privatization rather than nationalization is now the main topic in Zambia – but some
contributions reflect enduring patterns – for example, Ian Scott's contribution on party
and administration.

527   Decentralization and public sector reform in Zambia.
William Tordoff, Ralph A. Young. *Journal of Southern African Studies*, vol. 20, no. 2 (1994), p. 285-301.

This article is an offshoot of a consultancy report which the authors prepared for the Zambian government in 1993. It is therefore unsurprising that good intentions to decentralize are given prominence. The authors also note sympathetically that the Zambian government has opted for a phased approach to decentralization in the difficult financial circumstances in which it finds itself. The article offers a detailed description of the various functions of government at district and provincial level. Various initiatives in decentralization are mentioned, such as the institution of development co-ordinating committees and the introduction of a new Local Government Act in 1991. The general message conveyed, however, is that implementing decentralization is an uphill task. The section on local government finance illustrates this particularly well. The only substantial initiative mentioned as having been implemented is the establishment of the district health boards. The authors say optimistically: 'What remains to be done is to link the boards more closely to the existing district council structure'. It is for readers to decide whether that has taken place.

Foreign Relations

**528 Zambian crisis behaviour: confronting Rhodesia's unilateral
declaration of independence 1965-1966.**
Douglas C. Anglin.   Montreal; Kingston, Canada: McGill-Queen's
University Press, 1994. 389p. 2 maps. bibliog.
This is a curious book. It is comparatively recent, but deals with the Zambian reaction to
Rhodesia's Unilateral Declaration of Independence in 1965. It is definitely not meant as
an historical work, however, but aims to give a more general insight into crisis behaviour
in Zambian foreign policy. It is doubtful whether it has much to say about structural
features of Zambia's international relations, but it does contain an extremely detailed
inside account of Zambian policy making at a particular period. For example, British staff
work was almost unbelievably poor and the decision-making group in Zambia was
extremely small, consisting of Foreign Minister Kapwepwe, Finance Minister Arthur
Wina and Kaunda as the dominant voice (p. 179).

529 Zambia's foreign policy: studies in diplomacy and dependence.
Douglas G. Anglin, Timothy Shaw.   Boulder, Colorado: Westview
Press, 1979. 453p. 2 maps. bibliog.
This work synthesizes much of what these two international relations scholars have to say
about Zambia and Southern Africa. A densely written book, it is invaluable as a source
on these matters up to and including the mid 1970s. It contains, for instance, an overview
of the many attempts to forge unity among liberation movements. It contains chapters on
matters that seem now consigned to oblivion, but which at the time seemed to determine
Zambia's fate – for example, Zambia's role at an early stage of the Angolan civil war and
especially that difficult period of *détente* in the mid 1970s. It is a moot point whether the
study has transcended the particular period which it covers. For example, there is only one
reference to Robert Mugabe and nine to Ndabaningi Sithole. Their historical importance
appears now to be in the opposite order.

530 Kaunda and Southern Africa; image and reality in foreign policy.
Stephen Chan. London; New York: British Academic Press, 1992. 231p.

There are many conflicting images of Kaunda, and his image as a whole was subject to rapid change. The aim of this book is to demystify the intellectual history that has grown up around Kaunda's role in the liberation of Southern Africa. This valuable point of departure is followed, however, by a text of limited value. It lacks the narrative of a contemporary political history, and as an analysis of social situations it is flawed. For example, according to Chan, Kaunda's effectiveness was limited because he acted like an unguided missile, but he also argues that this could be very effective. Its value lies in its descriptions rather than the analysis of social situations. His descriptions of Kaunda's meeting with South African president De Klerk, or the visit of army officers with rumours about the Namibian situation, convey vividly the atmosphere in Zambia during the Southern African liberation struggle.

531 Zambia and the liberation of South Africa.
Kenneth Good. *Journal of Modern African Studies*, vol. 25, no. 3 (1987), p. 505-40.

This article deals more with domestic discontent and the government's reaction to it in the late Kaunda period than with the liberation of Southern Africa as such. It is informative in that respect, especially because it documents quite well the paranoia, xenophobia and scapegoating which could grip at least some sections of the Zambian population at that time. Good's preoccupation is – as usual – to debunk the myths around Kaunda. He speaks for example of 'Zambia's hostility to armed liberation movements and a readiness to co-operate covertly in various ways with South Africa and the United States to limit their success'. Such pronouncements can be considered overstatements; some indeed will consider them definitely wrong.

532 The high price of principles; Kaunda and the white south.
Richard Hall. Harmondsworth, England: Penguin Books, 1973. 285p. map.

Richard Hall was for many years the editor in chief of the *Times of Zambia*. He wrote contemporary history of the fight against white minority rule from the viewpoint of Kenneth Kaunda. In this book he gives a sympathetic account of Zambia's involvement in the Southern African liberation struggle. There are also some chapters on domestic politics which document important events such as the Skinner affair, when Kaunda gave in to demands from UNIP's youth wing and sacked Dennis Skinner, the Chief Justice. Hall – as a journalist – was himself a player in this struggle between the judiciary and arbitrary political power, and he lost or left the editorship of the *Times of Zambia* after writing editorials that were very critical of Kaunda. Nevertheless he makes a favourable judgement on Kaunda's use of power: 'It was not', he claims, 'in his nature to be autocratic' (p. 53), but circumstances forced him to be so. This judgement has not stood the test of time. Of course, there was a much more authoritarian leader in Southern Africa: Malawi's Dr Banda let Kaunda wait in the rain outside his house for an hour in 1961. This cameo is an illustration of this book's richness in anecdotes.

533 **The political economy of underdevelopment in Northern Rhodesia 1918-1960; a case study of customs; tariffs and railway freight policies.**
Ackson M. Kanduza.   Lanham, Maryland: University Press of America, 1986. 336p. 2 maps. bibliog.
This is a very detailed and informative study of the economic relations between Zambia and the rest of Southern Africa. It is couched in marxist jargon, but the issue with which Kanduza deals rises above the fashions of the day. His starting point is that Zambia is part of a double periphery: it is peripheral not only to the centres of world capitalism but also to the Southern African centre of capital. He therefore often resorts to the use of the expression 'fraction of capital': 'On the eve of the Second World War, the non-mining fraction of capital in Northern Rhodesia were engaged in a debate on how to encourage capital formation and industrialization in the country' (p. 162). The question of whether Zambia should aim to be more than a mere market for industries in Southern Africa has not lost its relevance. The railway, as the major connection with Southern Africa was therefore central to the problem.

534 **The Chitepo assassination.**
David Martin, Phyllis Johnson.   Harare: Zimbabwe Publishing House, 1985. 134p.
Herbert Chitepo was an important Zimbabwean politician who was killed by a car bomb in Lusaka in 1975. This episode is central to any understanding of Zambia's role in the liberation of Southern Africa. The Zambian government instituted a commission of enquiry whose members were drawn from all over the continent. The commission found that the murders (Chitepo was the most important one, but there were others) had been an internal matter within the Zimbabwean liberation movements, with tribalism and rivalry playing a major role. Martin and Johnson dispute this version of events, basing their argument on the testimony of an ex-Rhodesian Central Intelligence Organization officer. The commission's version was particularly convenient for the Zimbabwean leadership after independence as they were exonerated; another issue, of course, is how to balance the word of someone in Rhodesian security against the findings of a commission of enquiry. Such a commission has obviously far fewer vested interests in the events. This matter had long lasting effects on the relationship between Zambia and Zimbabwe.

535 **Politics of the Tanzania-Zambia rail project: a study of Tanzania-China-Zambia relations.**
Kasuka S. Mutukwa.   Washington, DC: University Press of America, 1977. 215p. map. bibliog.
This is primarily a study in international relations, documenting particularly the negotiations based on predictions of economic viability between the African countries, Western countries and mainland China. Mutukwa stresses Zambian reluctance: 'the Chinese may have not forgotten the suspicion, caution and hesitation on the part of Zambia to receive the loan offer for the Tanzania railway' (p. 201). The fact that the study ends before the railway came into operation does not diminish its value and one may wonder, for example, what has become of the thirty yearly instalments, beginning in 1983, by which the loan was to be repaid.

536 **Legal aspects of regional integration: COMESA and SADC on the regulation of foreign investment in Southern and Eastern Africa.**
Kenneth Kaoma Mwenda. *African Journal of International and Comparative Law*, vol. 9, no. 2 (1997), p. 324-49.

Despite the fact that Zambia does not figure in the title, the article discusses its position specifically in these two bodies – of which it is a member – aimed at promoting regional integration. It reviews Zambian legislation in the light of these treaties with respect to private foreign investment, transfer pricing and technology transfer. The information about Zambian legislation may be useful to some, but the relationship of this to the treaties remains vague. In general the article could have been rather more coherent.

537 **The Ndola crash and the death of Dag Hammerskjöld.**
Bengt Rosio. *Journal of Modern African Studies*, vol. 31, no. 4 (1993), p. 661-71.

The subject here is more an event that happened to take place within Zambia's borders than a Zambian event. The author was Swedish consul in Léopoldville (now Kinshasa) in 1961-62. He argues that, although certain events related to the air crash in which the UN Secretary General died are unexplainable, there is no positive indication of attempted murder. Above all, he argues that there was little motive to kill Hammerskjöld among the people accused of the supposed murder. The article is worth reading after a visit to the monument in Ndola.

538 **The aid relationship in Zambia; a conflict scenario.**
Oliver Saasa, Jerker Carlsson. Uppsala, Sweden: The Nordic African Institute; Lusaka: The Institute of African Studies, 1996. 170p. bibliog.

Four case studies on development co-operation are at the core of this book. They look at the Zambia educational materials project; the Western Province water supply and sanitation programme; the ground water development project in Southern Province; and drought emergency aid in Southern Africa as a whole in 1992. These cases are analysed with respect to the interaction between donors and host countries; conflict in this interaction is given a central place. The general plea is for more donor co-ordination, decentralization and participation. The authors have been consultants to aid organizations and their writing conveys a feeling for aid administration from the inside. The two chapters on macroeconomic development in, and aid flows to, Zambia contain some useful information which may be difficult to access in other forms.

539 **Friends, neighbours and former enemies: the evolution of Zambia-Zimbabwe relations in a changing regional context.**
James R. Scarrit, Solomon M. Nkiwane. *Africa Today*, vol. 43, no. 1 (1996), p. 7-32.

There is a dearth of writing on Zambian international relations in the Chiluba period. This article is therefore very welcome. It conscientiously moves through all possible fields of contact, including poachers, electricity generation, free trade blocks and regional security. It has a sharp eye for the ambiguities inherent in the relationships between Zambia and Zimbabwe. From time to time strong language is used, such as the following: 'However, it appears that Frederick Chiluba's MMD government holds Kaunda – and by association, Zimbabwe – personally responsible for Zambia's past and present economic woes' (p. 19).

540 The foreign policy of Zambia: ideology and interests.
Timothy M. Shaw. *Journal of Modern African Studies*, vol. 14, no. 1 (1976), p. 79-105.
The article aims to make the theoretical point that international relations are intimately linked to domestic politics. It tries to prove this point by studying Zambia's ambivalence towards the liberation struggle in Southern Africa. It is inspired by some major events in the mid 1980s: a new peace initiative in Zimbabwe; and the meeting of John Vorster, then the South African Prime Minister, and Kenneth Kaunda in a railway carriage on the bridge over the Zambezi. Shaw interprets Zambian domestic politics in terms of a debate on the national ideology: was Kaunda's Zambian humanism a nationalist or a socialist ideology? In these circumstances, *détente* is considered to have been successful to date because it advances both national and ideological interests in Zambia. That seemed a sensible position at the time, but *détente* with hindsight can be interpreted as the prelude to Zambia's deep involvement in the Zimbabwean liberation war. The article may have mistaken the events of a moment for a deep underlying trend.

541 Zambia; I changed my mind.
Michael Wright. London: Johnson, 1972. 172p.
Wright is a British liberal who was sympathetic to the Kaunda government. He came to work as a lecturer at Evelyn Hone College of Further Education in Lusaka in 1966. As the title says, he changed his mind about Kaunda after that. Chapter titles characterize the book well: 'Voting and the persecution of the opposition'; 'The hunting of the Chief Justice'; 'The plight of the religious'. Wright definitely exaggerates some of his judgements, for example when he talks about Chinese penetration of, and British collapse in, Zambia. Yet this is an interesting book as it gives a – perhaps somewhat biased – account of important political events in the 1960s. Wright also gives an intriguing impression of daily life in Lusaka for expatriates: theirs was a comfortable life.

Economy

542 Fiscal adjustment, financial liberalization and the dynamics of inflation: some evidence from Zambia.
Christopher Adam. *World Development*, vol. 23, no. 5 (1995), p. 735-50. bibliog.

Although Zambia has liberalized its economy considerably, this has not led to macroeconomic stabilization. This article deals with the following phenomenon, which the author terms perverse: why did inflation remain high despite quite tight monetary control on the part of the government? The explanation given is that there remained a high demand for money to convert into foreign exchange or high interest treasury bonds. This is a highly technical article in which models are built using terms such as 'laffer curve', 'variable eignoreige' and 'exogenous monetary growth'. It poses, however, very pertinent questions on the nature of the Zambian economy, which merit attention from more than just professional economists.

543 A nonlinear multisectoral simulation analysis of devaluation and import substitution in Zambia.
Michael J. Applegate. *Journal of Developing Areas*, vol. 24, no. 4 (1990), p. 543-56.

The model of the Zambian economy presented here is only accessible to econometrists. The general question posed is more widely pertinent, however, given the long-term slide of the Zambian *kwacha*: under what conditions does devaluation lead to the contraction rather than the stimulation of the economy? The article argues in favour of stimulation, despite allowing that there was an increase in domestic prices. According to the model, more strict controls on credit supply – especially government borrowing – would have prevented this increase.

170

544 The politics and economics of policy reform in Zambia.
Robert H. Bates, Paul Collier. *Journal of African Economies*,
vol. 4, no. 1 (1995), p. 115-43. bibliog.
There is no original research in this article, but it is worth noting as the authors are
influential in debates on structural adjustment. Their focus is the period 1985-87 and
theirs is one of the numerous attempts to interpret Kaunda's break with the IMF. The rise
in inflation played a central role in that event, and they argue that it was a one-off rise due
to the coincidence of foreign exchange auctioning and the abolition of price controls. It
was fuelled especially by expectations of further shortages of foreign exchange; a huge
increase in demand was the reason for the depreciation of the currency. They believe
therefore that the economy would have recovered if the government had persisted with
liberalization. The government did not do that as the structure of the one-party state
insulated the party bureaucracy from other interests in society.

**545 Zambia's economic reforms and their aftermath: the state and
the growth of indigenous capital.**
Carolyn Baylies. *Journal of Commonwealth and Comparative
Politics*, vol. 20, no. 3 (1982), p. 236-63.
This article discusses the effects of the measures by the Zambian state to diminish
expatriate control over the economy. It considers a latent tension between state capital and
indigenous capital. A Zambian capitalist class is believed to be emerging; this conclusion
is based on research in the land registry and the company registry. This class is seen as
still being too much in the process of formation to have much political clout, albeit that
members express interests through interest groups. A sobering conclusion could have
been given more prominence in the article: Baylies surveyed a considerable number of
enterprises and found that 'as many as forty per cent appeared to obtain little or no surplus
and perhaps a quarter of those were hovering on the brink of failure' (p. 249).

**546 Government revenue stabilisation in primary producing
countries: a model for Zambia.**
Michael W. Bell. *Journal of Modern African Studies*, vol. 21, no. 1
(1983), p. 55-76.
This article is mainly normative in character. Bell proposes a development stabilization
fund to cope with swings in fiscal receipts due to fluctuations or swings in the price of
primary products. According to him, such a fund could have overcome the depression
caused by the drop in copper prices since 1976. It contains a few lucid sections on
government finance in Zambia during the early 1980s when the author was working in
Zambia's Ministry of Finance.

547 African businessmen and development in Zambia.
Andrew A. Beveridge, Anthony Oberschall. Princeton, New
Jersey: Princeton University Press, 1979. 382p. 3 maps. bibliog.
This book, which first appeared when neo-marxism was in vogue, offered a perspective
which was unfashionable at that time, but which is considered highly relevant in today's
common neo-liberal ethos. It is based on elaborate research, covering virtually the whole
business community in Zambia. The main interest of the authors, the emergence of an
independent Zambian entrepreneurial class, is most apparent in a statistical analysis to

explain success. The conclusion that sixty-nine per cent of success can be explained by thirteen variables identified (p. 224) points to a weakness in the book: the assemblage of fragments of observations do not make a whole that is easy to comprehend. However, the book has a particular strength: it is overflowing with apt casual observations. For example, European and Asian businessmen are described as uncontrollably disgusted about their workforce (p. 150). The authors make also intriguing general points, for example on page 139 where they dispute the importance of religion in entrepreneurial success. Part of their work has been previously published in articles, which are mentioned in the preface.

548 Zambia country assistance review; turning an economy around.
Gladstone G. Bonnick.   Washington, DC: The World Bank;
Operations Evaluations Studies, 1997. 151p.

The country assistance reviews are evaluations of World Bank lending as well as documents recording contemporary economic history. This means they are of interest to various audiences. Readers who are interested to know that lending in the energy sector was most successful, and lending in the agricultural sector least so, may be a different group from those interested in a chronology of events or basic statistical data covering the period 1963 to 1996. Rather than presenting a novel analysis of Zambia's economic problems, the general tenor of the report emphasizes the need to involve Zambian stakeholders; bank donor collaboration; capacity building; donor co-ordination; and other measures in the management sphere. Yet there is little divergence between foreign donors and the government of Zambia: Bonnick states that, 'It is impossible to determine how much of this strategy Zambia really owns and how much the statement reflects Zambia's deep awareness of its financial dependence on donors' (p. 57).

549 The mines, class power, and foreign policy in Zambia.
Marcia M. Burdette.   *Journal of Southern African Studies*, vol. 10,
no. 2 (1984), p. 198-218.

This is primarily an article about the onset of Zambia's economic crisis in the 1970s, with special reference to the mining sector. The mines are crucial to any understanding of Zambia, and therefore all material on that subject is precious. For example, the discussion on page 212 on the gearing (indebtedness) of the mining companies should be noted. Burdette's analysis of class formation in which technocrats, civil servants, entrepreneurs and national politicians are distinguished remains speculative. She has some worthwhile observations on the complexities of Zambian foreign policy, but her argument remains disjointed in other respects. The value of the article lies in the information on the mines.

550 Industrial development in Zambia, Zimbabwe and Malawi: the primacy of politics.
Marcia M. Burdette.   In: *Studies in the economic history of Southern Africa; vol. I. The front line states.*   Edited by Z.A.
Konczacki, Jane L. Parpart, Timothy M. Shaw.   London: Frank
Cass, 1990, p. 75-127.

Even though Zambia is only one of the countries dealt with in a book which is not enormously thorough and comprehensive, this article may be useful as it sums up, albeit not completely, the formation of particular industries at particular times. Burdette concludes that the failure of Zambia's import substitution industries was predetermined by the inherited economic base, the events just after independence and the class character of the new regime. It is thus more an article on political economy than micro-economic analysis; however, this latter may be more useful in understanding what went wrong.

551 Zambia: debt and poverty.
John Clark, Caroline Allison. Oxford: Oxfam, 1989. 66p.
This introduction to Zambia's indebtedness and poverty is aimed at the broadest public. Boxes within the main text vividly describe the predicament of ordinary people. The authors argue that the responsibility for Zambia's debt is shared between Zambia and the donor community.

552 Third World countries and development options: Zambia.
Jonathan H. Chileshe.   New Delhi: Vikas Publishing House, 1986. 220p. 2 maps. bibliog.
This analysis of the Zambian economy, which concludes at the end of the 1970s, was not prescient. Although it sees major problems in Zambia, it airs the opinion that government participation in the economy through nationalization is a permanent fixture. This book can therefore be judged as outdated, but paradoxically that is its value. Chileshe was a high ranking civil servant and in his preface thanks especially Andrew Kashita and Alex Chikwanda who for a long time were close to Zambian economic decision making. It is therefore valuable as evidence of how the Zambian economy was seen up to 1976 from the inside of government rather than from an economic analysis point of view. It contains some remarkably astute observations on colonial history, such as its singling out Luapula Province in the development of African entrepreneurship or its pointing out that INDECO, the holding company in which most of the nationalized firms found a home, was formed as early as 1951.

553 Mukanashi: an exploration of some effects of the penetration of capital in North Western Zambia.
Kate Crehan.   *Journal of Southern African Studies*, vol. 7, no. 2 (1981), p. 82-93.
This is a short and impressionistic account of the role of money – in Crehan's words the penetration of capital – among the Kaonde in a remote area in North Western Province.

554 Constraints on the Zambian economy.
Charles Elliott.   Nairobi: Oxford University Press, 1971. 431p. 4 maps. bibliog.
This book is not outdated, despite the fact that it deals with the Zambian economy in the early 1960s, before the massive government intervention in the economy. Some chapters are outstanding, notably Richard Jolly's on the manpower constraint which was most binding in the early post-independence years when foreign exchange was in ample supply and demand was buoyant. Some of the book's remarks and terminology are strongly evocative of the times: 'an economy in which a cost-inflationary situation is compounded by excessive demand' or 'the aggressive – and some would say reckless – approach of the Industrial Development Corporation is likely to ensure that the planned targets on growth of manufacturing output will be met'. This volume is not only of historical interest, however, and it is regrettable that the massive amount of writing on the Zambian

economy does not refer to it. It is simply the best book ever written on the Zambian economy.

555 Zambia: reform and reversal.
Mohsen A. Fardi. In: *Restructuring economies in distress: policy reform and the World Bank.* Edited by Vinod Thomas, Ajay Chibber, Mansoor Dailami, Jaime de Melo. Oxford: Oxford University Press for the World Bank, 1991, p. 332-61.

This paper focuses on the relations between Zambia and the international financial institutions. Besides dealing with familiar general issues in the Zambian economy, the article is particularly informative on detailed issues concerning the negotiations up to 1987, when Kaunda broke with the IMF. It covers no more than four years of structural adjustment. Zambia's performance is seen at best as mixed in that period. Rigidities in the economic structure – caused by too much state involvement – are singled out as the major cause of the country's troubles. The lesson drawn is interesting: it is not sufficient that the elite accept a reform package; adequate incentives must be provided for the base of society. At the end of the article there is a discussion with Ben King and Edward Jaycox. Even though this book was published quite some time ago, it broaches themes that are still considered as central these days.

556 Economic dependence and the development of industry in Zambia.
Robin Fincham. *Journal of Modern African Studies*, vol. 18, no. 2 (1980), p. 279-313.

This is a subtly argued article which examines the thesis that Zambia's industrialization after independence was neo-colonial in character as argued by Anne Seidman (see item no. 589), that is, that it was excessively reliant on foreign inputs in management, raw materials, etc. As is common in import substitution, it was indeed increasingly dependent upon imports; the recession after 1970 led to redundancies in the productive sectors as compared to the service sectors; there was, however, a significant increase in locally added value; finally a much more complicated relationship than one of domination appeared between the state and foreign partners. Industrialization in Zambia was mainly located in the state sector, and Fincham argues that the state is a much more complicated arena of class struggle than is often suggested.

557 Understanding the failure of IMF reform: the Zambian case.
Jeffrey J. Hawkins Jr. *World Development*, vol. 19, no. 7 (1991), p. 839-49.

The object of this article is to clarify the political components involved in structural adjustment. According to Hawkins, reform implies a need to placate supporters of the old political regime and to promote new supporters successfully. The author tries in the first place to make a theoretical point, but illuminating insights and rare information about Zambia may be found in section four, which deals with the attempts at reform from 1984 to 1987. The reactions of the trade union movement to the initial reform programme may be especially worth noting.

558 Industrialisation and industrial promotion in the Western Province of Zambia.
Wim Hoppers, Aart van de Laar. The Hague: Institute of Social Studies Advisory Services, 1984. 130p. map. bibliog.

This is primarily of interest to those working on issues of regional development in Zambia. Government bureaucracy takes centre stage in this report which dates from the time when the working of the market was not seen as the prime mover in development. It may amaze people in this day and age that serious consideration was given to promoting industrial development in as unpropitious a location as Zambia's Western Province. The only concrete industries mentioned are in the agro-processing field: mangoes and meat.

559 The Seers Report in retrospect.
Richard Jolly. *African Social Research*, no. 11 (1971), p. 1-26.

Dudley Seers was chairman of a UN mission charged with mapping out a strategy for economic development at independence. This early article evaluates the recommendations and projections made. A comparison of projections and actual outcomes makes interesting reading. It is profitable at a time when the Zambian economy has declined so dramatically to read the doubts voiced before this decline set in. For example: 'The failure of investment to reach its 1970 target is almost entirely due to the failure to maintain the expansion of government expenditure after 1968' (p. 9). Such statements contrast with the spirit of the time in these neo-liberal days.

560 Zambia.
Igor Karmiloff. In: *Manufacturing Africa: performance and prospects of seven countries in sub-Saharan Africa.* Edited by Roger C. Riddell. London: James Currey, 1990, p. 297-323. bibliog.

This article deals with its subject in a very thorough manner. Karmiloff notes that 'public sector enterprises achieved commendable results in introducing a tight and up-to-date system of management reporting' to the International Monetary Fund; he probably benefited from that in writing this piece. Karmiloff discusses many familiar issues such as import substitution, the break with the IMF in 1997, and so on. This article stands out among the many dealing with such issues in the information it provides on the foreign exchange position. For example, ZIMCO, the parastatal holding company, earned $423 million in the first half of fiscal year 1987/88, but their total budgeted requirement of foreign currencies in the same period was $759 million. The allocation they actually received came only to $273 million or thirty-six per cent of what was necessary to honour their investments. It is obvious that productive capacity was run down on a tremendous scale. Although the book deals with manufacturing, the author also includes the mining industry under that heading.

561 Privatisation in Zambia.
Ephraim C. Kaunga. In: *Privatisation: a global perspective.* Edited by V.V. Ramanadham. London: Routledge, 1993, p. 373-96.

Kaunga was at the time of writing a director of ZIMCO – Zambia's conglomerate of state owned enterprises – and therefore he was well informed about policy making. This is mainly an historical record of the initiatives towards privatization at the end of the

Kaunda period (1990-91). Kaunga concludes that Zambia had only just embarked on the road to diminished state involvement in the economy. The radical changes that took place afterwards could not be foreseen then. The article is followed by a useful list of Zambian enterprises which are partly or wholly owned by government.

562 Growth from own resources: Zambia's fourth national development plan in perspective.
Steve Kayizzi-Mugerwa. *Development Policy Review*, vol. 8, no. 1 (1990), p. 59-77.

The fourth national development plan (1988-93) was the last plan produced. Just like the previous plans, it had mainly a symbolic function. Indeed, Kayizzi-Mugerwa concludes that perception of a plan's success rises or falls with the assumptions on which it is based. The prospects for this plan, given the susequent changes in Zambia, are therefore not particularly bright. The plan is discussed against the background of past failures to reach planned goals and in the context of the necessity for structural adjustment. Despite the fact that planning has had only a marginal significance in the Zambian economy, the article is worth noting for points other than those dealing with the plan alone. It gives a good flavour of the policy-making dilemmas faced during the period described and which have not lost relevance: the search for macroeconomic stability is still acute at the start of the 21st century.

563 External shocks and adjustment in a mineral dependent economy.
Steve Kayizzi-Mugerwa. *World Development*, vol. 19, no. 7 (1991), p. 851-65.

The economic modelling in this article is accessible only to econometrists. Kayizzi-Mugerwa's general conclusions have a more general application, however: standard explanations of the effects of high mineral prices on an economy (so-called Dutch disease) expect the reverse of these effects when the boom comes to an end. That did not happen in Zambia where both high mineral prices and low mineral prices were associated with a fall in manufacturing output. According to the author, agricultural activity is not affected by an upward movement in mineral prices, and he is silent about what happens in this sector when mineral prices fall. He concludes that the relationships between mineral revenues and the rest of the economy are complicated, but the question of the dynamic of these relationships remains open.

564 Zambia: 'stop-go' adjustment.
Angela Keller-Herzog, Monica L. Munachonga. In: *The gender dimension of economic reforms in Ghana, Mali and Zambia.* Edited by Lynn R. Brown, Joanne Kerr. Ottawa: The North-South Institute, 1997, p. 99-147. map. bibliog.

The Canadian International Development Agency (CIDA) commissioned this extensive study on gender and adjustment, of which the Zambian chapter is a part. It is thus policy oriented research. It reasons from an analysis through a problem/decision tree (based on experiences in Choma and Kasama), and provides an analysis of major barriers to making structural adjustment more effective. The exercise results in recommendations on policy options to increase the productivity of small-scale female producers. The work also contains the mixture of useful statistical information and general impressions to be found in consultants' reports. One finding should be noted as it may throw a different light on structural adjustment: 'It would be misleading to give the impression of a gradual, orderly, planned and pre-announced process of market liberalization. Liberalization occurred in fits and starts, driven by the fiscal deficits and SAP conditionality. Policy changes in general were not announced prior to the beginning of the planting season' (p. 120).

565 Structural adjustment in Zambia.
Stephen Jones. In: *Negotiating structural adjustment in Africa.* Edited by Willem van der Geest. London: James Currey for UNDP, 1994, p. 25-47. bibliog.

Although the article is dated, dealing as it does mainly with the period immediately before MMD came to power in 1991, it is highly informative. It gives an overview of all reform efforts from 1981 to 1991. It discusses in detail the effects of the auctioning system – which is evaluated positively – and the marketing of maize. According to Jones there is a cyclical pattern to efforts at structural adjustment in Zambia for three main reasons: weak policy design and implementation; inadequate external responses; and internal obstacles to reform. With respect to the latter, he sees a rift between technocrats in favour of market forces, who were supported by the president, and the party structure parallel to the government, which represented vested interests. The position which he thus assigns to Kaunda may be questionable. The author does not doubt that market reforms were in the public interest, but misunderstandings arose because of lack of comprehension of policy, failure of external promoters of adjustment to explain and justify policy prescriptions and a variety of other factors.

566 Rural labour markets in an adjusting mineral economy: Zambia.
John Loxley. In: *Structural adjustment and rural labour markets in Africa.* Edited by Vali Jamal. Basingstoke, England: Macmillan, 1995, p. 131-77.

Although the title suggests that the rural sector is the central focus of this piece, it is in fact one of the many articles devoted to Zambia's relations with the IMF. It deals therefore with the whole economy, rather than with the rural sector only. Its linchpin is Kaunda's break with the IMF in 1987. The description of the factors which drove Kaunda back to the IMF is lucid, and some attention is paid to events after 1990. The hybrid maize boom in outlying areas in the early 1980s, which was fuelled by government intervention, receives much attention. The urban working class is depicted as powerful in this article and is seen as a constraint on the implementation of an IMF programme of structural adjustment. After 1987 this resulted therefore, according to Loxley, in a deterioration of the terms of trade for the rural versus the urban sector.

567 An investigation into the change in the terms of trade between the rural and urban sectors of Zambia.
Fabian J.M. Maimbo, James Fry. *African Social Research*, no. 12 (1971), p. 95-110.

This is a sophisticated analysis of the statements made by Young (see item no. 604), which were immediately incorporated into a major speech by Kaunda. It combines statistical data collected by the Central Bureau of Statistics with the results of a budget survey among rural households in Pemba and Mzimba (Southern Province), and shows that the issues were more complicated and paradoxical than it seemed at first sight. Again, it is important to recognize the totally different starting points in considering economic policy compared to today's: 'one will have to wait until some kind of complete prices and incomes policy is implemented, covering rural as well as urban incomes' (p. 109).

568 Structural adjustment policies in Africa: designing chaos or chaos on implementation.
G.S. Maipose.   In: *Structural adjustment, reconstruction and development in Africa.*   Edited by Kempe Ronald Hope Sr.
Aldershot, England: Ashgate, 1997, p. 35-57.

There is little new material in this article, which traces Zambia's development strategies and economic fortunes since independence. It contains some information (three and a half pages) on structural adjustment since 1991, a period for which material is not abundant. Maipose treats structural adjustment problems in a political context, and the sensitive political judgements by a Zambian, from an internal perspective, make it worth noting. For example: 'the sequence of dominant public attitudes to democratization can be described as first euphoria, then disillusionment, and finally resignation and acceptance' (p. 55).

569 The global economy's impact on recent budgetary politics in Zambia.
John Markakis, Robert L. Curry.   *Journal of African Studies*, vol. 3, no. 4 (1976), p. 403-28.

The main argument made in this article is that Zambia needed to restrain its government expenditure after the drastic fall in copper prices, but that the Zambian government was beholden to a structure of privilege which it had itself created. It is a useful article, drawing attention to the role played by issues relevant at that time, such as the popular protests about food prices. The authors formulate one insight that unfortunately proved true: the government 'appears ready to embark on a venture that could be economically perilous – supplemental foreign borrowing' (p. 413).

570 Minding their own business: Zambia's struggle against western control.
Anthony Martin.   Harmondsworth, England: Penguin Books, 1975. 288p. map.

Martin is a journalist and therefore this book reads well and makes quite complicated material more accessible than academic writing. The chapter on 'How the Deal was Done' is an excellent introduction to the technicalities involved in nationalizing the copper mines. Although the mining industry is the centre of attention, the book is also an economic history of Zambia in the period 1964-70. Journalists are guided by a feel for what is relevant and therefore highlight issues that do not receive enough attention in the mental framework of academics. Martin demonstrates this trait, pointing out, for example, the way in which nationalizations gave opportunities to access loan capital, or singling out the fact that the Governor of the Bank of Zambia, Dr J.B. Zulu, was the only senior Zambian to oppose the deal with the mining companies. Zulu pointed to the danger of Zambia being committed to an unduly heavy outflow of foreign exchange after the nationalizations.

571 **Opportunities and prospects for energy conservation in an electrical utility: a Zambian case.**
Abel Mbewe. In: *African energy; issues in planning and practice.*
Edited by African Policy Research Network. London: Zed Books, 1990, p. 77-81.

This short note argues that the overall losses in the Zambian electricity system are low by African standards. The losses in the retail sector are substantial however, and electricity theft is a major topic of this paper.

572 **Planning and management in the African power sector; part 2 Zambia.**
Abel Mbewe. In: *Planning and management in the African power sector.* Edited by African Policy Research Network. London: Zed Books, 1998, p. 15-99.

The extremely valuable information contained in these papers is not immediately obvious. That is because this overview is written in a quite bureaucratic style and it ends in a set of recommendations which are self-evident. It contains, for example, tables on electricity demand, which give a general insight into the Zambian economy; and the projection of the mines' power demand gives valuable insight into their expected working lifetimes. An overview of the place of electricity in the cost structure of Zambia's major industries, such as Chilanga Cement and Nakambala Sugar Estates, is also highly informative. These papers would probably be especially fertile ground for an expert in the power sector.

573 **Structural adjustment and diversification in Zambia.**
Fons Meijer. *Development and Change*, vol. 21, no. 4 (1990), p. 657-92.

The economic term 'Dutch disease', referring to the effects on an economy of booming revenues from a mineral resource (copper in the case of Zambia), is central in this article. It traces the development of the Zambian economy over time since 1964 and stresses the postponement of adjustment. Meijer is sympathetic to the Zambian predicament and states that, 'It could be wondered whether any government would have been able to stabilize' after such a huge drop in income as happened in Zambia after 1974. It sees the solution in a diversification of tradeables which will necessarily have to be a medium-term strategy.

574 **African socialist ideologies and the IMF policies for economic development: the case of Zambia.**
Nsolo N.J. Mijere. *African Review*, vol. 15, no. 1 (1988), p. 41-59.

This mainly ideological article argues that the IMF wanted Zambia to divert from a socialist path. The tables presented on changes in the exchange rate and in prices during the period of auctioning of foreign exchange in 1985 are informative.

575 **Zambia.**
Thandika Mkandawire.   In: *The rocky road to reform: adjustment, income distribution, and growth in the developing world.*   Edited by Lance Taylor.   Cambridge, Massachusetts: The MIT Press, 1993, p. 457-75. bibliog.
Mkandawire describes policy responses in three distinct periods: 1964-68; 1968-74; 1975-87. The heart of the article is an economic model which highlights four characteristics. Firstly, Zambia is seen as a mineral rentier economy where government revenue is dependent upon copper. Secondly, higher capacity utilization in the economy as a whole leads to a reduction of the budget surplus, because of a highly subsidized, large parastatal sector. Private saving is crowded out by capital inflows, but rises strongly with capacity utilization. Thirdly, imports are sensitive to the real exchange rate, but liberalization seems to be associated with higher consumer imports and capital flight. Lastly, exports appear to be a function of capacity utilization, mainly because the copper industry is highly import dependent. The article ends with a discussion of the attempt at home-made adjustment after 1987 and policy changes up to 1993. Mkandawire's analysis concludes that rescheduling of debt is crucial to any possible revival of the economy.

576 **Contemporary issues in socio-economic reform in Zambia.**
Herrick C. Mpuku, Ivan Zyuulu.   Aldershot, England: Ashgate Publishing Ltd, 1997. 140p.
There is a dearth of literature on the Zambian economy since 1991 and a title like this may attract many readers. They will, however, be disappointed because none of the issues is discussed with any empirical depth. The book contains contributions on, among other things, financial reform; land tenure reform; housing and urbanization; and the health sector. The book originates from the Copperbelt University, and George Simwinga, the then vice-chancellor, contributes a chapter on managing that university. He complains bitterly in it about the unionized workers who resort to 'dirty tactics, manipulation of facts and realities including outright disinformation about the institution'. This illustrates how opinions rather than actual facts are to be found in this book. The usefulness of the book is therefore limited to those interested in such opinions.

577 **A needs assessment of the urban informal sector: a case study of market niches, product and service needs for the urban informal sector in Lusaka.**
Lawrence Mukuka.   Lusaka: Government of the Republic of Zambia; Gemeinschaft für Technische Zusammenarbeit, Step-in Programme, 1999. 108p. bibliog.
This study has to be situated in the neo-liberal belief in the market as the way out of poverty. A support programme for small business development commissioned it and it documents opportunities and constraints. The study is a survey of a stratified sample of businesses in five areas in Lusaka: Mtendere, Chaisa, Lilanda, Mandevu and Kanyama. The results are presented in a plethora of tables, which could be useful for further analysis in other contexts. The tables are broken down by gender, and from these it appears that, for females, setting up a small business is much more a question of necessity whereas, for males, it is more a question of grasping opportunities. Mukuka's conclusions may shock some readers. The concept of credit is not understood; it is seen as free money: 'The

general mentality of female and male operators is still that of expecting to get things for free' (p. 88).

578 Structural adjustment and drought in Zambia.
Mpanjilwa Mulwanda. *Disasters*, vol. 19, no. 2 (1995), p. 85-94.
The value of this article lies in a short description of the dramatic drought of 1992. The author is concerned with the effects of this drought on structural adjustment. The money supply increased in 1992 by ninety-nine per cent as against a target of thirty-five per cent, which according to Mulwanda, resulted from drought-related expenditure. It is an opinion worth noting in the general discussion about economic reform but, other than that, this article offers little of substance on either topic.

579 Too rich to be poor? A glimpse of the poverty situation in Zambia in the 1990s.
Gerry Nkombo Muuka, Denny H. Kalyalya. *Scandinavian Journal of Development Alternatives and Area Studies*, vol. 16, no. 1 (1997), p. 157-71.
Despite the fact that the authors are economists there is little in the way of economic data to be found in this article. There is a cursory review of causes of poverty against the background of their assumption that there is no reason for Zambia, given its natural resources, to be poor, but the most significant part of the article is a list of ways in which people cope with poverty. The authors do not limit themselves to the obvious ones, but mention, for example, gambling and increasing reliance on traditional healers as coping strategies of the poor.

580 The structural adjustment programme in Zambia: lessons from experience.
Allast Mwanza. Harare: SAPES Books, 1992. 47p.
The SAPES trust has the reputation of publishing radical views from African authors on recent events. This book may disappoint those who are looking for that, not only because this slim volume is announced as a monograph, but also because it contains little information beyond the mid 1980s, despite being published in 1992. The views expressed are also quite conventional. There is a defence of the home-grown structural adjustment advocated by Kaunda in the late 1980s, but the failure of that programme is seen as the result of a lack of foreign aid.

581 Chasing the winds and dependency syndrome; topical issues on Zambia's political economy.
Frederick K. Mwanza. Lusaka: MFK Management Consultancy Services, 1983. 41p.
Most of this pamphlet is comprised of a rather descriptive account of Zambia's political history. The most interesting part is in the last few pages, which are very sceptical about liberalization and privatization. The author was the first company secretary of INDECO, the parastatal holding company, and believes that, 'for the benefit of the young generation, it is important to reflect on the events leading to the creation of the parastatal sector' (p. 31).

582 World Bank and IMF supported programs – a Zambian perspective.
Jacob Mwanza. In: *Deepening structural reform in Africa; lessons from East Asia.* Edited by Laura Wallace. Washington, DC: International Monetary Fund, 1997, p. 129-46.

Mwanza is the governor of the Bank of Zambia and therefore this article is an authoritative statement on structural adjustment by a Zambian. It gives an historical overview of the genesis of reforms and a sector by sector treatment of the effects. As befits an article by a central bank governor, it is written objectively, from an internal perspective, but at the same time gives a clear opinion. Its generally positive attitude to reform is expressed in technical terms. For example: the treasury bill system is valued as it mops up excess liquidity that could put pressure on the exchange rate. The last two pages are extremely valuable as they contain a reasoned explanation for the disappointing results of reforms. For example: given the importance of the mining sector and the nature of its markets, one cannot expect a short-term response to liberalization and privatization.

583 The influence of the comparative price in the substitution of coal for woodfuel charcoal: the Zambian case.
A.N. Ng'andu (in collaboration with A.N. Mwanza). In: *African energy; issues in planning and practice.* Edited by African Policy Research Network. London: Zed Books, 1990, p. 106-11.

This short note argues that Zambia has substantial coal reserves, which are now used only in the mining industry. If coal were used for domestic fuel it could slow down deforestation. The article maintains that the cost of charcoal has been kept artificially low due to price controls. It would be interesting to see what has happened to the price of charcoal since such controls have disappeared.

584 Transforming a single-product economy; an examination of the first stage of Zambia's economic reform program, 1982-86.
Edited by Helen O'Neill. Washington, DC: Economic Development Institute of the World Bank, 1987. 243p.

Helen O'Neill wrote a substantial part of this report by Irish and Zambian economists as well as editing it. The report can best be described as a summary of thinking on economic reform at a point in time. It is interesting to note that the changes which took place after 1991 were at this time still unthinkable. Privatization of the mining industry, for example, is not mooted, and the concern is merely whether a new generation of better-trained Zambians will instil more commercial criteria into the industry. It contains much useful statistical material not easily available outside Zambia. The maize boom in outlying areas during the 1980s is well documented, for example. This document is, however, now primarily of historical interest rather than a treatment of essential themes in the study of the Zambian economy.

585 Food consumption and adjustment in Zambia.
Richard Pearce. In: *Negotiating structural adjustment in Africa.*
Edited by Willem van der Geest. London; Portsmouth, New
Hampshire: James Currey, 1994, p. 84-99.

This article is based on an evaluation of the food coupon system which the Kaunda
government introduced after riots about rises in maize prices in 1987. It identifies
resource poor households in urban and rural areas and argues that higher maize prices
may stimulate maize production, but may also make the position of these households
more difficult. It is therefore sympathetic to food subsidies, even though it also considers
administrative arrangements other than the coupon system. It recognizes the budgetary
constraint which forces government to cut subsidies.

586 Linkage creation, multinational companies and the Zambian economy.
N. Perdikis, P.G. Saunders. *Scandinavian Journal of Development
Alternatives*, vol. 10, no. 1/2 (1991), p. 172-89.

A questionnaire was sent in 1983 to all foreign subsidiaries in Zambia asking them about
the extent to which they used local sources of inputs. The response was rather low
(twenty-eight per cent) and showed that such backward linkages were underdeveloped.
The article gives a flavour of the attitude of expatriate business to the local economy.

587 Aid and economic reform in Africa: Zambia.
Lisa Rakner, Nicholas van der Walle, Dominic Mulaisho.
Washington, DC: The World Bank, 1999.

This is one report among many in a study of this topic by the World Bank research
department. In another influential World Bank report (*Assessing aid*, by principal
investigator David Dollar), Zambia is considered as an example of a country where aid
cannot be effective because of the poor policy environment. This report is not as
unsympathetic to Zambia as that. It portrays Zambia as quite a strong reformer, but
nevertheless tends towards a general conclusion of policy failure: there has been
no coherent growth strategy; reform has been only partial; and the policies in relation
to agricultural development are uneven. At the time of writing there is no
commercial paper version of the report. It can, however, be downloaded from
www.worldbank.org/research/aid/

**588 The IMF and Zambia: the contradiction of exchange rate
auctioning and de-subsidization of agriculture.**
Hans Otto Sano. *African Affairs*, vol. 87, no. 349 (1988),
p. 563-77.

Sano quotes the weekly *The Economist* at the beginning of the article: 'Mr Kaunda has
never known the first thing about economics...' and then argues that Kaunda's adversary,
the IMF, may itself have at best a limited understanding. He queries the latter's belief that
devaluation and de-subsidization of maize are in the interests of small farmers. Zambia
reduced subsidies in the structural adjustment programme, but maize farming in outlying
regions by small farmers came under threat as their cultivation is very import dependent.
Devaluation therefore raised their costs and, as a result, the government was forced to
raise subsidies. Sano argues that, contrary to IMF beliefs, subsidies have led to a

reduction in differences between urban and rural living standards. Within rural areas, large-scale farmers benefit from the unleashing of full market forces. He concludes that, 'Foreign parties involved should make an effort to understand the implications of what they are doing'.

589 The distorted growth of import-substitution industry: the Zambian case.
Ann Seidman. *Journal of Modern African Studies*, vol. 12, no. 4 (1974), p. 601-31.

This article is a product of its time, when dependency theory flourished. Seidman argues that Zambia's attempt at industrialization after independence has the common drawbacks of import substitution industries, namely that it serves mainly overseas and elite interests and 'may be expected to perpetuate and even aggravate the externally dependent economy' (p. 263). She therefore proposes an alternative long-term industrial strategy. Although much of this sounds dated, an enduring value of the article is the information on the institutional set up of industrialization in the early 1970s. The article is difficult to read, as the author bombards the reader with statements which do not always follow as straightforwardly as her conclusions would suggest.

590 Theoretical and practical implications of IMF conditionalities in Zambia.
Neva Seidman Makgetla. *Journal of Modern African Studies*, vol. 24, no. 3 (1986), p. 395-423.

Seidman's approach in this article is blunt: 'Given appropriate policies, the Zambian economy generated sufficient resources to repay debt and to maintain consumption of necessities' (p. 397). The difficulty in this statement on a crucial issue is, however, in the past tense used in the sentence. Is she referring here to the past or an alternative past in which there were such appropriate policies? Such ambiguity is typical of this article, which contains an overview of Zambia's economic problems in the mid 1980s in the light of the IMF's analysis and a critique of supply side economics which, according to Seidman, underlies that analysis. There are some very informative sections and some sharp remarks to be found, particularly in the section on foreign exchange and the operation of the auction system, but Seidman's argument is not convincing because it is not coherent enough. She accepts reform in principle, but does not make sufficiently clear what has gone so wrong in the Zambian economy that reform is necessary. She argues that the cost of shock treatment outweighs the gains in a Zambian context, but it is not obvious whether she is pleading for more gradualism in accepting IMF style reform or whether she is sticking to her rejection in principle of their economic proposals.

591 The impact of market liberalisation on food security in Zambia.
V. Seshamani. *Food Policy*, vol. 23, no. 6 (1998), p. 533-55.

This is an extremely valuable article. It is one of the rare publications which study the actual effects of economic reforms carried out since 1992; in this case, the liberalization of agricultural marketing is considered. On page 543 there is a useful overview of the actual policy measures put into effect. Seshamani evaluates the changes positively in the sense that there have been considerable macro- and microeconomic savings. The most notable effect of the liberalization is, however, that food production has declined. This negative supply response results from lower prices and the lack of a reliable private marketing structure. Seshamani, to a large extent, blames the way the policies were implemented, especially the sequencing of the reforms, for the negative effects, rather than the reforms themselves.

592 Trade regime and economic growth.
Charles L. Shanthunya, Victor Murinde. Aldershot, England: Applegate Publishing, 1998. 248p. bibliog.

Zambia and Malawi are the two countries which provide the major case studies in this book. Chapter 5 on Zambia consists of fifty pages. The book is recent but does not use any material from the 1990s. It is worth noting because of its conclusions, which go diametrically against the current pleas for an open trade regime, for example on page 183: 'All in all, import substitution helped the country to achieve better economic performance while trade liberalisation failed to resuscitate the economy from economic collapse and made things worse.'

593 Comparative financial policies: Zambia and Zaire.
Raj Sharma. In: *Natural resources and national welfare; the case of copper.* Edited by Ann Seidman. New York: Praeger Publishers, 1975, p. 341-44.

This very short article has an ominous conclusion: 'As against the very considerable increase in current expenditure, capital expenditure in Zambia during the period 1969-73 has consistently registered a downward movement' (p. 344).

594 Recent policy reform and industrial adjustment in Zambia and Ghana.
William F. Steel. *Journal of Modern African Studies*, vol. 26, no. 1 (1988), p. 157-64.

This short article is worth noting because it argues that the short-lived auction system of foreign exchange in 1986 led to a ten-fold increase in manufacturing exports, but that this was annihilated by a significant drop in export receipts from copper. This opinion is seldom voiced – at any rate not loudly – in the vast literature about that episode. It may significant that the author worked at the World Bank.

595 The informal sector and Zambia's employment crisis.
David M. Todd, Christopher Shaw. *Journal of Modern African Studies*, vol. 18, no. 3 (1980), p. 411-25.

The essence of this article is found on p. 418-24, where the authors try to estimate the size and importance of the informal sector on the basis of conjectures and conclusions from secondary material. The central conclusion is that Zambia's urban informal sector is sizeable and has grown faster than wage employment. The background of the study is the projected need to accommodate in the urban informal sector up to 22,000 unemployed per annum. Many of those have only a modicum of education. In its annotation, the article refers to useful grey literature on this subject from the 1970s.

596 Development in Zambia.
Edited by Ben Turok. London: Zed Press, 1979. 262p. map.
bibliog.

This collection of papers by people who were at one time on the staff of the University of
Zambia is a reflection of the academic spirit of the 1970s. Although this is definitely not
true of all contributions, most of them have a more or less radical neo-marxist orientation.
Quoting from Turok's own article: 'As other contributions in this book show, overcoming
dependence is a prerequisite for genuine development' (p. 84). Virtually all the papers
have also been published elsewhere. The entries by Turok, Seidman, Cliffe and Ndulo
will give an idea of what is to be found in this publication. It is also a work which presents
the first generation of Zambian scholars: Ndulo, Chikulo, Kashoki are among the names
here.

597 Control over the parastatal sector in Zambia.
Ben Turok. *Journal of Modern African Studies*, vol. 19, no. 3
(1981), p. 421-45.

The parastatal sector is in the process of being dismantled in Zambia. Therefore much of
the literature, e.g. by Johns or Simwinga (for both, see item no. 526) or Tangri (see item
no. 481), has only historical significance. The same can be said for this article, except that
it advocates a different line of reform from the other contributions. It does not advocate
more independence in decision making within the parastatal sector, but a more effective
involvement of the parastatals in the planning process to realize socially desirable goals.
Turok has a clear socialist perspective on the parastatal sector, and it may be paradoxical
that this was rare in a country committed to many socialist measures in its policy making.

**598 Structural adjustment and tradeables: a comparative study of
Zambia and Zimbabwe.**
John Weeks, Paul Mosley. In: *Post apartheid Southern Africa –
economic challenges and policies for the future.* Edited by Lennart
Petersson. London; New York: Routledge, 1998, p. 171-201.

Zambia is described here as a structural adjustment disaster, mainly as a result of
continuing policy uncertainties. For example, foreign investment is deterred because the
privatizations undertaken by the Chiluba government are seen as neither transparent nor
equitable. Zimbabwe's adjustment is characterized as incomplete rather than a failure.
This is not, however, explained in terms of differences in policy making but as a result of
initial conditions dating back to the colonial period. It is not surprising that the authors
repeatedly stress that they are making a complex argument, otherwise the reader might
suspect fuzzy thinking, or simply a lack of comprehension of what is going on.

599 Import support aid: experiences from Tanzania and Zambia.
Howard White. *Development Policy Review*, vol. 13, no. 1 (1995),
p. 41-65.

This article is informative about income support aid, a particular form of development aid
popular during the 1980s but virtually phased out during the 1990s. It is therefore of
interest to those studying the relationships between the donor community and the
Zambian government and economy. It contains very little information on the Zambian
economy as such.

600 Adjustment in Africa in the 1990s: the case of Zambia.
Howard White. *African Development Review*, vol. 9, no. 2 (1997),
p. 56-88.

There is a flood of literature on the breakdown of relations between the foreign donor community and the Kaunda government in the late 1980s. This is one of the first attempts to evaluate what happened after Chiluba came to power in 1991. It is also one of the first to note that the Chiluba government embarked on a sustained programme of economic reform in liberalizing the economy and therefore doing what the donors wanted. It did not bring the expected benefits, however, but instead a dismal growth record; deepening poverty; a ravaged manufacturing sector; and a sluggish supply response in agriculture. Howard White suggests moving to a different type of conditionality – *ex post* instead of *ex ante* – in which the Zambian government has freedom to manage the economy, and can then be rewarded or not depending on performance.

601 A black sheep among the reformers: programme aid to Zambia.
Howard White. Stockholm: Swedish International Development
Cooperation Agency, Sida evaluation 99/17:8, 1999. 92p.

This is the most elaborate of many studies on Zambia which White undertook for donor agencies. It concentrates on programme aid which is linked to policy reform. Such aid, mostly in the form of import support or budget support, provides foreign exchange and revenue for the government as part of a policy of economic reform. The evaluation contains a useful overview of reform and the relationships with the donors over time. It concludes that aid has not helped Zambia much, despite the fact that is has been a good reformer by the standards set by the international financial institutions. Zambia is so indebted that aid may ameliorate the immediate situation but is insufficient to give relief on the budget or stabilize the currency. This study is the best overview of the Zambian economy as it has operated since 1991.

602 Zambia.
I. Winawina. In: *The impact of structural adjustment on the
population of Africa.* Edited by Aderanti Adepoju. London:
James Currey; Portsmouth, New Hampshire: Heinemann, 1993,
p. 69-78.

This short article gives a few details about relations between Zambia and the IMF after the MMD government came to power. Its substance is composed of sections on the impact of structural adjustment on health, education and employment. Its conclusions are grim.

603 Zambia under the IMF regime.
Jurgen Wulf. *African Affairs*, vol. 87, no. 349 (1988), p. 579-94.

This is a macroeconomic analysis of Kaunda's break with the IMF in 1987. Wulf argues that the main ingredients of the IMF package made sense. However, he sees a contradiction between short-term needs for adjustment and longer-term needs for a restructuring of the economy. The latter implies, in the first place, shifting resources into new initiatives which are more productive than copper mining. Wulf argues therefore for structural adjustment plans which have a longer time perspective and more elaborately worked out policy targets and performance criteria reflecting such restructuring.

604   Rural-urban terms of trade.

C.E. Young.   *African Social Research*, no. 11 (1971), p. 91-94.

This article is typical of many debates on the Zambian economy in the 1970s. Young argues that the urban economy grew at the expense of rural areas, mainly because of stable food prices. He states that, 'To expect people to go back to the land under these conditions is to under-estimate their intelligence' (p. 94).

Finance and Banking

605 Financial policies and the banking system in Zambia.
Martin Brownbridge. In: *Banking in Africa.* Edited by Martin
Brownbridge, Charles Harvey. London: James Currey; Trenton,
New Jersey: Africa World Press; Nairobi: East African Publishing
House; Kampala: Fountain Publishers, 1998, p. 143-63.
This is an overview of what has happened in the Zambian banking sector since
independence, and the story is told with objective neutrality. Much attention is paid to the
problems of ZANACO, the bank established by the government in 1969; the failure of
four local banks in recent years is mentioned; and the notorious BCCI played a part in
Zambia also. Despite all this, the Zambian banking sector is described as healthy by
African standards. The reason for this is the significant presence of major foreign banks,
which refused to be nationalized in the 1960s. Banking in the highly regulated Kaunda
period appears to have been a relatively risk free business. Macroeconomic instability
changed that, especially after liberalization.

606 The control of credit in Zambia.
Charles Harvey. *Journal of Modern African Studies*, vol. 11, no. 3
(1973), p. 383-92.
The focus of this article is on lending institutions rather than on matters of monetary
policy. It discusses the nationalist attempt to gain control over the foreign owned banking
sector in the 1960s. It deals with the reforms which were carried through: a national bank
was established in 1965, rural credit was reformed, a government sponsored National
Commercial Bank was established. It also deals with the reform that was announced, but
not carried through, of the fifty-one per cent nationalization of Standard Bank and
Barclays Bank. The article has an insider feel to it. The discussion of the more technical
and indirect methods to control a foreign banking sector reads as particularly fresh. Later
in life, the author became the first governor of the Bank of Botswana.

607 **Rural credit in Zambia: access and exit.**
Charles Harvey. *Development and Change*, vol. 6, no. 2 (1975),
p. 89-105.

The most valuable part of this article is on pages 92-97. Harvey describes here the reform
of agricultural credit involved in the disbanding of the heavily politicized Credit
Organization of Zambia (COZ) and the establishment of its successor, the Agricultural
Finance Company (AFC). Harvey also proposes some general ideas on rural credit which
are summarized in 'On the irrelevance of rural credit to most farmers' (p. 101).

Trade, Mining and Industry

608 Mismanaged mineral depletion in Zambia.
Richard M. Auty. In: *Sustaining development in mineral economies; the resource curse thesis.* London: Routledge, 1993, p. 220-41.

The title suggests a detailed discussion of the mining sector, but this is mainly a general description of the various phases in the development of the Zambian economy. There is on pages 230-34, however, a succinct description of the decline of the mining industry. The gradual slide in copper production from 720,000 tons in 1969 to 416,000 tons in 1989 is a fact that should be borne in mind by anyone interested in Zambia. The book also contains interesting comparisons with comparable situations elsewhere, notably in Chile.

609 Economic independence and Zambian copper: a case study of foreign investment.
Edited by Mark Bostock, Charles Harvey. New York: Praeger Publishers, 1972. 274p. 3 maps. bibliog.

This is a collection of papers by people who were in Zambia at the time of the nationalization of the copper mines. Some were academics, but most of them were in or near the corridors of power as lawyers or economists. The book has a more technical orientation than other writing on the subject. This, compounded by the fact that the book was obviously composed in a hurry, makes it difficult to read. The legal framework of mining rights, prospecting, the details of the take-over and – above all else – taxation are the major topics. It is worth reading carefully the discussion of the advantages and disadvantages of the old and new tax system now that re-privatization of the mines is supposed to solve Zambia's problems.

610 Abe Galaun.
John Chileshe. Ndola, Zambia: Mission Press, 2000. 177p.

Galaun is a very prominent Zambian businessman. He is also an influential man in other respects, and it is not surprising that the photographs in the book show him in company with Kaunda as well as with Chiluba. His fortune originated in trading in Barotseland where the Litunga (local chief) did not want the Indian community to become established. This is, of course, told as a success story in which Mrs Galaun also plays a leading role as business co-pilot. Nevertheless, the biography also mentions more personal matters: 'he lived in Livingstone, but had very little contact with the Jewish community because of his close relations with African women' (p. 49). Later in life Galaun became very prominent in the Jewish community.

611 Economic adjustment, the mining sector and the real wage in Zambia.

Dennis Chiwele. In: *Constraints on the success of structural adjustment programmes in Africa.* Edited by Charles Harvey. New York: St. Martin's Press, 1996, p. 210-33. bibliog.

This article is mainly composed of a mathematical model to describe and explain the movements of real wages in the mining sector. The share of labour costs in GDP fell, as did real wages in the mining sector. The reason for this is not considered to be a fall in GDP, but rather structural adjustment. From 1983 there was a redistribution of income from labour costs to profits. Union power may have been strong in limiting economic reform, but it failed to stop a decline in real wages.

612 Case study two, Zambia.

James H. Cobbe. In: *Governments and mining companies in developing countries.* Edited by James H. Cobbe. Boulder, Colorado: Westview Press, 1979, p. 228-76. bibliog.

This version of the relations between the Zambian government and the mining companies is worthwhile for the section on bargaining positions, which covers the events in 1973 when – on the proceeds of a freak rise in copper prices – the Zambian government immediately redeemed the bonds which had financed the nationalization. Cobbe suggests that the aim was to gain more control and thus to get more grip on the transfer pricing techniques of the companies. The episode is seldom mentioned, but may be very important.

613 The copper industry in Zambia: foreign mining companies in a developing economy.

Simon Cunningham. New York: Praeger Publishers, 1981. 342p. map. bibliog.

This is primarily a study of decisions concerning investments and exploration, and is historical (covering the period up to the late 1960s). It will appeal therefore in the main to those who are interested in the technical and economic issues surrounding copper mining. The author considers the nationalization of the mines as an unfortunate example and is in general sympathetic to the mining companies. His conclusions about prospects of finding new copper deposits are pessimistic, although he stresses the uncertainty inherent in exploration.

614   Towards economic independence: papers on the nationalization of the copper industry in Zambia.
M.L.O. Faber, J.G. Potter.   Cambridge, England: Cambridge University Press, 1971. 134p.

Both authors worked for the Zambian government in the 1960s, and throughout these papers one has a sense of the pressures of policy making. Certain remarks give a strong sense of this: 'I recall a remark that was made by Muno Sipalo during a break in a meeting at State House' (p. vii). The first three papers are by Faber and give a general background – often historical – of the relations between government and the mining industry. The last paper is by Potter and deals with the nationalization. Although the authors are sympathetic to the Zambian government, the conclusion is prophetic: 'the result [of nationalization] is little change of net foreign exchange earnings at a profit per ton of above K400, but an increasing loss as profit per ton decreases below this level' (p. 121). As is well known, the copper price dropped. This book is highly recommended reading for anybody who wants to understand the dynamics of the nationalization process, but reading of it will entail dealing with complicated financial analyses.

615   Africa as a market for South African goods.
Adrian Guelke.   *Journal of Modern African Studies*, vol. 12, no. 1 (1974), p. 69-88.

Pages 77-80 of this article are devoted to Zambia, documenting how South Africa kept its share of imports into Zambia until 1970. The problematic of regional trading blocks has a new significance with the advent of majority rule throughout Southern Africa. Although this article deals with what are now historical situations, it has thus gained a new relevance.

616   Differentiation among small scale enterprises: the Zambian clothing industry in Lusaka.
Mwango Kasengele.   In: *African entrepreneurship: theory and reality*.   Edited by Anita Spring, Barbara E. McDade.   Gainesville, Florida: University Press of Florida, 1998, p. 93-109.

This short article reviews the whole range of activities that can be included under the heading of the small-scale clothing industry. The examples range from verandah tailors to wealthy women, married to important men, who design and make clothes competing with smart imports from overseas. The effect of the massive imports of second-hand clothes (*salaula*) is deplored, as is the competition from the Asian-owned local clothing companies. The article is more impressionistic than analytical and is therefore of limited value as social science.

617   Nationalization and the displacement of development policy in Zambia.
Ronald Libby, Michael E. Woakes.   *African Studies Review*, vol. 23, no. 1 (1980), p. 33-51.

This was one of the first articles to argue bluntly that it was a mistake to nationalize the mines. The fact that Mike Woakes is a mining engineer lends the judgement an authority that is absent in much other writing on the mines. There is in fact a dearth of accessible writing on the technical aspect of Zambia's copper mines. It is of course important to know that the nationalization of the mines caused the mines to become enormously indebted, but that does not require mining knowledge. Specialist knowledge is required, however, to know that the government's exploration policy after nationalization was a failure.

618   **The power of information: the contribution of information to the debate on the privatisation of the copper mining industry in Zambia.**
Maurice C. Lundu, Bernard Likubanga.   In: *The political economy of information; development, democracy and security in Southern Africa.*   Edited by Maurice Lundu.   Harare: SAPES Trust, 1996, p. 115-40. bibliog.

The article makes the important point that the nation, in whose interest the government owned the mines, was given very little information about what was happening in them. This message is most precisely delivered on pages 121-22. This article thus focuses relatively little on information about the mines; it is mainly prescriptive as to what should happen after democratization. Hopes were high, but the authors are now disillusioned. Symptomatic of continuing secrecy is the fact that the most important Kienbaum report on the privatization of the mines was kept secret by the government.

619   **Mining rights in Zambia.**
Muna Ndulo.   Lusaka: Kenneth Kaunda Foundation, 1987. 276p. map. bibliog.

Mining is crucial to any understanding of the development of Zambia, and this book treats mining law in a wide context: it relates it to its aim of an orderly exploitation of resources as well as the generation of government revenue. A large part of the book is, however, historical in nature. Up to page 119, Ndulo discusses the claims of the British South Africa Company. Thereafter he discusses mainly the changes brought about by the 1969 legislation, which was adapted to the new ownership pattern. It is regrettable that this book – in common with virtually all writing on mining in Zambia – contains so little information on what happened after 1970, despite its relatively recent publication date. The bibliography is interesting for some specialist interests. It covers, for example, relatively obscure writing on land use and ownership, as well as a list of publications on copper by Sir Ronald Prain. (Prain was the chairman of the Roan Selection Trust, one of the two companies that owned the Zambian copper mines before nationalization.)

620   **Copper and Zambia.**
Chukwuma F. Obidegwu, Mudziviri Nziramasanga.   Lexington, Massachusetts: Lexington Books, 1981. 221p. bibliog.

There are those who argue that there is an excess of empirical narrative, at the expense of theory building, in the study of the Zambian economy. Such people may appreciate this book. It is an exercise in model building, which requires a through grounding in mathematics if its full value is to be extracted. The argument is otherwise not accessible. One of the main conclusions, however, is worth noting by a broader public: stabilization of government expenditure, irrespective of receipts from mineral revenue, does not lead to stabilization of other major variables in the economy.

621 Foreign investment and the Zambian copper industry 1964-70.
Ciaran O'Faircheallaigh. In: *Mining and development.*
Beckenham, England: Croom Helm, 1984, p. 126-61.
The author worked in the late 1970s at the University of Papua New Guinea. That country
is, like Zambia, highly dependent upon copper revenues. This inspired him to undertake
a comparative study, and Zambia is the topic of one of the chapters in the resulting work.
It does not deal with recent developments and does not offer information that cannot be
found in more detail elsewhere. It is worth noting, however, for its wider interpretative
framework and bold conclusion on pages 148-54 that the nationalizations did not lead to
more Zambian control or to more revenue.

622 The mining multinationals and the Zambian economy.
F.O.E. Okafor. *African Review*, vol. 17, no. 1/2 (1990), p. 66-79.
This article does not add significantly to what is written elsewhere. Yet it may be
worthwhile to note because pages 72-75 summarize neatly the main issues involved in the
nationalization of the copper mines. The heart of the matter is formulated most succinctly
in a quotation from *The Economist* on page 74.

623 Zambia's mining industry: the first fifty years.
Roan Consolidated Mines. Ndola, Zambia: Public Relations
Department of Roan Consolidated Mines, 1978. 80p. 2 maps.
bibliog.
Company histories are by their nature inclined towards optimism, and this one has already
been out for quite some time. The reason for its inclusion here is not the dramatic and
often romantic history which the preface promises, but rather the introduction, rarely
found elsewhere, that the book offers to the general reader on the geology of the
Copperbelt and the technical aspects of the copper industry. The glossary in this
publication may also be useful for readers of other, more technical, publications.

**624 Zambia's policies towards foreign investment: the case of the
mining and non-mining sectors.**
Oliver Saasa. Uppsala, Sweden: Scandinavian Institute of African
Studies, 1987. 63p.
The emphasis in this short book is on the mining sector. This is a valuable publication as
it contains information about what happened in the sector in the 1970s and 1980s, about
which there is a considerable dearth of knowledge. On pages 41-45 one finds, for
example, information on the reintroduction of the mineral export tax and a proposal to
restructure and rehabilitate the mining industry in the 1980s. Saasa's analysis is imbued
by a strong realization that there is a continuing need for joint participation with foreign
investors in this important and complex sector.

625   The multinational corporation and a Third World host government in a mixed enterprise: the quest for control in the copper-mining industry of Zambia.
George K. Simwinga.   In: *Natural resources and national welfare; the case of copper.*   Edited by Ann Seidman.   New York: Praeger Publishers, 1975, p. 345-58.

Simwinga's article is critical of the mining companies, and he mentions several fields where the companies have remained dominant. He pays much attention in particular to Zambianization, voicing what may be called class interests: Zambian counterparts should get the same large salaries as the large numbers of expatriate staff. Financial arrangements are discussed more briefly and it appears that the companies remitted profits to their minority shareholders while borrowing money abroad for investment, so that the minority parent companies became richer and richer while the Zambian mines became more and more indebted. The article voices, probably accurately, how Zambian intellectuals viewed the nationalizations at the time. This makes it worthy of note.

626   Corporate power in an African state; the political impact of multinational mining companies in Africa.
Richard L. Sklar.   Berkeley, California: University of California Press, 1975. 245p. bibliog.

On the one hand, this book is contemporary history of the 1960s in Zambia, structured around the relationship between government and the mining companies. Some chapters – notably those on the relationships between labour and management and the context of the liberation struggle of Southern Africa – are situated specifically in a particular period and may be outdated. However, the chapters on the structure and nature of the mining industry and on the different viewpoints on revenue sharing and investment have a lasting relevance. The book seeks, however, to do more than simply provide a narrative. It gives a theoretical perspective on the relationship between multinational capital and developing countries. According to Sklar, there is no inherent conflict of interest between the multinational mining companies and 'the Zambian section of the managerial bourgeoisie'. Different national interests can be expressed in the context of the managers' wider perspective. This implies a very optimistic view of the relationships between the actors involved, which may not ring true for everybody.

627   The legal framework of copper production in Zambia.
C.M. Ushewokunze.   In: *Natural resources and national welfare; the case of copper.*   Edited by Ann Seidman.   New York: Praeger Publishers, 1975, p. 318-40.

This is a lawyer's article, which does not add much to what is written elsewhere, but looks at the subject from a slightly different angle. Its last section is a short comment by E. Alexander on the redemption of the bonds in 1973. Ushewokunze's indictment of the deal struck in 1969 is damning. Whereas sceptics like Potter (see item no. 614) stressed the underlying, faulty expectation that the copper price would rise as the weakness in the agreements, Ushewokunze rejects the agreements as a whole as inadequate.

Agriculture and Rural Development

628 The African husbandman.
William Allan. Edinburgh: Oliver & Boyd, 1965. 505p.
The title of this book suggests coverage of the whole of Africa, but actually most of its content is based on Zambian research. Allan was one among a group of brilliant ecologists and agronomists who worked in Zambia in the 1930s and 1940s. Their work has been attacked because they believed they could establish scientifically the number of people a certain agricultural area was capable of carrying given certain agricultural practices. A second criticism has been that they did not pay proper attention to local knowledge. The latter is definitely not true. The book gives detailed descriptions of a great variety of farm practices in Zambia. A diversity of *chitemene* practices (slash and burn agriculture), for example, is described. Allan does not champion any one practice, but sees advantages and limitations to all practices. Few books will give as much insight as this one into what happens in rural Zambia.

629 Seeking guidelines for poverty reduction in rural Zambia.
Jeffrey Alwang, Paul B. Siegel, Steen L. Jorgenson. *World Development*, vol. 24, no. 11 (1996), p. 1711-23.
A large part of this article is accessible only to those with mathematical knowledge. The general concern is to construct a poverty profile for Zambia's rural areas on the basis of primary data collected by the Central Statistical Office in 1991. The article concludes firstly that poverty is most severe in the most isolated provinces; secondly, that, although poverty is more widespread in female-headed households than in male-headed households, most of the poor live in male-headed households. Education makes a significant difference. The less education, the more likely there is to be poverty. The second part of the article extends this analysis to a household model in order to see the constraints faced in the light of market liberalization: 'Market liberalization should have a positive impact under ideal conditions'. The tenor of the article is upbeat: serious efforts are under way to realize these ideal conditions and 'a demand-driven community-based safety net is in operation' (p. 1721).

630 Rural responses to industrialization: a study of village Zambia.
Robert H. Bates. New Haven, Connecticut: Yale University Press, 1976. 380p. 4 maps. bibliog.

This book can be read on several levels. It can be seen as a theoretical treatise which laid the basis for Bates' influential, largely neo-liberal later works. He sees 'rural dwellers' primarily as strategic actors who treat political choices in the same way as market choices, calculating cost and benefit. He uses this analogy to explain why rural development is stagnating. Secondly, there is ethnographic material drawn from village life in Luapula, and it is, for example, worthwhile to read about the struggles around the headmanship. Thirdly, it is informative about the politics of the time when Simon Kapwepwe split off from UNIP; Bemba influence was a big issue then, and Luapula Province played an ambiguous role in national politics. The book has an authoritative tone but its representation is questionable. For example: Luapula is a much more heterogeneous area than Bates presents and, where the fishing industry is strong, it has quite a complicated connection to the cash economy.

631 Acquisition and alienation of cattle in Western Province.
Marie-Louise Beerling. Mongu, Zambia: Department of Veterinary and Tsetse Control Services, 1986. 140p.

This is a very detailed study of cattle ownership in Western Province. The author starts with a valuable overview of research already done on this topic and acknowledges that Gluckman's insights are still generally true. She proposes some additions, however. She notably makes the point that women have significant claims over cattle, and that this is much more widespread than is generally believed. A major part of the study is devoted to herding arrangements and the lending out of cattle in so-called *mafisa* contracts. The result is an extremely complex pattern of ownership in which actual ownership may be quite indeterminate. The limitations of the study or the indeterminacy of its findings could have been stressed more. This is a consultant's report based on a few months' research.

632 Planning for refugees in Zambia: the settlement approach to food self-sufficiency.
Richard Black, Thomas Mambwe. *Third World Planning Review*, vol. 14, no. 1 (1992), p. 1-20. maps.

In 1990 the authors carried out research among Mozambican refugees in the Ukimwi settlement scheme in Petauke district, Eastern Province. The scheme had the reputation of being an example of self-reliant development, mainly because much maize was sold to the co-operative marketing society. The authors question this image. The article remains relevant for two reasons, despite the fact that the Mozambican civil war ended in the 1990s. Firstly, it gives vivid impressions of grassroots relationships between Zambians and Mozambicans; secondly, it reveals important issues in development work – for example, the need to project an image of success in order to get further funding from donors.

633 Adopting improved farm technology: a study of smallholder farming in Eastern Province, Zambia.
Edited by Rafael Celis, John T. Milimo, Sudhir Wanmali.
Washington, DC: International Food Policy Research Institute, 1991.
409p. map. bibliog.

This study consists of sixteen papers by a variety of authors. The technological innovation involved here is mainly the cultivation of hybrid maize using fertilizer and ox drawn implements. At the heart of this book is a survey carried out among a stratified sample. Four variables are used for the stratification: status of the farmer; use of hybrid seed; use of oxen; and gender of the head of the household. The papers cover a wide range of topics not necessarily related to the survey, including, for example, the distribution of businesses in Eastern Province. As befits a book by economists, there are many tables, and regression analysis is the favoured statistical technique. The book is, however, fragmentary in its conclusions and it is difficult to distil a main message from it. The tabular information may, however, fit meaningfully into other people's work.

634 The state, technology and peasant differentiation in Zambia; a case study of the Southern Province 1930-1986.
Samuel N. Chipungu. Lusaka: Historical Association of Zambia, 1988. 259p. 4 maps. bibliog.

This book is a product of its time in the sense that it is imbued with the spirit of neo-marxism. It focuses on technological change – from hoe cultivation to the ox-plough and the tractor – and its relationship with peasant differentiation. The third analytical focus is on state involvement. It does not merely advocate a theoretical point of view however, but also contains much empirical material. It deals with the often-described miracle of peasant initiative against prevailing policies in the 1930s. He terms it the time of the reluctant state, which may be an understatement. A sizeable part of the book is devoted to the period after 1964, which is far less covered in the literature. He concludes that the period of the first republic – when this area, dominated by the ANC opposition, was discriminated against in government policy – was one of relative prosperity for the peasantry in Southern Province.

635 Private sector response to agricultural marketing liberalisation in Zambia: a case study of Eastern Province maize markets.
Dennis K. Chiwele, Pumulo Muyatwa-Sipula, Henrietta Kalinda.
Uppsala, Sweden: Nordiska Afrikainstitutet, 1996. 90p. bibliog.

This research was carried out in the same year as it was published – 1996 – and covered more than the title suggests. A pre-field test of the research instruments was held in Mumbwa district near Lusaka; Lusaka is included, as it is the main destination of the maize from Eastern Province. The report not only covers maize, but also makes comparative references to groundnuts and cotton. The fundamental belief of the authors is that market forces will establish a viable marketing structure if some constraints are removed, notably by improving the road network and providing more access to capital for the traders. Small traders (fewer than 100 bags in a season) have dominated the maize trade since liberalization, and profit margins are not high. It is a report from an unstable, new situation, and the picture that emerges from the research is not unambiguous. For example, millers (big operators) appear to be also very active in the trade. This is worthwhile reading for anybody interested in food supply in Zambia.

636 Agricultural credit management in Zambia: business development, social security or patronage?
James G. Copestake. *Development Policy Review*, vol. 16, no. 1 (1998), p. 5-29.

The liberalization of the Zambian food trade – especially in maize – in 1991 did not immediately lead to the emergence of a private marketing structure disciplined by the market. The Agricultural Credit Management Programme of 1994 aimed to stimulate the development of such a private sector. This article is a detailed analysis of the benefits of the programme for the various stakeholders involved. It appears that many long-standing problems resurfaced. Farmers were the main beneficiaries of the scheme, although only because of their failure to repay half their debts. The opportunity costs were high when looked at as the creation of a poverty safety net. Above all, the programme was inefficient with respect to business development. An appreciation of agricultural marketing is crucial to any understanding of the Zambian economy. The fact that there is little information available on developments after liberalization makes this article important, despite its limitations, which include a time scale limited to one year, and a dearth of substantial data about what actually happened 'down on the farm', or on the interaction between trader and farmer.

637 'Bishimi' and social studies: the production of knowledge in a Zambian village.
Kate Crehan. *African Affairs*, vol. 84, no. 334 (1985), p. 89-111.

This analysis takes issue with Gramsci's contention that organic intellectuals are not found in peasant societies. Crehan illustrates her thesis through the art of storytelling in a Kaonde village in Kasempa. This body of knowledge, however, meets antagonistic forces, for example through new state institutions. She discusses the school and the clinic. As one elderly informant said: 'The Europeans have killed our wisdom'. That is not necessarily so and the wise man M., a Jehovah's Witness, is depicted as creatively fabricating a cultural collage of the old and the new. The article is somewhat heavy on theory – providing essentially a modernization theory framework – and somewhat light on what *bishimi* actually entails.

638 The fractured community: landscapes of power and gender in rural Zambia.
Kate Crehan. Berkeley, California; Los Angeles: University of California Press, 1997. 258p. map. bibliog.

North Western Province includes isolated areas, which are relatively less integrated in Zambia's national and the international economy. The Kaonde communities studied by Kate Crehan in this book are an example. She describes life in the area, using the discourse of the people she studied. Kinship and hierarchy are overwhelmingly strong there, and that is the starting point of her analysis. The economic aspects of life, in particular, are approached through the relationships between male and female. Politics is treated in a separate chapter and a final chapter, 'The dangerous community', deals with the power of witchcraft. This is a very clearly written and easily accessible monograph about life in rural Zambia. It is therefore an excellent starting point for people who want to familiarize themselves with rural Zambia, but it should be borne in mind that the communities described here may be less typical than Crehan sometimes assumes. She also ignores many debates in other writing about rural Zambia and an over-simplification may be the result.

639   Understandings of 'development': an arena of struggle. The story of a development project in Zambia.
K. Crehan, A. von Oppen. *Sociologia Ruralis*, vol. 27, no. 2/3 (1988), p. 113-46.

The Lima project in North Western Province was remarkably successful. The cash income of many rural dwellers increased, and marketed agricultural output rose enormously. The project was planned and funded by the German aid agency GTZ (Gesellschaft für Technische Zusammenarbeit), and there seems every reason to be satisfied with the outcome. Crehan and von Oppen do not belittle these achievements, but they show how the project goals were modified, challenged and changed during implementation. It is difficult to do justice to the many complicated interactions described in this exemplary case study. A central theme is that patterns of client/patron relationships – which Crehan and von Oppen claim pre-date colonialism – pervade interaction between the German donors and the local population. It is therefore not surprising that the original ideal of self-reliant peasant groups who earned a cash income through production for the market was lost on the way. A vivid example of the way in which people (who are called 'target populations' in the jargon of planners) react is this angry outburst on page 126 from a politician against the planners who advocate small scale development: 'You have grown big and you want to keep us small! Worse than the colonialists!' This article is compulsory reading for anybody involved in planned intervention in rural Zambia as well as those looking for material on the hybrid maize boom there during the 1980s.

640   Planners and history; negotiating 'development' in rural Zambia.
Kate Crehan, Achim von Oppen.   Lusaka: Multimedia Publications, 1994. 319p. 9 maps. bibliog.

This is a useful publication, as it contains papers by a generation of scholars who wrote about rural Zambia at the time of the 1980s maize boom. The group includes expatriates, such as Han Seur, Jeremy Gould and Philip Gatter, as well as Zambians, such as Owen Sichone and Caleb M. Fundanga. The book captures a change in emphasis in the study of rural Zambia: the forces from below constructing ideas of development were being paid much more attention than before in rather rigid planning models. The article which Crehan and von Oppen published in *Sociologia Ruralis* (see item no. 639), in which they formulated these ideas most coherently, is part of this collection.

641   Why liberalization alone has not improved agricultural productivity in Zambia.
Klaus Deininger, Pedro Olinto.   Washington, DC: The World Bank, 2000. 22p.

This small publication is of great interest to those wishing to understand the Zambian economy in recent years. Zambia has liberalized its economy signficantly and this was intended to 'realize the efficiency gains that were expected from liberalization' (p. 1). These gains were defenitely not achieved in the agricultural sector. This paper anlayses data from a two-year panel of 5,000 rural households to find out why. The question is whether market imperfections are the cause, or whether more structural factors – in the technology of production – are the constraints. The authors conclude that market access is still the main limiting factor. That is one interpretation of the discovery that credit has a major productivity-increasing effect. Others may doubt whether commercially operating financial institutions (market forces) are likely to want to supply credit to Zambia's smaller farmers.

642 Animal traction survey in Zambia.

Henk Dibbits, Emmanuel Bwalya.   Lusaka: Government of the Republic of Zambia; Ministry of Agriculture, Food and Fisheries; Wageningen, The Netherlands: IMAG-DLO, 1993. 119p. 12 maps.

This study was carried out by engineers. It gives information about the number of trained oxen and the percentage of cultivated area in which oxen draught power was used in each district. Besides that, there is information on implements that can be drawn by oxen, their state of maintenance, the presence and effectiveness of extension staff, and so on. This publication merits the attention of everybody interested in Zambian agriculture and rural development. Ox-drawn ploughing is probably the most effective means by which to raise the productivity of smallholder farms, and it has important consequences for the sociological structure of farm enterprises. This survey gives, therefore, an excellent starting point for the study of the diversity in Zambian agriculture. Also, the fact that the number of trained oxen increased by forty-eight per cent between 1985 and 1990 is significant, as Zambian agriculture is so often described as stagnant. However, the spread of ox-drawn traction is very uneven throughout the country.

643 Developing interaction and understanding: rapid rural appraisal.

Michael Drinkwater.   In: *Beyond farmer first: rural people's knowledge, agricultural research and extension practice.*   Edited by Ian Scoones, John Thompson.   London: Intermediate Technology Publications, 1994, p. 32-41.

Knowledge, consciousness and prejudice: adaptive agricultural research in Zambia.

Michael Drinkwater.   In: *Beyond farmer first: rural people's knowledge, agricultural research and extension practice.*   Edited by Ian Scoones, John Thompson.   London: Intermediate Technology Publications, 1994, p. 133-39.

These short articles are highly ideological in nature, taking the wisdom of actual farm practices as a starting point. Agricultural extension and research, it is claimed, have to be in dialogue with those farm practices. The second paper argues that farm households have to be aggregated into clusters for effective research and extension. The case material in these papers is extremely limited, but they deal with issues that are important in the study of Zambian agriculture. To understand the articles, specialist knowledge is required about the cultivation of beans; compost and mounds; sorghum seed breeding; and dambo cultivation. The second article presents a striking contrast between success and disappointment on page 137.

644 Does the T and V extension assist female-headed families? Some recent evidence from Zambia.
Jean M. Due, Enock Sikapanda, Flavianus Magayans. *Eastern Africa Economic Review (new series)*, vol. 7, no. 1 (1991), p. 69-75. bibliog.

The Training and Visit (T and V) is a method of agricultural extension in which information is passed on from farmers who are regularly contacted by an extension officer to other farmers who are not. The main conclusion from a questionnaire, administered by Sikapanda in Eastern Province, is that the introduction of T and V has no impact at all on female-headed families and most impact on contact farmers. The article contains much statistical information that could undergo further interpretation.

645 Differences in earning, labour inputs, decision-making and perception of development between farm and market: a case study from Zambia.
Jean M. Due, Marcia White-Jones. *Eastern Africa Economic Review*, vol. 5, no. 2 (1989), p. 29-103. map. bibliog.

Jean Due has published many reports on surveys held in rural Africa, and Zambia figures prominently among them. This article reports on a questionnaire administered to 112 women on farms and thirty market women. It was administered in three areas and the differences in responses in the south and north are striking. For example, twenty-seven per cent of households in the south stated that husbands alone made decisions on cash income as compared to forty-six per cent in Northern Province. This type of research can degenerate into mindless data collection; on the other hand, isolated facts to be found in the tables here could stimulate further research questions.

646 Listening to farmers: participatory assessment of policy reform in Zambia's agricultural sector.
Paul A. Francis, John T. Milimo, Chosani A. Njobvu, Stephen P.M. Tembo. Washington, DC: World Bank, 1997. 36p.

Privatization, decentralization, demand driven extension and the like have been the buzzwords in agricultural policy in Zambia since 1991. In the jargon of economic reform, this report is a beneficiary assessment study on how farmers have adapted and coped to new circumstances, and it evaluates the changes. Chapter 4, on farmers' perception of agricultural services, makes the most telling reading. For example on page 27 it is stated that, 'Most of these recommendations (by farmers) appear to reflect a yearning for the bygone era of interventionist policy'.

647 Anthropology in farming systems research: a participant observer in Zambia.
Philip Gatter. In: *Practising development: social science perspectives.* Edited by Johan Pottier. London: Routledge, 1993, p. 153-87.

The setting of this article is Luapula Province in the 1980s, during the maize boom in outlying areas, where Gatter was working as an anthropologist in an Adaptive Research Planning Team. The primary purpose of the article, however, is to give insight into what may be termed as 'the production of knowledge' rather than an analysis of farming in Mabumba, Mansa district as such. The article is instructive about policy thinking on subjects other than hybrid maize in those years.

648 Pro-growth regulatory reforms for agricultural inputs in Malawi, Zambia and Zimbabwe.
David Gisselquist. In: *Southern African agribusiness: gaining through regional collaboration.* Edited by Steven Jaffee. Washington, DC: World Bank, 1998, p. 167-97. (Technical Paper no. 424).

Zambia plays a minor role in this paper which is – as the title indicates – quite ideological in nature, and therefore quite informative about neo-liberal thinking on agriculture. The difficult question faced is why these pro-growth reforms have not resulted in more significant growth in the agricultural sector. Rather than questioning the belief in the efficiency of the market, Gisselquist maintains that the impact of these reforms is masked by bad weather and disruptive macroeconomic and financial developments.

649 Systematic agricultural mismanagement: the 1985 'bumper' harvest in Zambia.
Kenneth Good. *Journal of Modern African Studies*, vol. 24, no. 2 (1986), p. 257-85.

This tragi-comic story of inefficiencies in agricultural marketing is well told. Although the experience in 1985 may have been extreme, it is representative of much of what went wrong when agricultural marketing was state dominated. Good quotes Kaunda at the beginning of the marketing season, commenting on an administrative reorganization in marketing: 'There must be somebody we can blame when things do not work out'. Blame, however, seems to be attributable everywhere in the unfolding story. Good tries to uncover the serious organizational and structural weaknesses in the Zambian state and political economy. He talks about an established and debilitating inter-linkage between a weak state and peasant agriculture, for which see also K. Good, 'The reproduction of weakness in the state and agriculture: the Zambian experience' (*African Affairs*, vol. 85, no. 339 [1986], p. 239-65). His theoretical statements, however, state generalities which do not do much to clarify much of the fascinating material presented here.

650 The direction of agricultural development in Zambia, Zimbabwe and Malawi.
Kenneth Good. In: *Studies in the economic history of Southern Africa; vol. I. The front line states.* Edited by Z.A. Konczacki, Jane L. Parpart, Timothy M. Shaw. London: Frank Cass, 1990, p. 127-59.

Zambia is only one of the countries dealt with in this article, and the situation is described more from a political economy perspective than from, for example, an agronomic one. Good's opinions on Zambia's agricultural strategy have been documented elsewhere as well (see item no. 649). In this article, however, there is an interesting class analysis of rural Zambia on the basis of World Bank research. Good concludes that Zambia has a much larger proportion of middle class and rich peasants than neighbouring countries. This fact is interesting in the light of the numerous negative verdicts on Zambia's rural development strategy. Good made this judgement before liberalization, which is supposed to create differentiation between rich and poor, affected Zambian agriculture.

651 Luapula: dependence or development.

Jeremy Gould. Lusaka: Zambia Geographical Association Regional Handbook 6; Finnish Society for Development Studies Monograph 3 (in co-operation with the Scandinavian Institute of African Studies), 1989. 229p. 7 maps. bibliog.

The first half of this monograph is a highly informative description of the demography, economy and social structures of Luapula Province. The second half is an overview of development interventions in the area. Gould's description of Luapula is pervaded by pessimism, although he argues that it is not poor and that the idea of it as a Cinderella province may need revision. The spread of market forces, he claims, marginalizes the poor and he pays special attention in this respect to the position of women. More importantly, however, an economic time-bomb is ticking away underneath the changes. His review of development policies stresses that, 'a collusion of political disinterest, uneven market development and administrative negligence has carved out of the regional economy a specific dependent niche for Luapula' (p. 153). He pleads for the more active involvement of rural producers in development planning as a way out.

652 Localizing modernity; action, interests and association in rural Zambia.

Jeremy Gould. Helsinki: The Finnish Anthropological Society, 1997. 286p. 2 maps. bibliog.

This is primarily a treatise on development theory, based on fieldwork in Luapula Province. The most substantial empirical work on Zambia is found in chapter 7, which describes the rise and fall of the Milambo Multipurpose Co-operative Society during the hybrid maize boom of the 1980s. This story is told against the background of neo-traditional politics among the Baushi people. Gould has a sharp eye for the tragic nature of this story and has a tendency to write provocatively. For example, rural Zambians 'put their trust in unknown and infamously unreliable agents, including cooperative managers, government agents and ancestral spirits' (p. 73). This book will offer more to those who like to philosophize about rural Zambia than to those who are looking for concrete information. Gould discusses classical monographs of the Manchester School extensively.

653 From the official future to a participatory future: rethinking development policy and practice in rural Zambia.

Guy Gran. *Africa Today*, vol. 30, no. 4 (1983), p. 5-22.

This is a review of what was at that time recent work on rural development in Zambia. Gran distils from these what he calls an 'official future', which is contrasted with a participative, alternative future. Such insights are caught in a particular time-warp in development theory, but this article is useful in that it foreshadows much of the important literature on rural development based on research during the 1970s.

654   Strengthening local linkages for socioeconomic development at regional level: a study of the rural economy of the Gwembe valley.

Hans Gsänger, Ulrike Muller-Glode, Thomas Selzer, Gunther Taube, Gabriele Trah, Roland Weiss.   Berlin: German Development Institute, 1986. 2 vols. map. bibliog.

Regional planning studies can be extremely detailed and the significance of the detail is often not made clear. That is the case here. There is a main report and a second volume with village studies, where one can read that there are two blacksmiths at Sinaimbwe and women usually drink *chibwantu*, a sweet non-alcoholic drink. Nevertheless this study is of interest because it adds to the already considerable literature on the Gwembe valley and so makes in-depth analysis possible. It is also of interest because of the history of – mostly ineffective – regional development in Zambia. This study is highly influenced by dependency theory and considers intra-regional import substitution policies as a major aim. According to the authors, however, viability depends on the local resource potential, and the Gwembe valley is poor.

655   Development prospects for the Zambezi valley in Zambia.

Edited by W.L. Handlos, G.W. Howard.   Lusaka: Kafue Basin Research Committee, 1985. 109p. 8 maps.

Although this collection of conference papers is edited by the Kafue Basin Research Committee, the papers deal especially with the Zambezi upstream from Livingstone, before the Kafue joins the big river. The papers are quite technical and cover topics such as hydrology, power generation, agricultural development and the like. One can find a description of the vegetation of the greater Zambezi drainage system, mean annual runoff coefficients, Zambezi streamflow records and so on. There are also lighter moments, especially in the reported discussions: Dennis Huckabey becomes almost lyrical when he envisages the possibility of a dam at Batoka gorge which would turn all the lower gorges into water skiing and boating areas.

656   The Kafue fishery: a case study of intensification.

Peter B. Hayward.   In: *Food systems in Central and Southern Africa*.   Edited by Johan Pottier.   London: School of Oriental and African Studies, University of London, 1985, p. 138-69. map. bibliog.

This article is based around a detailed study of one fishing crew. The construction of dams in the Kafue, combined with rapidly growing urban concentrations in the neighbourhood, provided favourable incentives for a fishing industry to develop. The article describes how pressure on stocks leads to intensification of fishing which in the short run leads to higher returns, but is highly damaging in the long run. Apart from its relevance for ecological studies, the article contains valuable material for the study of unfettered markets. One example is the following reported comment: "'As for investment", a fisherman explained, "We get so little money that all we can do is to drink it'" (p. 183).

657 Farm/non-farm growth linkages in Zambia.

Peter B.R. Hazell, Behjat Hojjati. *Journal of African Economies*, vol. 4, no. 3 (1995), p. 406-35. bibliog.

This article is based on a survey carried out by the International Food Policy Research Institute in Eastern Province in 1985 to 1986. The survey is used to model multiplier effects of income growth. This multiplier is said to be very high (2.5 as compared with an assumed 0.5 in the region as a whole). These multiplier effects are particularly strong in intra-regional sectors, and especially so within the agricultural sector. The effects of increased farm income are therefore substantial. Although a large part of the article is only accessible to readers with a strong grasp of mathematics, the general insights are of interest to a much wider public. Table 4 on household expenditure is particularly interesting, if only because expenditure on alcohol consumption is sizeable, but less substantial than is usually assumed.

658 Development in action: the experience of the Zambian extension worker.

Hans Hedlund. *Ethnos*, vol. 49, no. 3/4 (1985), p. 226-50.

According to Hedlund, anthropological fieldwork should pay more attention to the extension worker. He does so in this article on the basis of fieldwork in North Western Province. The article portrays one extension worker called Ndembu, whom Hedlund depicts with great empathy. Although the extension worker is not unimportant – he has passive influence – he is marginal in the local community: Hedlund comments, 'His poor resources and his frequently useless advice emphasized the low status of the department of agriculture' (p. 247). Above all he did not manage to attract resources through projects. This description will be recognizable to those who have experienced the work and life of the extension worker.

659 Migration and change in rural Zambia.

Hans Hedlund, Mats Lundahl. Uppsala, Sweden: The Scandinavian Institute of African Studies, 1983. 107p. 7 maps. bibliog.

The empirical material for this paper was collected in a base line survey undertaken for the Intensive Development Zone programme in Chipata, sponsored by the Swedish Agency of International Development. The authors challenge Heisler's contention (see item no. 515) that the Chewa were well adapted to a high labour migration rate. They found erosion and pressure on land, as well as a shortage of labour at peak periods, to be major problems in agriculture in their area. The more severe the labour shortage, the less circulatory is migration. The last two chapters deal with the changing role of beer – less used than previously for work parties in peak periods – and the possibility of solving problems through settlement schemes: the experience gives no reason for optimism.

660 Strategies and norms in a changing matrilineal society: descent, succession and inheritance amongst the Toka of Zambia.

Ladislav Holy. Cambridge, England: Cambridge University Press, 1986. 233p. 2 maps. bibliog.

This ethnography, set in Kalomo district in Zambia's Southern Province, provides detailed fieldwork, which is used to broach broad theoretical questions. Chapter 2, on ploughing arrangements, is central to the argument made. The introduction of ox-drawn ploughing necessitates the formation of ploughing teams and these tend to be made up of parent-son relationships. The parent-son relationship tends as a consequence to take precedence over matrilineal relationships. Holy does not, however, posit a linear and deterministic relationship between rules and particular forms of behaviour in society. Norms are a strategic resource which can be invoked, interpreted and changed into interaction. People can still adhere to a matrilineal normative and symbolic universe (the representational model) while their behaviour may be very different (the operational model). Holy presents a sophisticated view of matrilineal ideology, and the introduction of ox ploughing provides a valuable perspective on broader processes of social change in rural Zambia.

661 Agricultural policy and performance in Zambia; history, prospects and proposals for change.
Doris Jansen Dodge.   Berkeley, California: University of California, Institute of International Studies, 1977. 285p.
This book is still often quoted despite the fact that it is over two decades old. The policy frameworks within which it is situated have changed considerably: Jansen still takes state intervention in marketing, credit and pricing for granted. However, its great value lies in its historical overview of agricultural policies. The author comes to a damning conclusion with respect to the success or otherwise of policies in increasing employment and income in rural areas, diversifying the economy away from copper, and decreasing the dependence on imports. She asserts that the major cause of this is that farmers were taxed and not subsidized in the period 1964 to 1976, but this approach overlooks important changes which have taken place in Zambian agriculture since independence: the smallholder sector took over commercial maize production from the large-scale sector. The book was, however, written before the maize boom of the 1980s.

662 Zambia.
Doris J. Jansen.   In: *The political economy of agricultural pricing policy, vol.3 Africa and the Mediterranean.*   Edited by Anne O. Krueger, Maurice Schiff, Alberto Valdes.   Baltimore: The Johns Hopkins University Press for the World Bank, 1991, p. 286-328.
Jansen's contribution to this study can be seen as a follow-up to her study of the economics of Zambian agriculture published in the 1970s (see item no. 661). This paper contains time series up to 1986. Some of these time series may be seen as constructions for the benefit of economic modelling, for example those of nominal and effective rates of protection of maize. Others, however, such as a time series of the value of crop procurement in constant prices, are very valuable to a broad public. Her main message is that policy making by the government has compounded the problems in the agricultural sector: 'the least progressive option from the standpoint of agricultural development – taxing the farmer – is the most feasible solution from the standpoint of political expedience' (p. 320). A discussion of the maize boom of the 1980s is a striking omission from this paper.

663 Changing rural land use: evidence of a transition to sedentary agriculture among shifting cultivators of Solwezi district in North Western Province, Zambia.
Gear Kajoba. *Review of Rural and Urban Planning in Southern and Eastern Africa*, vol. 1 (1993), p. 6-32. bibliog.

Kajoba carried out research among the Kaonde people in 1991 to 1992. He first introduces the policy-making environment, involving government, missions and foreign donors. The second part of the article documents a shift to stable farms on which mainly maize is grown. Stable farms lead to a demand of fertilizer, and it is not surprising that sixty-five per cent of the farmers mentioned the high cost of fertilizers as their main problem.

664 The political economy of food security and agriculture in Zambia.
Kamima wa Chimika na Mwanza. In: *Food policy and agriculture in Southern Africa.* Edited by Richard Mkandawire, Khadole Mailosi. Harare: SAPES Books, 1993. 250p.

This paper is difficult to summarize as many arguments crop up in it. It is often more a collection of hypotheses than the statement of an argument. For example, the author suggests that the spread of education is a major factor stimulating a rural exodus. He concludes that Zambian food security is in trouble, mainly because export crops instead of food crops are stimulated. However, among the several interesting tables, there is one time series of marketed maize as compared to food needs. This shows an erratic time series rather than a declining trend in the supply of maize. This erratic time series is not addressed, as is the case in many similar studies.

665 History and agricultural change in Zambia.
Ackson M. Kanduza. *Transafrican Journal of History*, vol. 20 (1991), p. 97-110.

This short article is an example of historiography rather than actual writing of history. Kanduza's main concern is the relevance of history in the making of development policies. In this respect, he reviews a number of relatively recent studies critically. His concerns may not always be lucidly presented to the reader. A relatively concrete concern is linked to serious flaws in the analysis of the articulations of non-capitalist and capitalist processes of production.

666 Socio-economic change in Eastern Zambia: pre-colonial to the 1980s.
Edited by Ackson Kanduza. Lusaka: Historical Association of Zambia, 1992. 204p. 3 maps.

The title suggests a very long time span in these essays, but the late colonial period is the focus here. The Eastern Province Co-operative Marketing Association was launched at that time; then settlement schemes were started; and this was followed by extension efforts directed at farmer elites. This book is therefore useful reading for those interested in the emergence of Eastern Province as a cash-crop producing area. Most of the essays in the collection are written by people who are not professional historians. This may explain the variable quality of the contributions, but the writing on the late colonial period is the strongest part of this book.

667 Changes in Zambian agricultural policy since 1983: problems of liberalization and agrarianization.
Jonathan Kydd. *Development Policy Review*, vol. 4, no. 3 (1986), p. 233-60. bibliog.

Although this article has a broad focus on the effects of liberalization on the agrarian sector in Zambia, it offers most information on a much narrower issue: the liberalization of maize markets. Its view of production patterns in the 1980s may be questionable for some. Kydd certainly does not distinguish a maize boom in outlying areas, where maize cultivation was rather new as is often described. According to Kydd, maize production was fluctuating, and he mentions substantial increases only in areas where it is a staple food (along the line of the railway and in the east). This article is, however, of continuing interest because of the rare information it gives about the institutional experimentation with maize marketing in the middle 1980s. Maize marketing continues to be problematic in Zambia.

668 Coffee after copper?; structural adjustment, liberalisation and agriculture in Zambia.
Jonathan Kydd. *Journal of Modern African Studies*, vol. 26, no. 2 (1988), p. 227-53.

This article gives a very good overview of the various arguments made about, and events surrounding, the break of the Zambian government with the IMF in 1987. Although the article adopts a general macroeconomic perspective on the Zambian economy, most attention is paid to agriculture. It is especially enlightening on the issues of marketing and pricing in agriculture, while the section on foreign exchange auctioning may also be singled out as informative. Conflicting statements on the Zambian economy from various sources set the tone of the article. These show vividly the intense but often confusing trains of thought at that time. The article itself is more valuable as an impression of the times than as a neat and closely argued analysis of the Zambian economy. It rings true, however, as a reflection of a confusing period in Zambia's economic development.

669 The Goba of the Zambezi: sex roles, economics and change.
C.S. Lancaster.   Norman, Oklahoma: University of Oklahoma Press, 1981. 350p. 12 maps. bibliog.

The Goba are a Shona-speaking people who live in Zimbabwe and Zambia. This study was conducted on the Zambian side of the Zambezi where the Goba live among their Tonga-speaking neighbours straddling the confluence of the Zambezi and the Kafue. The Goba have a dual descent structure. The village system tends to be matrilocal, but patrilineal descent – argued here to be 'a residual from a patrilineal past' (p. 274) – is also important. The rise of a cash dominated economy has reversed this development: the cash economy is male dominated and, in particular, the monetization of the brideservice – financed from remittances – undermines the positions of influence of localized senior women. This monograph is extremely – maybe excessively – detailed. Its generalized conclusions are more oriented towards kinship theory – the dual descent system – than towards giving insight into social change in rural Zambia. The court cases in an appendix are worth noting and may be of particular value to anyone interested in gender issues.

670 **Farming co-operatives in the development of Zambian agriculture.**
C. Stephen Lombard. *Journal of Modern African Studies*, vol. 10, no. 2 (1972), p. 294-99.

This short article documents well the frantic enthusiasm for, and hopes placed in, co-operatives after independence and the disappointments at their actual functioning. The article ends with the recommendations of the first national co-operative conference held in January 1970. It was intended to rationalize the development of co-operatives as indicated in the first recommendation: defunct societies would have their registration cancelled.

671 **Social change and the individual: a study of the social and religious responses to innovation in a Zambian rural community.**
Norman Long. Manchester, England: Manchester University Press, 1968. 257p. 2 maps. bibliog.

This monograph, which is set among the Lala in Serenje district, can be read as a collection of separate essays on topics including farm management strategies; relations between urban and rural social ties or networks; cash crop agriculture; and the matrilineal system. Above all, however, it shows the importance of the Watchtower (Jehovah's Witnesses) beliefs in social life. It is by now a classic study, which introduced many themes which recur in later studies of rural Zambia. Its most striking pioneering aspect may be that it uses the anthropological or ethnographic approach to study much wider aspects of society than kinship, although the latter remains of crucial importance. Reading the case study of the visit of Pati, the townsman, may give the reader a feeling for life in Zambia which cannot be found elsewhere. This case is also very amusing.

672 **A cross-cultural examination of organizational structure and control: the Zambian agricultural sector.**
Robert E. Meyer. *Journal of Asian and African Studies*, vol. 27, no. 3-4 (1992), p. 244-59. bibliog.

This is more an article dealing with organization studies than with Zambia or the Zambian agricultural sector. The author measures formalization and centralization in sixteen agricultural planning and extension services – including some expatriate ones – in Central Province. It is not surprising to read that the Zambian organizations were highly centralized and were also very formal with an emphasis on sticking to the rules. The ultimate concern is to distinguish a particular Zambian pattern of organizational culture, which is discussed on page 256. Despite the seeming intellectual rigour, one can find in this paper statements such as: 'While none of the hypothesized relationships were statistically significant, five of six were in the direction predicted' (p. 255).

673 **Maize, markets and livelihoods; state intervention and agrarian change in Luapula Province, Zambia 1950-95.**
Gun Mickels Kokwe. Helsinki: Institute of Development Studies, University of Helsinki, 1997. 194p. 7 maps. bibliog.

Although the title suggests a much broader period, this is primarily a detailed description of the maize boom during the 1980s in Luapula Province. The research was initially geared to co-operative development, as marketing co-operatives were an essential part of this boom. The author is more positive than others have been about these institutions: they were, she maintains, 'virtually the only reliable and regular channel to the market'. The edifice on which the boom was built collapsed in the 1990s after economic liberalization. It is therefore not surprising that Mickels Kokwe observes that farmers in Luapula hanker after the days of controls. The significance of this study also derives from this point: the maize boom of the 1980s in fairly remote rural areas is highly salient to the discussion on state intervention and agricultural output in Zambia. This is probably the most informative and detailed study available of the maize boom.

674 **Cattle marketing in Zambia, 1965-1995; policies, institutions and cattle-owners in Western Province.**
Henk A.J. Moll, Desiree C.E. Dietvorst.   In: *Agricultural marketing in tropical Africa.*   Edited by H. Laurens van der Laan, Tjalling Dijkstra, Aad van Tilburg.   Aldershot, England: Ashgate, 1999, p. 185-205. bibliog.

The reluctance to sell cattle in Africa is a contentious issue in which the rationality of the farmer's behaviour is central. This is a much more empirical study of cattle marketing than is available elsewhere. It combines an analysis of statistics on cattle sales in Western Province with the results of a survey among farmers. The researchers find a great reluctance to sell cattle and that people will do so only when they have an urgent need for cash. Food self-sufficiency is therefore, not surprisingly, related to a reluctance to sell. The volume of cattle sales in a household is not related to herd size, a fact which also fits this central finding. An analysis of the secular trend in overall cattle sales in the province shows an increase in the number of sales however. This must presumably indicate a growing need for cash. The bibliography points to a considerable volume of grey literature about cattle in Western Province.

675 **The state, rural class formation and peasant participation in Zambia: the case of the Southern Province.**
Jotham Momba.   *African Affairs*, vol. 88, no. 352 (1989), p. 331-59. map.

Cash crop farming among peasants developed in Southern Province earlier than in other parts of Zambia. Momba starts from a neo-marxist inspired interest in these relatively well-to-do farmers, here denoted by the Russian word 'kulaks' dating from Leninist-Stalinist times, but he sees no Leninist-style linear pattern of evolution into capitalists and proletarians. Few capitalist-style enterprises developed even when the peasants moved out of villages onto state land or into settlement schemes. Neither does Momba see a contradiction of interests between rich and poor peasants. The second part of the article gives valuable insights into the politics of the ANC-dominated Southern Province. It is interesting to note that the introduction of the one-party state led to a reduction in tension between UNIP and ANC. Many of the ANC faithful were elected to leading position in the 1974 UNIP party elections. However, with a few exceptions, richer peasants were never drawn to UNIP.

676 **Cutting down trees; gender, nutrition and agricultural change in the Northern Province of Zambia, 1890-1990.**
Henrietta L. Moore, Megan Vaughan. London: James Currey, 1994. 278p. bibliog.

This highly praised and award-winning book (it was given the Hertzkovitz award) brings together a mass of information on agriculture in Northern Province. It deals with a range of materials varying from unpublished material to the classic studies of W. Allan and Audrey Richards. A central theme in the book is a reading of the discourse on the area and the way in which it shaped social realities, especially with regard to *chitemene* agriculture and gender relations. The authors' main argument is that there was much more diversity and local initiative than is suggested by the stereotype of a society undermined by the massive migration of men to the mines. It is helpful to be conversant with the work of Allan and Richards (see respectively item nos. 628, 165) to appreciate this book. The book is extremely detailed and, in its desire to be comprehensive, tends to include data of doubtful validity.

677 **Oxpower in Zambian agriculture and rural transport: performance, potential and promotion.**
Herbert Müller. Aachen, Germany: Edition Herodot, Rader Verlag, 1986. 150p. 7 maps. bibliog.

The author of this German doctoral thesis writes takes an engineering approach in this study. He believes strongly in the value of oxcarts – a view which is partly argued on the basis of returns from a survey among farmers. Anybody interested in the dispersion, adoption, spread and use of oxcarts will find information here, but also to accessible here are charts of the components used in oxcarts as well as the information that ninety per cent of such carts use the back of a pick-up truck or a pick-up axle. The oxcart is undoubtedly one of the major examples of technology adapted to the local environment.

678 **Expectations unfulfilled: the underdevelopment of peasant agriculture in Zambia: the case of Kabwe rural district.**
Maud Shimwaayi Muntemba. *Journal of Southern African Studies*, vol. 5, no. 1 (1977), p. 59-85.

The subject here is not as such the underdevelopment of agriculture in Kabwe rural district as a consequence of capitalism and imperialism. That is merely the background against which Muntemba sketches government initiatives since independence to bring about rural development. It offers close observation, albeit somewhat fragmented, of what resulted at the grass roots from policy instruments such as credit, mechanization, extension and the like. It is fairly critical with respect to issues of class formation and gender, but overall the article is imbued with sympathy for the UNIP government. The structural handicaps resulting from colonialism, however, are too great according to the author, and have been in some respects reinforced since independence.

679 **A spatial analysis of maize marketing policy reforms in Zambia.**
A. Mwanaumo, William A. Masters, Paul V. Prechel. *American Journal of Agricultural Economics*, vol. 79, no. 2 (1997), p. 514-23.

The authors plead for full liberalization of maize markets on the grounds that this would yield large and widespread benefits. The evidence for this is, however, based on a model, which begs the question as to what is actually happening in reality. The distinguishing feature of this model is that it discounts transport costs in the price of maize. The model is applied to maize marketing in one normal year (1989) and one drought year (1992) under three conditions: controlled marketing (as was the case before 1990); partially controlled marketing (as happened after 1990 where controls persisted on international trade and long distance flows of the crop); and in the purely hypothetical condition of fully liberalized markets. It is noteworthy that the authors are sceptical about the 1993 Food Security Act as it allows the government to use unspecified trade controls and storage schemes for price stabilization. They anticipate that governments will resort to these for political reasons which, in their view, are quite distinct from sound economic ones.

680   Farmers' organizations in Africa: a case study of the Zambian Cooperative Federation (ZCF).
Bonard Mwape.   *African Rural and Urban Studies*, vol. 1, no. 1 (1994), p. 91-110.
This is a highly informative article. It describes the evolution of co-operatives as a tool for agricultural development in Africa (the co-operative movement in Zambia was the subject of Mwape's PhD thesis, the particulars of which can be found in this article). Mwape rightly states that many so-called co-operatives or farmers' organizations must firstly be seen as an extension of government. He highlights the enormous growth of the movement in the 1980s. There were 1,680 societies by 1989 compared with 376 in 1983. Similarly, the membership increased from 101,000 in 1983 to 401,689 in 1989. This development was intimately connected to the marketing of maize during the maize boom in outlying areas. The article is particularly useful as a follow-up to the often quoted work by Quick (see item no. 689) which dates from the mid-1970s.

681   Experiment on rural development in an African state: Zambia, the Chunga irrigation scheme.
Melsome Nelson-Richards.   *Journal of African Studies*, vol. 8, no. 4 (1981-82), p. 146-63.
This is the story of a vegetable growing irrigation scheme near Lusaka. It originated from an unusual institution, the National Council for Scientific Research. The source of irrigation was also unusual: water from the Lusaka sewage works. It was built by the consulting engineer Simon Zukas, who later became the first MMD Minister of Agriculture. Nelson-Richards' main theme is that the scheme was let down by the bureaucracy which should have supported it. The article also contains a detailed analysis of cash income on the various plots of the scheme. The main conclusion there is that a well-cultivated plot did not result in higher income. The author moves rather unpredictably from the broad brush of theoretical concerns to details of the scheme. The latter may be of wider interest in the study of development projects in Zambia.

682 The case of Zambia.
Melsome Nelson-Richards. In: *Beyond the sociology of agrarian transformation; economy and society in Zambia, Nepal and Zanzibar.* Edited by Melsome Nelson-Richards. Leiden, The Netherlands: E.J. Brill, 1988, p. 27-78. 2 maps.

The topic here is a settlement scheme of the Tobacco Board of Zambia (TBZ) in Kaoma district to the west of Lusaka. The research was undertaken in 1976 and was followed up with a research visit in 1981-82. Tobacco has been a highly assisted crop as it threatened to disappear from Zambia when commercial farmers who grew the crop left at independence. Substantial sums of money were poured into the crop's cultivation through the TBZ without much result. One of the attempts to revive the crop was through settlement schemes as described here. Such schemes were highly stratified with management on top, settlers second and villagers who grew tobacco under an extension scheme third.

683 Zambia: country study and Norwegian aid review.
Siegfried Pausewang. Fantoft, Norway: The Chr. Michelsen Institute, 1986. 202p. map. bibliog.

The problems identified for Zambia have not changed much since this report was written. The book has a rather narrow focus on aid policies and is therefore – contrary to the suggestion in the title – not particularly valuable as a general introduction to Zambia. It does contain, however, a very useful summary of aid policies towards Zambia at that time. It reflects a great belief in the efficacy of quickly disbursed financial aid. For Northern Province, where Norway was involved in an intensive development zone, it proposes a specific agricultural programme for women.

684 The political uses of agricultural markets in Zambia.
James R. Pletcher. *Journal of Modern African Studies*, vol. 24, no. 4 (1986), p. 603-19.

Agricultural markets in the Kaunda era can, according to this article, only be seen in a political context. They are embedded in patterns of building political support and patronage. It follows logically that price-policy reforms threatened the Zambian state in various ways. This article may appeal to those interested in theoretical perspectives on rural Zambia. The article's informative content is low, however, and the article deals with a long-vanished past.

685 The politics of liberalizing Zambia's maize markets.
James Pletcher. *World Development*, vol. 28, no. 1 (2000), p. 129-43. bibliog.

The major research finding presented here is that maize marketing has been liberalized, but that there remains considerable intervention in the marketing of inputs: fertilizer and credit. The latter is commonly justified on redistributive grounds favouring smallholders, but Pletcher argues that a closer look reveals rentseeking. This article is primarily an analysis of the political interests involved, and the description of the Agricultural Credit Management Programme is particularly useful. The description of the actual measures taken is rather thin, partly because a substantial part of the article does not deal with maize marketing but with democratization and economic reform in Zambia generally.

686   Matrilineal ideology; male-female dynamics in Luapula, Zambia.
       Karla O. Poewe.   London: Academic Press, 1981. 140p. bibliog.
Only a third of this book deals with actual fieldwork carried out in Luapula. This is
embedded in a view on matriliny as an ideology, which is spelled out in the other,
theoretical chapters. Poewe sees a dialectical relation between matriliny and capitalism.
She concludes that, 'At this time of twilight of matriliny, a curious accommodation is
taking place between matrilineal and capitalist institutions'. Her view of matrilineal
descent systems is highly slanted by a feminist perspective, and many anthropologists
would dispute her assertion that the prevalence of a matrilineal descent system leads
automatically to female domination in power relationships. The research presented tends
to be superficial, but the pages also contain lively glimpses of life in Luapula. The
bibliography mentions several other writings by Poewe on matriliny, religion and
economics in Luapula.

**687   Reciprocity and the beer pot: the changing pattern of Mambwe
       food production.**
       Johan P. Pottier.   In: *Food systems in Central and Southern Africa.*
       Edited by Johan Pottier.   London: School of Oriental and African
       Studies, University of London, 1985, p. 101-37. 2 maps. bibliog.
Reflections on rural policies in the Kaunda era are contasted here with the realities as
found by Pottier in his fieldwork among the Mambwe (see item no. 688). Pottier
considers the ideology of humanism, village productivity committees and especially
intensive development zones and contrasts these with work parties in an historical
perspective. The role of beer is central: he claims that, 'African social worlds revolve
around and are expressed in beer transactions' (p. 110). Pottier's major contention is that
a so-called modern or progressive village – Ciwale – took on a traditional appearance by
organizing work parties cloaked in terms of Zambian humanism. The reality behind this
is, however, the penetration of modern commercial forms: work parties have become less
reciprocal and poor villagers must demand less from the richer.

**688   Migrants no more: settlement and survival in Mambwe villages;
       Zambia.**
       Johan Pottier.   Manchester, England: Manchester University Press,
       1988. 210p. 5 maps. bibliog.
For this book, Pottier went back to the area in Northern Province where Watson undertook
his seminal research (see entry no. 228). Watson had depicted Mambwe society as
cohesive and adaptive despite the effects of intensive labour migration. Pottier found a
more complex picture in the late 1970s. Labour migration had lost its overwhelming
importance and new economic activities had come to the fore. The most notable one
among those is the trade in food – mainly beans – and this trade straddled the nearby
Tanzanian border. Agriculture had changed considerably. Millet was decreasing in
importance; the cultivation of hybrid maize was taken up, especially by an elite; beans
were important as a cash crop for trade. Cash was much more a factor in agriculture than
had been reported by Watson. Pottier states that, 'The exploitation of labour has become
a recurrent feature of the Mambwe economy'. Pottier found much more fluidity and
diversity in the social structure than noted by Watson. A striking new development was
the frequent return of women to their home villages, where they lived with their male kin.
This book is rich in case material which documents kinship in action; attempts at
government intervention; and agricultural practices. Some main findings of his research

were reported earlier in Pottier's article, 'Defunct labour reserve? Mambwe villages in the post migration economy' (*Africa*, vol. 53, no. 2 [1983], p. 2-23).

689 Bureaucracy and rural socialism in Zambia.
Stephen A. Quick. *Journal of Modern African Studies*, vol. 15, no. 3 (1977), p. 379-400.
There are two aspects to this article. On the one hand, it is a study of how ideological concerns, which Quick calls 'micro socialism', are translated into reality. On the other hand, it is a case study of bureaucratic wrangling, obstruction and incompetence. In the first decade after independence, policy making in Zambia was often impulsive, with little consideration of implementation, and as such this case study is of wider relevance. This article also deals with the first report made on Zambia by the French agronomist René Dumont, which although important has been little studied.

690 Land use in Zambia; Part I: the basically traditional land use systems and their regions.
Jürgen Schultz. Munich, West Germany: Weltforum Verlag, 1976. 215p. 18 maps. bibliog.
Zambia's Ministry of Rural Development in the 1970s commissioned a land use mapping system; this book is the outcome. Schultz addresses in the first place the specialist reader, whose main interest may be in what Schultz has to add to the work of Trapnell and Clothier (see item no. 38). They certainly did not have the aerial photographs which Schultz uses extensively. Schultz also refers to the anthropological literature when describing the various land use systems. This book is also to be recommended for bibliographical reasons. The casual reader may be put off by Schultz's extensive use of classifications, but that would be regrettable. The thematic maps on land use, population and maize marketing, for example, are most informative. Above all, there is material in this book for anybody who wants to gain a greater appreciation of the Zambian landscape.

691 A history of development in the twentieth century: the Zambian portion of the middle Zambezi valley and the Lake Kariba basin.
Thayer Scudder. Worcester, Massachusetts: Clark University; Binghamton, New York: Institute of Development Anthropology, 1985. 84p. map. bibliog.
Thayer Scudder has observed over decades the changes among the Gwembe Tonga and the interventions to accelerate development. This paper deserves to be read not only by those interested in the Gwembe Tonga, but also by those who are interested in development interventions generally. The Gwembe Tonga were removed from their land in order to make space for Lake Kariba and in the course of that they have undergone their share of interventions. The following sentence is typical of the paper: 'It is hard to overemphasize the importance of the gillnet fisheries in spite of the fact that it collapsed within five years' (p. 27). Paradoxes like this and a clear eye for the unexpected nature of development (or, rather, the lack of development) provide important food for thought.

692   Sowing the good seed: the interweaving of agricultural change, gender relations and religion in Serenje district, Zambia.
Han Seur. Wageningen, The Netherlands: unpublished PhD thesis, Wageningen Agricultural University, 1992. 474p. 8 maps. bibliog.

Han Seur started out with the intention of restudying the area in Serenje district where Norman Long had carried out the research for his classic monograph. The result is a minutely detailed ethnography of changes in rural life, which is now only partly related to Long's study. Seur also deals with the subjects for which Long's book is best known: religion and farm management. The book's richness in case studies of farm management makes it indispensable reading for anybody interested in the effects of the plough on households or the way in which matriliny functions in a cash economy. Religion is dealt with but considered as less related to particular forms of social behaviour than in Long's book. The book covers other subjects however, which are minor or not mentioned in Long's book, such as the strategic ways in which local actors react to planned intervention and especially the interaction between the spread of cash crop farming and gender relations. Seur's description of the way in which successful female farming entrepreneurs emerged in Serenje is essential reading for anybody interested in gender issues in Zambia. The wealth of detail could be thematically better structured, but anybody who has any dealings with rural Zambia can get a flavour of real life by just dipping into the numerous case studies in this book. An example to start with can be found on page 234: the farm of Agnes Musonda Kalaka.

693   Rural development in Zambia: a spatial analysis.
David J. Siddle. *Journal of Modern African Studies*, vol. 8, no. 2 (1970), p. 271-84. 10 maps.

This is the article of a geographer who is fascinated by regional planning. His main interest is the diffusion of development through the location of government services or projects in appropriate places. Nodal points of government services are distinguished in two districts, Serenje and Mazabuka. Siddle advocates multi-nodal models of rural development.

694   Achievement motivation and economic development; farming behaviour in the Zambian railway belt 1912-1975.
David J. Siddle. *Third World Planning Review*, vol. 3, no. 3 (1981), p. 259-73. map.

This article is concerned with farming by European settlers along the lines of railways, and it tests out an evolutionary theory of farm development in frontier or settler areas. It tries to understand deviations from such an evolution in terms of the expectations of failure and success in the farming communities. The historical sketches of the mood in the settler farming communities, which are obviously founded on a thorough knowledge of their development, are interesting, but this article offers little else. It is worthwhile for people interested in interpretation, but it does not offer new information.

695 Indigenous soil categorisation in Northern Zambia.
Patrick Sikana. In: *Beyond farmer first: rural people's knowledge,
agricultural research and extension practice.* Edited by Ian
Scoones, John Thompson. London: Intermediate Technology
Publications, 1994, p. 244-45.
This is merely a note on the organization of farmers in village level participatory research
groups. It discusses changes made in the implementation of Adaptive Research Planning.

696 Patterns of agricultural development and foreign aid in Zambia.
William Smith, Adrian Wood. *Development and Change*, vol. 15,
no. 3 (1984), p. 405-34. map. bibliog.
The background to this article is the growing importance of foreign aid in Zambian rural
development: foreign technical assistance to the Ministry of Agriculture increased in four
years (1975-79) from half the size of its operating budget to twice the size of regular,
current, budgeted expenditure. A concomitant development was the regional
concentration of the efforts of particular foreign donors. Smith and Wood discuss this
development's pros and cons, especially in the light of a possible abdication of
responsibility for regional policy making on the part of the Zambian government. The
data in this article date from quite long ago, but regional specialization of donor efforts is
still prevalent, both in agriculture and in other sectors.

**697 A subsistence society under pressure: the Bemba of Northern
Zambia.**
Peter Stromgaard. *Africa*, vol. 55, no. 1 (1985), p. 37-58. 4 maps.
bibliog.
This research is situated in two villages – one west of Lake Bangweulu in Luapula
Province and one twenty kilometres south of Kasama. It provides an extremely detailed
study of the way people earn their livelihoods and an intensive analysis of residential and
kinship patterns, listing, for example, twelve types of trap used by villagers as well as
more than thirty foodstuffs that are eaten. Stromgaard's general conclusion is one of
disintegration: the uxorilocal settlement pattern is breaking down and the links in the
matrilineal kinship groups are loosening. New agricultural practices are being adopted, as
the old *chitemene* system of slash and burn is no longer practicable.

**698 The impact of Zambia's economic policy reform programme in
the agricultural sector.**
Scott Thomas, Wesley Weidemann. *Development Policy Review*,
vol. 6, no. 1 (1988), p. 51-75.
There is a multitude of articles on the events surrounding Kaunda's break with the IMF
in 1987. This one is noteworthy because it differs from many others in the opinions
presented. It argues that at the time of the break the beneficial effects of liberalization
were beginning to be felt in the rural sector: increases in hectarage of crops under
cultivation; rises in amounts of maize marketed; crop diversification; reduced capital and
import intensiveness; rising agricultural exports; and a reversal of the long-standing
decline of rural incomes, relative to urban. These conclusions run counter to the
widespread view that, while there was a agricultural boom in the 1980s, this boom –

virtually wholly in maize cultivation – was fuelled by subsidies and heavy state intervention. These authors maintain that the boom was the result of liberalization.

699   Politicians, bureaucrats and farmers: a Zambian case study.
Jan Kees van Donge.   *Journal of Development Studies*, vol. 19, no. 1 (1982), p. 88-108.

This article is based on research carried out in Mwase Lundazi in Eastern Province. It is a study of elite formation in a rural setting which challenges the common belief at the time that one would find a process of class formation there, driven by an interlocking elite of large-scale farmers, politicians and civil servants. This article argues that this is not necessarily the case and that one finds many relationships 'stranded' between these groups. For example, large-scale farmers preferred as a rule to maintain a distance from politics; politicians were mostly associated with failure in farming; and civil servants were a disillusioned group with few resources at their disposal. The article explains these phenomena as driven by different worldviews among these groups.

700   Rural-urban migration and the rural alternative in Mwase Lundazi, Eastern Province, Zambia.
Jan Kees van Donge.   *African Studies Review*, vol. 27, no. 1 (1984), p. 61-85.

Mwase Lundazi may be far away from major centres of employment, but migration to urban centres nevertheless plays a big role in life there. The article tries to explain the persistence of migration by males to urban areas in the face of declining economic opportunities in the cities. It presents the view from below, seeing the limited opportunities for young males in a rural setting where marriage and the establishment of a farming enterprise requires the support of older men. The latter, however, are in competition with the youths for marriage partners – polygyny is widespread – and like to tie dependent youngsters to their own farm enterprises. Given young males' difficulties in setting up a farming enterprise of their own in such circumstances, their continuing migration to urban areas becomes understandable.

701   Understanding rural Zambia today: the relevance of the Rhodes-Livingstone Institute.
Jan Kees van Donge.   *Africa*, vol. 55, no. 1 (1985), p. 60-76. bibliog.

In the first decades after independence, anthropology was often associated with colonialism. This was the case to an extreme degree in the 1970s and 1980s when neo-marxism was dominant. The main thrust of this article is that such an association was misplaced and that the ethnography written on the basis of research at the Rhodes-Livingstone Institute gives a more fruitful perspective on Zambia's rural life than the neo-marxist approaches then in vogue, as it allows for social change being moulded from below. The article is useful as a first encounter with the ethnography of Zambia and contains a case study on identities and the legal system which may be valuable.

702 **Exploitation and neglect: rural producers and the state in Malawi and Zambia.**
Megan Vaughan. In: *A history of Central Africa; the contemporary years since 1960.* Edited by David Birmingham, Phyllis M. Martin. London: Addison Wesley Longman Ltd., 1998, p. 167-203.

This article sums up the generally accepted views on the state and rural producers in Zambia. Zambia's rural development efforts during the years of the copper boom are seen as insufficient and ineffective. The maize boom of the 1980s in outlying areas is considered to be government sponsored and therefore not sustainable: by 1980, in the midst of economic crisis, the government was spending nineteen per cent of its shrinking revenue on agricultural subsidies. Structural adjustment, liberalization and a withdrawal by the state characterize recent times. The article contains witty anecdotes and serves well as a general introduction to rural Zambia's economic problems. The images produced are stereotypical, however, and received wisdom could have been challenged here more than it is.

703 **Farm production and the changing structure of Zambian agriculture.**
Adrian Wood. In: *Food systems in Central and Southern Africa.* Edited by Johan Pottier. London: School of Oriental and African Studies, University of London, 1985, p. 138-69. map. bibliog.

This paper is an overview of agricultural policy making in Zambia with a discussion of proposed changes. It predates the economic liberalization of the early 1990s: for example, it is considered great progress that the government is going to buy cassava nationwide (p. 154-55). At the same time it pleads for a return to economic pricing. This article is important for anyone interested in previous policy debates, or who wishes to understand how Zambian agriculture has been analysed in the past. The maize boom of the 1980s is of course crucial – as Wood points out, 'the quantity of maize marketed more than doubled between the 1979 and 1981 harvests' (p. 157).

704 **The dynamics of agricultural policy and reform in Zambia.**
Edited by Adrian P. Wood, Stuart Kean, John T. Milimo, Dennis Michael Warren. Ames, Iowa: Iowa State University Press, 1990. 682p. 10 maps. bibliog.

This is a massive tome containing thirty-three specialized contributions on Zambian agriculture. As the book has an agronomist's perspective and is therefore interdisciplinary in nature, one can find a very detailed table (3.2) of agro-ecological zones as well as a contribution on animal draught power. Most contributions are, however, social science based and chiefly economic in nature. The chapters on pricing and marketing are worth noting, as these issues remain consistently at the core of policy making in the area of rural development in Zambia. Many chapters suffer from a surfeit of formality – which is accentuated by the use of acronyms – and a normative slant which is not always supported by information. The book's heavy emphasis on policy making rather than empirical study of what happens on the farm reinforces these tendencies. This is more a book to browse through or to use as reference than to read. In fact, the pictures reproduced at the beginning of the book may be more informative about Zambian agriculture than many of the written contributions.

705 **The state and agriculture in Zambia; a review of the evolution and consequences of food and agricultural policies in a mining economy.**
Adrian P. Wood, Emmanuel C.W. Shula. In: *The state and agriculture in Africa.* Edited by Thandika Mkandawire, Nacour Bourenan. London: Codesria Books, 1987, p. 272-317.

This article is first and foremost a descriptive historical overview, which culminates in an analysis of the crisis in maize production during the late 1970s and early 1980s. It concludes with policy prescriptions aimed at ending that crisis, which seems puzzling as the 1980s was a decade of huge expansion in maize production. The authors' own data also show that maize production has been fluctuating very much along an upward trend since independence. They also describe a considerable shift from pure subsistence cultivation to some commercialization: in 1969 the least commercialized farms composed 75 per cent of all farm households as compared to 62.3 per cent in 1980. That decline shows itself in growth in the next level of commercialization, which was composed of 18.7 per cent of farms in 1969 and grew to 30.1 per cent in 1980. Zambian small-holder agriculture may be far less static than is usually assumed.

706 **Technology, marriage and women's work in the history of maize growers in Mazabuka, Zambia; a reconstruction.**
Marcia Wright. *Journal of Southern African Studies*, vol. 10, no. 1 (1983), p. 71-85.

Marcia Wright here culls, with great insight, material from secondary sources documenting an evolution in marriage practices. Brideservice, where the prospective husband works for the woman's family, was replaced by bridewealth, the payment of cattle or money for the right to marry the female and to claim the offspring. Later the influence of the wider kinship networks changed when paternal control over nuclear families based on polygyny became important. The technology in the title of the article refers to the introduction of ox-drawn ploughing, but the actual consequences of this for social organization are hardly discussed. This is regrettable, as the issue is central to the theoretical arguments which Wright attempts to make.

707 **Zambia.**
In: *A blighted harvest: the World Bank and African agriculture in the 1980s.* Edited by Peter Gibbon, Kjell J. Havnevik, Kenneth Hermele. London: James Currey; Trenton, New Jersey: Africa World Press, 1993, p. 82-103.

This is a very clear exposition of what happened in the Zambian agricultural sector in the 1980s, especially the boom in the cultivation of hybrid maize in outlying areas of the country. It argues most succinctly and relevantly that growth in agricultural output in Zambia was mainly due to government intervention: in particular, fertilizer and transport subsidies and the maintenance of pan-territorial pricing. This contradicts the assumption in thinking about structural adjustment that a withdrawal of the state and liberalization of agricultural marketing would lead to higher prices for the farmer and therefore to higher production. It argues on the basis of factual evidence in an area where assumption and emotion can easily gain the upper hand.

Transport and Communications

708 The Dar es Salaam transport corridor: an appraisal.
M.B. Gleave. *African Affairs*, vol. 91, no. 363 (1992), p. 249-67.
2 maps.
Zambia is landlocked and therefore information on transport routes is important to any
understanding of its economy. This article offers rare information on the actual operation
of the railway to Dar es Salaam in Tanzania. Data from the mid 1970s to the mid 1980s
show great fluctuations in utilization of the railway, but overall it worked at capacity
levels of only between 29.5 per cent and 17.4 per cent. There are intriguing facts among
the factors explaining this. For example, although eighty per cent of the railway's revenue
was generated in Zambia, sixty per cent of the costs arose in Tanzania. The result was that
the railway sometimes came to a standstill because no funds had been transferred.

**709 The Tanzania-Zambia railway: the Chinese loan and the pre-
investment analysis revisited.**
Ngila Mwase. *Journal of Modern African Studies*, vol. 21, no. 3
(1983), p. 535-43.
Mwase discusses here the feasibility study undertaken by Maxwell Stamp Associates for
the railway. This study concluded that the project was feasible. Thereafter he discusses
the benefits of the interest free Chinese loan. Mwase is sceptical with respect to all
calculations. He debunks the myth of the interest free Chinese loan by pointing out how
this was tied to imports from China and repayments in foreign exchange. The appreciation
of the Chinese *yuan* made this loan much more costly than its interest free nature would
suggest.

**710 Tazara: an analysis of Zambia's decision making in
transportation.**
Bertha Zimba Osei-Hwedie, Kwaku Osei-Hwedie. Lawrensville,
Virginia: Brunswick Publishing Corporation 1990. 117p. map.
The sequence of events leading to the construction of Zambia's railway is well described
here. While that story is well known – it has been told, for instance, in *Freedom railway:*

223

Transport and Communications

China and the Tanzania-Zambia railway link by Martin Bailey (London: Rex Collings, 1976) – the value of this book is in the attention paid to post-construction problems. Operational problems forced the Zambian government to reopen the alternative, Rhodesian route for copper and fertilizer transport in 1978. A cost cutting committee had to be established. Also in wider respects the operation of the railway was disappointing, as the expected economic development along the route did not materialize. The authors mention problems rather than give detailed descriptions. Similarly, they deliberate on problems rather than analyse them.

711 Southern African airtransport after apartheid.
Gordon M. Pirie. *Journal of Modern African Studies*, vol. 30, no. 2 (1992), p. 341-48.

Zambia hardly figures in this review. It was a prescient article, however, in that it foresaw a hub and spoke network connecting cities like Lusaka to Johannesburg.

Labour and Labour Relations

712 The trade union situation in Zambia: an overview of law, practice and the way forward; a monogram.
Darlington Amos Banda. Lusaka: Friedrich Ebert Stiftung, 1997. 36p.

This is a most useful booklet, which sketches the situation as it developed after the Industrial Relations Act 1993 in contrast with that pertaining under earlier legislation. The position of the Zambian Congress of Trade Unions (ZCTU) is central in this discussion. Democratization changed the position of the ZCTU drastically. Unions are free to affiliate with ZCTU; ZCTU has less power over affiliated unions; and internal democracy in ZCTU has been reinforced.

713 The colour of class on the copper mines; from African advancement to Zambianization.
Michael Buroway. Manchester, England: Manchester University Press, 1972. 121p. bibliog.

This is primarily a qualitative account, a narrative, of the changing relations between black and white labour or between local and expatriate personnel on the Zambian Copperbelt in the 1960s. The material is, unsurprisingly, definitely dated. The paper contains many verbatim quotations from individuals involved, and the analysis is close to discourse analysis. Buroway's later very successful career as a social theorist was highly influenced by this experience, and the book contains many theoretical references to, among other things, the nature of conservatism in the working class.

714 Africanisation, nationalisation and inequality; mining labour and the Copperbelt in Zambian development.
Philip Daniel. Cambridge, England: Cambridge University Press, 1979. 202p. 2 maps. bibliog.

This book is by an economist writing on matters that are always close to personnel policy. It is rich in description of the latter, especially from independence to the mid 1970s, when the relationship between expatriate and local labour was central. It is fitting that Daniel thanks the personnel officers of the mining companies warmly. As an economist he is also particularly interested in the effects on the national economy of replacing expatriate labour with local labour and, notably, the income inequalities in Zambia. The particular value of this book is that it gives some detailed, rare insights into what happened after nationalization. It is striking that the workforce grew significantly in the period from 1970 to 1976 (eighteen per cent) as compared with the period from 1964 to 1970 (six per cent). After 1970, however, the distribution of the wage bill started to disadvantage workers who had not been promoted in the drive to Zambianize.

715 Employment and income distribution in the African economy.
James Fry. London: Croom Helm, 1979, 186p.

Although Zambia is not mentioned in the title, this book examines two aspects of Zambian economic development: the growth of a wage sector and income inequality. The main story told in the book is what happened to the racially based income differentials after independence and the new ones that were then created on different grounds. James Fry is the most influential authority on the history of wage determination in the urban sector in the first decade after independence, but the rural/urban differential receives attention as well.

716 Domestic service in Zambia.
Karen Tranberg Hansen. *Journal of Southern African Studies*, vol. 13, no. 1 (1986), p. 57-81.

This is an informative article describing the changing role of domestic service over the years. It contains many figures on the size of the sector and seeks to give this group – described here as an underdog – a place in Zambia's labour history. The article does not contain the elegant historical gender analysis which is to be found in Hansen's book on domestic service in Zambia (see item no. 717).

717 Distant companions: servants and employers in Zambia 1900-1985.
Karen Tranberg Hansen. Ithaca, New York: Cornell University Press, 1989. 321p. 4 maps.

The poetic title conveys well the context in which this book is set: close relations amidst inequality in terms of race, gender and class. The central concern of the book is a sub-theme in that context: the persistence of domestic service as a male occupation. Sexual relations in colonial society form a necessary complement to understand this. The book contains fascinating material on concubinage: the worlds of servants and concubines were to be kept separate, and native females were seen as a threat in the house. African conceptions about the proper role of women also provided pressures to keep females out of the profession. Historical documents are the main sources in the first half of the book, with later sections based on fieldwork in Lusaka in the 1980s. The profession had changed: it had, of course, lost status as more and more reserved fields of employment became open to Africans. Various other influences led to a deskilling of the job. Moreover, Zambians themselves increasingly employed domestic servants. The profession remained predominantly male, however. Some women had entered it, but mostly in the area of childcare. This book is a theoretically informed sociological study of everyday life, but it is accessible to the general reader as well. Its richness in anecdotes will appeal to many.

718 **From school to work: youth, non formal training and employment in Lusaka.**
Wim Hoppers. The Hague: Centre for the Study of Education in Developing Countries (CESO), 1985. 267p. bibliog.

Hoppers traces the careers of people who drop out of the educational system early. He documents how they acquire skills through work experience. He traces the informal training which is given in this way and describes also the work of skills training centres which emerge from the voluntary sector, especially churches. This is a doctoral thesis and it has the thoroughness which a thesis requires. It is, however, arduous to undertake the painstaking interpretation of many tables to find conclusions which are often quite self-evident. For example, given the spectacular growth of education after independence, it is not surprising that apprentices tend to be better educated than the small entrepreneurs who employ them. This is obviously required reading for specialists in the field, but it is nevertheless also a good book to browse through, containing as it does pictures and life stories, for people trying to get a feel for Zambia's urban life. Hoppers has published many articles on this topic and there are useful references to these in the bibliography.

719 **Industrial training and labor market segmentation in Zambia: a historical analysis.**
Wim Hoppers. *African Studies Review*, vol. 29, no. 4 (1986), p. 43-61.

This is an historical overview of the various forms of skills training that developed from colonial times onwards. Towards the end of this work, Hoppers confirms the emergence of non-formal skills training as described in his published thesis (see item no. 718). The article contains many useful insights into the development of the labour market for semi-skilled jobs in the Southern African racial context over time. The persistent theme is a segmentation between privileged and non privileged labour. Hoppers has published widely on this topic and the fact that this article is published in a journal that is more widely available than others makes this work more accessible.

720 **The manpower approach to planning: theoretical issues and evidence from Zambia.**
Massiye Edwin Koloko. Denver, Colorado: University of Denver Graduate School of International Studies, 1980. 94p. (Monograph Series in World Affairs, vol. 18, book 1).

This is first and foremost a technical paper on manpower planning which applies a theoretical model to the Zambian situation. The data used in the model date from 1970 to 1973 and projections are made up to 1981. There are elements in Koloko's study which may clarify present day situations. One example is the fact that, 'The Zambian government failed to recognize that the requirements for technicians exceed by five times those of professional workers. Overemphasis has been put on the degree' (p. 75).

721 Industrial relations in Zambia: a country update report.
Francis Kunda.   In: *Labour relations in Southern Africa: proceedings of a conference on labour relations in Southern Africa.* Edited by Evance Kalula.   Braamfontein, South Africa: Friedrich Ebert Foundation, 1993, p. 20-25.

This is a very short paper, but it provides some interesting insights into the initial reactions of the trade union movement to democratization. They were anxious to say the least, having enjoyed their corporatist legal status in the one-party state. The paper also contains a table which suggests that democratization was accompanied by a wave of strikes. This is an aspect that the paper fails to develop.

722 Works councils and other committees: aspects of Zambian industrial relations.
Peter D. Machungwa, Tresform K. Mwaba.   Lusaka: M and M Management and Labour Consultants, 1989. 138p. bibliog.

Only the first three of the seven chapters of this book contain information specific to Zambia. Works councils were seen as central in the economic order envisaged by Kaunda's humanism. As such, it may be a publication tied to a particular era, but it should be noted that Machungwa has been Labour Minister during several periods in MMD governments. Any publication related to trade union matters in Zambia is relevant to an understanding of the country, and it is noteworthy to read that the introduction of works councils, 'generally has caused friction between the two bodies [i.e. trade unions and works councils]' (p. 36).

723 The political economy of a dual labour market in Africa.
Guy C.Z. Mhone.   London; Toronto, Canada: Associated University Presses, 1982. 254p. bibliog.

This study was carried out in the United States, as the author was refused a visa for a research visit. It is quite a qualitative narrative study, collecting as much material on labour as possible. For example, Mhone uses annual reports of the mining companies in an inventive manner. The data used end in 1969, and therefore before nationalization. A main thread in Mhone's argument is that, in reaction to rising wages for Africans, the mines substituted capital for labour. This resulted in an argument in favour of more labour intensive methods of production. According to Mhone this would mean a restructuring of the dual labour market, but his argument here is difficult to follow. The pattern of Africanization that emerged did not have this effect in Mhone's opinion.

724 Labour laws of Zambia.
A.M. Mtopa.   Lusaka: Kenneth Kaunda Foundation, 1989. 264p.

This is a comprehensive overview of labour laws at a particular moment: 1989. Labour law is more developed in Zambia than in other African countries because of the presence of the huge mining sector. It was also a major policy concern in the Kaunda era, but much may have changed in recent neo-liberal times.

725 **Supervisory women and men in Zambian work organisations.**
Pempelani Mufune, Lengwe Mwansa. Gaborone: M and M
Limited, 1993. 93p. bibliog.
This study may best be categorized as social psychology, because it uses as variables
elements such as self-esteem, power, perceptions of reward and the like. It reports the
results of survey research and much attention is paid to the survey design. The book
contains useful data on gender issues in employment. However, many of the findings
seem often to be self-evident: for example, we are told that, 'Increasing the power
position of both females and males may help enhance organisational effectiveness'
(p. 67).

726 **Labour and capital on the Zambian Copperbelt.**
Jane L. Parpart. Philadelphia: Temple University Press, 1983.
233p. 2 maps. bibliog.
Class consciousness and class action are the major preoccupations in this book.
Participation in industrial production is seen as a determining factor in the development
of class consciousness. With that perspective in mind, the book goes through a series of
familiar themes in the literature: the strikes, stabilization of labour and unionization.
Parpart sees a political impetus in labour conflicts, notably in the 1952 strike, where white
and black miners were in alliance during the days when the Federation of Rhodesia and
Nyasaland was in the making. She does not, however, deny the antagonism between the
unions and the nationalist movement. The historian Andrew Roberts said on reviewing
this book that there are too many of the wrong books on the Copperbelt. Roberts pleads
for more attention to matters such as entrepreneurial behaviour (see entry no. 145).
Indeed, the writing on the Copperbelt from a neo-Marxist perspective tends to be
repetitive and to interpret the same events over and over again. In Parpart's book it is not
always clear whether the interpretations stem from what the actors say or whether it is an
interpretation of Parpart herself.

727 **Trade unions in processes of democratisation.**
Lise Rakner. Fantoft, Norway: Department of Social Science and
Development of the Chr. Michelsen Institute, 1992. 177p. bibliog.
The fact that the Chr. Michelsen Institute published this Norwegian equivalent of a
master's thesis has left its mark on this publication. The first half of the thesis is obviously
intended more to satisfy examiners about Rakner's command of literature than it is to
inform people who want to know about Zambian trade unions. The second half of the
book is to be highly recommended, however. It contains a lucid discussion of the
relationships between trade unions and the political parties since 1971. The discussions
of the Industrial Relations Acts of 1971 and 1990 are especially valuable. Rakner
delineates sensitively the particular political space that the trade union movement
occupies in Zambia and which cannot be reduced to conventional terms. Witness this
quotation from a trade unionist: 'The truth is we [trade unions] were capitalist all the way,
you simply cannot have socialism in a country where productivity is as low as here' (p.
125).

728 **Adjustment, employment and labour market institutions.**
V. Seshamani, Ephraim Kaunga.   In: *Adjustment, employment and missing institutions in Africa: the experience in Eastern and Southern Africa.*   Edited by Willem van der Geest, Roland van der Hoeven.   London: James Currey, 1999.

This is an extremely informative article, which is an important source of reference for anybody writing on the Zambian economy. It gives a very detailed overview of economic reform and adjustment in Zambia. The core of the article deals with employment and the views of unions and employers on adjustment. There is information about a wide range of issues, from the phasing of tariff reductions to the time which cases take in the industrial court. Some insights evoke interest in further study: why do wage rates for the same levels of skill in Zambia differ so much from enterprise to enterprise? The article has a number of industrial case studies on the impact of structural adjustment on the labour market. The time series used ends in the mid-1990s, however, and it is to be hoped that the authors will write an update to this article soon.

729 **Management of human resources in the copper mining industry in Zambia.**
Geoffrey W. Silavwe.   Ndola, Zambia: The Author, 1995. 404p. 2 maps. bibliog.

Silavwe has substantial experience in social work and personnel administration in Zambia's mining industry. This may explain the bureaucratic and formal nature of his book. It reads as if it were for the most part composed of lecture notes written for various occasions. An exposition of Maslow's theory does not enlighten the reader about Zambia. Nevertheless, the book is informative on legal matters, and it probably provides important starting points in studying Zambianization in the mining industry. The photographs, which display optimistic, innocent and naïve people, may be revealing of the mood of the times: the 1970s were obviously the great period for those benefiting from Zambianization.

Statistics

730 Bank of Zambia statistics fortnightly.
Lusaka: Bank of Zambia, 1993- .
These have been published since 1993 and give up-to-date information on monetary matters. The information is also posted on the Bank of Zambia's website: www.boz.zmnet.zm/

731 Quarterly digest of statistics.
Central Statistical Office. Lusaka: Government of the Republic of Zambia, Central Statistical Office.
Statistical sources specifically dealing with Zambia emerged only after the break up of the Central African Federation. For many years, the Statistical Office published a monthly digest of statistics, but in the 1970s this became increasingly an occasional publication. It has now been succeeded by a quarterly digest of statistics, which is also irregular. New types of statistics are now incorporated in the quarterly digest. It is still predominantly economic in nature, but there is now more information on the social indicators: education and health.

732 1990 census of population, housing and agriculture: demographic projections 1990-2015.
Central Statistical Office. Lusaka: Government of the Republic of Zambia, Central Statistical Office, 1996. 289p.
The first census assessing the African population of Zambia was undertaken in 1963. Further enumerations of the population took place in 1969, 1980 and 1990. The 1990 census has been split into many volumes, with analytical reports by province, but this is the main summary. It provides data broken down by age group, sex and district with projections for future growth. The main conclusions show unabated population growth despite economic decline and the AIDS pandemic. The population grew from 5,661,801 in 1980 to 7,759,167 in 1990, an average growth of 3.7 per cent per year. Population density increased from 7.8 to 10.3 persons per square kilometre in the same period.

733 **National census of agriculture census report (1990/92) (Part 1).**
Central Statistical Office. Lusaka: Government of the Republic of
Zambia, Central Statistical Office, 1996. 289p. 4 maps.

The summary in this report offers easy access to important facts on regional agricultural
variations in Zambia. Maps illustrate the distribution of crops and cattle throughout the
country. The second half of this volume consists of tables showing regional diversity.
Particular attention is paid in this survey to female headed households.

734 **The evolution of poverty in Zambia 1991-1996.**
Central Statistical Office. Lusaka: Government of the Republic of
Zambia, 1997. 161p. bibliog.

An increase in poverty is often believed to accompany structural adjustment. As a
consequence, the international financial institutions consider poverty in their
negotiations. In Zambia, as in many other countries, this has led to a new role in statistical
offices: that of monitoring. This publication compares three surveys carried in 1991, 1993
and 1996. All of them report widespread poverty. One of this report's most striking
findings is that, 'Total poverty generally decreased from 1991-1996 for households whose
heads were less educated and generally increased for the more educated' (p. 64).

735 **Living conditions monitoring survey report 1996.**
Central Statistical Office. Lusaka: Government of the Republic of
Zambia, Central Statistical Office, 1997. 355p. 2 maps.

This survey is more comprehensive than previous ones, which were mostly concerned
with a headcount and measuring depth of poverty. This one not only paid attention to such
measures and other social indicators in health and education, but asked about income
generating activities, household assets, household coping strategies, and so on. The
following will give an impression of the kinds of finding this survey contains: 'the
extremely poor households have less access to clean water (thirty-six per cent) than the
moderately poor households (fifty-four per cent) and the non-poor households (sixty-nine
per cent)' (p. 175).

736 **Zambia demographic and health surveys 1992 and 1996:
preliminary report.**
Central Statistical Office. Lusaka: Government of the Republic of
Zambia, Central Statistical Office, Ministry of Health, 1997. 23p.
**Trends in demographic, family planning and health indicators in
Zambia 1980-1996.**
Central Statistical Office. Lusaka: Government of the Republic of
Zambia, Central Statistical Office, Ministry of Health, 1997. 17p.

These demographic and health surveys provide information on marriage, fertility, family
planning, fertility preferences and maternal and child care; mothers' and children's
nutritional status; infant and child mortality. They often make depressing reading. Child
survival rates, for example, have been decreasing since the mid 1980s. These two reports
are accessible to a wide public, but people with a genuine research interest can access the
whole database through the Internet.

737   Living conditions in Zambia (1998); preliminary report.
Central Statistical Office.   Lusaka: Government of the Republic of
Zambia, Central Statistical Office, 1999. 134p. 2 maps.

This is the fourth living conditions monitoring survey carried out in Zambia, but it makes
systematic comparisons only with the 1996 and 1998 surveys. It finds an increase in
poverty from 69.2 per cent to 72.9 per cent in this period. This increase – in tandem with
an increase in extreme poverty – may be attributed to an increase in urban poverty. It is,
however, the rural areas which are most affected by poverty.

738   Zambia in figures, 1999.
Central Statistical Office.   Lusaka: Government of the Republic of
Zambia, Central Statistical Office, 2000. 20p. map.

This short publication provides essential demographic and economical data on Zambia. It
offers often dramatic reading: lending interest rates have dropped from 69 per cent to 40.4
per cent in the period 1996 to 1999. The purchasing power of the *kwacha* halved between
1996 and 1999.

Education

739 Implementing educational policies in Zambia.
Paul P.W. Achola. Washington, DC: World Bank, Africa Technical
Department, 1990. 54p. bibliog. (Discussion Paper Series, no. 90).
This is an overview of the development of education in Zambia with special attention
given to policy making. It identifies problems and mentions plans to deal with them. The
paper contains valuable statistical material, for example on enrolment, although the time
series only goes as far as 1984.

**740 The effects of civic education on political culture: evidence from
Zambia.**
Michael Bratton, Philip Alderfer, Georgina Bowser, Joseph Tembo.
World Development, vol. 27, no. 5 (1999), p. 807-24.
The perception of a need for civic education is brought about by a pessimistic assessment
of democratic practices after the reintroduction of multipartyism. The article reports the
results of a questionnaire administered in the course of three civic education exercises:
one organized by the monitoring organization FODEP (whose original brief was the
monitoring of elections); the second sponsored by an American organization and carried
out by a Civic Action Fund; the third involving the retraining of civics teachers to revamp
civics teaching at junior secondary school. The results show positive effects of these
exercises on citizens' knowledge, but little effect on political behaviour, with one
important exception: the likelihood of registering to vote has increased. The effects were
also mostly to be seen among those who were already educated and informed. This
research is meticulously designed and offers insights into a branch of political activity –
civic education – which is seen as very important after the return to multipartyism. In the
end, however, one has to ask whether a great deal of trouble has been taken to find the
obvious.

741 Denominational secondary schooling in post-independence Zambia: a case study.

Brendan P. Carmody. *African Affairs*, vol. 89, no. 355 (1990), p. 247-91.

Jesuits founded Canisius Secondary School near Chisekesi in Southern Province in 1949. This article discusses the development, mainly in the period after independence, of this school in the light of two issues. First, the school's Catholic character changed as increasing numbers of teachers and students were of other denominations after independence. In the late 1970s there was a reaction against that and an attempt was made to maintain or recreate its Catholic character. Second, the article discusses the role of the school as the source of elite formation. The colonial government feared that the founding of the school had the danger of creating an 'intellectual unemployed proletariat'. Around independence, Zambia was faced with a large shortage of manpower, and secondary school education of a high standard naturally became extremely valuable. New concerns cropped up in later decades in the light of growing unemployment among the educated and disquiet about growing inequities in Zambian society: Carmody reports the conclusion that, 'Canisius needs to adopt a religiously rooted critical stance towards the educational and social system'.

742 Education in Zambia: Catholic perspectives.

Brendan Carmody. Lusaka: Bookworld Publishers, 1999. 195p. 6 maps. bibliog.

The greater part of this book is a history of Catholic education in Zambia. One finds relevant information about the backgrounds of famous Catholic schools, such as Chikuni in Southern Province, but it is perhaps the last part that is the most interesting. There, Carmody discusses the loss of the primary schools which were taken over by the government – a decision that there is now a tendency to regret. Secondly, he writes about the ideological battle between the church and the government which he considers to have lasted from 1974 to 1995.

743 The struggle against underdevelopment in Zambia since independence: what role for education?

Tom Draisma. Amsterdam: Free University Press, 1987. 523p. 5 maps. bibliog.

The major topic in this book is the debate on the educational reforms which Kaunda announced in 1976. The purpose of these reforms was to adapt education for the developmental problems of Zambia, and a major plank of the reforms was the introduction of 'production units' in schools. That topic is discussed from p. 229 onwards. Draisma followed the education debate closely for six months. The book can be read merely to get an idea of people's approach to education in Zambia. The section on education and the churches from p. 339 onwards can still be profitably read for that purpose twenty-five years later. Secondly, the work can be read as a study of policy making under Kenneth Kaunda. Thirdly, it can function as a reference work on education until the early 1980s. One can read, for example, on p. 415 about protest against marxist influence in political education during the 1980s. Finally, Draisma has been a secondary school teacher and inside knowledge informs this massive tome which brings authoritatively together much that was previously dispersed.

744 **The origins and development of education in Zambia; from pre-colonial times to 1996. A book of notes and readings.**
Edited by M.J. Kelly. Lusaka: Image Publishers Ltd., 1999. 365p.
Kelly has gathered together in this collection a very wide selection of readings. It is unsurprising to find a good section on the history of education as that has been reasonably well studied, but Kelly also presents a section on HIV/AIDS and education, and another on education, poverty reduction and structural adjustment. Some of the authors covered are to be found in this bibliography also, including Coombe (see item no. 129), Carmody (see item nos. 282, 741, 742) and Hoppers (see item nos. 718, 719), but others have been retrieved from the grey literature to be found in bureaucracies – for example a survey of conditions in twenty-five Zambian primary schools by Dennis Aspinwall which makes stark reading. His estimate that only about fifty-seven per cent of school-age children are actually enrolled in school is interesting in the light of official statistics.

745 **'No girl leaves the school unmarried'; Mabel Shaw and the education of girls at Mbereshi, Northern Rhodesia.**
Sean Morrow. *The International Journal of African Historical Studies*, vol. 19, no. 4 (1986), p. 601-34.
Mabel Shaw was Principal of Mbereshi girl's boarding school from 1915 until 1944. This article gives a richly detailed account of the mixture of concerns regarding girls' education that motivated her: feminist ('a kind of sex pride'); discipline ('convent-like exclusion'); tradition (the school as a 'tribe in miniature'); marriage ('a western form of *chisungu* – Bemba initiation); reactions to migration and urbanization; and above all the building up of a Christian character. The article ends with the demise of Shaw's ideal to train African girls for what Shaw considered Christian marriage. Her attempt at neo-traditional education was, it is concluded, too isolated from the European as well as from the African communities.

746 **Research study report on out of school youth.**
Lawrence Mukuka, Record Mulango, Gilbert Masiye, Harriet Ntalasha. Lusaka: Government of the Republic of Zambia: Ministry of Education, 1995. 115p. bibliog.
Economic decline means less money for education. Absolute enrolment numbers are not declining in Zambia, but this statistic is not adjusted to take account of population growth. This study estimates that eighty-three per cent of the potential Grade 1 population fail to get a place, but this estimate seems to be on the high side. This study reports on a survey among 368 respondents stratified according to geographical criteria – two urban and two rural provinces – and sex. The information in tabular form reveals one of the most convincing descriptions of poverty, wherein the position of females is the worst. Yet the authors conclude also that, 'The perception of agriculture by most out-of-school youth was still that of a less prestigious and brutish way of life associated with the illiterate rural people' (p. 101).

747 **The impact of rapid population growth and economic decline: Zambia.**
Mwelma Musambachime. *Review of African Political Economy*, no. 48 (1990), p. 89-92.

This is one of a number of contributions on the theme of education and cultural production. It is more a statement of the situation, containing useful figures, than an interpretation. It documents the enormous expansion of Zambian education from a small base after independence. Thereafter came the decline when the system could not cope with ever increasing demand. More importantly, the economic decline undermined the system from within: teachers were demoralized by low pay, large classes, many shifts and the lure of jobs abroad. The article ends by mentioning cost sharing, which led to rioting at the University of Zambia.

748 **Party, polity and bureaucracy: the Zambian education debate, 1974-77.**
Dan O'Brien. *African Affairs*, vol. 81, no. 323 (1982), p. 207-30.

O'Brien's conclusion in this article is that the educational debate of the 1970s brought little change. Ultimately the party (UNIP), where he locates the origin of the debate, conceded that the education system should aim at the production of academically competent pupils who could compete on the international scene. The ideas of gearing education to the needs of those who drop out or of suiting education to the particular needs of Zambia – mainly agricultural – were dropped. This is an informative article, which gives an overview of the debate and situates it imaginatively in the power structure of Zambian society.

749 **Higher education and the labour market in Zambia: expectations and performance.**
Bikas C. Sanyal, John H. Chase, Philip S. Dow, Mary E. Jackman. Paris: The Unesco Press; Lusaka: The University of Zambia, 1976. 371p. bibliog.

This is one of several studies which traced the careers of secondary school leavers in various African countries on the labour market. The study is technocratic in nature: data collection and computing, it assumes, will provide the basis for educational planning. The book contains numerous tables, which usually make projections up to 1981. The book does not read easily: the reader's attention can get lost in a multitude of facts that are not obviously related to each other. Yet it may be of benefit to know the attrition rate among teachers in the early 1970s (about twenty per cent per year) or to know that among the 194 graduates in the Ministry of Rural Development in 1971, there were only 37 Zambians.

750 **Secondary education and the formation of an elite; the impact of education on Gwembe district, Zambia.**
Thayer Scudder, Elizabeth Colson. New York: Academic Press, 1980. 190p. map. bibliog.

The authors followed, in a longitudinal survey over twenty years (1956-76), the first 500 men and women from Gwembe district who attended secondary school. The title and theoretical focus of the book suggest the emergence of a particular cohesive elite out of this education, but that is hardly the case. The book gives first and foremost an insight into the diversity of experience and individual struggles for advancement in life. The section on financing an education is particularly telling. It reveals starkly the great cost of education in a situation where education was 'free'. The kinship system was the main source of support and increasingly became the only one. The book contains also challenging information on conceptualizations and realities of 'the good life'. It mentions, for example, the 'felt poverty of the lowest paid secondary school leavers' in sharp contrast with 'the steady progress among the most successful village farmers'. This observation is made against the background of the authors' adherence to the view that there is a strong urban bias in the Zambian economy.

751 The significance of schooling; life journeys in an African society.
Robert Serpell. Cambridge, England: Cambridge University Press, 1993. 345p. map. bibliog.

The subject of this study is the role of education in a Chewa village near Katete, Eastern Province. The study is the outcome of an almost lifelong involvement with the cultural context within which cognitive development of children takes place. The book is very rich in themes and data and defies summary. Among the topics it covers are: a confrontation of the notion of intelligence with Chewa concepts; a discussion of test outcomes during various periods in people's lives; and the role of community drama in relation to education. Serpell has an impressive grasp of the wider literature in his subject and therefore the book has a wider significance than for Zambia alone. The book is not only of interest to specialists in education however, because it also gives much insight into everyday life. In Serpell's chapter on life journeys, for example, it becomes apparent how few people in Zambia succeed in a school career: thirty-three per cent of the cohort studied effectively ignored the school system. Serpell does not, however, belittle the meaning and importance of the school as is especially evident in his chapter on educational planning. One chapter, 'Wenzelu ndani?', which gives a Chewa perspective on child development and intelligence, can be strongly recommended as an excellent introduction to the huge differences in cultural assumptions which have to be faced by foreigners who come to live and work in Zambia.

752 Memory and becoming chosen others: fundamentalism and elite making in a Zambian Catholic mission school.
Anthony Simpson. In: *Memory and the postcolony; African anthropology and the critique of power.* Edited by R. Werbner. London: Zed Books, 1998, p. 209-29.

The author spent a total of twenty years teaching in the school concerned and also carried out anthropological fieldwork there. It is therefore an internal view of 'born again' Christianity, which is widespread in Zambia. Simpson explains the appeal of such beliefs as a response to the experience of failure and speaks about the moral discourse of failure. Secondary school students are an elite in Zambia, but they face a very uncertain future due to the economic decline of the country. Anybody who is familiar with this form of evangelical Christianity will be struck by the veracity of Simpson's account. He claims, for example, that, 'Repetition is a striking feature of the preaching style adopted'.

Literature and the Arts

753 Women = masks: initiation arts in North Western Province, Zambia.
Elizabeth L. Cameron. *African Arts*, vol. 31, no. 2 (1998),
p. 50-61.
The journal in which this article appeared is lavishly illustrated and that may be the reason why it often disappears from libraries. This article on the Makisi culture has therefore not been seen by the compiler.

754 Zambia's traditional dances.
Frank Chingwalu. *Z Magazine*, no. 39 (1972), p. 16-18; no. 40
(1972), p. 24-25; no. 41 (1972), p. 16-18; no. 42 (1972), p. 16-17;
no. 44 (1973), p. 13-15; no. 45 (1973), p. 16-21; no. 47 (1973),
p. 16-19.
Dancing and drumming are art forms in which Zambia excels. This is a series of articles describing (in order of publication) *vimbuza* (a healing performance, danced by the Tumbuka in eastern Zambia); *nyau* (the masked dances among the Chewa); *kalela* (found in the Copperbelt, Luapula and Northern Provinces); *icila* (a dance of the Lala in Serenje district, Central Province, danced at night only); *umutomboko* (a dance associated with the Kazembe chiefs of the Lunda in Luapula); and *makisi* (found in Western and North Western Provinces). The illustrations are beautiful and the articles provide a good introduction to Zambian dance as a vibrant and vivid culture.

755 Life among the cattle-owning Plateau Tonga; the material culture of a Northern Rhodesia native tribe.
Elizabeth Colson. Livingstone, Zambia: The Rhodes Livingstone Museum, 1949. 40p.
Colson has written extensively on the Tonga, and this is her first published work. The booklet bears the hallmarks of a first write-up after fieldwork. It is devoid of theory and primarily describes everyday life structured by the objects (material culture) which the

Tonga use. It is therefore useful as an introductory text for people interested in the Plateau Tonga. Secondly, it is useful to get a feel about how the area looked in the 1940s through the eyes of an anthropologist. Some remarks, however, rise above time and place, such as the comment that, 'The chief pleasure of the adults seems to lie in talk' (p. 35). This is true of rural Zambia in general, both at that time and much later, and it has not received the anthropological attention it deserves.

756 Patronage, the state and ideology in Zambian theatre.
Stewart Crehan. *Journal of Southern African Studies*, vol. 16, no. 2 (1990), p. 290-307.

Although popular theatre is thriving in Zambia, this has, Crehan claims, not led to 'a revolutionary synthesis of traditional and modern, popular and elite forms'. This thesis is discussed against the background of the struggle to develop an indigenous Zambian theatre and the role of patronage therein. Firstly, there was a struggle within and against 'white enclave' theatre. Secondly, there was a struggle for recognition by and support from party, government and president. This came to a dead end when state control became more of a concern than state support. The next generation of patrons discussed are aid agencies and NGOs who use theatre for educational and awareness raising programmes. Finally, institutional theatre is mentioned where organizations – mainly parastatals – adopt theatre groups just as they may adopt football clubs. A good number of plays produced in Zambia are discussed.

757 Songs of Zambia.
Compiled and edited by Jackie Ehlers, Joan Child. Lusaka: Longman, 1975. 107p.

These songs have been collected for educational purposes. The texts in the original languages are printed with musical notations and a commentary stating theme, source and language in which they are sung. These are not, however, innocent children's songs as may be suggested by the educational flavour of the book. To give one example: *Moye* is a song about a girl who goes off from her village dancing and comes back walking as if she had a disease. This song predates the AIDS scourge.

758 Zambian traditional art.
Ladislav Holy with photographs by Jirina Lukesova. Lusaka: Zambia Information Services, 1971. 47p.

With its twenty pages of text and twenty-seven of photographs, this is more a brochure than a book. It draws attention to the collection of Zambian traditional art in the Livingstone Museum – for example, their large collection of masks of Europeans, which are striking in their veracity. This brochure is very useful, as Holy sums up the types of art one finds among the various people in Zambia. It is not widely known, for instance, that the clay toys made by the Subiya are so remarkable. The pictures are beautiful and typical of what one might find in Zambia as traditional art.

759 Theatre and social change in Zambia; the Chikwakwa theatre.
Patrick E. Idoye. Lewiston, New York: The Edwin Mellen Press, 1996. 178p.

In the late sixties, the Chikwakwa theatre was built of mud near the Great East Road campus of the university. This book deals not only with the plays performed there but also with those staged on tour – often under the name of 'development theatre' – in various rural areas. The book is primarily informative as it introduces the reader to the most important names and it provides as comprehensive as possible a list of the productions. Idoye stresses the emancipatory nature of this theatre, where Africans could find a voice of their own outside the European dominated theatre clubs. The situation was slightly more complicated, as is evident from the fact that two Europeans – Michael Etherington and David Kerr – have been most influential in creating the theatrical tradition. It is regrettable that there is no mention made of the deportation of Etherington in 1971, which is highly relevant in a political analysis of the Chikwakwa theatre.

760 **African music in Northern Rhodesia and some other places.**
A.M. Jones. In: *Occasional papers of the Rhodes-Livingstone Museum 1-16.* Manchester, England: Manchester University Press, 1974, p. 73-143.

Jones was already studying Zambian music in the 1940s, and he has published a considerable number of papers on the topic. This publication brings several of them together. Most of the content is beyond comprehension for people who do not have a musicological training. A chapter on how African songs are composed will, however, also be of interest to students of oral literature. The author's admiration for Zambian musicians shines through the often cerebral text: 'The transcriber has to listen to six variant rhythms simultaneously, and each rhythm has its own main beat which may not coincide with that of the other. This is quite beyond the most brilliant musician, it simply cannot be done'.

761 **The messages of tourist art; an African semiotic system in comparative perspective.**
Bennetta Jules-Rosette. New York: Plenum Press, 1984. 266p. bibliog.

This is primarily a sociology of the tourist scene in Africa as a whole. While it draws heavily on Zambian material, there are no separate chapters devoted to Zambia as such. One can, however, find subheadings within chapters entitled, for example: 'three cottage industries in Marrapodi' (Lusaka); 'pottery as a woman's craft in Lusaka'; and 'the Kanyama [Lusaka] painters' circle'. It is a good book to browse through for somebody interested in Zambian art in particular; this pleasure is enhanced by the evocative black and white photographs. Its sociological content may also from time to time be of interest to a general audience: one example is the table on p. 160 indicating how painters adapt their subject to their audience. Here it is explained that pictures of the mines on the Copperbelt, for example, are for the local proletariat, while the pictures of Mount Kilimanjaro produced in Zambia are intended for the international tourist. On the same page is a reproduction of a beautiful picture of Mount Kilimanjaro which is almost Japanese in style.

762 **The treasures of Zambian art.**
Introduced by Simon Mwansa Kapwepwe. Lusaka: National Museums Board, 1970.

This is the catalogue of an exhibition of treasures – and that is the right word – at the national museum in Livingstone. It lists the works exhibited and contains many illustrations. The art mainly originates from North Western and Western Province. This catalogue would be a good starting point for people studying Zambian art.

763 Wood carvers of Zambia.
Bonnie B. Keller. Livingstone, Zambia: National Museums of
Zambia, 1967. 57p. map. bibliog.
Livingstone attracts by far the most tourists in Zambia and thus provides a ready market
for African wood carvers. This work is a study of the social background of this distinct
occupational group. It is not a purely sociological treatment however, but discusses both
their market and what they make.

**764 Dance, media entertainment and popular theatre in South-East
Africa.**
David Kerr. Bayreuth, West Germany: Eckhard Breitinger, 1988.
286p. bibliog. (Bayreuth African Studies Series, no. 43).
David Kerr has been a force in the development of African theatre, working from the
University of Zambia and the University of Malawi. The book covers both these countries
and is written against the background of a general quest to establish whether there has
been cultural imperialism. He concludes that the content of much television and most
radio entertainment is far more hybrid than is usually assumed. It is worthwhile to read
Kerr's discussion of Andrew Masiye's play about Kazembe and the Portuguese to see
how he unravels the way themes can adapt and function in a Zambian context. Above all,
however, this is a reference work which introduces a great variety of popular dramatic art
to the reader.

765 Traditional Zambian pottery.
Text by Bente Lorenz, photography by Margaret Plesner. London:
Ethnographica, 1989. 47p.
Art in Zambia is often expressed in utensils: baskets and pottery are the prime examples.
This book shows that clearly. Bente Lorenz, who wrote the introduction, is a gifted potter
and a central figure in the Zambian art scene.

766 Music and dance in Zambia.
Atta Annan Mensah. Lusaka: NECZAM, 1973. 18p.
This is a short and informative pamphlet. Mensah describes very briefly the main
characteristics of Zambian music; the main categories of instruments used; and the role
of dance. The last section of the paper deals with the way music functions in social
contexts. The second half of the book, where pages are not numbered, consists of
illustrations of musical instruments.

**767 Form and significance in the art of the Lunda, Luvale, Luchazi
and Chokwe of Zambia: a Boasion approach.**
Kafungulwa Mubitana. *Zambia Museums Journal*, vol. 1 (1970),
p. 22-27.
The writer of this article, Kafungulwa Mubitana, was a brilliant art historian and
anthropologist who died tragically in a car accident. This work is a quite philosophical
piece, which discusses the symbolism in the objects made by the groups of people of the
title. They are distinguished from other groups in Zambia as a result of their rich culture
in carving objects.

768 Stools and headrests in Zambia.
Kafungulwa Mubitana. *Zambia Museums Journal*, vol. 2 (1971), p. 7-38.
The title of this article is self explanatory. The work catalogues the collection to be found in the Livingstone museum. The numerous illustrations are annotated with texts on area of origin, decoration, and symbolic and other functions.

769 The tongue of the dumb.
Dominic Mulaisho. London: Heinemann Educational Books, 1971. 249p.
Mulaisho is the only Zambian writer of fiction who has gained international recognition. This book explains his success as it not only keeps the attention of the reader easily, but also gives a very good introduction to village life: notably the struggles for leadership positions, the attempt to build up a following and the place of witchcraft. The major rift in the community is between traditionalists and those influenced by the Catholic mission. It is stated at the beginning of the book that the events are fictional but, according to Father O'Shea (see item no. 178), it is recognizably set in Katondwe mission in the Luangwa valley.

770 The smoke that thunders.
Dominic Mulaisho. London: Heinemann Educational Books, 1979. 277p.
The smoke that thunders is *Musi-O-Tunya*, the Victoria Falls. In this novel, Mulaisho fictionalized elements from the Zambian and Zimbabwean independence struggle. It is advisable to read Mulaisho's other novel first (see item no. 769) as it is much stronger than this one. The characters here are too one-dimensional and lack the tragedy, ambiguity and paradoxes to be found in the historical events to which the novel refers.

771 Ticklish sensation.
Gideon Phiri. Lusaka: Zambia Educational Publishing House, 1994. Rev. ed. 196p.
This novel is not great literature, but it has remained extremely popular since it was first published in 1973. This account of the transition from boyhood to adulthood gives readers, who come from all walks of life, a good insight into the worldviews of the book's characters, not only with regard to the ticklish sensations emerging in a teenager, but also with regard to how life in school is perceived.

772 The battle for control of the camera in late nineteenth century Western Zambia.
Gwyn Prins. *African Affairs*, vol. 89, no. 354 (1990), p. 97-107.
Eight photographs, taken by the missionary François Coillard, form the centrepiece of this article. Photography is described as part of the struggle for control between the mission and the Lozi establishment. Prins maintains that these photographs provide insights which cannot be obtained from other types of data.

773   **The material culture of the peoples of the Gwembe Valley.**
Barrie Reynolds.   Manchester, England: Manchester University
Press, 1968. 262p. 2 maps. bibliog.

Reynolds was part of the team that studied the Gwembe Tonga before their land and villages in the lower Zambezi were flooded as a result of the Kariba dam. He made a seemingly exhaustive inventory of the artefacts which they used. The various areas covered include art and recreation; pounding grain and tubers; building houses; smelting and smithing; basket making; and tobacco and snuff. The book has no narrative and is to be used for reference. This is important because many of the skills and objects Reynolds describes can be found much more widely than just in the vanished culture of the Valley (Gwembe) Tonga.

774   **Nadine Gordimer's 'A guest of honour': a failure to understand Zambian society.**
Jan Kees van Donge.   *Journal of Southern African Studies*, vol. 9,
no. 1 (1982), p. 59-85.

This is part of a special issue on literature and society in Southern Africa. 'A guest of honour' is situated in an imaginary country, but one which greatly resembles Zambia. The article confronts the question of whether the novel is believable for people who know Zambia well. It concludes that it is not, but that analysing the novel spurs speculation about the nature of Zambian politics.

775   **Makisi of Zambia.**
P. André Vrydagh.   *African Arts*, vol. 10, no. 4 (1977), p. 12-19.
map.

This article is well worth attention, as it contains some magnificent illustrations. Vrydagh accompanies the pictures with a clear text on these masked dances of groups living close to the Angolan border in western Zambia. He describes the dancers, the occasions on which they perform, who makes the masks, and so on, in a flowing narrative based on his own experiences. He is especially informative about the interrelations of the *Makisi* dancers (who are not Lozi) with the Lozi capital.

776   **Seeing makishi: an anthropological study of West Zambian art.**
Bert Witkamp.   Leiden, The Netherlands: Institute of Cultural
Anthropology, University of Leiden, 1987. 115p. 5 maps. bibliog.

This is an unpublished MA thesis, but it contains exceptionally valuable information. *Makishi* dancing is famous for its masks. It is found virtually throughout the western part of Zambia and is associated with the Luchazi, Luvale and Mbunda. Witkamp speaks about the West Central Bantu, who spread far into Angola as well. He gives an elaborate description of the dances he has seen and interprets the meaning of the dances, which are especially associated with boys' circumcision rituals (*mukanda*). The book also contains much factual information about how the masks are made and the colour symbolism in them. There are two annexes: one of drawings of masks by Teddy Malite and the other a photographic record of *Makishi* masks at the Livingstone Museum.

Mass Media

General

777 The freedom of the press.
Fackson Banda. Lusaka: Zambia Independent Media Association, 1997. 68p.
Banda presents a lucid statement on the limitations of press freedom in Zambia as the background for a content analysis comparing the government-owned with the privately-owned press. It is not surprising that the MMD got overwhelming coverage in the government-owned press. The privately-owned press gave much more attention to other parties – *The Post* notably to the Zambian Democratic Congress. *The Post* was, however, primarily in favour of UNIP's boycott.

778 Press freedom in Zambia: a brief review of the press during the MMD's first five years in office.
Chris H. Chirwa. Lusaka: Zambia Independent Media Association, 1996. 71p.
This rather loosely structured little book is very useful. It provides, for example, an overview of the periodicals which appeared during democratization and which have now perished, and the circulation figures of the major daily papers. It is very critical in tone: MMD has kept the major media under government control; there is quite a lot of legislation that needs to be withdrawn lest it present a threat to press freedom; it mentions that *The Post* has been involved in over 100 court cases, of which it has lost only two. However, it also mentions that Zambian editors often want to, and can, act independently of the owners of the papers. It also has a section on the criticisms of the government voiced by its own papers.

779 **The press in Zambia; the development, role and control of national newspapers in Zambia 1906-1983.**
Francis P. Kasoma, with a foreword by Richard Hall.   Lusaka: Multimedia Publications, 1986. 244p. 3 maps. bibliog.
About half of this book is devoted to newspapers in colonial times, while the other half deals with the much shorter post-independence period. The former part is mainly historical, but in the second part there is more stress on detailed content analysis in order to create a more quantitative idea of the independence of the papers: whether their writing suggested a pro-government stance or not. It documents vividly how the newspapers remained critical of government, despite attempts to control them. The book contains many interesting personal details. Kasoma suggests without hesitation that Richard Hall, the gifted *Times of Zambia* editor after independence, resigned because he had fallen out of favour with the political elite. He was succeeded by Dunstan Kamana who was even more critical. The book pays attention not only to the major newspapers, but even to a newspaper that never appeared at all: in 1983, Sikota Wina had intended to publish a paper called *Sunday Drum*.

780 **The Kapelwa Musonda file.**
Kapelwa Musonda.   Lusaka: NECZAM, 1972. 140p.
Kapelwa Musonda, in daily life, was an ordinary chemist who worked with Shell Chemicals. In public life, however, he had an influence which went far beyond that. His friendly satire could make pompous people hopelessly ridiculous. When young politicians in MMD declared themselves to be Young Turks, he said they could be identified by their suits. They were even said to sleep in suits. Given that that was written in the mid 1990s, Musonda's columns clearly continued for a long time in the *Times of Zambia* after the appearance of this collection. The articles in it have, in general, not lost their relevance, however, and they remain refreshing to read. Particularly recommended is the column on the pay rise (p. 43).

Newspapers

781 **The Monitor.**
Lusaka: Afronet, 1998 - . weekly.
This weekly has emerged after the closure of virtually all privately owned newspapers. It has a fiercely independent tone, but it is richer in opinions than in news gathering. Afronet is a network of non-governmental organizations.

782 **National Mirror.**
Lusaka: Multimedia Zambia, 1972 - . weekly.
This paper is owned by the Christian Multimedia complex. During the one-party state, it was one of the few public platforms in Zambia which were not under the control of the party. It is now a weekly and remains independent, while offering, relatively speaking, quite a lot of church news.

783 Newspaper index; topical guide to newspaper articles in the Zambian print media 1998-1999.
Lusaka: Special Collections of the Library of the University of Zambia, [n.d.]. 2 vols.

These two volumes are the first products of an ongoing project to index articles appearing in the major national newspapers. The topics are nominally arranged alphabetically, although quite a number of entries find their place seemingly at random. It nevertheless is a most useful tool: for example, the entries mentioned under the name Jack Chisi lead directly to articles about the 1997 coup attempt.

784 The Post.
Lusaka: Post Newspapers Ltd., 1990, weekly; 1995, bi-weekly; 1996 - . daily.

This paper – at one time a weekly – was the voice of the demand for liberalization and multipartyism in 1990. It was for a time by far the best selling paper in Zambia. Its circulation has now fallen drastically, however. *The Post* did not become the voice of the new MMD government, but on the contrary was very critical of it. It even started to identify with Kenneth Kaunda in his bid to become president again. Its original muckraking investigative journalism changed to an aggressive accusing tone without much substance to its allegations, but it voices the opinion of an important section of the Zambian public – especially the intellectuals who are active in non-governmental organizations. Its website address is www.zamnet.zm/post/

785 Times of Zambia.
Ndola, Zambia: Times Newspapers Zambia Ltd., 1965 - . daily.

This paper is a successor to newspapers owned by the South African Argus group before independence. The group withdrew after independence and sold their papers to Lonrho, who opted for this name. Lonrho owned the paper until 1975 when the government nationalized it. It is still owned by the government after democratization. The paper has, however, always shown an independent spirit and is probably the most widely read paper in Zambia. It has a special issue on Sunday and offers a financial and economic supplement. Its website's address is www.zamnet.zm/times/

786 Zambia Daily Mail.
Lusaka, 1969 - . daily.

This paper originated in 1960 as the weekly *African Mail*. It became a government owned paper in 1965 as the government did not want Lonrho to hold a monopoly. In 1969 it became a daily paper. It continued in government ownership after the change of government in 1991. It covers virtually the same news as the *Times of Zambia*, but lacks the journalistic flair of that paper. Although it is a moot point – a change has perhaps been apparent in recent years – the paper is considered to show more loyalty to the government than the *Times* does. It has a special issue on Sunday and offers a financial and economic supplement. Its website address is www.daily_mail.co.zm/

Bibliographical periodicals

787   Africa bibliography.
International African Institute.   Edinburgh: Edinburgh University
Press, 1983 - .

This is published on behalf of the International African Institute, which has a long history
of bibliographical work on Africa. It is nowadays brought out as an annual publication,
but there can be long delays in publication. It is divided into a general section and regional
sections, where there is a category on Zambia. These latter sections are then subdivided
into particular topics. Over the years, more subjects outside the social sciences have
gradually been included. Until recently, book reviews were also included, and this gave
easy access to opinion and debate. This series is particularly good on edited volumes, as
individual chapters are listed separately.

**788   African studies abstracts. The abstracts journal of the African
Studies Centre, Leiden.**
African Studies Centre.   Leiden, The Netherlands; East Grinstead,
England: Bowker/Saur, 1969 - .

This is a most useful journal, as it includes many abstracts of journal articles. The
abstracts are published in English, but sourced from a variety of languages: German,
French, Afrikaans and Portuguese. The journal has numbered its volumes from 1969, but
it was for a long time known under the Dutch title *Dokumentatieblad*. It has improved
over the years, with geographical organization especially much better than it was.

789   A current bibliography of African affairs.
Edited by Roger W. Moelidz.   Amityville, New York: Baywood
Publishing Co., 1969/70 - .

This bibliography covers a very wide selection of journals which are not necessarily
Africanist. It is especially useful as it covers more of the natural sciences than other
bibliographies. It appears four times a year and is subdivided into a general and a regional
section. In the latter, a section on Zambia can be found in each issue.

**790   International African bibliography; current books, articles and
papers in African studies.**
Edited by David Hall.   East Grinstead, England: Bowker/Saur,
1971 - .

This periodical appears four times a year and is subdivided into two sections: articles and
books. Both of these are geographically subdivided and give access to Zambia. It is
almost completely oriented towards the arts and social sciences. Slight attention is
devoted to sources outside the English language. The entries are not annotated.

791 Quarterly index to periodical literature; Eastern and Southern Africa.
Library of Congress.   Nairobi: Library of Congress Office, 1991 - .
This is a very useful source, as it concentrates on subjects relevant to the region published within the region. Periodicals within Africa often emanate from obscure sources and as a rule appear highly irregularly. Publications are listed alphabetically by author. There is no annotation, but an index is given for keywords as well as for the region. The publication has a website: www.icipe.org/LOCNAIROBI/

Current affairs publications

792 Africa confidential.
Edited by Patrick Smith.   London, Miramoor Publications, 1960 - .
fortnightly.
This is a widely read fortnightly publication on current affairs in Africa. It does not aim to be systematic and has no regularity in the reports on particular countries. The journal will publish an article on a particular country whenever it seems relevant. The articles are anonymously written and are often muckraking in nature. It has an annual register with geographic entries.

793 Africa contemporary record: annual survey and documents.
Edited by Colin Legum.   New York: Africana Publishing Company, 1968/69 - .
Veteran journalist Colin Legum puts his personal stamp clearly on this publication. It consists of a number of thematic essays; a country-by-country review of events; a section of statistical tables; and reproductions of important documents. It has a bias towards international relations, and outside this field the information is often fragmentary and loosely organized. There tend to be long delays between publications.

794 Africa research bulletin.
Exeter, England: Africa Research Limited, 1963 - . fortnightly.
Two series of this bulletin are published: one devoted to political, social and cultural issues, the other to economic, financial and technical topics. They present an overview of current affairs fortnightly, broken down on a country-by-country basis. Their sources are newspapers, which are mentioned below the entries. It publishes an index yearly, where the combination between geographical area and a subdivision in topics is particularly handy.

795 Africa review.
Essex: Waldon Publishers, 1978 - . annual.
This review is subtitled 'The economic and business report', and this is apt. This annual publication is geared first and foremost towards essential facts for the (business) visitor

who has to form an opinion quickly about a country. Each country section has a map; a country profile; an overview of key statistical indicators; and a review of the past year.

796 Regional surveys of the world: Africa south of the Sahara.
London: Europa Publications, 1971 - . annual.
This excellent reference work is produced annually. The book is subdivided into country sections, which are listed alphabetically. Each country section is subdivided into geographical, historical, political/recent history and economic section. These essays, mostly by respected authorities, are followed by a statistical survey and a directory of, among other things, the cabinet; diplomatic missions; recent election results; periodicals published in the country; and political organizations.

Publications of societies and institutions in Zambia

797 African social research.
Lusaka: Institute for African Studies/Institute for Economic and Social Research, University of Zambia, 1966 - .
This is the successor to the journal of the Rhodes-Livingstone Institute. It has appeared irregularly, and increasingly so in recent years. The journal has also veered over the years more towards policy oriented articles and opinion than towards factual material.

798 Bank of Zambia annual reports.
Lusaka: Bank of Zambia.
These reports understandably emphasize monetary issues: interest and exchange rates; inflation and money supply. They are not, however, bank documents in the narrow sense but also contain information on matters such as redundancies during structural adjustment, or the movement of copper and cobalt prices. These reports have, of course, become more interesting since liberalization. The governor of the Bank has much more independence. This publication is extremely useful for anybody who needs immediate access to information on the Zambian economy.

799 Comments on the budget.
Lusaka: University of Zambia, Department of Economics.
Since 1993, the University of Zambia's economics department has published in this work a set of essays commenting on the government's budget for the year.

800 Economic report presented to the national assembly.
Lusaka: Government of the Republic of Zambia.
The annual government budget in Zambia is accompanied by an economic report on the state of the economy which is usually subdivided into assessments of the world economy;

the state of the national economy; and subsectors in the national economy. The reports occasionally pay particular attention to subjects, depending upon their political salience: examples include parastatals in the 1980s or the environment in the 1990s. The general macroeconomic chapter is usually the most informative one, and it contains the up-to-date statistical information available on the economy at that moment.

801 Human problems in British Central Africa.
Lusaka: Rhodes-Livingstone Institute, 1944-65.

This was the journal of the Rhodes-Livingstone Institute. It is recommended reading for anybody interested in the ethnography of the country. As is the case with the monographs as well, these articles have a freshness and actuality that belie the conservative title.

802 Northern Rhodesia journal.
Livingstone, Zambia: The Rhodes-Livingstone Museum, 1950-65.

This may be seen as a rival journal to *Human problems in British Central Africa*. It demonstrates a completely different attitude to what is interesting in the country. Archaeology, colonial history and settler nostalgia are the main topics of interest. It is, however, extremely informative on these topics.

803 Zambia law journal.
Lusaka: School of Law, University of Zambia, 1969 - .

This journal has been in existence for a long time now and appears more regularly than the other scholarly journals in Zambia. It represents a great resource for anybody interested in the Zambian legal system and profession.

804 Zango: Zambian journal of contemporary issues.
Lusaka: University of Zambia, 1976 - .

The word *zango* means 'forum', 'debate' or 'arena for exchanging views'. The journal was founded in the process of the Zambianization of the university. The newer members of staff wanted more direct access to publication and a journal that was more oriented towards the problems of Zambia and Southern Africa. The result is a journal that is primarily oriented towards the formation of opinions. It appears more and more irregularly.

805 Z-magazine.
Lusaka: Government of Zambia: Zambia Information Services, 1971-83.

This was a delightful magazine, which devoted space to articles and essays on sports, politics, economics and especially the arts. It reflects the era as one in which Zambians were emerging into areas which had previously been considered the province of whites: the painter Aquila Simpasa writes and draws on the theme of witchcraft; Mumba Kabumpa directs a play on Che Guevara, and so on. It reflects strongly a feeling of optimism, especially prevalent in the 1970s.

Occasional publications

806   Department of National Parks and Wildlife; Wildlife Society.
At time of writing, there is no regular publication in this field. The Wildlife Society used to publish a journal called *Black Lechwe*. The Department of National Parks and Wildlife used to publish occasional papers under the name *The Puku*.

807   Farmers.
Zambia's large scale farmers – who were then virtually all white – published a periodical called *Commercial Farming* from 1965 to 1974. This was then renamed *Productive Farming*. In the mid 1990s, the name was again changed to *The Zambian Farmer*, and produced very good journalism for some time. The Ministry of Agriculture published a periodical called *Farming in Zambia* in the 1960s and 1970s. It is difficult to establish the actual times that these periodicals appeared and they are also usually irregular. At the time of writing, there is no longer a specific periodical dedicated to farming in Zambia.

808   Historical Association of Zambia.
Since 1969 this association has been publishing a research bulletin, which became *History in Zambia* in 1980. At time of writing, however, it has not appeared for quite some time. The association also publishes occasional papers.

809   Zambia Chamber of Commerce and Industry.
This society published the periodical *Profit* during the 1990s. Again, it is not possible to establish exactly the period in which it appeared or its regularity. It is an important source however, as it gives a running commentary on the economic liberalization – notably privatization – carried out by the Chiluba government.

810   Zambia Geographical Society.
This society has published the *Zambia Geographical Journal*, occasional papers, school supplements and conference handbooks. The last are especially valuable as they were dedicated to the place where the conference was held.

811   Zambia Ornithological Society.
The Zambian Ornithological Society has a long history of publications. From 1969 until 1984, its chief publication was the *Bulletin of the Zambian Ornithological Society*. The society also produced occasional papers, and in the years 1997 and 1998 two Zambia Bird Reports appeared: *Sightings*. The primary preoccupation in these publications, as the name suggests, is with sightings of birds, but they are useful for a broader public to acquire an idea of the various environments in which the birds have been sighted.

Bibliographies

812 An annotated bibliography of research on the urban informal sector in Zambia: suggestions for further research and support.
Raj Bardouille. Lusaka: The Finnish Development Agency (Finnida) and The University of Zambia Press, 1991. 234p.

Bardouille retrieved for this bibliography much that could have been lost: mimeographed papers, commissioned reports, seminar papers and so on. This bibliography has 126 elaborately annotated entries and is a comprehensive collection of the literature available at the time of compilation. The concept of the informal sector has lost popularity and therefore less is being written about it, so the bibliography retains current value. The chapters are introduced with interpretative commentaries. As the title says it is more than merely a bibliography. It contains much food for thought, as may be illustrated by a remark from Bardouille herself: 'The informal sector businesses in Zambia are small with low turnover and the potential to accumulate capital and expand businesses beyond the mere subsistence level is low' (p. 117).

813 Research on Zambian women in prospect and retrospect.
Raj Bardouille. Lusaka: Swedish International Development Agency (SIDA), 1992. 179p.

This, as is usually the case with Bardouille's bibliographies, is a most useful document. There are introductory essays to the various sections, which consist of 154 entries. These entries are elaborately annotated and continue therefore to be valuable if some of the more obscure materials cannot be traced. The obvious statement or the platitude seems, however, to be a danger in writing about gender and development. To give one example, we are told in one case that, 'the paper argues that accessibility to food is a big constraint to rural household food security to the extent that starvation and malnutrition are crippling the health status of the population' (p. 85).

814 **Women in Zambia: a bibliographical guide and directory.**
A.M. Chitambo. Lusaka: Women and Law in Southern Africa
Research Project, 1991. 89p.
Chitambo says in her introduction that this is the third bibliography on women in Zambia.
More such bibliographies have been published since. This one has many entries, 307 in
all, and covers newspaper articles. A separate section lists conference, seminar and
workshop proceedings and reports. It also contains a directory of women's organizations
– thirty-two all told – in Zambia.

815 **A select bibliography; Zambia.**
Robin Fincham. In: *Industry and accumulation in Africa.* Edited
by Martin Fransman. London: Heinemann Educational Books Ltd.,
1982, p. 426-28.
Zambia had a successful industrialization record in the first decade after independence.
After 1975, when copper prices fell, that sector appeared to be particularly vulnerable.
This bibliography contains much literature that gives insight into the debates surrounding
industrialization, before privatization became the main option.

816 **An annotated bibliography of identified and published research
activities related to the Zambian family from 1964-1993.**
Ministry of Community Development and UNICEF. Lusaka:
Ministry of Community Development and UNICEF, 1994. 56p.
This bibliography was compiled to commemorate the year of the family. It is not
particularly extensive – consisting of fifty-six entries – but the annotations fully
summarize the literature. A short essay introduces each section. It is divided into seven
parts, the most substantial of which are, in descending order of size: 'Women in the
family', 'Structural adjustment' and 'Family size and planning'.

817 **Kaunda's Zambia: a select and annotated bibliography.**
Naomi Musiker. Johannesburg: South African Institute of
International Affairs, 1993. 426p. map.
This bibliography contains 1,657 entries. It covers not only books and academic
periodicals, but also magazines and publications which update information, such as *Africa
Confidential.* Alternative access is provided by a subject index. The annotations are
neutral and informative. While this bibliography may be particularly useful for students
of Zambia's recent political history, it contains entries on a wide range of topics. A typical
example is Entry 441, which discusses the potential of BOTZAM, a network of roads
between Botswana and Zambia, for regional co-operation and integration.

818 **Bibliography of Zambian theses and dissertations; from 1930-
1989.**
Ilse Mwanza. Lusaka: Institute for African Studies, University of
Zambia, 1990.
This is a most useful compilation of theses on Zambian subjects. The entries are ordered
alphabetically by author and cover a wide range of universities, including some outside
the Anglo-Saxon sphere of influence – for example: Potchefstroom in South Africa and

the Free University, Amsterdam. Ms. Mwanza has continued registering theses and is willing to provide an updated list, if requested, from imwanza@zamtel.zm

819 Agricultural development in SADDC countries; volume 8, Zambia.
Thiendou Niang, project leader.   Wageningen, The Netherlands: CTA, 1990. 373p.

This bibliography, containing 3,452 entries, takes its information from six national and international databases, all compiled outside the region. Most of the publications mentioned also originate from outside Southern Africa. They are arranged in chronological order, starting in 1948 and ending in 1988. The number of yearly entries increases considerably over time. A subject and author index makes it possible, however, to access the information easily. The entries are not annotated, but each entry is provided with keywords. The bibliography covers all aspects of agriculture, but over forty per cent of the entries relate to plant and animal science. It offers therefore a useful entrance to technical aspects of agriculture which are not covered in this bibliography.

820 A bibliography of pre-independence Zambia: the social sciences.
William E. Rau.   Boston, Massachusetts: G.K. Hall, 1979. 357p.

This is an impressive piece of work, listing nearly 4,000 entries. It is not a bibliography of what appeared in pre-independence Zambia, but rather of what appeared on pre-independence Zambia until 1979. It lists PhD theses as well as published work; it does not restrict itself to English, but also contains material written in German or French. It includes major recent works as well as old publications which one would expect to have fallen into oblivion. An example of the latter: a periodical entitled *Echoes of Service*, which appeared in the 1890s.

821 Bibliography on human settlement with emphasis on households and residential environment – Zambia.
Ann Schlyter, Jairos Chanda.   Lusaka: University of Zambia, Institute of African Studies; Lund, Sweden: School of Architecture, Department of Building Function Analysis, 1982. 137p.

This bibliography is wide ranging and covers planned settlement in urban as well as rural settings. Besides that, one can also find entries about Zambian foods and cooking as well as about health problems in Lusaka. The real strength of this bibliography lies in the access it gives to grey literature on housing in the urban situation.

822 HIV/AIDS bibliography: an annotated review of research on HIV/AIDS in Zambia.
UNICEF and National Programmes.   Lusaka: UNICEF and National AIDS/STD/TB and Leprosy Programme, 1996. 189p. map.

This bibliography has relatively few entries (218), but these are elaborately annotated. The annotations give an abstract of the articles and pay much attention to the scientific procedure followed. The particular value of this bibliography is that it focuses not only on public and academic research, but also on the research done within and for Zambian institutions. The annotations note precisely the institutional location of research undertaken.

823 Zambia; a bibliography of geographical writing 1900-1979.
Geoffrey J. Williams. Lusaka: Zambia Geographical Association, 1982. 33p.

This bibliography aimed to be comprehensive, at any rate with respect to publications in the English language. It contains entries published in thirty-three countries. An overview of the development of geography in Zambia precedes the listing of entries.

824 Independent Zambia: a bibliography of the social sciences; 1964-1979.
Geoffrey J. Williams. Boston, Massachusetts: G.K. Hall & Co., 1984. 538p.

This bibliography has close to 4,500 entries. It is as comprehensive as can be and is an amazing achievement. To give an idea of its range, entries 3,722-3,727 cover publications in Afrikaans, Silozi and Polish as well as English. It covers not only regular publications, but also government directories, handbooks, etc. The brochure *Zambia goes metric* is an obscure example. Grey publications at the university are another area covered – for example a study by J. Momba and R. Nglase, then students, of Zambian permanent secretaries. The bibliography is also less limited to the social sciences than the title suggests. There is a section on archaeology, and in the section on linguistics one can find lists of plant names in Chichewa as well as in Chibemba. The book regularly includes notes on the authors as well as notification of reviews of the books mentioned.

Indexes

There follow three separate indexes: authors (personal or corporate); titles; and subjects. Title entries are italicized and refer either to the main titles, or to other works cited in the annotations. The numbers refer to bibliographical entry rather than page number. Individual index entries are arranged in alphabetical sequence.

Index of Authors

257

259

261

Index of Titles

278

Index of Subjects

288

Tshombe, Moise 452
Tuberculosis 385
Tumbuka 281, 312
  dictionary 279
  vimbuza 754
Turnout (electoral) 408
Twin Palm 365

U

Ubutwa 81
Umutomboko 754
Unionization 726
Unionized workers 576
UNIP 25, 116, 138, 153,
  155, 175, 281, 303, 330,
  332, 408, 423, 425, 427,
  433, 448-49, 462
  and administrative
    reform 520
  and education 748
  and Kapwepwe 630
  and rural development 678
  and the ANC 675
  and the press 777
  and the refutation of one-
    party state argument
    437
  and the trade union
    movement 431
  and women 428
  archives 447
  general conference 1967
    473
  in Luanshya 432
  landslide victory 444
  national congress 1967
    479
  National Council
    meeting 1986 479
United Church of Zambia
  170
United Party 462
University of Zambia
  (UNZA) 430, 469, 478,
  596, 747

Upgrading *see* Squatter
  settlements
UPP 119, 453, 466
  trade union movement 431
Urban sector 325, 371
  agriculture 359
  life 146, 718
  poverty 356
  settings 142, 302
  society 325, 328, 331,
    427
  wage determination 715
  working class 566
Urbanization 29, 123, 325-
  27, 330, 338, 340-46,
  515, 576
  and language 235
User charges 390, 396,
  403, 506, 747
User fees *see* User charges
Ushi 652
Uyombe 153

V

Vampires 97, 184-85
Vegetable growing 681
Vegetation of the Zambezi
  655
Victoria Falls 13, 770
Village life 769
Vimbuza 312, 754
Vorster, John 540
Voter registration 411

W

Wage determination 715
Wage employment 595
Wage policy 406
Wage sector 715
Wages and salaries 112
Walensa, Lech 470
War 104
Water supply 322
Weeds 71

Welensky, Roy 114, 148
Welfare associations 95
Welfare societies 136,
  427
Western Province 4, 6,
  538
  art 762
  cattle 631, 674
  cattle sales statistics 674
  health care 403
  regional development
    558
  see also Barotseland
White farms 135
White Fathers 172-73,
  184, 203, 293
White mine workers 207
Widows and inheritance
  491
Wildlife 3, 11, 21, 24, 31,
  47, 52, 58, 186
  aerial surveys 27
  and political patronage
    25
  depletion of 23
  mammals 54, 61
  plant uses 68
  poaching 26
  publications 806
Wilson, Godfrey 123-24
Wina brothers 155, 443
Wina, Arthur 528
Wina, Sikota 479, 779
Winawina 156
Wisa *see* Bisa
Witch finding 280
Witchcraft 173, 286, 300,
  303, 318, 353, 492,
  638, 769, 805
Witchcraft Ordinance
  402
Women 96, 133, 140-41,
  312, 331, 359, 377,
  383, 515
  and agricultural
    development aid 683

Map of Zambia

This map shows the more important features.

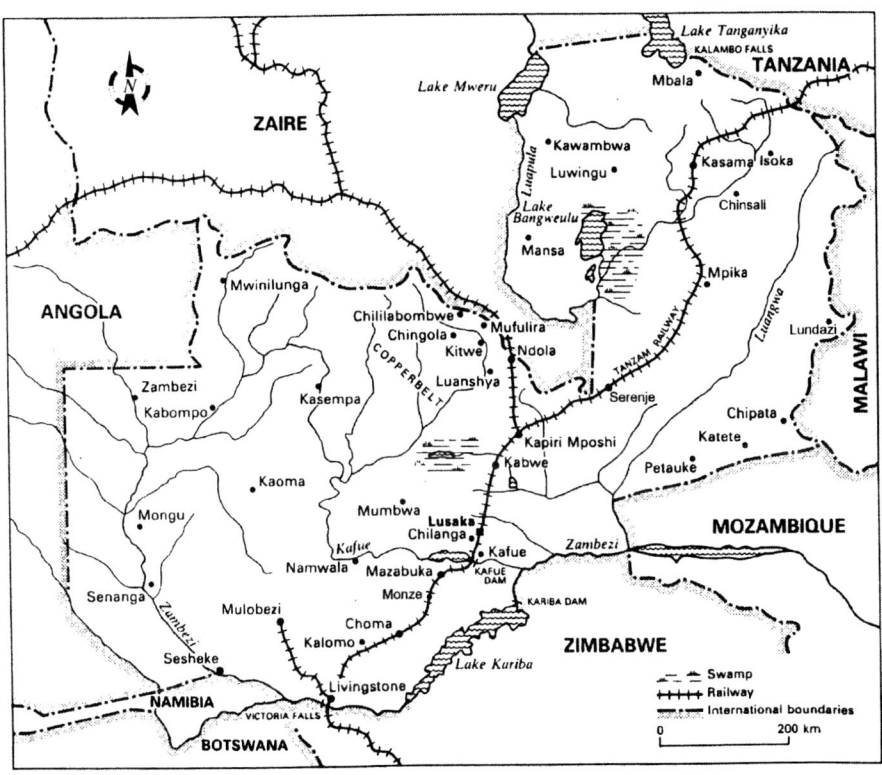

ALSO FROM CLIO PRESS

INTERNATIONAL ORGANIZATIONS SERIES

Each volume in the International Organizations Series is either devoted to one specific organization, or to a number of different organizations operating in a particular region, or engaged in a specific field of activity. The scope of the series is wide ranging and includes intergovernmental organizations, international non-governmental organizations, and national bodies dealing with international issues. The series is aimed mainly at the English-speaker and each volume provides a selective, annotated, critical bibliography of the organization, or organizations, concerned. The bibliographies cover books, articles, pamphlets, directories, databases and theses and, wherever possible, attention is focused on material about the organizations rather than on the organizations' own publications. Notwithstanding this, the most important official publications, and guides to those publications, will be included. The views expressed in individual volumes, however, are not necessarily those of the publishers.

VOLUMES IN THE SERIES

1 *European Communities*, John Paxton
2 *Arab Regional Organizations*, Frank A. Clements
3 *Comecon: The Rise and Fall of an International Socialist Organization*, Jenny Brine
4 *International Monetary Fund*, Anne C. M. Salda
5 *The Commonwealth*, Patricia M. Larby and Harry Hannam
6 *The French Secret Services*, Martyn Cornick and Peter Morris

7 *Organization of African Unity*, Gordon Harris
8 *North Atlantic Treaty Organization*, Phil Williams
9 *World Bank*, Anne C. M. Salda
10 *United Nations System*, Jospeh P. Baratta
11 *Organization of American States*, David Sheinin
12 *The British Secret Services*, Philip H. J. Davies
13 *The Israeli Secret Services*, Frank A. Clements